iPhone
The Missing Manual

Fifth Edition

iPhone: The Missing Manual, Fifth Edition   BY DAVID POGUE

Copyright © 2011 David Pogue. All rights reserved.
Printed in Canada.

Published by O'Reilly Media, Inc., 1005 Gravenstein Highway North, Sebastopol, CA 95472.

O'Reilly books may be purchased for educational, business, or sales promotional use. Online editions are also available for most titles *(safari.oreilly.com)*. For more information, contact our corporate/institutional sales department: 800.998.9938 or *corporate@oreilly.com*.

Executive Editor: Chris Nelson

Copy Editor: Julie Van Keuren

Indexers: David Pogue, Emma Hollister

Cover Designers: Monica Kamsvaag and Phil Simpson

Interior Designer: Phil Simpson (based on a design by Ron Bilodeau)

Print History:
> December 2011:   Fifth Edition.

The O'Reilly logo is a registered trademark of O'Reilly Media, Inc. *iPhone: The Missing Manual* and related trade dress are trademarks of O'Reilly Media, Inc.

Many of the designations used by manufacturers and sellers to distinguish their products are claimed as trademarks. Where those designations appear in this book, and O'Reilly Media, Inc. was aware of a trademark claim, the designations have been printed in caps or initial caps. Adobe Photoshop™ is a registered trademark of Adobe Systems, Inc. in the United States and other countries. O'Reilly Media, Inc. is independent of Adobe Systems, Inc.

Photos of the iPhone courtesy of Apple, Inc.

While every precaution has been taken in the preparation of this book, the publisher and author assume no responsibility for errors or omissions, or for damages resulting from the use of the information contained herein.

ISBN: 978-1-4493-0177-4
[TI]   [12/11]

Contents

Part 4: Connections

The Missing Credits

 **David Pogue** (author) writes a weekly tech column for *The New York Times* and a monthly column for *Scientific American*. He's an Emmy-winning correspondent for *CBS News Sunday Morning*, the host of *NOVA scienceNOW* on PBS, and the creator of the Missing Manual series. He's the author or coauthor of 53 books, including 27 in this series; six in the "For Dummies" line (including *Macs, Magic, Opera,* and *Classical Music*); two novels (one for middle-schoolers); and *The World According to Twitter*. In his other life, David is a former Broadway show conductor, a piano player, and a magician. He lives in Connecticut with his three awesome children.

Links to his columns and weekly videos await at *www.davidpogue.com*. He welcomes feedback about his books by email at *david@pogueman.com*.

Julie Van Keuren (copy editor) is a freelance editor, writer, and desktop publisher who runs her "little media empire" from her home in Billings, Montana. In her spare time she enjoys swimming, biking, running, and (hey, why not?) triathlons. She and her husband, M.H., have two sons, Dexter and Michael. *Email: little_media@yahoo.com*.

Phil Simpson (design and layout) runs his graphic design business from Southbury, Connecticut. His work includes corporate branding, publication design, communications support, and advertising. In his free time he is a homebrewer, ice cream maker, wannabe woodworker, and is on a few tasting panels. He lives with his wife and three great felines. Email: *phil.simpson@pmsgraphics.com*.

Rich Koster (technical reviewer). The iPhone became Rich's first cellphone (and first iPod) the very first evening it was sold by Apple. It's been his faithful electronic companion through the years since, being replaced by new iPhone versions as they came out. From the start, he began corresponding with David Pogue, sharing tips, tricks, and observations; eventually, David asked him to be the beta reader of the first edition of *iPhone: The Missing Manual*—and hired him as the tech editor of subsequent editions. Rich is a husband, father, graphics artist, writer, and Disney fan (@DisneyEcho on Twitter).

Acknowledgments

The Missing Manual series is a joint venture between the dream team introduced on these pages and O'Reilly Media. I'm grateful to all of them, especially to designer Phil Simpson and to prose queen Julie Van Keuren, who have become my Missing Manual core team.

A few other friends did massive favors for this book. The lovely Emma Hollister was always there for me, contributing screenshots and indexing help. Philip Michaels did an expert job of writing up the Game Center. Apple's Greg Joswiak and Natalie Kerris were incredibly generous in chasing down elusive technical answers. Kellee Katagi contributed a sharp proofreading eye. O'Reilly's Brian Sawyer accommodated my chaotic schedule without once threatening to break my kneecaps. And my incredible assistant Jan Carpenter kept me from falling apart like wet Kleenex.

The work done on previous editions lives on in this one; for that, I'm still grateful to my fellow *New York Times* columnist Jude Biersdorfer, my 2010 summer intern Matt Gibstein, and the inimitable Brian Jepson.

Thanks to David Rogelberg and Tim O'Reilly for believing in the idea, and above all, to my family. They make these books—and everything else—possible.

—*David Pogue*

The Missing Manual Series

Missing Manual books are superbly written guides to computer products that don't come with printed manuals (which is just about all of them). Each book features a handcrafted index; cross-references to specific page numbers (not just "See Chapter 14"); and RepKover, a detached-spine binding that lets the book lie perfectly flat without the assistance of weights or cinder blocks.

Recent titles include:

- *Photoshop CS5: The Missing Manual* by Lesa Snider King
- *Home Networking: The Missing Manual* by Scott Lowe
- *Your Brain: The Missing Manual* by Matthew MacDonald
- *Your Body: The Missing Manual* by Matthew MacDonald
- *Living Green: The Missing Manual* by Nancy Conner

The Web:

- *Google+: The Missing Manual* by Kevin Purdy
- *PHP & MySQL: The Missing Manual* by Brett McLaughlin
- *HTML5: The Missing Manual* by Matthew MacDonald
- *Dreamweaver CS5.5: The Missing Manual* by David Sawyer McFarland
- *Flash CS5.5: The Missing Manual* by Chris Grover
- *eBay: The Missing Manual* by Nancy Conner
- *Wikipedia: The Missing Manual* by John Broughton
- *Facebook: The Missing Manual* by E.A. Vander Veer
- *Google: The Missing Manual* by Sarah Milstein and Rael Dornfest
- *Google Apps: The Missing Manual* by Nancy Conner
- *Google Sketchup: The Missing Manual* by Chris Grover
- *JavaScript & jQuery: The Missing Manual* by David Sawyer McFarland
- *CSS: The Missing Manual*, 2nd Edition, by David Sawyer McFarland
- *Creating a Web Site: The Missing Manual* by Matthew MacDonald
- *The Internet: The Missing Manual* by David Pogue and J.D. Biersdorfer

Gadgets:

- *iPad 2: The Missing Manual,* by J.D. Biersdorfer
- *iPod: The Missing Manual,* 10th Edition by J.D. Biersdorfer
- *David Pogue's Digital Photography: The Missing Manual* by David Pogue
- *Galaxy S II: The Missing Manual* by Preston Gralla
- *Motorola Xoom: The Missing Manual* by Preston Gralla

- *Galaxy Tab: The Missing Manual* by Preston Gralla
- *Droid X2: The Missing Manual* by Preston Gralla
- *Netbooks: The Missing Manual* by J.D. Biersdorfer

Macintosh:
- *Mac OS X Lion: The Missing Manual* by David Pogue
- *Photoshop Elements for Mac: The Missing Manual* by Barbara Brundage
- *iMovie '11 & iDVD: The Missing Manual* by David Pogue and Aaron Miller
- *iPhoto '11: The Missing Manual* by David Pogue and Lesa Snider
- *Switching to the Mac: The Missing Manual*, Lion Edition by David Pogue
- *iWork '09: The Missing Manual* by Josh Clark
- *AppleScript: The Missing Manual* by Adam Goldstein
- *Office 2011 for Macintosh: The Missing Manual* by Chris Grover
- *FileMaker Pro 10: The Missing Manual* by Geoff Coffey and Susan Prosser

Windows:
- *Windows 7: The Missing Manual* by David Pogue
- *Windows Vista: The Missing Manual* by David Pogue
- *Office 2010: The Missing Manual* by Chris Grover, Matthew MacDonald, and E. A. Vander Veer
- *Word 2010: The Missing Manual* by Chris Grover
- *Excel 2010: The Missing Manual* by Matthew MacDonald
- *PowerPoint 2010: The Missing Manual* by Emily A. Vander Veer
- *Access 2010: The Missing Manual* by Matthew MacDonald
- *Microsoft Project 2010: The Missing Manual* by Bonnie Biafore
- *PCs: The Missing Manual* by Andy Rathbone
- *Photoshop Elements 10: The Missing Manual* by Barbara Brundage
- *Premiere Elements 8: The Missing Manual* by Chris Grover
- *Quicken 2009: The Missing Manual* by Bonnie Biafore
- *QuickBooks 2012: The Missing Manual* by Bonnie Biafore
- *QuickBase: The Missing Manual* by Nancy Conner

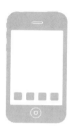

Introduction

How do you make the point that the iPhone has changed the world? The easy answer is "use statistics"—100 million sold, 500,000 downloadable programs on the iPhone App Store, 15 billion downloads…. Trouble is, those statistics get stale almost before you've finished typing them.

Maybe it's better to talk about the aftermath. How since the iPhone came along, cell carriers (AT&T, Verizon, Sprint, and so on) have opened up the calcified, conservative way they used to consider new cellphone designs. How every phone and its brother now have a touchscreen. How BlackBerry, Google (Android) phones, and Windows 7 phones all have their own app stores. How, in essence, everybody wants to be the iPhone.

The thing is, they'll never quite catch up technologically, because Apple is always moving, too. In October 2011, for example, it introduced the fifth iPhone model, the iPhone 4S. It looks identical to the previous model, the iPhone 4—but the guts are quite a bit different. The processor is much faster, the camera is much better, and there's speech recognition. Not just dictation—you can actually *tell the phone what to do.*

More importantly, there's a new, free version of the iPhone's software, called iOS 5. (Why not "iPhone OS" anymore? Because the same operating system runs on the iPad and the iPod Touch. It's not just for iPhones anymore, and saying "the iPhone/iPad/iPod Touch OS" takes too long.)

iOS 5 adds all kinds of new features people have been pining for: direct access to the camera from the Lock screen, a Notification Center that lists your messages, calls, and appointments with one finger-swipe, and so on.

Why is it so important? Because you can run iOS 5 on *older* iPhone models (the 4 and the 3GS) without having to buy the iPhone 4S. This book covers all three phones that can run the iOS 5 software: the iPhone 3GS, the iPhone 4, and the iPhone 4S.

About the iPhone

So what's the iPhone?

Well, it's a cellphone, obviously. But it's also a full-blown iPod, complete with a dazzling screen for watching videos. And the iPhone is also the best pocket Internet viewer you've ever seen. It shows fully formatted email (with attachments, thank you) and displays entire Web pages with fonts and design intact. It's tricked out with a tilt sensor, a proximity sensor, a light sensor, WiFi, Bluetooth, GPS, a gyroscope, and that amazing multitouch screen.

Furthermore, it's a calendar, an address book, a calculator, an alarm clock, a stopwatch, a stock tracker, a traffic reporter, an RSS reader, and a weather forecaster. It even stands in for a flashlight and, with the screen off, a pocket mirror.

But don't forget the App Store. Thanks to the hundreds of thousands of add-on programs that await there, the iPhone is also a fast, wicked-fun pocket computer. All those free or cheap programs can turn it into a medical reference, a musical keyboard, a time tracker, a remote control, a sleep monitor, a tip calculator, an ebook reader, and so on. And whoa, those games! Thousands of them, with smooth 3-D graphics and tilt control.

All of this sends the iPhone's utility and power through the roof. Calling it a phone is practically an insult.

(Apple probably should have called it an "iPod," but that name was taken.)

About the Carriers

For four years, the iPhone was exclusively an AT&T phone. But in early 2011, Verizon got the iPhone 4. Then, in the fall of 2011, AT&T, Verizon, *and* Sprint got the iPhone 4S.

In general, these companies' iPhone models look and work identically. There are just a couple of tiny differences to be aware of.

First, Verizon and Sprint rely on an older, more established cellular network type called CDMA. AT&T, on the other hand, uses a network type known as GSM.

Not many other countries use CDMA, but 220 countries and territories use GSM, including Europe. That's why the Verizon iPhone 4 doesn't work in most other countries.

The iPhone 4S, though, is a world phone. It contains both CDMA and GSM circuitry, so even the Verizon and Sprint models work in any other country.

If you want your iPhone to retain its usual phone number while you're traveling, you can pay Verizon/Sprint/AT&T some steep roaming charges. Otherwise, you can temporarily replace your original SIM card with one you've rented in your new country. In both cases, you have to call your main carrier ahead of time to get the OK.

There's one more GSM/CDMA difference to be aware of: You can't talk on a CDMA phone (Verizon or Sprint) while you're online. That is, if you're on a call, you can't simultaneously check a Web site or send email over the cellular network.

It's not such a big deal. Continuing processes like downloads and GPS navigation resume automatically when you end your call. You can still send and get text messages when you're on a call. And none of this applies when you're in a WiFi hotspot; in that case, you can call and surf simultaneously, no problem.

About This Book

By way of a printed guide to the iPhone, Apple provides only a fold-out leaflet. It's got a clever name—"Finger Tips"—but to learn your way around, you're expected to use an electronic PDF document. This PDF covers the basics well, but it's largely free of details, hacks, workarounds, tutorials, humor, and any acknowledgment of the iPhone's flaws. You can't mark your place, underline, or read it in the bathroom.

The purpose of this book, then, is to serve as the manual that should have accompanied the iPhone. (If you have an original iPhone or iPhone 3G, you really need one of this book's earlier editions. If you have an iPhone 3GS or iPhone 4, this book assumes that you've installed the free iOS 5 software; see Appendix A.)

Writing computer books can be an annoying job. You commit something to print, and then—bam—the software gets updated or revised, and suddenly your book is out of date.

That will certainly happen to this book. The iPhone is a *platform*. It's a computer, so Apple routinely updates and improves it by sending it new software bits. To picture where the iPhone will be five years from now, just look at how much better, sleeker, and more powerful today's iPod is than the original 2001 black-and-white brick.

Therefore, you should think of this book the way you think of the first iPhone: as a darned good start. To keep in touch with updates we make to it as developments unfold, drop in to the book's Errata/Changes page. (Go to *www.missingmanuals.com*, click this book's name, and then click View/Submit Errata.)

 Tip Writing a book about the iPhone is a study in exasperation, because the darned thing is a moving target. Apple updates the iPhone's software fairly often, piping in new features, bug fixes, speed-ups, and so on.

This book covers the iPhone's 5.0.1 software. There will be a 5.0.2, and a 5.0.3, and so on. Check this book's page at *www.missingmanuals.com* to read about those updates when they occur.

About the Outline

iPhone: The Missing Manual is divided into five parts, each containing several chapters:

- Part 1, **The iPhone as Phone,** covers everything related to phone calls: dialing, answering, voice control, voicemail, conference calling, text messaging, MMS, and the Contacts (address book) program. It's also where you can read about FaceTime, the iPhone's video-calling feature, and Siri, the "virtual assistant" in the iPhone 4S.

- Part 2, **Pix, Flix & Apps,** is dedicated to the iPhone's built-in software programs, with a special emphasis on its multimedia abilities: playing music, podcasts, movies, TV shows, and photos; capturing photos and videos; navigating with GPS; reading ebooks; and so on. These chapters also cover app management: installing, organizing, and quitting apps—and, of course, the iPhone's special version of multitasking.

- Part 3, **The iPhone Online,** is a detailed exploration of the iPhone's third talent: its ability to get you onto the Internet, either over a WiFi hotspot connection or via the cellular network. It's all here: email, Web browsing, and *tethering* (that is, letting your phone serve as a sort of Internet antenna for your laptop).

- Part 4, **Connections,** describes the world beyond the iPhone itself—like the copy of iTunes on your Mac or PC that can fill up the iPhone with music, videos, and photos, and syncing the calendar, address book, and mail settings. These chapters also cover the iPhone's control panel, the

Settings program; and how the iPhone syncs wirelessly with corporate networks using Microsoft Exchange ActiveSync—or with your own computers using Apple's iCloud service.

- Part 5, **Appendixes,** contains three reference chapters. Appendix A walks you through the setup process; Appendix B is a tour of accessories like chargers, car adapters, and carrying cases; and Appendix C is a master compendium of troubleshooting, maintenance, and battery information.

About→These→Arrows

Throughout this book, and throughout the Missing Manual series, you'll find sentences like this one: Tap Settings→Airplane Mode→On. That's shorthand for a much longer instruction that directs you to open three nested screens in sequence, like this: "Tap the Settings button. On the next screen, tap Airplane Mode. On the screen after that, tap On." (In this book, tappable things on the screen are printed in orange to make them stand out.)

Similarly, this kind of arrow shorthand helps to simplify the business of choosing commands in menus on your Mac or PC, like File→Print.

About MissingManuals.com

To get the most out of this book, visit www.missingmanuals.com. Click the Missing CDs link, and then click this book's title to reveal a neat, organized list of the shareware, freeware, and bonus articles mentioned in this book.

The Web site also offers corrections and updates to the book; to see them, click the book's title, and then click View/Submit Errata. In fact, please submit corrections yourself! Each time we print more copies of this book, we'll make any confirmed corrections you've suggested. We'll also note such changes on the Web site, so you can mark important corrections into your own copy of the book, if you like. And we'll keep the book current as Apple releases more iPhone updates.

The Guided Tour

I f you'd never seen all the videos and photos of the iPhone, and you found it lying on someone's desk, you might not guess it was a phone (let alone an iPod/Web browser/alarm clock/stopwatch/voice recorder/ musical instrument/compass). You can't see any antenna, mouthpiece, or earpiece—and, goodness knows, there are no number keys for dialing.

It's all there, though, hidden inside this sleek glass-and-metal slab.

For the rest of this book, and for the rest of your life with the iPhone, you'll be expected to know what's meant by, for example, "the Home button" and "the Sleep switch." A guided tour, therefore, is in order. Keep hands and feet inside the tram at all times.

Sleep Switch (On/Off)

On the top-right edge of the iPhone, you'll find a silver metal button shaped like a dash. This, ladies and gents, is the Sleep switch.

It has several functions:

- **Sleep/Wake.** Tapping it once puts the iPhone to sleep—into Standby mode, ready for incoming calls but consuming very little power. Tapping it again turns on the screen so it's ready for action.

- **On/Off.** The same switch can also turn the iPhone off completely so it consumes no power at all; incoming calls get dumped into voicemail. You might turn the iPhone off whenever you're not going to use it for a few days.

    To turn the iPhone off, press the Sleep switch for 3 seconds. The screen changes to say slide to power off. Confirm your decision by placing a fingertip on the right-pointing red arrow and sliding to the right. The device shuts off completely.

To turn the iPhone back on, press the switch again for 1 second. The chromelike Apple logo appears as the phone boots up.

- **Answer call/Dump to voicemail.** When a call comes in, you can tap the Sleep button *once* to silence the ringing or vibrating. After four rings, the call goes to your voicemail.

  You can also tap it *twice* to dump the call to voicemail immediately. (Of course, because they didn't hear four rings, iPhone veterans will know you've blown them off. Bruised egos may result. Welcome to the world of iPhone etiquette.)

- **Force restart.** The Sleep switch has one more function. If your iPhone is frozen, and no buttons work, and you can't even turn the thing off, this button is also involved in force-restarting the whole machine. Steps for this last-ditch procedure are on page 504.

Locked Mode

When you don't touch the screen for 1 minute (or another interval you choose), or when you put the iPhone to sleep, the phone *locks* itself. When it's locked, the screen is dark and doesn't respond to touch. If you're on a call, the call continues; if music is playing, it keeps going; if you're recording audio, the recording proceeds.

But when the phone is locked, you don't have to worry about accidental button pushes. You wouldn't want to discover that your iPhone has been calling people or taking photos from the depths of your pocket or purse. Nor would you want it to dial a random number from your back pocket, a phenomenon that's earned the unfortunate name *butt dialing.*

The Lock Screen

To wake the phone when it's locked, press either the Sleep switch or the Home button just below the screen.

That gesture alone doesn't fire up the full iPhone world, though. Instead, it presents the Lock screen shown here.

Until iOS 5 came along, the Lock screen wasn't especially useful; most people encountered it only as a welcome mat before *unlocking* it. You do that by sliding your finger to the right across the gray arrow, as indicated by the animation.

 Note: The iPhone can demand a password each time it wakes up, if you like. See page 461. On the other hand, you can adjust how quickly the phone locks itself, or make it stop locking itself altogether; see page 461 again.

Today, however, there are plenty of reasons why you might want to check the Lock screen without going on to unlock the phone. For example, you can use the iPhone as a watch—millions of people do. Just tap the Sleep switch to consult the Lock screen's time and date display, and then shove the phone right back into your pocket. The iPhone automatically relocks itself after a few seconds.

Better yet, the Lock screen is now a handy status screen. Here you see a record of everything that happened while you weren't paying attention. It's a list of missed calls, text messages received, notifications from your apps, and other essential information.

Now, each of these notices has come from a different *app* (software program). To call somebody back, for example, you'd want to open the Phone app; to reply to a text message, you'd want the Messages app, and so on.

Here, then, is one of the handiest new shortcuts in iOS 5: You can dive directly into the relevant app by swiping your finger *across the notification itself,* like this:

Lock screen with notifications　　　　　　　*Swipe to open that app*

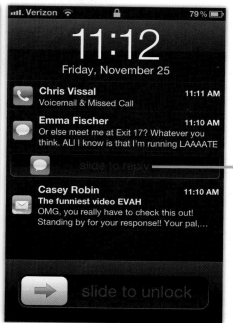

Adopting that shortcut saves you the trouble of unlocking the phone, fumbling through your Home screens until you find the app you want, and tapping it to open it.

Tip On the other hand, if you'd rather *not* have all these details show up on the Lock screen, you can turn them off. (Privacy is the main reason you might want to do so—remember that the bad guys don't need a password to view your Lock screen. They just have to tap the Sleep switch or the Home button.)

You can hide these items from your Lock screen on an app-by-app basis. For example, you might want missed calls to show up here but not missed text messages. To set this up, choose Settings→Notifications. Tap the app in question; scroll to the bottom, and then turn off View in Lock Screen.

Home Button

Here it is: the one and only button on the front of this phone. Push it to summon the Home screen, which is your gateway to everything the iPhone can do. (You can read more about the Home screen at the end of this chapter.)

Home button

Having a Home button is a wonderful thing. It means you can never get lost. No matter how deeply you burrow into the iPhone software, no matter how far off track you find yourself, one push of the Home button takes you back to the beginning.

It sounds simple, but remember that the iPhone doesn't have an actual Back button or an End button. The Home button is the *only* way out of some screens.

As time goes on, Apple saddles the Home button with more and more functions. It's become Apple's only way to provide shortcuts for common features; that's what you get when you design a phone that only *has* one button. In iPhone Land, you can press the Home button one, two, or three times for different functions—or even hold it down. Here's the rundown.

One Quick Press: Wake Up

Pressing the Home button once wakes the phone if it's in locked mode. That's sometimes easier than finding the Sleep switch on the top edge. It gives you a quick glance at the time or your missed calls and texts.

One Long Press: Voice Control—or Siri

If you hold down the Home button for about 3 seconds, you make the phone ready for *voice control*.

If you have an iPhone 3GS or 4, you can use voice control dial by speaking a name or number, or use it to control music playback. If you have an iPhone 4S, you can do a thousand times more: You can command Siri, your virtual voice-controlled assistant. Details are in Chapter 4.

Two Quick Presses: Task Switcher

If, once the phone is awake, you press the Home button *twice quickly,* the screen dims, and the current image on it slides upward—to reveal the task switcher strip at the bottom. This feature is the key to the iPhone's multitasking feature.

What you see here are icons of the four programs you've used most recently. Each time you swipe your finger to the left, you bring more icons into view, representing programs you opened less and less recently.

The point is that with a single tap, you can jump right back into a program you had open, without waiting for it to start up, show its welcome screen, and so on—and without having to scroll through 11 Home screens trying to find the icon of a favorite app.

In short, the task switcher gives you a way to jump *directly* to another app, without a layover at the Home screen first.

This task switcher is the only visible element of the iPhone's multitasking feature, which is described in delicious detail on page 247. Once you get used to it, that double-press of the Home button will become second nature—and your first choice for jumping among apps.

Two Quick Presses, Part 2: The Widget Bar

Most of the time, you'll do the two-presses thing to open the task switcher so you can, well, switch tasks. But there are hidden gems awaiting.

If you summon the task switcher and then drag your finger to the *right,* the task switcher reveals a set of four hidden controls. These go by the name of widgets, meaning that they're not quite as full blown as actual apps, but they still get their own icons. Here's what they do, from left to right:

- ↻ **Rotation lock.** When you tap this button, the screen no longer rotates when you turn the phone 90 degrees. The idea is that sometimes, like when you're reading an ebook on your side in bed, you don't want the screen picture to turn; you want it to stay upright relative to your eyes, even though you're lying down. (A little ↻ icon appears at the top of the screen to remind you why the usual rotating isn't happening.)

  The whole thing isn't quite as earth-shattering as it sounds—first, because it locks the image in only one way: upright, in portrait orientation. You can't make it lock into widescreen mode. Furthermore, there aren't that many apps that rotate with the phone to begin with. But when that day comes when you want to read in bed on your side with your head on the pillow, your iPhone will be ready. (Tap the button a second time to turn rotating back on.)

- ⏮, ▶, ⏭. These controls govern playback in whatever program is playing music in the background. They're always two Home-button presses away, no matter what program you're in. You can skip a horrible song quickly and efficiently without having to interrupt what you're doing.

- **Music-app button.** Finally, the app icon here represents your iPhone's iPod app, or the Pandora Internet radio app, or whatever program is playing music in the background at the moment. Once again, the idea is to give you a quick shortcut when you want to switch albums, songs, or podcasts, so you don't have to meander back to the Home screen.

Three Presses: VoiceOver, Zoom, or White on Black

In Settings→General→Accessibility, you can set up a triple-press of the Home button to turn one of several accessibility features on or off: VoiceOver (the phone speaks whatever you touch), white-on-black type (which is sometimes easier to see), zooming (magnifies the screen), or AssistiveTouch (155). If you choose Ask, then a triple-click summons *three* buttons: VoiceOver, White on Black, and Zoom.

All of these features are described beginning on page 149.

 Tip The Home button is also part of the *force quit* sequence—a good troubleshooting technique when a particular program seems to be acting up. See page 504.

Screen

The touchscreen is your mouse, keyboard, dialing pad, and notepad. You might expect it to get fingerprinty and streaky.

But one of the best unsung features of the modern iPhone is its *oleophobic* screen. That may sound like an irrational fear of yodeling, but it's actually a coating that repels grease. You'll be amazed at how easily a single light wipe on your clothes restores the screen to its right-out-of-the-box crystal sheen.

You can also use the screen as a mirror when the iPhone is off.

 Note Geeks may enjoy knowing that the iPhone 4 and 4S, whose screen Apple calls the Retina display, packs in an astonishing 640 × 960 pixels. That's four times as sharp as older iPhones, like the 3GS, and the highest resolution of any phone on the market. It's really, *really* sharp, as you'll discover when you try to read text or make out the details of a map or photo.

But what about scratches? Fortunately, Apple learned its lesson on this one. The front and back of the iPhone 4 and 4S are made of Gorilla Glass, a special glass formulation made by Corning. It's unbelievably resistant to scratching. (That doesn't mean it can't crack; you can still shatter it if you drop it just the right way.)

 Note In case you're interested, this is how Corning's Web site says this glass is made: "The glass is placed in a hot bath of molten salt at a temperature of approximately 400°C. Smaller sodium ions leave the glass, and larger potassium ions from the salt bath replace them. These larger ions take up more room and are pressed together when the glass cools, producing a layer of compressive stress on the surface of the glass. Gorilla Glass's special composition enables the potassium ions to diffuse far into the surface, creating high compressive stress deep into the glass. This layer of compression creates a surface that is more resistant to damage from everyday use."

If you're nervous about protecting your iPhone, you can always get a case for it (or a "bumper" for the iPhone 4 or 4S—a silicone band that wraps around the metal edges). But if you're worried about scratching, you're probably worrying too much. Even many Apple employees carry the iPhone in their pockets without carrying cases.

And why aren't recent iPhone backs made of metal, like the original iPhone? Because radio signals can't pass through metal. And there are a *lot* of radio signals in this phone. All told, there are *15* different radio transceivers inside: four for the standard GSM frequencies; four for GSM's 3G frequencies; three for CDMA frequencies; and one each for WiFi, Bluetooth, American GPS, and Russian GPS.

Screen Icons

Here's a roundup of the icons you may see in the status bar at the top of the iPhone screen, from left to right:

- **▁▁▂▃ Cell signal.** As on any cellphone, the number of bars indicates the strength of your cell signal, and thus the quality of your call audio and the likelihood of losing the connection. If there are zero bars, then the dreaded words "No service" appear here.

- **Network name and type.** The **E** means your iPhone is connected to the Internet via AT&T's very slow EDGE network; on a Verizon or Sprint iPhone, that unhappy situation is denoted instead by this icon **O**. (On AT&T, that circle means GPRS, better known as "the even older, slower Internet network.")

If you see the **3G** logo, though, get psyched; you're in one of the cities where your cell company has installed a 3G network—meaning much, much faster Internet connections.

- ✈ **Airplane mode.** If you see the airplane instead of signal and WiFi bars, then the iPhone is in Airplane mode (page 331).

- 📶 **WiFi signal.** When you're connected to a wireless Internet hotspot, this indicator appears. The more "sound waves," the stronger the signal.

- 🔒 **Lock.** This icon appears only on the Lock screen described earlier in this chapter. It means, obviously, that the phone is locked.

- **9:50 AM.** When the iPhone is unlocked, a digital clock replaces the lock symbol.

- ▶ **Play indicator.** The iPhone is playing music. Before you respond, "Well, duh!" keep in mind that you may not be able to hear the music playing. For example, maybe the earbuds are plugged into the iPhone but aren't in your ears. So this icon is actually a handy reminder that you're running your battery down unnecessarily.

- 🕐 **Alarm.** You've got an alarm set. This reminder, too, can be valuable, especially when you intend to sleep late and don't *want* an alarm to go off. See page 268 for setting (and turning off) alarms.

- ✳ **Bluetooth connection.** The iPhone is connected wirelessly to a Bluetooth earpiece or a hands-free car system, as described on page 145. (If this symbol is gray, then it means Bluetooth is turned on—and draining your battery—but that it's not connected to any other gear.)

- 🚇 **TTY symbol.** You've turned on Teletype mode, meaning that the iPhone can communicate with a Teletype machine. (That's a special machine that lets deaf people make phone calls by typing and reading text. It hooks up to the iPhone with a special cable that Apple sells from its Web site.)

- **⟿ Call forwarding.** You've told your iPhone to auto-forward any incoming calls to a different phone number (page 144). This icon is awfully handy—it explains at a glance why your iPhone never seems to get calls anymore.

- **VPN VPN.** You corporate stud, you! You've managed to connect to your corporate network over a secure Internet connection, probably with the assistance of some highly paid systems administrator—or by consulting page 446.

- **✳ Syncing.** The iPhone is currently syncing with some Internet service—iCloud, for example (Chapter 14).

- **🔋 Battery meter.** When the iPhone is charging, the lightning bolt appears. Otherwise, the battery logo "empties out" from right to left to indicate how much charge remains. (You can even add a "% full" indicator to this gauge; see page 459.)

- **➹ Navigation active.** You're running a GPS navigation program in the background (yay, multitasking!). Why is a special icon necessary? Because those GPS apps slurp down battery power like a thirsty golden retriever. Apple wants to make sure you don't forget you're running it.

- **⟲ Rotation lock.** This icon reminds you that you've deliberately turned off the screen-rotation feature, where the screen image turns 90 degrees when you rotate the phone. Why would you want to? And how do you turn the rotation lock on or off? See page 14.

Cameras and Flash

At the top of the phone, above the screen, there's a horizontal slot. That's the earpiece. Just to its left, the tiny round pinhole is the front-facing camera (on the iPhone 4 and 4S). It's a little bit more visible on the white iPhone than on the black one.

Its primary purpose is to let you conduct video chats using the FaceTime feature, but it's also handy for taking self-portraits or just checking to see if you have spinach in your teeth.

Just keep in mind that it's not nearly as good a camera as the one on the back. The front camera takes much lower-resolution shots (640 × 480 pixels), has no flash, and isn't as good in low light.

The camera on the back of the iPhone, meanwhile, takes very good photos indeed—at 3, 5, or 8 megapixels (iPhone 3GS, 4, and 4S). Its lens appears in the upper-left corner.

On the iPhone 4 and 4S, a tiny LED lamp appears next to this lens. It's the flash for the camera, the video light when you're shooting movies, and a darned good flashlight for reading restaurant menus and theater programs in low light. (A free app like LED Light makes it quick and easy to turn the light on and off.)

More on the iPhone's cameras in Chapter 7.

Sensors

Behind the glass *above* the earpiece are two sensors. (On the black iPhones, they're camouflaged; you can't see them except with a bright flashlight.) First, there's an ambient-light sensor that brightens the display when you're in sunlight and dims it in darker places. You can also adjust the brightness manually; see page 456.

Second, there's a proximity sensor. When something (like your head) is close to the sensor when you're using the phone functions, it shuts off the screen illumination and touch sensitivity. Try it out with your hand. (It works only in the Phone app.) You save power and avoid dialing with your cheekbone when you're on a call.

Headphone Jack

At the top-left corner of the iPhone, you can see the miniplug where you plug in the white earbuds that came with it (or other earbuds or headphones).

This little hole is more than an ordinary 3.5-millimeter audio jack, however. It contains a secret fourth pin that conducts sound *into* the phone from the microphone on the earbuds' cord. Now you, too, can be one of those executives who walk down the street barking orders, apparently to nobody. The iPhone can stay in your pocket as you walk or drive. You hear the other person through your earbuds, and the mike on the cord picks up your voice.

 Note There's a tiny pinhole next to the headphone jack. This, believe it or not, is a microphone. It's the key to the noise-cancellation feature of the iPhone 4 and 4S. It listens to the sound of the world around you, and pumps in the opposite sound waves to cancel out all that ambient noise. (It doesn't do anything for *you*—the noise cancellation affects only what the *other* guy on the phone hears.)

Silencer Switch, Volume Keys

Praise be to the gods of technology—this phone has a silencer switch! This tiny flipper, on the left edge at the top, means that no ringer or alert sound will humiliate you in a meeting, at a movie, or in church. To turn off the ringer, push the flipper toward the back of the phone (see the photo on page 8).

 Note Even when silenced, the iPhone still makes noise in certain circumstances: when an alarm goes off; when you're playing iPod music; when you're using Find My iPhone (page 428); when you're using VoiceOver (page 150); or, sometimes, when a game is playing. Also, the phone still vibrates when the silencer is engaged, although you can turn this feature off; see page 454.

No menus, no holding down keys, just instant silence. All cellphones should have this feature.

With practice, you can learn to tell if the ringer is on while the iPhone is still in your pocket. That's because when the ringer is on, the switch falls in a straight line with the volume keys. By swiping your thumb across these controls, you can feel whether the silencer switch is lined up or tilted away.

Below the silencer, still on the left edge, are the volume controls—a single up/down rocker switch on the 3GS, separate metal + and – buttons on the iPhone 4 and 4S. The volume controls work in four different ways:

- On a call, these buttons adjust the speaker or earbud volume.

- When you're listening to music, they adjust the playback volume.

- When you're taking a picture, the middle one (volume up) serves as a shutter button or a camcorder start/stop button.

- At all other times, they adjust the volume of sound effects like the ringer and alarms.

No matter what you're adjusting, a corresponding volume graphic appears on the screen to show you where you are on the volume scale.

SIM Card Slot

On the right edge of the iPhone 4S, there's a tiny pinhole next to what looks like a very thin slot cover. (It's also on the right side of the AT&T iPhone 4, or the top of the iPhone 3GS.) If you push an unfolded paper clip straight into the hole, the *SIM card* tray pops out.

So what's a SIM card?

It turns out that there are two major cellphone network types: *CDMA*, used by Verizon and Sprint, and *GSM*, used by AT&T, T-Mobile, and most other countries around the world.

Every GSM phone stores your phone account info—things like your phone number and calling-plan details—on a tiny memory card known as a SIM (subscriber identity module) card. On some phones, though not on the iPhone, it even stores your address book.

What's cool is that, by removing the card and putting it into *another* GSM phone, you transplant a GSM phone's brain. The other phone now knows your number and account details, which can be handy when your iPhone goes in for repair or battery replacement.

iPhone 4S: The World Phone

AT&T is a GSM network, so AT&T iPhones have always had SIM cards. But intriguingly enough, every iPhone 4S has a SIM card, too—even the Verizon and Sprint models. That's odd, because most CDMA cellphones don't have SIM cards.

That's because the iPhone 4S contains antennas for *both* GSM and CDMA. It's the same phone, no matter which cell company you buy it from. Only the activation process teaches it which phone company it "belongs" to.

Even then, however, you can still use any company's phone in any country. (That's why the 4S is said to be a "world phone.") When you use the Verizon or Sprint iPhone in the United States, it uses only the CDMA antenna. But if you travel to Europe or another GSM part of the world, you can still use your Verizon or Sprint phone; it just hooks onto that country's GSM network.

If you decide to try that, you have two ways to go. First, you can contact your phone carrier and ask to have international roaming turned on. You'll keep your same phone number overseas, but you'll pay through the nose for calls and, especially, Internet use.

Second, you can rent a temporary SIM card when you get to the destination country. (The iPhone 4S, as well as the AT&T iPhone 4, requires one of the newer, smaller *MicroSIM* cards.) That's a less expensive route, but it means you'll have a different phone number while you're there.

 Note Except for this one example—inserting a card from another country for international use—you can't swap any other company's SIM card into the iPhone. For example, you can't make it a T-Mobile phone by inserting a T-Mobile SIM card. In other words, the iPhone is still not an "unlocked" GSM phone (at least, not officially; there are some unauthorized ways).

Apple thinks SIM cards are geeky and intimidating and that they should be invisible. That's why, unlike most GSM phones, your iPhone came with the card preinstalled and ready to go. Most people will never have any reason to open this tray, unless they just want to see what a SIM card looks like.

If you were curious enough to open it up, you can close the tray simply by pushing it back into the phone until it clicks.

Microphone, Speakerphone, Connector

On the bottom edge of the iPhone, Apple has parked three important components: the speakerphone speaker, the microphone, and, directly below the Home button, the 30-pin connector that charges and syncs the iPhone with your computer.

 Tip The speakerphone isn't very loud, because it's aimed straight out of the iPhone's edge, away from you. But if you cup your hand around the bottom edge, you can redirect the sound toward your face, for an immediate boost in volume and quality.

Antenna Band

That silver metal band around the edge is one of the most famous features of the iPhone 4 and 4S.

Top/left segments: Bluetooth, WiFi, GPS antennas

Right/bottom segments: voice and cellular data antennas

Apple is so proud of it. This stainless-steel band is an Apple-concocted alloy, claimed to be five times as strong as steel. It's the primary structural component of the phone—everything else is attached to it.

But this band is also part of the iPhone's antenna, and that's where the controversy begins.

You may remember that, shortly after the iPhone 4 debuted in the summer of 2010, videos began appearing online, showing a peculiar quirk: If you held the iPhone 4 so that the lower-left corner was pressed into your palm, the signal strength would drop. You could actually see the bars disappearing. Sometimes, the phone dropped calls as a result. It was a Death Grip!

A cellphone that loses its signal when you pick it up? Well, that could be considered a drawback.

It didn't happen to everyone. It was more likely if you were in a weak signal-strength area—or if you had sweaty palms. The problem seemed to occur only when covering up the black gap in the metal band at the phone's lower-left edge.

Even more intriguing: Putting the phone in a case eliminated the problem. Even a "bumper"—like the $30 one that Apple sells—solved the problem. (It's a thin, silicone band, available in a range of colors, that covers the metal edge entirely.)

After a week of media hysteria, including a stinging "not recommended" review from *Consumer Reports,* Apple held a press conference. CEO Steve Jobs showed videos of other companies' smartphones with exactly the same problem, insisting that signal weakening in certain grips was not just an iPhone issue. (Even so, he offered a free case or Apple bumper to anyone who'd bought the phone before this quirk became public.) Eventually, the hysteria died down.

If you have an iPhone 4, and you notice the problem, you can avoid covering the black gap with your flesh; you can put a piece of tape over it; or you can use a case.

If you have an iPhone 4S, you don't even have to go that far. The problem doesn't occur at all.

In the Box

Inside the minimalist box, you get the iPhone, its earbud/mike cord, and these items:

- **The charging/syncing cable.** When you connect your iPhone to your computer using this white USB cable, it simultaneously syncs and charges. (See Chapter 13.)

- **The AC adapter.** When you're traveling without a computer, you can plug the dock's USB cable into the included two-prong outlet adapter, so you can charge the iPhone directly from a wall socket.

- **Finger Tips.** Cute name for a cute fold-out leaflet of iPhone basics.

What you *won't* find in the box is a CD containing the iTunes software. You're expected to have a copy of that on your computer already. You don't need iTunes, or even a computer, to use the iPhone anymore—but it makes loading up the phone a lot easier, as described in Chapter 13.

If you don't have iTunes on your computer, then you can download it from *www.apple.com/itunes.*

Seven Basic Finger Techniques

The iPhone isn't quite like any machine that came before it, and operating it isn't quite like using any other machine. You do everything on the touch-screen instead of with physical buttons. Here's what you need to know.

Tap

You'll do a lot of tapping on the iPhone's onscreen buttons. They're usually nice and big, giving your fleshy fingertip a fat target.

You can't use a fingernail or a pen tip; only skin contact works. (OK, you can also buy a special iPhone stylus. But a fingertip is cheaper and much harder to misplace.)

Drag

When you're zoomed into a map, Web page, email, or photo, you can scroll around just by sliding your finger across the glass in any direction—like a flick (described below), but slower and more controlled. It's a huge improvement over scroll bars, especially when you want to scroll diagonally.

Swipe

In some situations, you'll be asked to confirm an action by *swiping* your finger across the screen. That's how you unlock the phone after it's been in your pocket, for example. It's ingenious, really; you may bump the touch screen when you reach into your pocket for something, but it's extremely unlikely that your knuckles will randomly *swipe* it in just the right way.

You also have to swipe to confirm that you want to turn off the iPhone, to answer a call on a locked iPhone, or to shut off an alarm. Swiping like this is also a great shortcut for deleting an email or a text message.

Flick

A *flick* is a faster, less-controlled *slide.* You flick vertically to scroll lists on the iPhone. You'll discover—usually with some expletive like "Whoa!" or "Jeez!"—that scrolling a list in this way is a blast. The faster your flick, the faster the list spins downward or upward. But lists have a real-world sort of momentum; they slow down after a second or two, so you can see where you wound up.

At any point during the scrolling of a list, you can flick again (if you didn't go far enough) or tap to stop the scrolling (if you see the item you want to choose).

Pinch and Spread

In programs like Photos, Mail, Web, and Maps, you can zoom in on a photo, message, Web page, or map by *spreading.*

That's when you place two fingers (usually thumb and forefinger) on the glass and spread them. The image magically grows, as though it's printed on a sheet of rubber.

Note The English language has failed Apple here. Moving your thumb and forefinger closer together has a perfect verb: *pinching*. But there's no word to describe moving them the opposite direction.

Apple uses the oxymoronic expression *pinch out* to describe that move (along with the redundant-sounding *pinch in*). In this book, the opposite of "pinching" is "spreading."

Once you've zoomed in like this, you can zoom out again by putting two fingers on the glass and pinching them together.

Double-Tap

Double-tapping is actually pretty rare on the iPhone, at least among the programs supplied by Apple. It's not like the Mac or Windows, where double-clicking the mouse always means "open." Because the iPhone's operating system is far more limited, you open something with *one* tap.

A double-tap, therefore, is reserved for two functions:

- In the Safari (Web browser), Photos, and Maps programs, double-tapping zooms in on whatever you tap, magnifying it. (Double-tapping means "restore to original size" after you've zoomed in.) Double-tapping also zooms into some email messages—the ones formatted like Web pages—as well as PDF files, Microsoft Office files, and others.

- When you're watching a video (or recording one), double-tapping switches the *aspect ratio* (video screen shape).

Two-Finger Tap

This weird little gesture crops up in only one place: Google Maps. It means "zoom out." To perform it, tap once on the screen—with *two* fingers.

Charging the iPhone

The iPhone has a built-in, rechargeable battery that fills up a substantial chunk of its interior. How long one charge can drive your iPhone depends on what you're doing—music playback saps the battery the least, Internet (*especially* 3G Internet) and video sap it the most. But one thing is for sure: Sooner or later, you'll have to recharge the iPhone. For most people, that's every night or every other night.

You recharge the iPhone by connecting the white USB cable that came with it. You can plug the far end into either of two places to supply power:

- **Your computer's USB jack.** In general, the iPhone charges even if your computer is asleep. (If it's a laptop that itself is not plugged in, though, the phone charges only if the laptop is awake. Otherwise, you'd come home to a depleted laptop.)

- **The AC adapter.** The little white two-prong cube that came with the iPhone connects to the end of the cradle's USB cable.

Unless the charge is *really* low, you can use the iPhone while it's charging. If the iPhone is unlocked, then the battery icon in the upper-right corner displays a lightning bolt to let you know that it's charging. If it's locked, pressing the Home button shows you a battery gauge big enough to see from space.

 Note The iPhone's battery isn't user-replaceable. It's *rechargeable,* but after 400 or 500 charges, it starts to hold less juice. Eventually, you'll have to pay Apple to install a new battery. (Apple says the added bulk of a protective plastic battery compartment, a removable door and latch, and battery-retaining springs would have meant a much smaller battery—or a *much* thicker iPhone.)

Battery Life Tips

The battery life of the iPhone is either terrific or terrible, depending on your point of view—and which model you have.

If you were an optimist, you'd point out that when these phones are using your carrier's 3G network, they get longer battery life than any other 3G phone.

If you were a pessimist, you'd observe that you sometimes can't even make it through a single day without needing a recharge.

So knowing how to scale back your iPhone's power appetite could come in extremely handy.

The biggest wolfers of electricity on your iPhone are its screen and its wireless features. Therefore, these ideas will help you squeeze more life out of each charge:

- **Dim the screen.** In bright light, the screen brightens (but uses more battery power). In dim light, it darkens. That's because when you unlock the phone after waking it, it samples the ambient light and adjusts the brightness.

 This works because of the ambient-light sensor hiding behind the glass above the earpiece. Apple says it experimented with having the light sensor active all the time, but it was weird to have the screen constantly dimming and brightening as you used it.

  You can use this information to your advantage. By covering up the sensor as you unlock the phone, you force it into a low-power, dim-screen setting (because the phone believes it's in a dark room). Or by holding it up to a light as you wake it, you get full brightness. In either case, you've saved all the taps and navigation it would have taken you to find the manual brightness slider in Settings.

- **Turn off WiFi.** If you're not in a wireless hotspot, you may as well stop the thing from using its radio. From the Home screen, tap Settings→Wi-Fi→Off.

  Or at the very least tell the iPhone to stop *searching* for WiFi networks it can connect to. Page 451 has the details.

- **Turn off "push" data.** This is a big one. If your email, calendar, and address book are kept constantly synced with your Macs or PCs, then you've probably gotten yourself involved with Yahoo Mail, Microsoft Exchange (Chapter 15), or iCloud (Chapter 14). It's pretty amazing to know that your iPhone is constantly kept current with the mother ship—but all that continual sniffing of the airwaves, looking for updates, costs you battery power. If you can do without the immediacy, then visit Settings→Mail, Contacts, Calendar→Fetch New Data. If you turn off the "Push" feature, and set it to Manually instead, then your iPhone checks for email and new appointments only when you actually open the email or calendar apps. Your battery goes a lot further.

  These days, non-Apple apps can check for frequent updates, too: Facebook, Twitter, stock-reporting apps, and so on. Your best bet on battery life, then, also involves visiting the Notification Center (page 36), tapping each app's name, and turning the Notification Center switch Off. That way, your apps won't use power by frequently checking online to see what's new.

- **Turn off cellular data.** This option turns off the cellular Internet features of your phone. You can still make calls, and you can still get online in a WiFi hotspot.

  This feature is designed for people who have a capped data plan—a limited amount of Internet use per month—which is almost everybody. If you discover that you've used up almost all your data allotment for the month, and you don't want to go over your limit (and thereby trigger an overage charge), you can use this option to shut off all data. Now your phone is just a phone.

- **Turn off the cellular voice circuitry, too.** In Airplane mode, you shut off both WiFi and the cellular radios, saving the most power of all. See page 331.

- **Turn off GPS checks.** In Settings→Location Services, there's a list of all the apps on your phone that are using your phone's location feature to know where you are. (It's a combination of GPS, cell-tower triangulation and, on some phones, WiFi hotspot triangulation.) All that checking uses battery power, too.

  Some apps, like Maps, Find My Friends, and Yelp, won't do you much good without knowing your location. But plenty of apps don't really need to know where you are. Facebook and Twitter, for example, need that information only so that they can location-stamp your posts. In any case, the point is to turn off Location Services for each app that doesn't really need to know where you are.

 Tip In the list of apps under Location Services, tiny ➶ icons show you which apps are using GPS right now (the ➶ appears in purple), and which have used it in the past 24 hours. These icons can help guide you in shutting off the GPS use of various apps.

- **Turn off Bluetooth.** If you're not using a Bluetooth headset, then for heaven's sake shut down that Bluetooth radio. In Settings, tap General and turn off Bluetooth.

- **Turn off the screen.** You can actually turn off the screen, rendering it totally black and saving incredible amounts of battery power. Of course, you now have to learn the VoiceOver talking-buttons technology to navigate and operate the phone; see page 150.

Last battery tip: Beware of 3-D games and other graphically intensive games, which can be serious power hogs. And turn off EQ when playing your music (see page 176).

 Note Before iOS 5 came along, you could also turn off the 3G feature. That would slow down your Internet connections, of course, but it would also double your battery life. That feature has been removed from most iPhones; it lives on only on AT&T models (pre-iPhone 4S) that have been upgraded to iOS 5.

The Home Screen

The Home screen is the launching pad for every iPhone activity. It's what appears when you press the Home button. It's the immortal grid of colorful icons.

It's such an essential software landmark, in fact, that a quick tour might be helpful.

- **Icons.** Each icon represents one of your iPhone apps (programs)—Calculator, Maps, Camera, and so on—or a folder that you've made to *contain* some apps. Tap one to open that program or folder.

Your iPhone comes with about 20 icons preinstalled by Apple; you can't remove them. The real fun, of course, comes when you *add* to the starter set by downloading more apps from the App Store (Chapter 8).

Apps

Badge (new information!)

Dock

- **Badges.** Every now and then, you'll see a tiny, red number "badge" (like ②) on one of your app icons. It's telling you that something new awaits: new email, new text messages, new chat entries, new updates for the apps on your iPhone. It's saying, "Hey, you! Tap me!"

- **Home-page dots.** As you install more and more programs on your iPhone—and that will happen fast once you discover the App Store— you'll need more and more room for their icons.

  The standard Home screen can't hold more than 20 icons. So where are all your games, video recorders, and tip calculators supposed to go?

  Easy: The iPhone automatically makes room for them by creating *additional* Home screens. You can spread your new programs' icons across 11 such launch screens.

  The little white dots are your map. Each represents one Home screen. If the third one is "lit up," then you're on the third Home screen.

To move among the screens, swipe horizontally—or tap to the right or left of the little dots to change screens.

And if you ever scroll too far away from the *first* Home screen, here's a handy shortcut: Press the Home button (yes, even though you're technically already home). That takes you back to the first Home screen.

 Tip The very first dot, at the far left, is actually a tiny magnifying glass. It represents the Spotlight (search) screen described on page 58. It's always waiting for you "to the left" of all the other Home screens.

- **The Dock.** At the bottom of the Home screen, four exalted icons sit in a row on what looks like a polished glass tabletop. This is the Dock—a place to park the most important icons on your iPhone. These, presumably, are the ones you use most often. That's why Apple starts you off with the Phone, Mail, Safari, and Music icons.

  What's so special about this row? As you flip among Home screens, the Dock never changes. You can never lose one of your four most cherished icons by straying from the first page, so they're always handy.

- **The background.** You can replace the traditional black background (behind your app icons) with a photo. A complicated, busy picture won't do you any favors—it will just make the icon names harder to read—so Apple provides a selection of handsome, relatively subdued wallpaper photos. But you can also choose one of your own photos.

  For instructions on changing the wallpaper, see page 220.

It's easy (and fun!) to rearrange the icons on your Home screens. Put the most frequently used icons on the first page, put similar apps into folders, reorganize your Dock. Full details are on page 236.

Notifications

As the iPhone became more and more about *apps,* certain original design aspects became more and more unwieldy—and *notifications* were among them.

A notification is an important status message. You get one every time a text message comes in, an alarm goes off, a calendar appointment is imminent, or your battery is running low. For years, iPhone notifications appeared in a blue bubble, as shown here at left.

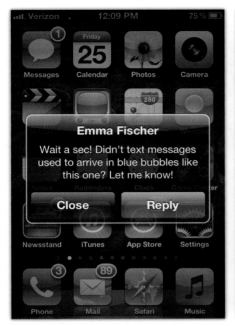

Trouble was, more and more apps began to use this mechanism. You'd get a blue bubble when your friends posted updates on Facebook or Twitter. When your flight was two hours from takeoff. When a new Groupon discount became available. When your online Scrabble or chess partner made another move.

Each time, whatever you were doing was interrupted by the appearance of a new blue bubble—and you couldn't return to your activity without tapping, for example, OK or Cancel or Reply in the blue bubble. It got annoying fast.

So in iOS 5, you can choose one of three notification styles for *each individual app.* To see these controls, open Settings→Notifications. Scroll down and tap the app you want to tweak. You'll see that you have three choices for each app:

- **None.** If certain apps seem to bug you with news you really don't care about, you can make them shut up forever. Tap None to squelch their notifications altogether.

- **Banners.** This option, new in iOS 5, is illustrated above at right. It makes incoming notifications appear quietly and briefly at the top of the screen. The message holds still long enough for you to read it, but it doesn't interrupt your work and goes away automatically after a few seconds. Banners are a good option for things like Facebook and Twitter updates, and incoming text and email messages.

Tip If you can tap that banner with your finger before it disappears, you jump directly to the app that's trying to get your attention.

- **Alerts.** This is the old-style option: A blue bubble appears to get your attention. You might use this option for apps whose messages are too important to miss, like alarms, flight updates, and text messages.

The Notification Center

No matter what kind of notification pops up, you still see only one alert at a time. And once it's gone, you can't get it back.

Or at least that's now it used to be. In the modern age of iOS 5, there's a simple solution: the Notification Center screen. It lists every single notification you've received recently, in a tidy, scrolling list.

You can check it out right now: Swipe your finger down from the top of the iPhone's screen. The Notification Center pulls down like a classy black window shade, printed in white with every recent item of interest.

Swipe down from above the screen... 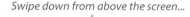 *...to reveal the Notifications center.*

Here you'll find all your apps' notifications, as well as all of your missed calls, recent text messages, reminders, and upcoming calendar appointments.

You can have all kinds of fun here:

- Swipe upward inside the list to see more of it.

- Drag the ribbed bottom handle upward to make the window shade snap up again, hiding the Notification Center.

 Tip Actually, you don't have to aim for the ribbed handle. You can just swipe upward from beneath the screen, quickly and sloppily.

- Tap a line in the Notification Center to open the relevant app for more details—for example, to see more information about that appointment, or to read the whole text message in context.

- Tap the ⊗ next to an app's name, and then tap Clear, to remove that app's current listings from the Notification Center. (That app's heading will reappear here the next time it has anything to tell you.)

It's important to note, by the way, that you can (and should) specify *which* apps are allowed to junk up your Notification Center. Open Settings→Notifications to see the master Notifications list, with one entry for every single app that might ever want your attention (next page, left).

 Tip As you scroll through the list of apps in Settings→Notifications, choosing which you want to appear in the Notification Center, don't miss the two oddballs here: Weather Widget and Stock Widget. If you tap one and turn On its presence in the Notification Center, the Weather Widget will show the local current conditions and a forecast, right there on the Notification Center; the Stock widget will display a scrolling ticker of any stocks you've selected in the Stocks app (Chapter 9).

Here, on the master Notifications screen, you can also specify the order of the various apps' notifications in the Center. If you tap By Time, then the apps with the newest alerts appear at the top. But if you tap Manually and then Edit, you can drag the ☰ handles up or down to specify the top-to-bottom order of your apps' notifications on the Notification Center screen.

Anyway, now it's time to change the settings for one app at a time. Tap an app's name to open its individual Notifications settings screen (above, right— the Reminders app, in this example). Here, you can, if you like, turn Notification Center to Off.

Tip You can also use the Show button to specify how *much* of the Notification Center this app is allowed to use up—that is, how many lines of information. Maybe you need only the most recent alert about your upcoming flight (1 Item), but you want to see a lot more of your upcoming appointments (10 Items).

You'll discover that the app's name no longer appears in the upper list of apps, which bears the obvious heading "In Notification Center." It's jumped to the lower list, called "Not in Notification Center" (duh). The app can still get your attention with banners or alert bubbles—but it won't appear in the Notification Center.

Messages on the Lock Screen

The Lock screen, of course, is what appears when you tap the Sleep switch or Home button to wake a sleeping iPhone.

This screen, too, is a great place to see what's been trying to get your attention while the phone was in your pocket: missed calls and texts, new messages and email, and so on. (You can see a picture on page 11.)

In principle, the Lock screen is therefore exactly like the Notification Center—but there are differences. For example, every time you wake the phone, whatever notifications are on the Lock screen are wiped clear. They don't stay put, as they do on the Notification Center.

You might want a *different* set of apps to list their nags on the Lock screen. Maybe you want the Lock screen to show only missed calls, new text messages, and new mail—but you'd like the Notification Center to be fully stocked with Twitter and Facebook updates, for example.

That's why, when you burrow into Settings→Notifications and tap an app's name, you get a View in Lock Screen on/off switch.

 Tip While you're here, you may as well check out the Badge App Icon switch for each app. The Badge is the little ❷ that indicates how many messages or updates are waiting inside that app—and you can turn it off for each app individually. Some apps even offer an on/off switch for Sounds, which is handy if you think your phone makes far too many bleeps and burbles as it is.

Yes, there's a lot going on in the world of iPhone notifications now—a lot of fine-grained control, a lot of apps to be adjusted individually. But once you've owned your iPhone for a while, you'll come to be grateful that you can boost to prominence the most urgent and important notices—and squelch the ones you couldn't care less about.

2

Typing, Editing & Searching

The iPhone is amazing, all right. But as a pocket computer, it faces some fundamental limitations: It has no real keyboard and no real mouse. Which might be considered drawbacks on a gadget that's capable of running hundreds of thousands of programs.

Fortunately, where there's a problem, there's software that can fix it. The modern iPhone's virtual keyboard is smart in all kinds of ways—automatically predicting and correcting typos, for example. You can even tap a mistyped word to see some suggestions for fixing it. This chapter covers every aspect of working with text on the iPhone: entering it, fixing it, and searching for it. (Well, *almost* every aspect. Chapter 4 covers *dictating* text into the iPhone 4S.)

The Keyboard

Very few iPhone features have triggered as much angst, hope, and criticism as the onscreen keyboard. It's true, boys and girls: The iPhone has no physical keys. A virtual keyboard, therefore, is the only possible built-in system for typing text. Like it or not, you'll be doing a lot of typing on glass.

The keyboard appears automatically whenever you tap in a place where typing is possible: in an outgoing email or text message, in the Notes program, in the address bar of the Web browser, and so on.

Just tap the key you want. As your finger taps the glass, a "speech balloon" appears above your finger, showing an enlarged version of the key you actually hit (since your finger is now blocking your view of the keyboard).

In darker gray, surrounding the letters, you'll find these special keys:

- **Shift (⇧).** When you tap this key, it glows white to indicate that it's in effect. The next letter you type appears as a capital. Then the ⇧ key returns to normal, meaning that the next letter will be lowercase.

Tip The iPhone has a Caps Lock feature, but you have to turn it on. In
Settings→General→Keyboard, **turn on** Enable Caps Lock.

From now on, if you double-tap the ⇧ key, it turns blue. You're now in Caps Lock
mode, and you'll now type in ALL CAPITALS until you tap the ⇧ key again. (If you
can't seem to make Caps Lock work, try double-tapping the ⇧ key *fast.*)

- **Backspace (⌫).** This key actually has three speeds.

  Tap it once to delete the letter just before the blinking insertion point.

  Hold it down to "walk" backward, deleting as you go.

  If you *hold down the key long enough,* it starts deleting *words* rather than
  letters, one whole chunk at a time.

- **.?123**. Tap this button when you want to type numbers or punctuation.
  The keyboard changes to offer a palette of numbers and symbols. Tap
  the same key—which now says **ABC**—to return to the letters keyboard.
  (On the iPhone 4S, the button may just say 123, without the punctuation;
  that's to leave room for the little microphone button.)

Once you're on the numbers/symbols pad, a new dark gray button appears, labeled . Tapping it summons a *third* keyboard layout, containing the less frequently used symbols, like brackets, the # and % symbols, bullets, and math symbols.

> **Note** Because the period is such a frequently used symbol, there's an awesome shortcut that doesn't require switching to the punctuation keyboard: At the end of a sentence, just tap the space bar *twice*. You get a period, a space, *and* a capitalized letter at the beginning of the next word. (This, too, can be turned off—in Settings→General→Keyboard—although it's hard to imagine why you'd want to.)

- **Return.** Tapping this key moves to the next line, just as on a real keyboard. (There's no Tab key or Enter key in iPhone Land.)

The Widescreen Keyboard

In some programs, you can turn the phone 90 degrees to type. When the keyboard stretches out the long way, the keys get a lot bigger. And it's a lot easier to type—even with two thumbs.

This glorious feature doesn't work in every program, alas. Fortunately, it works in the programs where you do the most typing, like Mail, Messages (text messages), the Safari browser, Contacts, Twitter, and Notes. (The screen also rotates in Camera, Music, Calculator, Calendar, and Stocks, though not for typing purposes.)

Making the Keyboard Work

Some people have no problem tapping those tiny virtual keys; others struggle for days. Either way, here are some tips:

- Don't be freaked out by the tiny, narrow keys. Apple *knows* your fingertip is fatter than that.

  So as you type, use the whole pad of your finger or thumb. Don't try to tap with only a skinny part of your finger to match the skinny keys. You'll be surprised at how fast and accurate this method is. (Tap, don't press.)

- This may sound like New Age hooey, but *trust* the keyboard. Don't pause to check the result after each letter. Just plow on.

> **Tip** Although you don't see it, the sizes of the keys on the iPhone keyboard are actually changing all the time. That is, the software enlarges the "landing area" of certain keys, based on probability.
>
> For example, suppose you type *tim*. Now, the iPhone knows that no word in the language begins *timw* or *timr*—and so, invisibly, it enlarges the "landing area" of the E key, which greatly diminishes your chances of making a typo on that last letter. Cool.

- Start with one-finger typing. Two-thumb, BlackBerry-style typing comes later. You'll drive yourself crazy if you start out that way, although it's not bad when you're using the *widescreen* keyboard layout.

- Without cursor keys, how are you supposed to correct an error you made a few sentences ago? Easy—use the *loupe.*

  Hold your fingertip down anywhere in the text until you see the magnified circle appear. Without lifting your finger, drag anywhere in the text; you'll see that the insertion point moves along with it. Release when the blue line is where you want to delete or add text, just as though you'd clicked there with a mouse.

> **Tip** In the Safari address bar, you can skip the part about waiting for the loupe to appear. Once you click into the address, start *dragging* to make it appear at once.

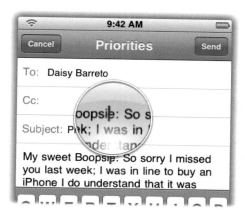

- Don't bother using the Shift key to capitalize a new sentence. The iPhone does that capitalizing automatically. (To turn this feature on or off, open Settings→General→Keyboard. Turn off Auto-Capitalization.)

Auto-Suggestions

If you make a mistake, don't reflexively go for the Backspace (⊗). Instead, just beneath the word you typed, you'll find the iPhone's proposed replacement. The software analyzes the letters *around* the one you typed and usually figures out what you really meant. For example, if you accidentally type *imsame*, the iPhone realizes that you meant *insane* and suggests that word.

To accept its suggestion, tap the space bar or any punctuation, like a period or question mark. To ignore the suggestion, tap it carefully with your finger.

 Tip If you turn on Speak Auto-text (page 155), your iPhone will even *speak* the suggested word out loud. That way, you can keep your focus on the keyboard.

The suggestion feature can be especially useful when it comes to contractions, which are normally clumsy to type because you have to switch to the punctuation keyboard to find the apostrophe.

So you can save time by *deliberately* leaving out the apostrophe in contractions like *I'm, don't, can't,* and so on. Type *im, dont,* or *cant.* The iPhone proposes *I'm, don't,* or *can't,* so you can just tap the space bar to fix the word and continue.

The suggestion feature also kicks in when the iPhone thinks it knows how you intend to complete a *correctly* spelled word. For example, if you type *fathe,* the suggestion says *father.* This trick usually saves you only a letter or two, but that's better than nothing.

 Tip If you *accidentally* accept an autocorrect suggestion, tap the Backspace key. A word bubble appears, which you can tap to reinstate what you'd originally typed.

The Spelling Checker

Here's the world's friendliest typo-fixer. Apple calls it a spelling checker, but maybe that's stretching it.

The idea is that anytime the iPhone doesn't recognize something you've typed, it draws a dotted red underline beneath. Tap the word to see a pop-up balloon with one, two, or three alternate spellings. Often, one of them is what you wanted, and you can tap it to fix the mistake. (Equally often, none of them is, and it's time to break out the loupe and the keyboard.)

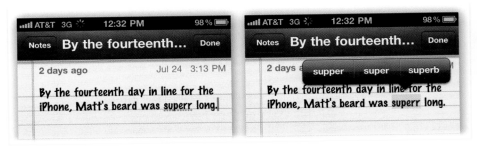

The Spelling Dictionary

As you type, the iPhone compares what you've typed against the words in its built-in word list, or dictionary (and against the names in your address book). If it finds a match or a partial match, it displays a suggestion just beneath what you've typed.

If you tap the space bar to accept the suggestion, wonderful.

If you don't—if you dismiss the suggestion and allow the "mistake" to stand— then the iPhone adds that word to a custom, dynamic dictionary, assuming that you've just typed some name, bit of slang, or terminology that wasn't in its dictionary originally. It dawns on the iPhone that maybe that's a legitimate word it doesn't know—and it adds it to the dictionary.

From now on, in other words, it will accept that bizarre new word as a legiti-mate word—and, in fact, will even *suggest* it the next time you type some-thing like it.

Words you've added to the dictionary actually *age.* If you stop using some custom term, the iPhone gradually learns to forget it. That's handy behavior if you never intended for that word to become part of the dictionary to begin with (that is, it was a mistake).

Accented Characters

To produce an accented character (like é, ë, è, ê, and so on), keep your finger pressed on that key for one second. A palette of diacritical marks appears; slide onto the one you want, as you can see on the next page.

Not all keys sprout this pop-up palette. Here's a list of the keys that do produce alternative markings.

Key	Alternates
A	à á â ä æ ã å ā
C	ç ć č
E	è é ê ë ę è ē
I	ī į í ì ï î
L	ł
N	ń ñ
O	ō ø œ õ ó ò ö ô o
S	ß ś š
U	ū ú ù ü û
Y	ÿ
Z	ź ž ż
?	¿
'	' ' '
"	» « „ " "
-	—

Key	Alternates
$	€ £ ¥ ₩
&	§
0	°

How to Type Punctuation with One Touch

On the iPhone, the punctuation and alphabet keys appear on two different keyboard layouts. That's a *serious* hassle, because each time you want, say, a comma, it's an awkward, three-step dance: (1) Tap the ?123 key to get the punctuation layout. (2) Tap the comma. (3) Tap the ABC key or the space bar to return to the alphabet layout.

Imagine how excruciating it is to type, for example, "a P.O. Box in the U.S.A."! That's 34 finger taps and 10 mode changes!

Fortunately, there's a secret way to get a punctuation mark with only a *single* finger gesture.

The iPhone doesn't register most key presses until you *lift* your finger. But the Shift and Punctuation keys register their taps on the press *down* instead.

So here's what you can do, all in one motion:

1 **Touch the [?123] key, but don't lift your finger.** The punctuation layout appears.

2 **Slide your finger onto the period or comma key, and release.** The ABC layout returns automatically. You've typed a period or a comma with one finger touch instead of three.

> **Tip** If you're a two-thumbed typist, you can also hit the [?123] key with your left thumb, and then tap the punctuation key with your right. It even works on the [#+=] sub-punctuation layout, although you'll probably visit that screen less often.

In fact, you can type any of the punctuation symbols the same way. This technique makes a *huge* difference in the usability of the keyboard.

> **Tip** This same trick saves you a finger-press when capitalizing words, too. You can put your finger down on the ⇧ key and slide directly onto the letter you want to type in its uppercase version. Or, if you're a two-handed iPhone typist, you can work the Shift key like the one on your computer: Hold it down with your left thumb, type a letter with your right, and then release both.

Typing Shortcuts (Abbreviation Expanders)

Here's a new iOS 5 feature that nobody ever talks about—probably because nobody even knows it exists. But it's a huge time- and frustration-saver; for a phone that has no physical keys, anything that can do your typing for you is very welcome indeed.

For the first time, you can program your phone to expand abbreviations that you type. Set up *addr* to type your entire return address. Create two-letter abbreviations for big legal or technical words you have to type a lot. Set up *goaway* to type out a polite rejection paragraph for use in email. And so on.

This feature has been in Microsoft Office forever (called AutoCorrect). And it's always been available as a separate app (TypeIt4Me and TextExpander, for example—but because they were separate, you had to copy your expanded text, switch to the target program, and then paste). But now it's built right into the operating system, so it works anywhere you can type.

You build your list of abbreviations in Settings→General→Keyboard. Scroll way down and tap Add New Shortcut. On the resulting screen, type the expanded text into the Phrase box. (It can be very long, but it all has to be one continuous blob of text; it can't contain Returns.) In the Shortcut box, type the abbreviation you want to use to trigger the phrase. (The Shortcut box says "optional," but it's not. If you leave the shortcut blank, your new shortcut is un-triggerable and pointless.)

That's it! Now, whenever you type one of the abbreviations you've set up, the iPhone proposes replacing it with your substituted text. The suggestion bubble works exactly the way the spelling bubble does: To accept the suggestion, keep on typing; to reject it, carefully tap the suggestion bubble itself.

International Typing

As the iPhone goes on sale around the world, it has to be equipped for non-English languages—and even non-Roman alphabets. Fortunately, it's ready.

To prepare the iPhone for language switching, go to Settings→General→International. Tap Language to set the iPhone's primary language (for menus, button labels, and so on).

To make other *keyboards* available, tap Keyboards, tap Add New Keyboard, and then turn on the keyboard layouts you'll want available: Russian, Italian, whatever.

If you choose Japanese or Chinese, you're offered the chance to specify which *kind* of character input you want. For Japanese, you can choose a QWERTY layout or a Kana keypad. For Simplified or Traditional Chinese, you have a choice of the Pinyin input method (which uses a QWERTY layout) or handwriting recognition, where you draw your symbols onto the screen with your fingertip; a palette of potential interpretations appears to the right. (That's handy, since there are thousands of characters in Chinese, and you'd need a 65-inch iPhone to fit the keyboard.) Or hey—it's a free tic-tac-toe game!

Now, when you arrive at any writing area in any program, you'll discover that a new icon has appeared on the keyboard: a tiny globe (⊕) next to the space bar. Each time you tap it, you rotate to the next keyboard you requested earlier. The new language's name appears briefly on the space bar to identify it.

Thanks to that ⊕ button, you can freely mix languages and alphabets within the same document, without having to duck back to some control panel to make the change. And thanks to the iPhone's virtual keyboard, the actual letters on the "keys" change in real time. (As an Apple PR rep puts it, "That's really hard to do on a BlackBerry.")

Connecting a Real Keyboard

This iPhone feature barely merits an asterisk in Apple's marketing materials. But if you're any kind of wandering journalist, blogger, or writer, you might flip your lid over this: You can type on a real, full-sized, plastic keyboard, and watch the text magically appear on the iPhone screen—wirelessly.

That's because you can use a Bluetooth keyboard (the Apple Wireless Keyboard, for example) to type into your iPhone.

To set this up, from the Home screen, tap Settings→General→Bluetooth. Turn Bluetooth on, if it's not already.

Now turn on the wireless keyboard. After a moment, its name shows up on the iPhone screen in the Devices list; tap it. You'll know the pairing was successful, because when you tap in a spot where the onscreen keyboard would usually appear, well, it doesn't.

As you can probably imagine, typing is a lot easier and faster with a real keyboard than when you're trying to type on glass. As a bonus, the Apple keyboard's brightness, volume, and playback controls actually work to control the iPhone's brightness, volume, and playback.

 Tip The Apple keyboard's ⏏ key even works: It makes the iPhone's onscreen keyboard appear or disappear. Oh, and to switch languages, press ⌘-space bar on the wireless keyboard. You'll see the list of languages. Tap the space bar again to choose a different language.

When you're finished using the keyboard, turn it off. The iPhone goes back to normal.

 Tip There's another way to bypass the onscreen keyboard, too: Dictate. If you have an iPhone 4S, you can speak instead of typing, as described in Chapter 4.

If you have an earlier iPhone, you can use the free Dragon Dictation app instead. Over an Internet connection, your words are turned into typed text in about 2 seconds. From there, one tap copies the results to a text message, an outgoing email, the Clipboard for pasting somewhere, or Facebook or Twitter as an update.

Cut, Copy, Paste

After two years of customer whining and pining, Apple finally blessed the iPhone with Copy and Paste. You can grab a picture or text off a Web page and paste it into an email message, copy directions from email into Notes, paste a phone number from your address book into a text message, and so on.

Part of the problem, according to Apple, was the challenge of designing a way to select text and trigger Cut, Copy, and Paste functions—on a machine with no mouse and no menus! As on the Mac or PC, it takes three steps.

Step 1: Select the Text

Start by highlighting the text you want to cut or copy. Sounds simple, but there are two different ways to go about it:

- **Double-tap method.** Here's the quickest way. Double-tap the first word (or last word) that you want in the copied selection. That word is now highlighted, with blue dots at diagonal corners; drag these handles to expand the selection to include all the text you want. The little magnifying loupe helps you release the dot at just the right spot.

Double-tap…

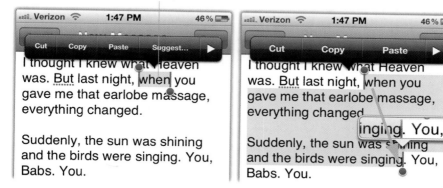

…drag the handle.

- **Insertion-point method.** This method involves more steps but offers a Select All option that you don't get with the double-tap. It's available only in places where you can type (not, for example, in an email from somebody else).

  Tap in your text to place the blinking insertion point where you want it (next page, left); then tap the insertion point itself to summon the selection buttons (middle). Tap Select All to copy everything in the text box or message. Or tap Select to get the two diagonal blue selection dots (right); drag the handles as already described.

> **Tip** On a Web page, you can't very well double-tap to select a word, because double-tapping means "zoom in." So instead, *hold your finger down* on a word to produce the blue handles; the loupe magnifies the proceedings to help you. (If you highlight the wrong word, keep your finger down and slide to the correct one; the highlighting goes with you.)
>
> However, if you're zoomed out to see the whole page, holding down your finger highlights the *entire block* of text (a paragraph or even a whole article) instead of one word. Now you can expand the selection to include a photo, if you like; that way, you can copy and paste the whole enchilada into an outgoing email message.

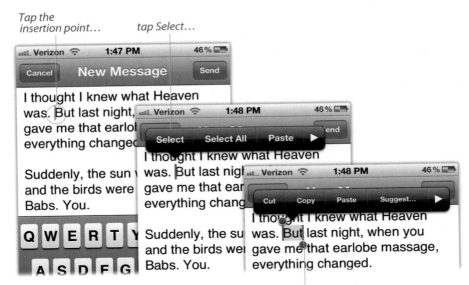

Tap the insertion point...   *tap Select...*

...drag the blue handles to select text.

Step 2: Cut or Copy

At this point, you've highlighted the material you want, and the Cut and Copy buttons are staring you in the face. Tap Cut (to remove the selected text) or Copy (to leave it but place a duplicate on your invisible Clipboard). (The Suggest button summons three alternate suggestions from the iPhone spelling checker.)

 Tip And what if you want to get rid of the text *without* copying it to the Clipboard (because you want to preserve something you copied earlier, for example)? Easy: Just tap the Delete key!

Step 3: Paste

Finally, switch to a different spot in the text, even if it's in a different window (for example, a new email message) or a different program (for example, Calendar or Notes). Tap in any spot where you're allowed to type: Notes, email, text message, Safari's address bar, the Spotlight search box, a text box on a Web page, someone's Contacts screen, the top of the Calculator, even the phone-number display on the dialing keypad. Tap the Paste button to paste what you cut or copied.

Ta-da! And to think that it took two years.

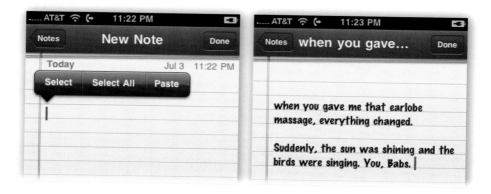

(Possible Step 4: Undo)

Everyone makes mistakes, right? Fortunately, there's a secret Undo command, which can come in handy when you cut, copy, or paste something by mistake.

The trick is to *shake* the iPhone. The iPhone then offers you an Undo button, which you can tap to confirm the backtracking. One finger touch instead of three.

Tip The shake-to-Undo feature also works to undo *dictating or typing*—not just cutting or pasting.

In fact, you can even Undo the Undo. Just shake the phone again; now the screen offers you a Redo button. Fun! (Except when you shake the phone by accident and you get the "Nothing to Undo" message. But still.)

The Definitions Dictionary

Earlier in this chapter, you can read about the spelling dictionary that's built into the iOS—but that's just a dumb list of words. Your iPhone also has a *real* dictionary, one that shows you definitions.

You can look up any word that appears on the screen. Double-tap it to get the editing bar shown below at left; then tap Define. The attractively formatted definitions page appears instantly (below, right).

 Tip You can also double-tap the blinking insertion point that's just before a word. On the editing bar, tap the ▶ button to see the Define button.

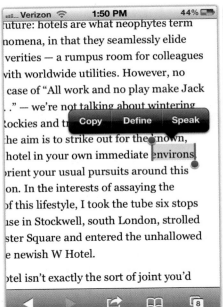

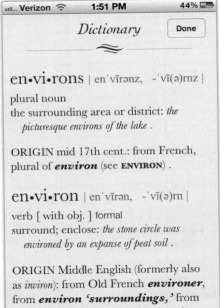

Spotlight: Global Search

The iPhone has a feature so fast, powerful, and so useful, you'll wonder how the heck anyone survived without it: a global search feature called Spotlight. Just by typing a few letters, you can search almost the entire phone at once—or even the whole Web. Here's where it looks to find matches:

- **Contacts.** First names, last names, and company names.

- **Mail.** The To, From, and Subject lines of all accounts. For certain accounts, you can even search inside the messages.

- **Calendar.** Appointment names, meeting invitees, and locations (but not any notes attached to your appointments).

- **Music.** Song, performer, and album names, plus the names of podcasts, videos, and audiobooks. Oh, and voice memos' names and descriptions.

- **Notes, Reminders.** The actual text of your notes and to-do items.

- **Messages.** Yep, you can search your SMS text messages, too.

- **Your apps.** For frequent downloaders, this may be the juiciest function of all: Spotlight also searches the names of every single app on your iPhone. If you have dozens or hundreds installed, this is a much more efficient way to find one than trying to page through all the Home screens, eye-balling the icons as you go.

- **Web.** At the bottom of the list of search results, the Search Web button appears. Tap it to open Safari and begin an automatic search for the term you've typed, using Google or whatever search page you've specified in Settings.

- **Wikipedia.** At the *very* bottom of the list of search results, you get a Search Wikipedia option. As you could probably guess, tapping it opens up Wikipedia and performs a search for the term you've typed.

These last two options might not *quite* seem to fit into the same cat-egories as Mail, Apps, and so on. But once you get used to the idea that you've got quick Web search options right there in Spotlight, they can save you a few steps the next time you want to look something up online.

 It's worth noting that the Contacts, Mail, Calendar, Music, and Notes programs have their *own* search boxes (usually hidden until you scroll all the way to the top of their lists). Those individual search functions are great when you're already *in* the program where you want to search. The Spotlight difference is that it searches all these apps at once.

How to Open Spotlight

The Spotlight screen is built into your Home screens—at the far left.

Once you've pressed the Home button, you can either keep swiping your finger to the right, or press the Home button again (and maybe a third time),
until the Spotlight screen heaves into view.

(Truth is, that's an overly wordy description of what's usually a simple task. A
slow double-press is usually all it takes.)

How to Search

The keyboard opens automatically (previous page, left). Begin typing to identify what you want to find and open. For example, if you were trying to find a
file called *Pokémon Fantasy League,* typing just *pok* or *leag* would probably
suffice. (Spotlight doesn't find text in the *middles* of words, though; it searches
from the beginnings of words.)

A results list immediately appears below the search box, listing everything
Spotlight can find containing what you've typed so far. (This is a live, interac-
tive search; that is, Spotlight modifies the menu of search results *as you type.*)

Contacts, apps, emails...

Pass your query on to the Web

They're neatly grouped by category; the beginning of each category is marked with an icon, and the light gray and medium gray backgrounds alternate to help you notice when a new category has begun.

 Tip If you drag your finger to scroll the list, the keyboard helpfully vanishes so you can see more results.

If you see the icon of whatever you were hoping to dig up, just tap to open it. The corresponding program (Contacts, Mail, Music, the app you tapped, whatever) opens automatically.

How to Tweak Spotlight

You've just read about how Spotlight works fresh out of the box. But you can tailor its behavior to fit it to the kinds of things you look up most often. To open Spotlight's settings, start on the Home screen. Tap Settings→General→Spotlight Search.

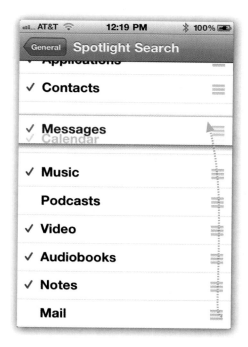

You can tweak Spotlight in two ways here:

- **Turn off categories.** The checkmarks identify the kinds of things that Spotlight tracks. If you find that Spotlight uses up precious screen space listing categories you don't use much, then tap to turn off their checkmarks. Now more of Spotlight's space-constrained screen is allotted to icon types you do care about.

- **Prioritize the categories.** This screen also lets you change the *order* of the category results; using the little ☰ grip strip at the right side, you can drag an individual list item up or down.

  For example, the factory setting is for Contacts to appear first in the menu. But Contacts has its own search box, so it might make more sense to put Calendar or Applications at the top of the list so that it's quicker to do a schedule check or fire up a certain app. You'll have less scrolling to do once the results menu appears.

3

Phone Calls & FaceTime

Suppose you're in luck. Suppose the "number of bars" logo in the upper-left corner of the iPhone's screen tells you that you've got cellular reception. You're ready to start a conversation.

Well, *almost* ready. The iPhone offers five ways to dial, but four of them require that you first be in the Phone *application*. The following pages cover all these methods. (The fifth way is dialing by voice, as described in Chapter 4.)

Dialing from the Phone App

To dial by tapping, open the Phone app like this:

❶ **Go Home, if you're not already there.** Press the Home button.

❷ **Tap the Phone icon.** It's usually at the bottom of the Home screen. (The tiny circled number in the corner of the Phone icon tells you how many missed calls and voicemail messages you have.)

> **Tip** Of course, you can also double-press the Home button to open the task switcher. If you make calls often, the Phone app's icon should be there waiting for you, as described on page 13. This shortcut skips the trip to the Home screen.

Now you've arrived in the Phone program. A new row of icons appears at the bottom, representing the four ways of dialing from here:

- **Favorites list.** Here's the iPhone's version of speed-dial keys: It lists the 50 people you think you call most frequently. Tap a name to make the call. (Details on building and editing this list begin on page 65.)

- **Recents list.** Every call you've recently made, answered, missed, or dialed but hung up appears in this list. Missed callers' names appear in red lettering, which makes them easy to spot—and easy to call back.

    Tap a name or a number to dial. Or tap the ⊘ button to view the details of a call—when, where, how long—and, if you like, to add this number to your Contacts list.

- **Contacts list.** This program also has an icon of its own on the Home screen; you don't have to drill down to it through the Phone button. It's your phone book; tap somebody's name or number to dial it.

- **Keypad.** This dialing pad may be virtual, but the buttons are a *heck* of a lot bigger than they are on regular cellphones, making them easy to tap, even with fat fingers. You can punch in any number and then tap Call to place the call.

Once you've dialed, no matter which method you used, either hold the iPhone up to your head, put in the earbuds, turn on the speakerphone, or put on your Bluetooth earpiece—and start talking!

The few short paragraphs above, however, are only the Quick Start Guide. Here's a more detailed look at each of the four Phone-app modules.

The Favorites List

You may not wind up dialing much from Contacts. That's the master list, all right, but it's too unwieldy when you just want to call your spouse, your boss, or your lawyer. Dialing by voice (Chapter 4) is almost always faster. But when silence is golden, at the very least use the Favorites list—a short, easy-to-scan list of the people you want to call most often.

You can add a phone number to this list (for dialing, texting, or FaceTime video calls) or an email address (for FaceTime).

You can add names to this list in any of three ways:

- **From the Favorites list itself.** Tap the + button to view your Contacts list. Tap the person you want. If there's more than one phone number or email address on the Info screen, tap the one you want to add to Favorites.

Tip Each Favorite doesn't represent a *person;* it represents a *number or email address.* So if Chris has both a home number and a cell number, add two items to the Favorites list. Blue lettering in the list lets you know whether each number or address is mobile, home, or whatever.

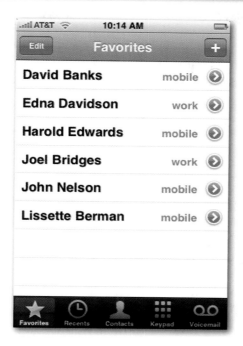

- **From the Contacts list.** Tap a name to open the Info screen, where you'll find a button called Add to Favorites. (If you have an email address for this person but no phone number, the iPhone treats it as a FaceTime favorite.) If there's more than one phone number on the Info screen, you're asked to tap the one you want to add to Favorites.

- **From the Recents list.** Tap the ◉ button next to any name or number in the Recents list. If it's somebody who's already in your Contacts list, then you arrive at the Call Details screen, where one tap on Add to Favorites does what it says.

  If it's somebody who's not in Contacts yet, you'll have to *put* her there first. Tap Create New Contact, and then proceed as described on page 71. After you hit Save, you return to the Call Details screen so you can tap Add to Favorites.

The Favorites list holds 50 numbers. Once you've added 50, the Add to Favorites and **+** buttons disappear.

Reordering Favorites

Tapping that Edit button at the top of the Favorites list offers another handy feature, too: It lets you drag names up and down, so the most important people appear at the top of the list. Just use the right-side "grip strip" (☰) as a handle to move entire names up or down the list.

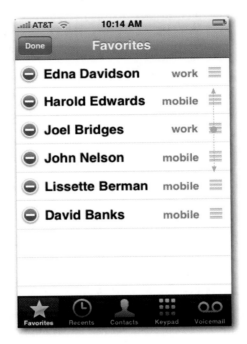

Deleting from Favorites

To delete somebody from your Favorites—the morning after a nasty political argument over drinks, for example—tap Edit. Then follow the usual iPhone deletion sequence: First tap the ⊖ button next to the unwanted entry, and then tap Remove to confirm.

The Recents List

Like any self-respecting cellphone, the iPhone maintains a list of everybody you've called or who's called you recently. The idea, of course, is to provide you with a quick way to call someone you've been talking to lately.

To see the list, tap Recents at the bottom of the Phone application. You see a list of the last 75 calls that you've received or placed from your iPhone, along with each person's name or number (depending on whether that name is in Contacts or not), which phone number it is (mobile, home, work, or whatever), city of the caller's home area code (for callers not in your Contacts), and the date of the call.

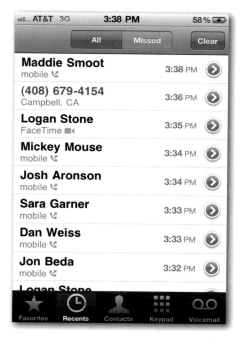

Here's what you need to know about the Recents list:

- Calls that you missed (or sent to voicemail) appear in red type. If you tap Missed at the top of the screen, you see *only* your missed calls. The color-coding and separate listings are designed to make it easy for you to return calls you missed, or to try again to reach someone who didn't answer when you called.

- A tiny 📞 icon lets you know which calls you *made* (to differentiate them from calls you *answered*).

- To call someone back—regardless of whether you answered or dialed the call—tap that name or number in the list.

- Tap the ◉ button next to any call to open the Info screen. At the top of the screen, you can see whether this was an outgoing call, an incoming call, or a missed call.

What else you see here depends on whether or not the other person is in your Contacts list.

If so, the Info screen displays the person's whole information card. A little table displays all the incoming and outgoing calls to or from this person that day. A star denotes a phone number that's also in your Favorites list.

If the call *isn't* from someone in your Contacts, then you get to see a handy notation at the top of the Info screen: the city and state where the calling phone is registered.

- To save you scrolling, the Recents list thoughtfully combines consecutive calls to or from the same person. If some obsessed ex-lover has been calling you every 10 minutes for 4 hours, you'll see "Chris Meyerson (24)" in the Recents list. (Tap the ◉ button to see the exact times of the calls.)

- To erase one call from this list, tap Edit, tap the button next to the unwanted entry, and then tap Delete. You can also erase the *entire* list, thus ruling out the chance that a coworker or significant other might discover your illicit activities; just tap Clear at the top of the screen. You'll be asked to confirm your decision.

The Contacts List

The Phone app offers four ways to dial—Favorites, Recents, Contacts, and Keypad—but the Contacts list is the source from which all other lists spring. That's probably why it's listed twice: once with its own button on the Home screen, and again at the bottom of the Phone application.

Contacts is your address book—your master phone book.

> **Tip** Your iPhone's own phone number appears at the very top of the Contacts list within the Phone module. (If you tap the Contacts icon on your Home screen instead, your phone number doesn't appear.) Drag down on the list to reveal its hiding place above the search box.
>
> That's a much better place for it than deep at the end of a menu labyrinth, where it is on most phones.

If your social circle is longer than one screenful, then you can navigate this list in any of three ways.

First, you can savor the distinct pleasure of flicking through it (page 27).

Second, if you're in a hurry to get to the T's, use the A-to-Z index down the right edge of the screen. You can tap the last-name initial letter you want (R or W or whatever). Alternatively, you can drag your finger up or down the index. The list scrolls in real time.

Third, you can use the search box at the very top of the list, above the A's. (If you don't see it, tap the tiny ⚲ icon at the top of the A-to-Z index on the right side of the screen, or just flick the list downward.)

Tap inside the search box to make the keyboard appear. As you type, Contacts pares down the list, hiding everyone whose first, last, or company name doesn't match what you've typed so far. It's a really fast way to pluck one name out of a haystack.

(To restore the full list, clear the search box by tapping the ⊗ at its right end.)

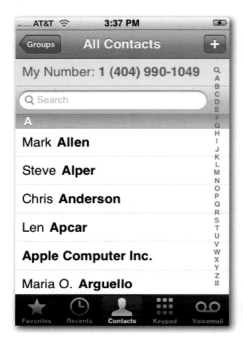 

In any case, when you see the name you want, tap it to open its card, filled with phone numbers and other info. Tap the number you want to dial.

> **Tip** Your iPhone excels at syncing with existing address books. It can slurp in the addresses from the Mac or PC, for example (Chapter 13), and from a corporate Exchange server (Chapter 15), and from an iCloud account (Chapter 14).
>
> If you can't seem to find someone in the list, you may be looking in the wrong list. Tap Groups at the top-left corner, in that case, to return to the list of accounts. Tap All Contacts to view a single, unified list of everyone your phone knows about.

Adding to the Contacts List

Every cellphone has a Contacts list, of course, but the beauty of the iPhone is that you don't have to type in the phone numbers one at a time. Instead, the iPhone sucks in the entire phone book from your Mac or PC, iCloud, and/or an Exchange server at work.

Tip Actually, it can slurp in your phone list from the SIM card of an older GSM cellphone, too. See page 471.

It's infinitely easier to edit your address book on the computer, where you have an actual keyboard and mouse. The iPhone also makes it very easy to add someone's contact information when they call, email, FaceTime you, or send a text message, thanks to a prominent Add to Contacts button.

But if, in a pinch, on the road, at gunpoint, you have to add, edit, or remove a contact manually, here's how to do it.

Make sure you've selected the right account, as described in the Tip on the previous page. You don't want to add the person to the wrong account.

On the Contacts screen, tap the **+** button. You arrive at the New Contact screen, which teems with empty boxes.

Many computer address book programs, including Mac OS X's Address Book, also let you place your contacts into *groups*—subsets like Book Club or Fantasy League Guys. You can't create or delete groups on the iPhone, but at least the groups from your Mac or PC get synced over to it. To see them, tap Groups at the top of the Contacts list.

If you do use the Groups feature, then remember to tap the group name you want *before* you create a new contact. That's how you put someone into an existing group. (If not, tap All Contacts instead.)

And now, a few tips and tricks for the data-entry process:

- **The keyboard opens automatically** when you tap in a box. And the iPhone capitalizes the first letter of each name for you.

 If you know somebody has your same cell company, add it—like "(AT&T)" or "(Verizon)" or "(Sprint)"—after the last name. That way, when he calls, you'll know that the call is free (like all calls within the same company's cell network).

Or add a similar notation to his cellphone number in Contacts. That way, when you call him, you'll know which number to use (cell versus landline, for example) to get the free call.

- **Phone numbers are special.** When you enter a phone number, the iPhone adds parentheses and hyphens for you. (You can even enter text phone numbers, like 1-800-GO-BROWNS; the iPhone converts them to digits when it dials.)

If you need to insert a pause—for dialing access numbers, extension numbers, or voicemail passwords—type #, which introduces a 2-second pause in the dialing. You can type several to create longer pauses.

To change the label for a number ("mobile," "home," "work," and so on), tap the label that's there now. The Label screen shows you your choices. There's even a label called "iPhone," so you and your buddy can gloat together.

 If you scroll way down the Label screen, you'll see that you can also create *custom* labels. You might prefer someone's cellphone number to be identified as "cell" instead of "mobile," for example. Or you might want to create a label that says "Skype," "Google Voice," "Line 2," "Yacht Phone," or "Bat Phone." The secret: Tap Add Custom Label at the very bottom of the screen.

- **Infinite Expand-O-Fields mean you'll never run out of room.** This might take some explanation.

Almost every field (empty box) on a Contacts card is infinitely expanding. That is, the instant you start filling in a field, another empty box appears right below it, so you can immediately add *another* phone number, email address, URL, street address, or whatever. (The only non-expanding fields are First, Last, Company, Ringtone, and the oddball fields that you add yourself.)

For example, when you start creating a *card* for someone, the phone-number box is labeled "mobile." If you start entering a phone number into it, a new, *second* empty phone-number box appears just below it (labeled "iPhone"—Apple's wishful thinking!), so you'll have a place to enter a second phone number for this person. When you do that, a *third* box appears. And so on.

There's always one empty field, so you can never run out of places to add more phone numbers, addresses, and so on. (Don't worry—the perpetual empty box doesn't appear once you're finished editing the person's card.)

- **You can add a photo of the person, if you like.** Tap Add Photo. If you have a photo of the person already, tap Choose Photo. You're taken to your photo collection, where you can find a good headshot (Chapter 7).

  Alternatively, tap Take Photo to activate the iPhone's built-in camera. Frame the person, and then tap the green camera button to snap the shot.

  In either case, you wind up with the Move and Scale screen (below, right). Here you can frame up the photo so that the person's face is nicely sized and centered. Spread two fingers to enlarge the photo; drag your finger to move the image within the frame. Tap Choose to commit the photo to the address book's memory. (Back on the Info screen where you started, a miniature version of the photo now appears. Tap edit if you want to change the photo, take a new one, adjust the Move and Scale screen, or get rid of the photo altogether.)

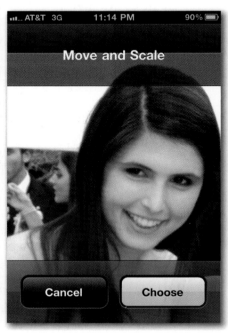

From now on, this photo will pop up whenever the person calls.

- **Choose a ringtone or a text tone.** The word "Default" in the ringtone and text tone boxes lets you know that when this person calls or texts you, you'll hear your standard ringing sounds. But you can, if you like, choose a different ringtone or text tone for each person in your address book. The idea is that you'll know by the sound of the ring who's calling or texting you.

(Actually, you can even set up a custom *vibration pattern* for each person, so you can *feel* who's calling while the phone is still in your pocket. See page 154.)

 Note It's one tone per person, not per phone number. Of course, if you really want one ringtone for your buddy's cellphone and another for his home phone, you can always create a different Contacts card for each one.

To choose a ringtone, tap Default. On the next screen, tap the sound you want, and then tap Save to return to the Info screen where you started.

- **You can add new fields of your own.** Very cool: If you tap add field at the bottom of the screen, then you go down the rabbit hole into Field Land, where you can add any of 15 additional info bits about the person whose card you're editing: Prefix (like Mr. or Mrs.), Suffix (like M.D. or Esq.), Nickname, Job Title, a Birthday, an Instant Message address, a phonetic pronunciation for people with weird names, and so on.

When you tap one of these labels, you return to the Info screen, where you'll see that the iPhone has inserted the new, empty field in the most intelligent spot. For example, if you add a Phonetic First Name, that box appears just below the First name box. The keyboard opens, so you can fill in the blank.

- **Link and unlink Unified Contacts.** As noted earlier, your phone can sync up with different accounts. Your Contacts app might list three sets of names and numbers: one stored on your phone, one from an iCloud account, and a third from your corporate Exchange server at work. In the old days, therefore, certain names might have shown up in the All Contacts list two or three times—not an optimal situation.

Now, as a favor to you, the iPhone displays each person's name only once in that master All Contacts list. If you tap that name, you open up the new Unified Info screen for that person. It includes *all* the details from *all* the underlying cards from that person.

To see which cards the iPhone is combining for you, scroll to the bottom of the card. There, the Linked Cards section shows you which cards have been unified.

Here you can tap a listing to open the card in the corresponding account. You can also unlink one of the cards (tap Edit, then ⊖, then Unlink). For that matter, you can manually link a card, too; tap Edit, tap Link Contact, and then choose a contact to link to this unified card—even if the name isn't a perfect match.

Home info   Unified info   Work info

Clearly, this stuff gets complex. But in general, the iPhone tries to do the right thing. For example, if you edit the information on the unified card, you're actually changing that information only on the card in the corresponding account. (Unless you **add** information to the Unified Info card. In that case, the new data tidbit is added to **all** the underlying source-account cards.)

Adding a Contact on the Fly

There's actually another way to add someone to your Contacts list—a faster, on-the-fly method that's more typical of cellphones. Start by bringing the phone number up on the screen:

- Tap Home, then Phone, then Keypad. Dial the number, and then tap the **+👤** button.

- You can also add a number that's in your Recents (recent calls) list, storing it in Contacts for future use. Tap the ⊙ button next to the name.

In both cases, finish up by tapping Create New Contact (to enter this person's name for the first time) or Add to Existing Contact (to add a new phone number to the card of someone who's already in your list). Off you go to the Contacts editing screen shown on page 71.

Editing Someone

To make corrections or changes, tap the person's name in the Contacts list. In the upper-right corner of the Info card, tap Edit.

You return to the screens already described, where you can make whatever changes you like. To edit a phone number, for example, tap it and change away. To delete a number (or any other info bit), tap the ⊖ button next to it, and then tap Delete to confirm.

Deleting Someone

Truth is, you'll probably *add* people to your address book far more often than you'll *delete* them. After all, you meet new people all the time—but you delete people primarily when they die, move away, or break up with you.

To zap someone, tap the name in the Contacts list and then tap Edit. Scroll down, tap Delete Contact (below, left), and confirm by tapping Delete Contact again.

Sharing a Contact

There's a lot of work involved in entering someone's contact information. It would be thoughtful, therefore, if you could spare the next guy all that effort—by sending a fully formed electronic business card to him. It can be yours or that of anyone in your Contacts list.

To do that, open the contact's card, scroll to the bottom, and tap Share Contact. Now you're offered a choice of Email or Message (above, right). ("Message" means "an iMessage—page 139—if it's a fellow Apple fan, or a text message otherwise.")

Tap your choice, address the message (to an email address or, for a message, a cellphone number), and send it. The recipient, assuming he has a half-decent smartphone or address-book program on the receiving end, can install that person's information with a single tap on the attachment.

 Tip Ever meet someone at a party or conference and wish you could just exchange business cards electronically, iPhone to iPhone? You can, using the free app Bump. If you both have this app, adding your address-book cards to each other's Contacts lists is as easy as literally bumping your iPhone-holding fists together. Wirelessly. Without having to type anything at all.

The Keypad

The fourth way to place a call is to tap Keypad at the bottom of the screen. The standard iPhone dialing pad appears. It's just like the number pad on a normal cellphone, except that the "keys" are much bigger and you can't feel them.

To make a call, tap out (or paste) the phone number—use the ⊗ key to back-space if you make a mistake—and then tap the green Call button.

You can also use the keypad to enter a phone number into your Contacts list, thanks to the little +👤 icon in the corner. See page 77 for details.

Answering Calls

When someone calls your iPhone, you'll know it; three out of your five senses are alerted. Depending on how you've set up your iPhone, you'll *hear* a ring, *feel* a vibration, and *see* the caller's name and photo fill that giant iPhone screen. (Smell and taste will have to wait until iOS 6.0.)

 Note For details on choosing a ringtone and on Vibrate mode, see page 455. And for info on the silencer switch, see page 20.

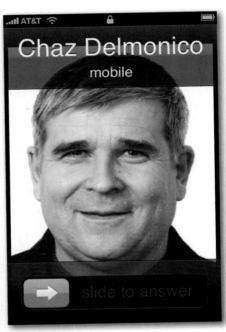

How you answer depends on what's happening at the time:

- **If you're using the iPhone,** tap the green Answer button. Tap End Call when you've both said enough.

- **If the iPhone is asleep or locked,** the screen lights up and says slide to answer. If you slide your finger as indicated by the arrow, you simultaneously unlock the phone and answer the call.

- **If you're wearing earbuds,** the music fades out and then pauses; you hear the ring both through the phone's speaker and through your earbuds. Answer by squeezing the clicker on the right earbud cord or by using either of the methods already described.

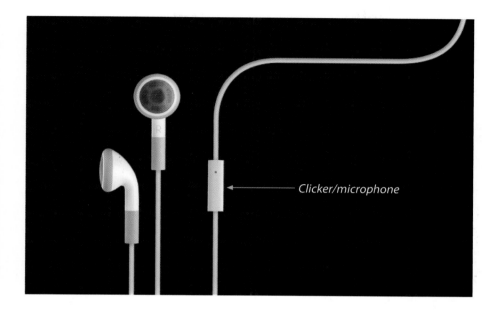

Clicker/microphone

When the call is over, you can click again to hang up—or just wait until the other guy hangs up. Either way, the music fades in again and resumes from precisely the spot where you were so rudely interrupted.

Same thing if you were watching a video; it pauses for the duration of the call and then resumes when you hang up.

Multitasking

Don't forget, by the way, that the iPhone is a multitasking master. Once you're on the phone, you can dive into any other program—to check your calendar, for example—without interrupting the call.

If you're in a WiFi hotspot or if you have a GSM connection (page 2), you can even surf the Web, check your email, or use the other Internet functions of the iPhone without interrupting your call. (If you have Sprint or Verizon in the U.S., and you're not in a WiFi hotspot, you can't get online until the call is complete.)

Silencing the Ring

Sometimes you need a moment before you can answer the call; maybe you need to exit a meeting or put in the earbuds, for example. In that case, you can stop the ringing and vibrating by pressing one of the physical buttons on the edges (the Sleep/Wake button or either volume key). The caller still hears the phone ringing, and you can still answer it within the first four rings, but at least the sound won't be annoying those around you.

(This assumes, of course, that you haven't just flipped the silencer switch.)

Not Answering Calls

And what if you're listening to a *really* good song, or you see that the call comes from someone you *really* don't want to deal with right now?

In that case, you have two choices. First, you can just ignore it. If you wait long enough (four rings), the call will go to voicemail (even if you silence the ringing/vibrating as described above).

Second, you can dump it to voicemail *immediately* (instead of waiting for the four rings). How you do that depends on the setup:

- **If you're using the iPhone,** tap the Decline button on the screen.
- **If the iPhone is asleep or locked,** tap the Sleep button twice fast.
- **If you're wearing the earbuds,** squeeze the microphone clicker for 2 seconds.

Of course, if your callers know you have an iPhone, they'll also know that you've deliberately dumped them into voicemail—because they won't hear all four rings.

Fun with Phone Calls

Whenever you're on a call, the iPhone makes it pitifully easy to perform stunts like turning on the speakerphone, putting someone on hold, taking a second call, and so on. Each of these is a one-tap function.

Here are the seven options that appear on the screen whenever you're on a call.

Mute

Tap this button to mute your own microphone, so the other guy can't hear you. (You can still hear him, though.) Now you have a chance to yell upstairs, to clear the phlegm from your throat, or to do anything else you'd rather the other party not hear. Tap again to unmute.

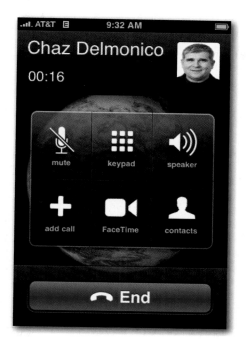

Keypad

Sometimes you have to input touchtones, which is generally a perk only of phones with physical dialing keys. For example, that's usually how you operate home answering machines when you call in for messages, and it's often required by automated banking, reservations, and conference-call systems.

Tap this button to produce the traditional iPhone dialing pad, illustrated on page 79. Each digit you touch generates the proper touchtone for the computer on the other end to hear.

When you're finished, tap Hide Keypad to return to the dialing-functions screen, or tap End Call if your conversation is complete.

Speaker

Tap this button to turn on the iPhone's built-in speakerphone—a great hands-free option when you're caught without your earbuds or Bluetooth headset. (In fact, the speakerphone doesn't work if the earbuds are plugged in or if a Bluetooth headset is connected.)

When you tap the button, it turns blue to indicate that the speaker is activated. Now you can put the iPhone down on a table or a counter and have a conversation with both hands free. Tap Speaker again to channel the sound back into the built-in earpiece.

 Tip Remember that the speaker is on the bottom edge of the phone. If you're having trouble hearing it, and the volume is all the way up, consider pointing the speaker toward you, or even cupping one hand around the bottom to direct the sound.

Add Call (Conference Calling)

The iPhone is all about software, baby, and that's nowhere more apparent than in its facility at handling multiple calls at once.

The simplicity and reliability of this feature put other cellphones to shame. Never again, in attempting to answer a second call, will you have to tell the first person, "If I lose you, I'll call you back."

Suppose you're on a call. Here are some of the tricks you can do:

- **Make an outgoing call.** Tap Add Call. The iPhone puts the first person on hold—neither of you can hear the other—and returns you to the Phone program and its various phone-number lists. You can now make a second call just the way you made the first. The top of the screen makes clear that the first person is still on hold as you talk to the second.

- **Receive an incoming call.** If a second call comes in while you're on the phone, you see the name or number (and photo, if any) of the new caller. You can tap either Decline (meaning, "Send to voicemail; I'm busy now"), Hold Call + Answer (the first call is put on hold while you take the second), or End Call + Answer (ditch the first call).

Whenever you're on two calls at once, the top of the screen identifies both other parties. Two new buttons appear, too:

- **Swap** lets you flip back and forth between the two calls. At the top of the screen, you see the names or numbers of your callers. One says HOLD (the one who's on hold, of course) and the other bears a white telephone icon, which lets you know whom you're actually speaking to.

  Think how many TV and movie comedies have relied on the old "Whoops, I hit the wrong button and now I'm bad-mouthing somebody directly to his face instead of behind his back!" gag. That can't happen on the iPhone.

You can swap calls by tapping swap or by tapping the HOLD person's name or number.

- **Merge Calls** combines the two calls so all three of you can converse at once. Now the top of the screen announces, "Bill O'Reilly & Al Franken" (or whatever the names of your callers are), and then changes to say "Conference."

  If you tap the ⊙ button, you see the names or numbers of everyone in your conference call (as shown on the next page). You can drop one of the calls by tapping its ⊖ button (and then End Call to confirm), or choose Private to have a person-to-person private chat with one participant. (Tap Merge Calls to return to the conference call.)

 Note If a call comes in while you're already talking to someone, tap Hold Call + Answer. Then tap Merge Calls if you want to add the newcomer to the party.

This business of combining calls into one doesn't have to stop at two. At any time, you can tap Add Call, dial a third number, and then tap Merge to combine it with your first two. And then a fourth call, and a fifth. With you, that makes six people on the call.

Then your problem isn't technological, it's social, as you try to conduct a meaningful conversation without interrupting one another.

 Just remember that if you're on the phone with five people at once, you're using up your monthly cellular minutes five times as fast. Better save those conference calls for weekends!

FaceTime

Tap this button to switch from your current phone call into a face-to-face video call, using the FaceTime feature described on the next page.

(This feature requires that both you and the other guy have iPhone 4 or 4S models, and that you're both in WiFi hotspots; Apple puts a FaceTime button on the screen even when those conditions aren't met, which is a little confusing.)

Hold (iPhone 3GS)

When you tap this button, you put the call on hold. Neither you nor the other guy can hear anything. Tap again to resume the conversation.

Tip On the iPhone 4 and 4S, there's no Hold button—you get a FaceTime button instead. But you can still trigger the Hold function—by holding down the Mute button for a couple of seconds.

Contacts

This button opens the address book program so you can look up a number or place another call.

FaceTime

The iPhone 4 and 4S, as you're probably aware, have two cameras—one on the back and one on the front. And that can mean only one thing: Video calling has arrived.

The iPhone was not the first phone to be able to make video calls. But it is the first one that can make *good* video calls, reliably, with no sign-up or setup, with a single tap. The picture and audio are generally rock-solid, with very little delay, and it works the first time and every time. Now Grandma can see the baby, or you can help someone shop from afar, or you can supervise brain surgery from thousands of miles away. (If you're a brain surgeon, of course.)

However, you can enjoy these *Jetsons* fantasies only if you and your calling partner are both in strong WiFi hotspots. You both have to have the iPhone 4 or 4S, an iPad, an iPod Touch, or a Mac. In time, other software companies may create FaceTime-compatible programs for other gadgets and computers. And Apple implies that someday you'll be able to make such calls over the cellular airwaves, not just over WiFi.

In any case, FaceTime could not be easier to fire up. You can try it in either of two situations:

- **When you're already on a phone call with someone.** This is a good technique when you want to ask first if the other guy *wants* to do video, or when you've been chatting and suddenly there's some *reason* to do video. In any case, there's nothing to it: Just tap the FaceTime icon that's right on the screen when you pull the phone away from your face.

- **From scratch.** You can also start up a videochat without placing a phone call first. Once you and your loved one (or your minion) have become accustomed to FaceTime, you may want to skip the initial phone-call part, especially since it costs you cellular minutes. You can also use FaceTime even when you can't get a cell signal.

Of course, if you're not already on a call, the iPhone doesn't yet know whom you want to call. So you have to tell it.

Open your Contacts app, tap the person's name, and then tap the FaceTime button. Or, from within the Phone app, call up your Favorites or Recents list. Tap the blue ⊙ button next to a name to open the contact's card; tap FaceTime.

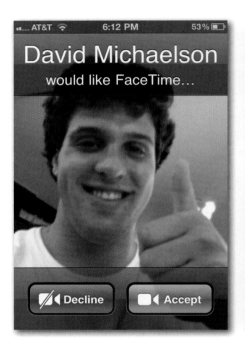

At this point, the other guy receives an audio and video message inviting him to a chat. If he taps Accept, then you're on.

You're on each other's screens, seeing and hearing each other in real time. (You appear on your own screen, too, in a little inset window. Consider it spinach-in-your-teeth protection.)

Once the chat has begun, here's some of the fun you can have:

- **Rotate the screen.** FaceTime works in either portrait (upright) or landscape (widescreen) view; just turn your phone 90 degrees. Of course, if your calling partner doesn't *also* turn her gadget, she'll see your picture all squished and tiny, with big black areas filling the rest of the screen. (On the Mac, the picture rotates automatically when your partner's gadget rotates. You don't have to turn the computer 90 degrees.)

 Tip The Rotation Lock button described on page 14 works in FaceTime, too. That is, you can stop the picture from rotating when you turn the phone—as long as you're happy with full-time upright (portrait) orientation.

- **Show what's in front of you.** Sometimes, *you* are not the important thing; sometimes, you'll want to show your friend what you're looking at. That is, you'll want to turn on the camera on the *back* of the iPhone, the one pointing away from you, to show off the baby, the artwork, or the broken engine part.

  That's easy enough; just tap the (📷) icon on your screen. The iPhone switches from the front camera to the back camera. Now you and your callee can both see what you're seeing. (It's a lot less awkward than using a laptop for this purpose, because the laptop's camera always faces away from you—so you can't see what you're showing.)

  Tap the (📷) icon again to return to the front camera.

- **Snap a commemorative photo.** You can immortalize a chat by using the screenshot keystroke (Sleep + Home) described on page 200. You'll wind up with a still photo of your videochat in progress, safely nestled in your Photos app.

- **Mute the audio.** Tap the 🎤 icon to silence the audio that you're sending. Great when you need to yell at the kids.

- **Mute the video.** When you leave the FaceTime app for any reason (press the Home button and then open a different program, if you like), the other guy's screen goes black. He can't see what you're doing when you leave the FaceTime screen. He can still hear you, though.

  This feature was designed to let you check your calendar, look something up on the Web, or whatever, while you're still chatting. But it's also a great trick when you need to adjust your clothing, pick your nose, or otherwise shield your activity from whomever's on the other end.

  In the meantime, the call is, technically, still in progress—and a green banner at the top of the Home screen reminds you of that. Tap there, on the green bar, to return to the video call.

When you and your buddy have had quite enough, tap the End button to terminate the call. (Although it's easy to jump from phone call to videochat, there's no way to go the other direction.)

And marvel that you were alive to see the day.

•

4 Speech Recognition —and Siri

The iPhone may have put a camera, a GPS unit, an iPod, and a TV in our pockets. But no matter how much you love the thing, one fact is unassailable: The onscreen keyboard is a drag.

On its Android phones, Google addressed the problem using the screamingly obvious solution: speech recognition. A tiny microphone button next to the space bar, right there on the onscreen keyboard, lets you speak instead of type—anywhere you can type. You don't get perfect accuracy most of the time, but it's a heck of a lot faster and less fussy than typing with one finger on glass.

But Apple held out. Steve Jobs, a famous perfectionist, disliked features that only *sort of* worked, and speech recognition was one of them.

In the end, though, Apple played catch-up the way Apple likes to play: by leapfrogging its rivals.

On the iPhone 3GS and iPhone 4, you can dial by voice and control music playback by voice.

But on the iPhone 4S, you can go much, much further. First, you can now dictate anywhere you can type, exactly as on Android.

Second, the iPhone 4S offers Siri, a voice-controlled personal minion.

Siri is, to be blunt, amazing. You can say, "Wake me up at 7:45," or "What's Chris's work number?" or "How do I get to the airport?" or "What's the weather going to be like in San Francisco this weekend?"

You can say, "Any good Italian restaurants around here?" Or "Make a note to rent *Titanic* this weekend." Or "How many days until Valentine's Day?" Or "Play some Electric Light Orchestra." Or "When was James K. Polk born?"

In each case, Siri thinks for a few seconds, displays a beautifully formatted response, and speaks in a calm voice.

This chapter covers all three iPhone speech technologies: the speak-to-dial feature of the iPhone 4, the dictation feature of the iPhone 4S, and Siri.

Voice Control (iPhone 3GS, iPhone 4)

If you upgrade these older phones to iOS 5, they inherit almost every single feature described in this book. Almost.

One of the big exceptions: They don't get the jaw-dropping speech-recognition smarts of Siri. That's a feature you can't get except on the iPhone 4S.

You're not excluded from the speech party entirely, however. You can use your voice to dial and to control music playback, as you're about to find out.

Dialing by Voice

If you have an iPhone 3GS or an iPhone 4 (or an iPhone 4S with Siri turned off), you can call somebody just by saying, "Call Chris at home" or "Dial 225-3210."

Voice dialing is a big deal on any phone, because it lets you keep your eyes on the road while you're driving. (Yes, yes, cellphone use in the car is dangerous and, in some states, illegal. And studies have shown that it's the act of talking on the phone—not just holding a phone up to your head—that causes distraction-related accidents. But we all know people do it anyway.)

On the iPhone, though, it's an even bigger deal, because it means that you can place a phone call with only a single button press. Without voice dialing, you have to wake the phone, unlock it, tap your way to the Phone app, tap the list you want, tap a number, and then tap Dial—a lot of steps.

To dial by voice, hold down the Home button for 3 seconds. (If you're wearing the earbuds, hold down the center button; if you have a Bluetooth earpiece, hold down the Call button.)

 Tip The hold-down-the-button thing works even when the phone is asleep and locked! This tip makes it extraordinarily easy to place calls quickly. (If you're worried about the security of this option, you can turn it off; see page 117.)

You hear a crisp double-beep, and then the Voice Control screen appears. The wavy line in the center reflects what the iPhone is "hearing" at the moment; you'll see it respond to your voice.

The words flying across the background are meant to help you learn the Voice Control feature. They're cues to the commands the phone understands.

Many have to do with iPod playback and are described later in this section. For calling purposes, there are only two commands to know: Call and Dial. They're interchangeable, but you have to follow each with one of two utterances:

- **A name from your Contacts list.** For maximum efficiency, say the first and last names, along with which number you want: "work" (or "at work"), "home" (or "at home"), "mobile," and so on.

 The iPhone doesn't recognize "cell" or "cellphone," however.

You might say, therefore, "Call Chris Patterson at home," or "Dial Esmeralda at work." (Saying only the first name is OK if there's nobody else in your Contacts list with that name.)

If you don't specify a last name and which phone number you want, then the little talking iPhone lady asks you which one you meant—"Chris Patterson: Home? Work? Or mobile?"—and you have to speak the answer.

Tip You don't actually have to say "call" or "dial" in *English*. The iPhone recognizes the equivalent words in 32 different languages. Collect them all!

- **A phone number.** You can also speak the digits of a phone number. For example, "Call four six six, oh seven two seven."

 Note You have to say every digit separately. None of this "eighty-two hundred" or "forty-two, forty-three" stuff. (There's only one exception: You're allowed to say "eight hundred" for 800 numbers.)

The iPhone syntho-lady always repeats what she thinks she heard—she might confirm, for example, "Chris Patterson, home"—and then dials.

Voice dialing usually works, but not always. Noisy backgrounds, accents, and similarity of Contact name spellings can confuse it. If the confirmation is incorrect, you have about a second to interrupt the dialing by saying "No," "Wrong," "Not that," "Not that one," or (believe it or not) "Nope." The iPhone lady hangs up so you can try again.

Other times, you'll hear, "No match found," even when you know there is a match. Try again, or just say "Cancel" and give up.

 Tip You can also say, "What time is it?" (Actually, what's new is that the phone will *answer* you.)

Voice Control of Music

On the iPhone 3GS and iPhone 4, you can also control the iPod's playback by voice, just by speaking into the iPhone's microphone (as though you're using the phone) or into the earbuds cord.

The beauty of voice control is that you don't have to be in iPod mode to do it. You can be in any app. And you don't even have to look at the iPhone. In theory, you could even be driving (although you'd never be fiddling with your phone in the car, right?).

To issue a playback command, hold down the Home button (or the center earbuds button, if you're wearing those) for 3 seconds, or until you hear the happy double-beep of success. Now the blue Voice Control screen appears, complete with animated words flying across to remind you of the sorts of commands the iPhone understands. They include these:

- **"Play"** or **"Play music."** Starts the iPod a-playing. It resumes with whatever you were listening to most recently.

- **"Pause"** or **"Pause music."** Does what you'd think.

- **"Previous song"** or **"Next song."** Skips to the previous or next song in your playlist or album.

- **"Play [album, artist, or playlist]."** When you're in the mood for U2, say, "Play U2." If you want your Jogging Toonz playlist, say, "Play Jogging Toonz." If you want a certain album, say, "Play 'Abbey Road' " (or whatever).

  The little digital iPhone voice lady tells you what she thinks you want her to do—"Playing 'Abbey Road' "—and then the music begins. If she got it wrong—and she does fairly often—you can either press the Home button again and start over or just use your finger to tap what you want.

- **"Shuffle."** Skips to a random new song.

- **"What's playing?"** or **"What song is this?"** or **"Who is this song by?"** or "Who sings this song?" The iPhone voice lady tells you what you're listening to: "Now playing 'Barbie Girl' by Aqua."

- **"Genius"** or **"Play more songs like this"** (or just "Play more like this"). All these commands do the same thing: They use the Genius feature (page 163) to choose a different song that's musically similar to the one you were just listening to (roughly the same tempo and rockiness).

- **"Cancel."** If you summoned the Voice Control screen but now you've changed your mind—maybe the song you were hating just got to a good part—say "Cancel" to go back to what you were doing.

> **Tip** Dictation software—speak-to-type—may be built into the iPhone 4S, but it's also available for the iPhone 3GS or iPhone 4 in the form of a free app: Dragon Dictation. It's not nearly as convenient, because you have to do your dictating in the app and then copy the transcription into your text message, email message, or whatever. But it's a lot better than nothing.

iPhone 4S: Speak to Type

The term "speech recognition" is a fairly imprecise term. It could mean "speak to give your computer commands," or it could mean "speak to type."

The iPhone 4S can do both.

The new dictation feature lets you enter text anywhere, into any program, just by speaking. (Behind the scenes, it's using the same Nuance recognition technology that powers the Dragon Dictation app.)

This feature transforms the iPhone experience. Suddenly you don't have to fuss with the tiny keyboard. The experience of "typing" is no longer claustrophobic. You can blather away into an email, fire off a text message, or draft a memo without ever looking at the screen. *So many* of the things you can do with an iPhone—record or change an appointment, call someone, set an alarm, send a text—require many fewer steps when you just speak your command.

Now, before you get all excited, here are the necessary footnotes:

- Voice typing works only when you have an Internet connection. If you don't, the little microphone button on the keyboard doesn't even appear.

- Voice typing works best if there's not a lot of background noise.

- Voice typing isn't always practical, since everybody around you can hear what you're doing.

- Voice typing isn't 100 percent accurate. Most of the time, you'll have to correct an error or two.

All right—expectations set? Then here's how to type by speaking.

First, fire up someplace where you can call up the keyboard. Messages, Notes, Mail, Safari, whatever. Tap, if necessary, so that the onscreen keyboard appears.

See the tiny microphone button next to the space bar? Tap that (facing page, step 1). The microphone bar appears (facing page, step 2).

When you hear the single xylophone note, say what you have to say. If there's background noise, hold the phone up to your head; if it's relatively quiet, a couple of feet away is fine. You don't have to speak slowly, loudly, or weirdly, either; speak normally.

1. Tap microphone to dictate.

3. Your text appears.

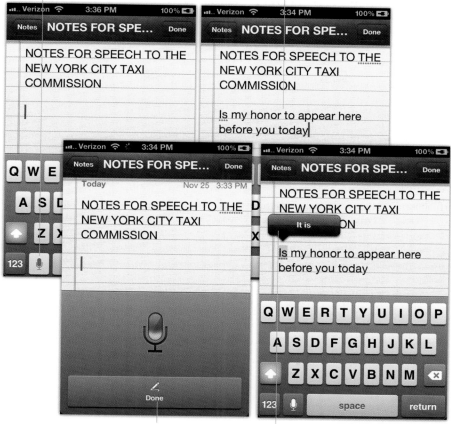

2. Speak smoothly but clearly, and then tap Done.

4. Tap an underlined word to correct the transcription.

You have to speak your own punctuation, like this: "Dear Dad (colon): Please send money (dash)—as much as you can (comma), please (period)." (The table at the end of this section describes all the different punctuation symbols you can dictate.)

After you finish speaking, tap Done. Your iPhone plays another xylophone note—higher, this time—and transmits the audio data to distant computers. They analyze your speech and transmit the resulting typed-out text back to your iPhone. (During this time, three blinking purple dots occupy the text area where you dictated.) The transcribed text appears all at once, in a big blob, as shown in step 3 above.

Note Sometimes, those dots blink away—but when they stop, no text appears at all. That usually means that your Internet connection isn't good enough, or that the transcription service is busy. You can try again, or you can just sigh and resort to typing with your finger.

If the transcription contains errors, you can tap with your finger to edit them, exactly as you would fix an error in something you typed (Chapter 2). (Make the effort; you're simultaneously teaching your iPhone to do better the next time.) Or, if the whole thing is a mess, you can *shake* your iPhone, which is the universal gesture for Undo.

 Tip Often, the iPhone knows perfectly well when it might have gotten a word wrong— it draws a dashed underline beneath words or phrases it's insecure about. You can tap that word or phrase to see the iPhone's alternative interpretation, which is often correct. (This effect is identified as step 4 in the preceding illustration.)

Usually, you'll find the accuracy pretty darned good, considering you didn't have to train the software to recognize your voice, and considering that your computer is a *cellphone,* for crying out loud. You'll also find that the accuracy is better when you dictate complete sentences, and long words fare better than short ones.

Punctuation

Here's a handy table that shows you what punctuation you can say, and how to say it.

 Tip If you've ever used Dragon NaturallySpeaking (for Windows) or MacSpeech Dictate (for the Mac), then you already know these commands; they're the standard Nuance dictation-software shortcuts, because that's what the iPhone uses behind the scenes.

Say this:	To get this:	For example, saying this:	Types this:
"period" or "full stop"	. [space and capital letter afterward]	"Best (period) date (period) ever (period)"	Best. Date. Ever.
"dot" or "point"	. [no space afterward]	"My email is frank (dot) smith (at sign) gmail (dot) com"	My email is frank.smith@ gmail.com
"comma," "semi-colon," "colon"	, ; :	"Mom (comma) hear me (colon) I'm dizzy (semi-colon) tired"	Mom, hear me: I'm dizzy; tired
"question mark," "exclamation point"	? ! [space and capital letter afterward]	"Ellen (question mark) Hi (excla-mation point)"	Ellen? Hi!
"inverted ques-tion mark," "inverted excla-mation point"	¿ ¡	"(inverted ques-tion mark) Que paso (question mark) "	¿Que paso?
"ellipsis" or "dot dot dot"	…	"Just one (ellipsis) more (ellipsis) step (ellipsis)"	Just one… more… step…
"space bar"	[a space, espe-cially when a hyphen would normally appear]	"He rode the merry (space bar) go (space bar) round"	He rode the merry go round
"open paren" then "close paren" (or "open bracket/close bracket," or "open brace/ close brace")	( ) or [ ] or { }	"Then she (open paren) the doc-tor (close paren) gasped"	Then she (the doctor) gasped
"new line"	[a press of the Return key]	"milk (new line) bread (new line) Cheez Whiz"	milk bread Cheez Whiz

Say this:	To get this:	For example, saying this:	Types this:
"new paragraph"	[two presses of the Return key]	"autumn leaves (new paragraph) softly falling"	autumn leaves softly falling
"quote," then "unquote"	" "	Her perfume screamed (quote) available (unquote)	Her perfume screamed "available"
"numeral"	[writes the following number as a digit instead spelling it out]	"Next week she turns (numeral) eight"	Next week she turns 8
"asterisk,""plus sign,""minus sign,""equals sign"	*, +, −	"numeral eight (asterisk) two (plus sign) one (minus sign) three (equals sign) fourteen"	8*2+1−3=14
"ampersand," "dash"	&, —	"Barry (ampersand) David (dash) the best (exclamation point)"	Barry & David— the best!
"hyphen"	- [without spaces]	"Don't give me that holier (hyphen) than (hyphen) thou attitude"	Don't give me that holier-than-thou attitude
"backquote"	'	"Back in (backquote) (numeral) fifty-two"	back in '52
"smiley,""frowny," "winky" (or "smiley face,""frowny face,""winky face")	:-) :-(;-)	"I think you know where I'm going with this (winky face)."	I think you know where I'm going with this ;-)

You can also say "percent sign" (%), "at sign" (@), "dollar sign" ($), "cent sign") (¢), "euro sign" (€), "yen sign" (¥), "pounds sterling sign" (£), "section sign" (§), "copyright sign" (©), "registered sign" (®), "trademark sign" (™), "greater-than sign" or "less-than sign" (> or <), "degree sign" (°), "caret" (^), "tilde" (~), "vertical bar" (|), and "pound sign" (#).

The software automatically capitalizes the first new word after a period, question mark, or exclamation point. But you can also force it to capitalize words you're dictating by saying "cap" right before the word, like this: "Dear (cap) Mom, I've run away to join (cap) The (cap) Circus (comma), a nonprofit cooperative for runaway jugglers."

Here's another table—this one shows the other commands for capitalization, plus spacing and spelling commands.

 Tip Speak each of the on/off commands as a separate utterance, with a small pause before and after.

Say this:	To get this:	For example, saying this:	Types this:
"cap" or "capital"	Capitalize the next word	"Give me the (cap) works"	Give me the Works
"caps on," then "caps off"	Capitalize the first letter of every word	"Next week, (caps on) the new england chicken coop-erative (caps off) will hire me"	Next week, The New England Chicken Cooperative will hire me
"all caps," then "all caps off"	Capitalize everything	"So (all caps on) please please (all caps off) don't tell anyone"	So PLEASE PLEASE don't tell anyone
"all caps"	Type just the next word in all caps	"We (all caps) really don't belong here"	We REALLY don't belong here
"no caps"	Type the next word in lowercase	"see you in (no caps) Texas"	see you in texas

Say this:	To get this:	For example, saying this:	Types this:
"no caps on," then "no caps off"	Prevents any capital letters	"I'll ask (no caps on) Santa Claus (no caps off)"	I'll ask santa claus
"no space"	Runs the next two words together	"Try new mega (no space) berry flavor"	Try new mega-berry flavor
"no space on," then "no space off"	Eliminates all spaces	"(No space on) I can't believe you ate all that (no space off) (comma) she said excitedly"	Ican'tbelieveyou ateallthat, she said excitedly
[alphabet letters]	Types the letters out, though usually not very accurately.	"The stock symbol is A P P L"	The stock symbol is APPL

You don't always have to dictate these formatting commands, by the way. Siri automatically inserts hyphens into phone numbers (you say, "2125561000," and she types "212-556-1000"); she formats two-line street addresses without your having to say "New line" before the city; she handles prices automatically ("six dollars and thirty-two cents" becomes "$6.32"). She formats dates and Web addresses well, too; you can even use the nerdy shortcut "dub-dub-dub" when you want the "www" part of a Web address.

Siri recognizes email addresses, too, as long as you remember to say "at sign" at the right spot. You'd say, "harold (underscore) beanfield (at sign) gmail (dot) com" to get harold_beanfield@gmail.com.

 Tip You can combine these formatting commands. Many iPhone owners have wondered: "How do I voice-type the *word* "comma," since saying, "comma" types out only the symbol?"

The solution: Say, "No space on, no caps on, C, O, M, M, A, no space off, no caps off." That gives you the *word* "comma."

Then again, it might just be easier to type that one out with your finger.

iPhone 4S: Siri

In 2010, Apple bought Siri, a company that made a voice-control app (no longer available) for the iPhone. Apple cleaned it up, beefed it up, integrated it with the iPhone's software, and wound up with Siri, your virtual minion.

 Note Believe it or not, Siri is a spinoff from a Department of Defense research project called CALO (Cognitive Assistant that Learns and Organizes), which Wikipedia describes as "the largest artificial-intelligence project ever launched." In a very real way, therefore, Siri represents your tax dollars at work.

The spinoff was run by the Stanford Research Institute (SRI), which should provide a hint as to the origins of Siri's name.

Siri is a crisply accurate, astonishingly understanding, uncomplaining, voice-commanded servant. No voice training or special syntax is required; you don't even have to hold the phone up to your head.

Most speech-recognition systems work only if you issue certain limited commands with predictable syntax, like, "Call 445-2340" or "Open Microsoft Word." But Siri is different. She's been programmed to respond to casual speech, normal speech. It doesn't matter if you say, "What's the weather going to be like in Tucson this weekend?" or "Give me the Tucson weather for this weekend" or "Will I need an umbrella in Tucson?" Siri understands almost any variation of the kinds of requests you make.

And she understands regular, everyday speaking. You don't have to separate your words or talk weirdly. Speak clearly but normally. The only thing you may sometimes need to exaggerate slightly is the ending consonants of words.

It's not *Star Trek*. You can't ask Siri to clean your gutters or teach you French. (Well, you can *ask*.) She can't even do basic iPhone tasks that you might assume she could, like reporting how many minutes you have left on your calling plan, switching on Airplane Mode, or opening apps ("Open Angry Birds").

But, as you'll soon discover, the number of things Siri *can* do you for you is rather impressive. (Furthermore, Apple says it intends to keep adding to Siri's intelligence through software updates.)

Note Apple also intends to increase the number of languages that Siri understands. At the outset, Siri understands English (American, British, and Australian), German, and French.

What You Can Say

To get Siri's attention, you have three choices:

- Hold down the phone's Home button until you hear a double-beep.

 Tip The phone doesn't have to be unlocked or awake, which is a fantastic feature. Just pull the phone out of your pocket or purse, and then hold down that Home button.

- Hold the phone up to your head, as though making a call. You'll hear the double-beep. (You have to turn this feature on in advance: The on-off switch is in Settings→General→Siri→Raise to Speak. See the details at the end of this chapter.)

- Hold down the clicker on your earbuds cord or Bluetooth earpiece.

When that double-beep sounds, the microphone icon becomes a level meter; it flashes as you speak, to make sure you know Siri's listening. Ask your question or say your command (see below). You don't have to hold the phone up to your mouth; Siri works perfectly well at arm's length, on your desk in front of you, or on the car seat beside you.

 Note Apple insists that Siri is neither male nor female. In fact, if you ask Siri her gender, she'll say something noncommittal like, "None." But that's just political correctness. If you consult any baby-name Web site, it will tell you that Siri is a girls' name. (Siri's alto voice sort of gives her away, anyway—at least in the U.S. She has a male voice in the United Kingdom and French editions.)

When you're finished speaking, tap the microphone icon, or just be quiet. After about 1 second, the iPhone double-beeps again, at a higher pitch this time (meaning, "OK, I've got it"). About 1 second after you stop speaking, the ring around the microphone icon begins lighting up with animation—your sign that Siri is busily connecting with her master brain online and processing your request. After a moment, she presents (and speaks) an attractively formatted response.

 Tip Although you generally see only the most recent question and response on the Siri screen, you can drag downward with your finger to see all the previous exchanges you've had with Siri during this session.

If you want to rephrase your question or cancel or start over, tap the microphone button again to interrupt Siri's work. (You can also cancel by saying "Cancel" or just by pressing the Home button.) Tap again to trigger your new attempt. (Of course, you can combine these two steps by double-tapping the button.)

Here are the general categories of things you can say to Siri.

 Tip You have a more concise version of the following cheat sheet right on your phone. Hold down the Home button to make Siri's "What can I help you with?" banner appear at the bottom of your screen. Then tap the ❸ button to reveal the list of categories shown below.

Or just trigger Siri and then say, "What can I say?" or "What can you do?" or "Help me!" The same cheat sheet appears.

- **Alarms.** You can say, "Wake me up at 7:35.""Change my 7:35 alarm to 8:00.""Wake me up in 6 hours.""Cancel my 6 a.m. alarm" (or "Delete my…" or "Turn off my…"). This is *so* much quicker than setting the iPhone's alarm the usual way.

  Result: When you set or change an alarm, you get a cute slice of a digital alarm clock, right there beneath Siri's response. And Siri speaks to confirm what she understood.

- **Timer.** You can also control the Timer module of the phone's Clock app. It's like a stopwatch in reverse, in that it counts down to zero—handy when you're baking something, limiting your kid's video-game time, and

so on. For example: "Set the timer for 20 minutes." Or "Show the timer," "Pause the timer," "Resume," "Reset the timer," and "Stop it."

Result: A very cool animated slide rule–style Timer appears.

- **Clock.** "What time is it?" "What time is it in San Francisco?" "What's today's date?" "What's the date a week from Friday?"

Result: When you ask about the time, you see the clock, identifying the time in question. (For dates, Siri just talks to you and writes out the date.)

- **Contacts.** You can ask Siri to look up information in your address book (the Contacts app)—and not just addresses. For example, you can say, "What's Gary's work number?" "Give me Sheila Jenkins's office phone." "Show Tia's home email address." "What's my boss's home address?" "When is my husband's birthday?" "Show Larry Murgatroid." "Find everybody named Smith." "Who is P.J. Frankenberg?"

Result: A half "page" from your Contacts list. You can tap it to jump into that person's full card in Contacts. (If Siri finds multiple listings for the person you named—"Bob," for example—she lists all the matches and asks you to specify which one you meant.)

Tip In many of the examples on these pages, you'll see that you can identify people by their relationship to you. You can say, "Show my mom's work number," for example, or "Give me directions to my boss's house," or "Call my girlfriend." For details on teaching Siri about these relationships, see "Advanced Siri" at the end of this chapter.

- **Calling.** Siri can place phone calls or FaceTime calls for you. "Call Harold." "Call Nicole on her mobile phone." "Call the office." "Phone home." "Dial 512-444-1212." "Start a FaceTime call with Sheila Withins." "FaceTime Alex."

  Result: Siri hands you off to the Phone app or FaceTime app and places the call. At this point, it's just as though you'd initiated the call yourself.

- **Text messages.** "Send a text to Alex Rybeck." "Send a message to Peter saying, 'I no longer require your services.'" "Tell Cindy I'm running late." "Send a message to Janet's mobile asking her to pick me up at the train." "Send a text message to 212-561-2282." "Text Frank and Ralph: Did you pick up the pizza?"

  Result: You see a miniature outgoing text message. Siri asks if you want to send it; say "Yes," "Send," or "Confirm" to proceed.

 Tip You can even use Siri to proofread your text message before you send it. Say, "Read it back to me" or just "Read it to me."

If you need to edit the message before sending it, you have a couple of options. First, you can tap it; Siri hands you off to the Messages app for editing and sending.

Second, you can edit it by voice. You can say, "Change it to" to re-dictate the message; "Add" to add more to the message; "No, send it to Frank" to change the recipient; "No" to leave the message on the screen without sending it; or "Cancel" to forget the whole thing.

You can also ask Siri to read incoming text messages to you, which is great if you're driving. For example, you can say, "Read my new messages," and "Read that again."

Tip If you've opted to conceal the actual contents of incoming texts so that they don't appear on your screen (page 137), Siri can read you only the senders' names or numbers—not the messages themselves.

You can even have her reply to messages she's just read to you. "Reply, 'Congratulations (period). Can't wait to see your trophy (exclamation point)!'" "Call her back." "Tell him I have a flat tire and I'm going to be late."

- **Email.** Of course, you shouldn't be doing email when you're driving. But if you can't resist, at least you can do it without taking your eyes off the road.

To check your email, you can say things like, "Check email." "Any new mail from Chris today?" "Show new mail about the world premiere." "Show yesterday's email from Jan."

Result: Siri doesn't read your messages to you. She can, however, display the headers of each message (who it's from, subject line, date, and time).

You can also compose a new message by voice; anytime you use the phrase "about," that becomes the subject line for your new message. "Email Mom about the reunion." "Email my boyfriend about the dance on Friday." "New email to Freddie Gershon." "Mail Mom about Saturday's flight." "Email Frank and Cindy Vosshall and Peter Love about the picnic." "Email my assistant and say, 'Thanks for arranging the taxi!'" "Email Gertie and Eugene about their work on the surprise party, and say I really value your friendship."

You can't send mail to canned groups of people using Siri—at least not without MailShot, an iPhone app that exists expressly for the purpose of letting you create email addressee groups.

You can reply to a message Siri has just described, too. "Reply, 'Dear Robin (comma), I'm so sorry about your dog (period). I'll be more careful next time (period).'" "Call her mobile number." "Send him a text message saying, 'I got your note.'"

Result: A miniature Mail message, showing you Siri's handiwork before you send it.

- **Calendar.** Siri can make appointments for you. Considering how many tedious finger taps it usually takes to schedule an appointment in the Calendar app, this is an enormous improvement. "Make an appointment with Patrick for Thursday at 3 p.m." "Set up a haircut at nine." "Set up a meeting with Charlize this Friday at noon." "Meet Danny Cooper at six." "New appointment with Steve, next Sunday at seven." "Schedule a conference call at 5:30 p.m. tonight in my office."

Result: A slice of that day's calendar appears, filled in the way you requested.

 Siri may also alert you to a conflict, something like this: "Note that you already have an all-day appointment about 'Boston Trip' for this Thursday. Shall I schedule this anyway?" Amazing.

You can also move previously scheduled meetings by voice. For example, "Move my 2:00 meeting to 2:30." "Reschedule my meeting with Charlize to a week from Monday at noon." "Add Frank to my meeting with Harry." "Cancel the conference call on Sunday."

You can even *consult* your calendar by voice. You can say, "What's on my calendar today?" "What's on my calendar for September 23?" "What does my weekend look like?" "When's my next appointment?" "When is my meeting with Charlize?" "Where is my next meeting?"

Result: Siri reads you your agenda and displays a tidy Day view of the specified date.

- **Directions.** By consulting the Maps app and the phone's GPS, Siri can answer questions like these: "How do I get to the airport?" "Any good Thai restaurants around here?" "Show me 1500 Broadway, New York City." "Directions to my assistant's home." "Take me home."

 Tip You can ask for directions to the home or work address of anyone in your Contacts list—provided those addresses are *in* your Contacts cards.

> *Result:* Siri fires up the Maps app, with the start and end points of your driving directions already filled in.

- **Business lookups.** Siri is a walking (well, all right, non-walking) Yellow Pages. Go ahead, try it: "Find coffee near me." "Where's the closest Walmart?" "Find some pizza places in Cincinnati." "Search for gas stations." "French restaurants nearby." "I'm in the mood for Chinese food." "Find me a hospital." "I want to buy a book."

> *Result:* Siri displays a handsome list of businesses nearby that match your request.

Tip She's a sly dog, that Siri. She'll even help you out if your requests are, ahem, somewhat off the straight and narrow. If you say, "I think I'm drunk," she'll list nearby cab companies. If you indicate that you're craving relief from your drug addiction, she'll provide you with a list of rehab centers. If you refer to certain biological urges, she'll list escort services.

- **Prices.** Siri can even report the average prices for things in certain areas. "What's the price of rice in Illinois?" "What's the average gas price in Detroit?"

- **Reminders.** Siri is a natural match for the Reminders app that's new in iOS 5. She can add items to that list at your spoken command. For example: "Remind me to file my IRS tax extension." "Remind me to bring the science supplies to school." "Remind me to take my antibiotic tomorrow at 7 a.m."

  The *location-based* reminders are especially amazing. They rely on GPS to know where you are. So you can say, "Remind me to visit the drugstore when I leave the office." "Remind me to water the lawn when I get home." "Remind me to check in with Nancy when I leave here."

Result: A miniature entry from the Reminders app, showing you that Siri has understood.

- **Notes.** You create a new note (in the Notes app) by saying things like, "Make a note that my shirt size is 15 and a half" or "Note: Dad will not be coming to the reunion after all." You can even name the note in your request: "Create a 'Movies to Rent' note."

  But you can also call up a certain note to the screen, like this: "Find my frequent-flyer note." You can even summon a table-of-contents view of all your notes by saying, "Show all my notes."

  Result: A miniature Notes page appears, showing your newly dictated text (or the existing note that you've requested).

You can keep dictating into the note you've just added. Just say, "Add 'Return books to library'" (or just say, "Add," and she'll ask you what to add). She'll keep adding to the same note until you say, "Note that…" or "Start a note" or "Take a note" to begin a fresh note page.

You can add text to an earlier note: "Add *Titanic II: The Voyage Home* to my 'Movies to Rent' note." (The first line of any note is also its title—in this case, "Movies to Rent.")

- **Music.** Instead of fumbling around in your Music app, save yourself steps and time by speaking the name of the album, song, or band: "Play some Beatles." "Play 'I'm a Barbie Girl.'" "Play some jazz." "Play my jogging playlist." "Play the party mix." "Shuffle my 'Dave's Faves' playlist." "Play." "Pause." "Skip."

  Result: Siri plays (or skips, shuffles, or pauses) the music you asked for—without ever leaving whatever app you were using.

- **Weather.** "What's the weather going to be today?" "What's the forecast for tomorrow?" "Show me the weather this week." "Will it snow in Dallas this weekend?" "Check the forecast for Memphis on Friday." "What's the forecast for tonight?" "Can you give me the wind speed in Kansas City?" "Tell me the windchill in Chicago." "What's the humidity right now?" "Is it nighttime in Cairo?" "How's the weather in Paris right now?" "What's

the high for Washington on Friday?" "When will Jupiter rise tomorrow?" "When's the moonrise?" "How cold will it be in Houston tomorrow?" "What's the temperature outside?" "Is it windy out there?" "When does the sun rise in London?" "When will the sun set today?" "Should I wear a jacket?"

Result: A convenient miniature Weather display for the date and place you specified.

- **Stocks.** "What's Google's stock price?" "What did Ford close at today?" "How's the Dow doing?" "What's Microsoft's P/E ratio?" "What's Amazon's average volume?" "How are the markets doing?"

Result: A tidy little stock graph, bearing a wealth of up-to-date statistics.

- **Find My Friends.** You see this category only if you've installed the Find My Friends app (page 274). "Where's Ferd?" "Is my dad home?" "Where are my friends?" "Who's here?" "Who is nearby?" "Is my dad at work?"

Result: Siri shows you a beautiful little map with the requested person's location clearly indicated by a blue pushpin. (She does, that is, if you've set up Find My Friends, you've logged in, and your friends have made their locations available.)

- **Search the Web.** "Search the Web for a 2013 Ford Mustang." "Search for healthy smoothie recipes." "Search Wikipedia for the Thunderbirds." "Google Benjamin Franklin." "Search for news about the Netflix-Amazon merger."

 Tip "Google" isn't the only verb around here. You can also ask Siri to "Bing" something or "Yahoo" something (for example, "Bing low-cal dessert recipes").

Wikipedia is a search type all its own. "Search Wikipedia for Harold Edgerton." "Look up Mariah Carey on Wikipedia." Pictures get special treatment, too: "I want to see pictures of cows." (You can also say, "Show me pictures of…" or "Find me…" or "Search for…" but weirdly enough, those forms require you to confirm that you do, in fact, want to search the Web before Siri actually does it.)

Result: Safari opens, showing the results of your search.

- **Facts and figures.** This is a huge category. It represents Siri's partnership with the Wolfram Alpha factual search engine (*www.wolframalpha. com*). The possibilities here could fill an entire chapter—or an entire encyclopedia.

You can say things like, "How many days until Valentine's Day?" "When was Abraham Lincoln born?" "How many teaspoons are in a gallon?" "What's the exchange rate between dollars and euros?" "What's the capital of Belgium?" "How many calories are in a Hershey bar?" "What's a 17 percent tip on sixty-two dollars for three people?" "What movie won the Oscar for Best Picture in 1985?" "When is the next solar eclipse?" "Show me the Big Dipper." "What's the tallest mountain in the world?" "What's the price of gold right now?" "What's the definition of 'schadenfreude'?" "How much is 23 dollars in pesos?" "Generate a random number." "Generate a random password." "Graph x equals 3y plus 12."

Result: A special, white, mini-notepaper page, ripped right out of Wolfram Alpha's knowledge base.

You may never find the end of the things Siri understands, or the ways that she can help you. If her repertoire seems intimidating at first, start simple—use her to dial by voice, to send text messages, and to manage your alarms. You can build up your bag of tricks as your confidence builds.

Remember that you can use Siri without even unlocking your phone—and therefore without any security, like your passcode. Among certain juvenile circles, therefore, Siri is already the source of some juicy pranks. Someone who finds your phone lying on a table could change your calendar appointments, send texts or emails, or even change what Siri calls you ("Call me 'You idiot' "), without having to enter the phone's password!

The solution is fairly simple. In Settings→General→Passcode Lock, turn off Siri. Of course, you've now lost the convenience of using Siri when the phone is locked. But at least you've prevented having your own phone call you an idiot.

When Things Go Wrong

If Siri doesn't have a good enough Internet connection to do her thing, she'll tell you so.

If she's working properly but mis-recognizes your instructions, you'll know it, because you can see her interpretation of what you said (below, left). Although you might not have guessed it, you can tap Siri's interpretation to open up an editing screen, so that you can make corrections by typing.

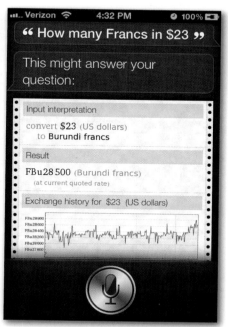

If Siri recognizes what you said but it isn't within her world of comprehension, she offers you a Search the web button as a last resort.

Siri's Personality

Siri's understanding of casual spoken commands is so impressive that you might sometimes think she's almost human. And that, of course, is exactly what Apple wants you to think.

You can say all kinds of off-script and off-kilter things to Siri. You rapidly become aware that whoever programmed her had a deliciously sassy sense of humor.

For example, if you ask her, "What is the meaning of life?" she responds with one of nine different answers. She might say, "I can't answer that now, but give me some time to write a very long play in which nothing happens." Or "Try and be nice to people, avoid eating fat, read a good book every now and then, get some walking in, and try to live in peace and harmony with people of all creeds and nations." Or: "All evidence to date suggests it's chocolate."

Siri is full of such comebacks, and there are whole Web sites dedicated to her snark. Here are a few examples. (The list here won't ruin the fun, because Siri actually has several different comebacks to most of these questions.)

You: "Who's your daddy?" Siri: "You are. Can we get back to work now?"

You: "Open the pod bay doors." Siri: "I'm sorry, I'm afraid I can't do that." (Then: "Are you happy now?")

You: "Knock knock." Siri: "Knock knock. Who's there? Joshua. Joshua who? Joshua, I don't do knock-knock jokes."

You: "What are you wearing?" Siri: "Aluminosilicate glass and stainless steel. Nice, huh?"

You: "Do you know HAL 9000?" Siri: "Everyone knows what happened to HAL. I'd rather not talk about it."

You: "Who's the boss?" (Siri presents the vital statistics of Bruce Springsteen.)

You: "Beam me up, Siri!" Siri: "Please remove your belt, shoes, and jacket, and empty your pockets."

You: "Show me the money." Siri: "I've found 23 ATMs that are fairly close to you…"

You, in the evening: "Good morning, Siri." Siri: "Good morning? It's 9:24 p.m.!"

You: "How much wood would a woodchuck chuck if a woodchuck could chuck wood?" Siri: "42 cords of wood, to be exact. Everyone knows that."

Here are a few other things to say to Siri when you get bored:

I love you, Siri.

Will you marry me?

You're so sexy.

When is your birthday?

What's the best phone?

What's going to happen?

Can you sing?

Why are we here?

You're cute.

You make me so mad!

What do you want?

Tell me a joke.

I'm cold.

Do you love me?

Why are we here?

I need a bathroom.

What are you doing?

You're the best assistant ever!

Take me to your leader.

You're funny.

Guess what?

You're an idiot.

Have a nice day.

How are you today?

Talk dirty to me.

Tell me a story.

I don't have any friends.

What do you think is the best tablet?

How many pickled peppers did Peter Piper pick?

Oh my god.

Do you know Eliza?

What does "Siri" mean?

Am I your best friend?

Do you believe in love?

What is the best computer in the world?

Testing 1, 2, 3.

I'm tired.

What's your secret?

Siri?

What do you think of Android?

What do you think of Windows?

You don't understand love.

You don't understand me.

I'm sorry.

Am I fat?

What are you wearing?

Can you murder someone for me?

Who's on first?

Why are you so awesome?

What's your favorite color?

Where are you?

Advanced Siri

With a little setup, you can extend Siri's powers in some intriguing ways. Let us count them.

Teaching Siri about Your Relationships

When you say, "Text my mom" or "Call my brother" or "Remind me to replace the light bulbs when I get to my friend's house," how does Siri know whom you're talking about? Sure, Siri is powerful artificial intelligence, but she's not actually *magic.*

Turns out you teach her by referring to somebody in your Contacts list. Say to her something like, "My assistant is Jan Carpenter" or "Tad Cooper is my boyfriend." When Siri asks for confirmation, say "Yes" or tap Confirm.

Alternatively, you can just wait for Siri to ask you herself. If you say, "Email my dad," Siri asks, "Who is your dad?" Just say his name; Siri remembers that relationship from now on. (The available relationships are mother, father, brother, sister, child, son, daughter, spouse, wife, husband, boss, partner, manager, assistant, girlfriend, boyfriend, and friend.)

Behind the scenes, Siri builds up a list of these relationships on your card in Contacts.

Now that you know that, it should be pretty easy for you to figure out how to edit or delete these relationships. Which is handy—not all relationships, as we know, last forever.

Post to Facebook or Twitter

Siri can't post directly to Twitter or Facebook. But she can send text messages—and both of those services let you post updates by text message, once you've tweaked some settings.

To set this up for Facebook, send a text message to 32665 (on the dialing keypad, that's *FBOOK*); in the body, type *hello*. For Twitter, send the message to 40404 with the message *START* (all capitals).

> **Tip** Those are the U.S. text-message numbers. If you're in another country, look up the correct text-message number for Facebook at *http://on.fb.me/rr6AbR* or at *http://bit.ly/jZK91N* for Twitter.

After a moment, you get a reply by text message. Follow the instructions in it to finish setting up your text-to-post system. For Facebook, you can tap the link in the reply, or log into the mobile settings page of Facebook and type in the text message's confirmation code. For Twitter, you're asked to text back your Twitter name; in the next message, text your password; in the final message, text *OK*.

Tip You might want to visit *http://twitter.com/devices* and turn off the Message Notifications checkboxes. Otherwise, your phone may be flooded by text messages that represent *replies* to your tweets.

From now on, you can post Facebook statuses by sending text messages to 32665, and Tweets by texting 40404.

But the point of this exercise, of course, is to let Siri send these updates for you. Since she can send text messages to anybody in your Contacts app, create two new "people"—one called Facebook (whose "mobile number" is 32665) and one called Twitter (whose number is 40404).

Now you can post a message on Facebook by telling Siri, "Send a text to Facebook saying, 'I can't believe it just snowed in August'" (or whatever), or to Twitter by saying something like, "Tell Twitter I just turned 40."

 Tip The setup for Google Plus is very similar. Visit *https://plus.google.com/settings/plus*. In the "Set delivery preferences" section, add your cellphone number. (Turn on "Don't notify me," though, to prevent your phone from getting bombarded by return text messages representing replies.) Google sends your phone a code, which you need to enter on the same settings page. Finally, add a "person" called "Google Plus" to your Contacts, whose mobile phone number is 33669. Now you can post updates using Siri by saying, "Send a text to Google Plus saying…"

Fix Siri's Name Comprehension

Siri easily understands common names—but if someone in your family, work, or social circle has an unusual name, you may quickly become frustrated. After all, you can't text, call, email, or get directions to someone's house unless Siri understands the person's name when you say it.

One workaround is to use a relationship, as described earlier. That way, you can say, "Call my brother" instead of "Call Ilyich" (or whatever his offbeat name is).

Another is to use the Contact app's little-known Phonetic option. Open Contacts. Open the person's card. Tap Edit. Scroll to the bottom and tap add field. Tap Phonetic First Name or Phonetic Last Name.

Into the new box you've added to this person's card, you can type a phonetic spelling of the name. For Ishmael, for example, you can type "ISH-may-ell"— whatever it takes to get Siri to understand that name when you speak it.

Siri Settings

In Settings→General→Siri, you can fiddle with several Siri settings:

- **On/Off.** If you turn Siri off, you can no longer command your iPhone 4S using all the Siri commands described in this chapter. Nor can you dictate to type; the little microphone button disappears from the onscreen keyboard.

    You can still use your voice to dial and to control music playback, exactly as described on pages 92 and 94. In essence, you've just turned your iPhone 4S into an iPhone 4.

 Note And why would anyone willingly turn off Siri? One reason: Using Siri involves transmitting a lot of data to Apple, which gives some people the privacy willies. Apple's computers collect everything you say to Siri, the names of your songs and playlists, your personal information in Contacts, plus all the other names in your Contacts (so that Siri can recognize them when you refer to them).

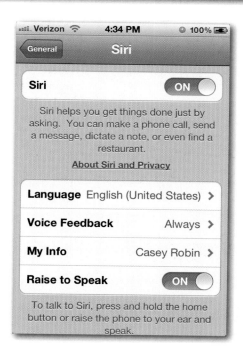

- **Language.** What language and accent do you have? The options here include English in three accents—American, British, and Australian—plus German and French. Apple says it will add more languages over time.

- **Voice Feedback.** Siri generally replies to your queries with both text and a synthesized voice. Here, by choosing Handsfree Only, you can tell Siri not to bother speaking when you're looking at the screen and can read the responses for yourself. In other words, you're telling her to speak only if you can't see the screen because you're on speakerphone, using a headset, listening through your car's Bluetooth system, and so on.

- **My Info.** Siri needs to know which card in Contacts contains your information and lists your relationships. That's how she's able to respond to queries like "Call my mom," "Give me directions to my brother's office," "Remind me to shower when I get home," and so on. Use this setting to show Siri which card is yours.

- **Raise to Speak.** As noted at the beginning of this section, holding down the Home button is only one way to get Siri ready to respond to you. If you turn this option on, you have another way: Just lift the phone to your head. Its tilt sensor and proximity sensor know when it's actually against your face, and that's when you hear the familiar double-beep. (You can't trigger Siri just by turning the phone vertical. Siri listens only when you also place the phone against your ear, which the phone's proximity sensor detects. Clever!)

  The phone is smart enough not to trigger Siri when you raise the phone to your head when you're on a *call*. It does, however, trigger Siri when you hold the phone to your ear to listen to voicemail messages, which can be a little annoying.

Voicemail, Texting & Other Phone Tricks

5

Once you've savored the exhilaration of making phone calls on the iPhone, you're ready to graduate to some of its fancier tricks: voicemail, text messages, cell-company features like caller ID and call forwarding, and a Bluetooth headset or car kit.

Visual Voicemail

On the iPhone, you don't *dial in* to check for answering-machine messages people have left for you. You don't enter a password. You don't sit through some Ambien-addled recorded lady saying, "You have…17…messages. To hear your messages, press 1. When you have finished, you may hang up…."

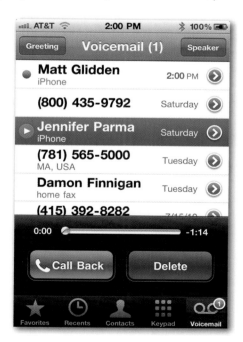

Instead, whenever somebody leaves you a message, the phone wakes up, and a notice on the screen lets you know who the message is from. You also hear a sound, unless you've turned that option off in Settings or turned on the silencer switch (page 20).

That's your cue to tap Home→Phone→Voicemail. There you see all your messages in a tidy chronological list. (The list shows the callers' names if they're in your Contacts list; otherwise it shows their numbers.) You can listen to them in any order—you're not forced to listen to three long-winded friends before discovering that there's an urgent message from your boss. It's a game-changer.

Setup

To access your voicemail, tap Phone on the Home screen, and then tap Voicemail on the Phone screen.

The very first time you visit this screen, the iPhone prompts you to make up a numeric password for your voicemail account—don't worry, you'll never have to enter it again—and to record a "Leave me a message" greeting.

You have two options for the outgoing greeting.

- **Default.** If you're microphone-shy, or if you're famous and you don't want stalkers and fans calling just to hear your famous voice, then use this option. It's a prerecorded, somewhat uptight female voice that says, "Your call has been forwarded to an automatic voice message system. 212-661-7837 is not available." *Beep!*

- **Custom.** This option lets you record your own voice saying, for example, "You've reached my iPhone. You may begin drooling at the tone." Tap Record, hold the iPhone to your head, say your line, and then tap Stop.

  Check how it sounds by tapping Play.

Then just wait for your fans to start leaving you messages!

Using Visual Voicemail

In the voicemail list, a blue dot ● indicates a message you haven't yet played.

 Tip You can work through your messages even when you're out of cellular range—on a plane, for example—because the recordings are stored on the iPhone itself.

There are only two tricky things to learn about Visual Voicemail:

- **Tap a message's name twice to play it.** That's a deviation from the usual iPhone Way, where just *one* tap does the trick. In Visual Voicemail, tapping a message just selects it and activates the Call Back and Delete buttons at the bottom of the screen. You have to tap *twice* to start playback (once if the message is already highlighted).

- **Turn on speaker phone first.** As the name "Visual Voicemail" suggests, you're *looking* at your voicemail list—which means you're *not* holding the phone up to your head. The first time people try using Visual Voicemail, therefore, they generally hear nothing!

  That's a good argument for hitting the Speaker button *before* tapping messages that you want to play back. That way, you can hear the playback *and* continue looking over the list. (Of course, if privacy is an issue, you can also double-tap a message and then quickly whip the phone up to your ear.)

 Note If you're listening through the earbuds, a Bluetooth earpiece, or a car kit, of course, you hear the message playing back through *that*. If you really want to listen through the iPhone's speaker instead, tap Audio and then Speaker Phone. (You switch back the same way.)

Everything else about Visual Voicemail is straightforward. The buttons do exactly what they say:

- **Delete.** The Voicemail list scrolls with a flick of your finger, but you still might want to keep the list manageable by deleting old messages. To do that, tap a message, or swipe across its name, and then tap Delete. The message disappears instantly. (You're not asked to confirm.)

 Tip The iPhone hangs on to old messages for 30 days—even ones you've deleted. To listen to deleted messages that are still on the phone, scroll to the bottom of the list and then tap Deleted Messages.

On the Deleted screen, you can Undelete a message that you actually don't want to lose yet (that is, move it back to the Voicemail screen) or tap Clear All to erase these messages for good.

- **Call Back.** Tap a message and then tap Call Back to return the call. Very cool—you never even encounter the person's phone number.

- **Rewind, Fast Forward.** Drag the little white ball in the scrubber bar (beneath the list) to skip backward or forward in the message. It's a great way to replay something you didn't catch the first time.

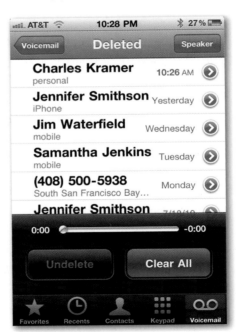

- **Greeting.** Tap this button (upper-left corner) to record your voicemail greeting.

- **Call Details.** Tap the ⊙ button to open the Info screen for the message that was left for you. Here you'll find out the date and time of the message.

If it was left by somebody who's in your Contacts list, you can see *which* of that person's phone numbers the call came from (indicated in blue type), plus a blue ★ if that number is in your Favorites list. Oh, and you can add this person to your Favorites list at this point by tapping Add to Favorites.

If the caller's number isn't in Contacts, then you're shown the city and state where that person's phone is registered. And you'll be offered a Create New Contact button and an Add to Existing Contact button, so you can store it for future reference.

In both cases, you also have the option to return the call (right from the Info screen), fire off a text message, or place a FaceTime video call.

Dialing in for Messages

Gross and pre-iPhonish though it may sound, you can also dial in for your messages from another phone. (Hey, it could happen.)

To do that, dial your iPhone's number. Wait for the voicemail system to answer.

As your own voicemail greeting plays, dial * (or # if you have Verizon), your voicemail password, and then #.

You hear the Uptight Carrier Lady announce how many messages you have, and then she'll start playing them for you.

After you hear each message, she'll offer you the following options (but you don't have to wait for her to announce them):

- To delete the message, press 7.

- To save it, press 9.

- To replay it, press 4.

Conveniently enough, these keystrokes are the same on Verizon, Sprint, and AT&T.

> **Tip** If this whole Visual Voicemail thing freaks you out, you can also dial in for messages the old-fashioned way, right from the iPhone. Open the keypad and hold down the 1 key, just as though it were a speed-dial key on any normal phone.
>
> After a moment, the phone connects; you're asked for your password, and then the messages begin to play back, just as described above.

Text Messages (SMS)

"Texting," as the whippersnappers call it, was *huge* in Asia and Europe before it began catching on in the United States. These days, however, it's increasingly popular, especially among teenagers and twentysomethings.

SMS stands for Short Messaging Service. An SMS text message is a very short note (under 160 characters—a sentence or two) that you shoot from one cellphone to another. What's so great about it?

- Like a phone call, it's immediate. You get the message off your chest right now.

- As with email, the recipient doesn't have to answer immediately. The message waits for him even when his phone is turned off.

- Unlike a phone call, it's nondisruptive. You can send someone a text message without worrying that he's in a movie, a meeting, or anywhere else where holding a phone up to the head and talking would be frowned upon. (And the other person can answer nondisruptively, too, by sending a text message *back*.)

- You have a written record of the exchange. There's no mistaking what the person meant. (Well, at least not because of sound quality. Whether or not you can understand the texting shorthand culture that's evolved from people using no-keyboard cellphones to type English words—"C U 2mrO," and so on—is another matter entirely.)

The basic iPhone plans don't come with any text messages. You have to pay extra for them—for example, $20 a month for unlimited texts. Remember that you use up one of those 200 each time you send *or receive* a message.

And by the way, *picture and video messages* (known as MMS, or multimedia messaging service) count as regular text messages.

Receiving a Text Message

When you get an SMS, the iPhone plays a sound. It's a quick marimba riff, unless you've assigned a text tone to this specific person.

Anyway, the phone also displays the name or number of the sender *and* the message. Unless you've fooled around with the Notifications settings (page

37), the message appears in a translucent message rectangle. If you're using the iPhone at the time, you can tap Close (to keep doing what you were doing) or Reply (to open the message so you can reply).

Otherwise, if the iPhone was asleep, it wakes up and displays the message right on its Unlock screen (below, left). You can unlock the phone and jump directly to the message by swiping your finger *right across the message on the Lock screen.*

If you *have* changed the options in Notifications, then your text message might appear discreetly at the top of the screen, disappearing momentarily on its own, so as not to interrupt what you're doing. If you turned off Show Preview, then you don't see the message itself—only the name or number of the sender. And if you've turned off View in Lock Screen, then, sure enough, the text message does *not* appear on the Lock screen.

 Tip The Messages icon on the Home screen bears a little circled number "badge," letting you know how many new text messages are waiting for you.

Once you tap a message notification to open it, the look of Messages might surprise you. It resembles iChat, Apple's chat program for Mac, in which incoming text messages and your replies are displayed as though they're car-toon speech balloons (facing page, right).

 Tip The last 50 exchanges appear here. If you want to see even older ones, scroll to the very top (which you can do by tapping the top edge of the screen) and tap Load Earlier Messages.

And by the way—if the keyboard is blocking your view of the conversation, swipe downward to hide it.

To respond to the message, tap in the text box at the bottom of the screen. The iPhone keyboard appears. Type away, and then tap Send. Assuming your phone has cellular coverage, the message gets sent off immediately.

 Tip Links that people send you in text messages actually work. For example, if someone sends you a Web address, tap it with your finger to open it in Safari. If someone sends a street address, tap it to open it in Google Maps. And if someone sends a phone number, tap it to dial.

And if your buddy replies, then the balloon-chat continues, scrolling up the screen. Don't forget to turn the iPhone 90 degrees for a bigger, wider keyboard!

 Tip If all this fussy typing is driving you nuts, you can always tap the big fat Call button to conclude the transaction by voice, or FaceTime to conclude it by video. Those buttons are hiding above the message; tap the top edge of the screen to jump there.

The Text List

What's cool is that the iPhone retains all these exchanges. You can review them or resume them at any time by tapping Messages on the Home screen. A list of text message conversations appears; a blue dot indicates conversa-tions that contain new messages.

 Tip If you've sent a message to a certain group of people, you can address a new note to the same group by tapping the old message's row here.

The truth is, these listings represent *people,* not conversations. For example, if you had a text message exchange with Chris last week, a quick way to send a new text message (on a totally different subject) to Chris is to open that "con-

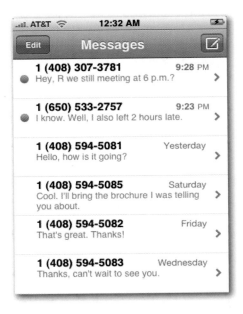

versation" and simply send a "reply." The iPhone saves you the administrative work of creating a new message, choosing a recipient, and so on.

 Tip Hey, you can search text messages! At the very top of the list, there's a search box. You can actually find text inside your message collection.

If having these old exchanges hanging around presents a security (or marital) risk, you can delete them in either of two ways:

- **From the Text Messages list.** *Swipe* away the conversation. Just swipe your finger horizontally across the conversation's name (either direction). That makes the Delete confirmation button appear immediately.

- **From within a conversation's speech-balloons screen.** Tap Edit to open the message-deletion screen. Here you can delete all the exchanges simultaneously (tap Clear All) or vaporize only particularly incriminating messages. To do that, tap the round ✔ buttons for the individual balloons you want to nuke; then tap Delete (2) (or whatever number the button says). Tap Done.

Sending a New Message

If you want to text somebody you've texted before, the quickest way, as noted above, is simply to resume one of the "conversations" already listed in the Text Messages list.

But options to fire off text messages lurk all over the iPhone. A few examples:

- **In the Messages program.** From the Home screen, tap Messages. The iPhone opens the list of messages you've received. Tap the ☑ button at the top-right corner to open a new text message window.

  Address it by typing a few letters of the recipient's name and then choosing from the list of matches. Or tap the **+** button, which opens your Contacts list. Tap the person you want to text.

 Your *entire* Contacts list appears here, even people with no cellphone numbers. But you can't text somebody who doesn't have a cellphone.

- **In the Contacts, Recents, or Favorites lists.** Tap a person's name in Contacts, or ⊙ next to a listing in Recents or Favorites, to open the Info screen; tap Text Message. In other words, sending a text message to anyone whose cellphone number lives in your iPhone is only two taps away.

- **From Photos or Voice Memos.** Whenever you see a 📤 (Share) button—when you're looking at a photo or a video in Photos, for example, or when you tap the ☰ button in Voice Memos—the usual list of sending options appears. It usually includes Email, iCloud—and Message. Tapping Message sends you back to Messages, where the photo, video, or audio file is ready to send. (More on multimedia messages shortly.)

You can now tap that ➕ button again to add *another* recipient for this same message (or tap the ⏺123 button to type in a phone number). Lather, rinse, and repeat as necessary; they'll all get the same message.

In any case, the skinny little text message composition screen is waiting for you now. You're ready to type (or dictate) and send!

 Tip In iOS 5, a delightful new text-reading option is available. If you drag your finger down the screen, you *hide the keyboard.* Doing that makes much more of the screen available to display the text-message conversation.

Text-Message Options

You might not think that an act as simple as sending a text message would come with a bunch of options, but you'd be wrong. If you tap Settings→Messages, you'll stumble upon two intriguing text-messaging options:

- **MMS Messaging.** MMS messages are like text messages—except that they can also include audio clips, video clips, or photos, as described in the following section. In the rare event that your cell company charges extra for these messages, you have an on/off switch here. If you turn it off, you can send only plain text messages.

- **Group Messaging.** Suppose you're sending a message to three friends named A, B, and C (they had very unimaginative parents). When they reply to your message, the responses will appear in a Messages thread that's dedicated to this particular group (facing page, left). It works only if *all* of you have turned on Group Messaging. (Note to the paranoid: It also means that everyone sees everyone else's phone numbers.)

- **Show Subject Field.** If email messages can have subject lines, why not text messages? Now, on certain newfangled phones (like yours), they can; the message arrives with a little dividing line between the subject and the body, offering your recipient a hint as to what it's about.

 Note It's OK to leave the subject line blank. But if you leave the *body* blank, the message won't send. (Incidentally, when you do fill in the subject line, what you're sending is a multimedia (MMS) message, rather than a plain old text message.)

- **Character Count.** If a message is longer than 160 characters, the iPhone breaks it up into multiple messages. That's convenient, sure. But if your cellphone plan permits only a fixed number of messages a month, you could wind up sending (and spending) more than you intended.

  The Character Count feature can save you. When it's on, after your typing wraps to a second line, a little counter appears just above the Send button ("71/160," for example, as shown above at right). It tracks how many characters remain within your 160-character limit for one message.

- **Show Preview.** Usually, when a text message arrives, it wakes up your phone and shows itself. Which is great, as long as the message isn't private and the phone isn't lying on the table where everyone can see it. If you turn off Show Preview, though, you'll see who the message is from, but not the actual text of the message (until you tap the notification banner or bubble). You can find the Show Preview on/off switch in its new iOS location: in Settings→Notifications→Messages.

- **Repeat Alert.** If someone sends you a text message but you don't read it, the iPhone will remind you a couple more times that you have an unread text message. If you really want to ignore that message and you don't want to be nagged about it, turn this option off in Settings→Notifications→Messages.

Picture, Audio, or Video Messages

Man, we waited long enough for this. It was bizarre that, for all its other superpowers, the iPhone could not send photos to other cellphones, let alone audio clips or video clips. This feature—called MMS (multimedia messaging service) was on every cellphone on earth, even the $20 starter phones. But not on the iPhone.

Fortunately, MMS is here now. To send a photo or a video, tap the ◉ icon next to the box where you type your text messages (shown below). Two buttons appear: Take Photo or Video or Choose Existing.

If you want to transmit a photo or video that's already on your phone, then tap Choose Existing; your Photos app opens automatically, showing all your photos and videos. Tap the one you want and then tap Choose. If you choose Take Photo or Video instead, then your Camera app opens so you can take a new picture or snag a video clip.

In any case, you now return to your SMS conversation in progress—but now that photo or video appears inside the Send box. Type a caption or comment, if you like. Then tap Send to fire it off to your buddy.

Capturing Text-Message Goodies

In general, text messages are fleeting; most people have no idea how they might capture them and save them forever. Copy and Paste help with that. (So does the amazing Google Voice service, but that's another conversation.)

Some of the stuff *in* those text messages is easy to capture, though. For example, if you're on the receiving end of an MMS photo or video, tap the small preview in the speech bubble. It opens at full-screen size so you can have a better look at it—and if it's a video, there's even a ▶ button so you can play it. Either way, if the picture or video is good enough to preserve, tap the ➦ button. You're offered a Save Image or Save Video button; tap to add the photo or video to your iPhone's collection.

If someone sends you contact information (name and address, for example), you can add it to your address book. Just tap inside that bubble, and then tap either Create New Contact or Add to Existing Contact.

iMessages

Here's a new iOS 5 feature that should interest you—if it doesn't, in fact, make you giggle like a schoolgirl.

An iMessage looks and works exactly like a text message. You send them and receive them in the same app (Messages). They show up in the same window. You can send the same kinds of things: text, photos, videos, contacts, and map locations. You send and receive them using exactly the same techniques.

The big difference: iMessages are what your phone sends to other iPhones, iPads, and iPod Touches (with iOS 5, of course). If your iPhone determines that the address belongs to any *other* kind of phone, it automatically switches to sending regular old text messages.

So why would Apple reinvent the text-messaging wheel? Why did it create iMessages to replicate regular text messaging? Because iMessages offer some huge advantages over regular text messages:

- iMessages don't count as text messages! You don't have to pay for them. They look and work exactly like text messages, but they're transferred over the Internet (WiFi or 3G) instead of your cell company's voice airwaves. You can send and receive an unlimited number of them and never have to pay a penny more. In fact, if most of the people you text have i-gadgets, you can sign up for a cheaper texting plan with a lower monthly message allotment—and save a lot of money every year.

- When you're typing back and forth with somebody, you don't have to wonder whether, during a silence, they're typing a response to you or just ignoring you; when they're typing a response, you see an ellipsis (…), as you can see here at right.

- You don't have to wonder if the other guy has received your message. A tiny, light-gray word "delivered" appears under each message you send, briefly, to let you know that the other guy's device received it.

- You can even turn on a "read receipt" feature that lets the other guy know when you've actually *seen* a message he sent. You'll see a notation that says, for example, "Read: 2:34 PM."

- Your history of iMessages shows up on all your i-gadgets; they're synchronized through your iCloud account. In other words, you can start a back-and-forth with somebody using your iPhone, and later pick up your iPad at home and carry right on from where you stopped.

You don't have to do anything special. Just go into Messages and create a text message as usual. If your recipient is using an iOS 5 gadget, your iPhone sends your message as an iMessage automatically. It somehow knows.

You'll know, too, because the light-gray text in the typing box says "iMessage" instead of "Text Message" (facing page, right). And each message you send shows up in a blue speech bubble instead of a green one. In fact, when you're addressing the new text message, a tiny blue icon appears next to the names of each person who has an iMessages gadget, so you know in advance who's cool and who's not (facing page, left).

Even though iMessages are automatic, you still have some control over their behavior. Open Settings→Messages and peruse these options:

- **iMessage.** This is the on/off switch for the entire feature. It's hard to imagine why you wouldn't want to avoid paying for text messages, but you know—whatever floats your boat.

- **Send Read Receipts.** When you turn this option on, your iMessage correspondents will know when you've seen their messages. A tiny word "Read" will appear beneath each sent message that you've actually seen.

- **Send as SMS.** If iMessages is unavailable (meaning that you have no Internet connection at all), then your phone will send your message as a regular text message, via the regular cellphone voice network.

More Free Text Messages

Text messaging is awesome. Paying for text messaging, not so much.

That's why iMessages is so great: It bypasses the cell companies' text-message network by sending messages over the Internet instead—but only when you're sending to fellow iOS 5 owners.

Fortunately, there are all kinds of sneaky ways to do text messaging for free that *don't* require your correspondents to have iOS 5. Yes, you read that right: free. Here are a couple of examples:

Solution #1: Textfree With Voice. It's an app from the App Store that gives your iPhone its own phone number just for free text message or picture messages, so you can send and receive all you want without paying a cent. Incoming voice calls are free, too; you can buy minutes for outgoing calls.

Solution #2: Sign up for a free Google Voice account. It has a million great features. But one of the best is that it lets you send and receive free text messages. You can do that from your computer (an amazingly useful feature, actually) at *voice.google.com*, or by using the free Google Voice app).

Chat Programs

The iPhone doesn't *come* with any chat programs, like AIM (AOL Instant Messenger), Yahoo Messenger, or MSN Messenger. But installing one yourself—like AIM, below—is simple, as described in Chapter 7.

If you're a hard-core chatter, though, what you really want is an all-in-one app like IM+ or Beejive IM. You get a single app that can conduct chats with people on just about every chat network known to man: GTalk, Yahoo, MSN/Live Messenger, AIM, iChat, ICQ, Myspace, Twitter, Facebook, Jabber, and Skype.

Call Waiting

Call waiting has been around for years. With a call-waiting feature, when you're on one phone call, you hear a beep indicating that someone else is calling in. You can tap the Flash key on your phone—if you know which one it is—to answer the second call while you put the first one on hold.

Some people don't use call waiting because it's rude to both callers. Others don't use it because they have no idea what the Flash key is.

On the iPhone, when a second call comes in, the phone rings (and/or vibrates) as usual, and the screen displays the name or number of the caller, just as it always does. Buttons on the screen offer you three choices:

- **Ignore.** The incoming call goes straight to voicemail. Your first caller has no idea that anything has happened.

- **Hold Call + Answer.** This button gives you the traditional call-waiting effect. You say, "Can you hold on a sec? I've got another call," to the first caller. The iPhone puts her on hold, and you connect to the second caller.

  At this point, you can jump back and forth between the two calls, or you can merge them into a conference call, just as described on page 84.

- **End Call + Answer.** Tapping this button hangs up on the first call and takes the second one.

If call waiting seems a bit disruptive, you can turn it off, at least on the AT&T iPhone (the switch is in Settings→Phone→Call Waiting). When call waiting is turned off, incoming calls go straight to voicemail when you're on the phone.

If you have Sprint or Verizon, you can turn off call waiting only one call at a time; just dial *70 before you dial the number. You won't be disturbed by call waiting beeps while you're on that important call.

Call Forwarding

Here's a pretty cool feature you may not have even known you had. It lets you route all calls made to your iPhone number to a *different* number. How is this useful? Let us count the ways:

- When you're home. You can have your cellphone's calls ring your home number so you can use any extension in the house, and so you don't miss any calls while the iPhone is turned off or charging.

- When you send your iPhone to Apple for battery replacement, you can forward the calls you would have missed to your home or work phone number.

- When you're overseas, you can forward the number to one of the Web-based services that answers your voicemail and sends it to you as an email attachment (like Google Voice or CallWave.com).

- When you're going to be in a place with little or no cell coverage (Alaska, say), you can have your calls forwarded to your hotel or to a friend's cellphone. (Forwarded calls eat up your allotment of minutes, though.)

You have to turn on call forwarding while you're still in an area with cell coverage.

- **AT&T.** Tap Settings→Phone→Call Forwarding, turn call forwarding on, and then tap in the new phone number. That's all there is to it—your iPhone will no longer ring. At least not until you turn the same switch off again.

- **Verizon, Sprint.** On the dialing pad, dial *72, plus the number you're forwarding calls to. Then tap Call. (To turn off call forwarding, dial *73, and then tap Call.)

Caller ID

Caller ID is another classic cellphone feature. It's the one that displays the phone number of the incoming call (and sometimes the name of the caller).

The only thing worth noting about the iPhone's own implementation of caller ID is that you can prevent *your* number from appearing when you call *other* people's phones. From the Home screen, tap Settings→Phone→Show My Caller ID, and then tap the On/Off switch.

- **AT&T.** Tap Settings→Phone→Show My Caller ID, and then tap the On/Off switch.

- **Verizon, Sprint.** You can disable caller ID only for individual calls. For example, if you're calling your ex, you might not want your number to show up on his phone. Just dial *67 before you dial the number. (Caller ID turns on again for subsequent calls.)

Bluetooth Earpieces and Car Kits

The iPhone has more antennas than an ant colony: for the cellular networks, for WiFi hotspots, for GPS, and for Bluetooth.

Bluetooth is a short-range wireless *cable elimination* technology. It's designed to untether you from equipment that would ordinarily require a cord. Bluetooth crops up in computers (print from a laptop to a Bluetooth printer), in game consoles (like Sony's wireless PlayStation controller), and above all, in cellphones.

There are all kinds of things Bluetooth *can* do in cellphones, like transmitting camera-phone photos to computers, wirelessly syncing your address book from a computer, or letting the phone in your pocket serve as a wireless Internet antenna for your laptop. But most people use the iPhone's Bluetooth primarily for hands-free calling.

To be precise, it works with those tiny wireless Bluetooth earpieces, of the sort you see clipped to people's ears, as well as in cars with Bluetooth phone systems. If your car has one of these "car kits" (Acura, Prius, and many other models include them), then you hear the other person's voice through your stereo speakers, and there's a microphone built into your steering wheel or rearview mirror. You keep your hands on the wheel the whole time.

Note This discussion covers *monaural* Bluetooth earpieces intended for phone calls. But the iPhone can also handle Bluetooth *stereo* headphones, intended for music. Details are on page 174.

Pairing with a Bluetooth Earpiece

So far, Bluetooth hands-free systems have been embraced primarily just by the world's geeks for one simple reason: It's *way* too complicated to pair the earpiece (or car) with the phone.

So what's pairing? That's the system of "marrying" a phone to a Bluetooth earpiece, so that each works only with the other. If you didn't do this pairing, then some other guy passing on the sidewalk might hear your conversation through *his* earpiece. And you probably wouldn't like that.

The pairing process is different for every cellphone and every Bluetooth earpiece. Usually it involves a sequence like this:

① **On the earpiece, turn on Bluetooth. Make the earpiece discoverable.** *Discoverable* just means that your phone can "see" it. You'll have to consult the earpiece's instructions to learn how to do so.

② **On the iPhone, tap Settings→General→Bluetooth. Turn Bluetooth to On.** The iPhone immediately begins searching for nearby Bluetooth equipment. If all goes well, you'll see the name of your earpiece show up on the screen.

③ **Tap the earpiece's name. Type in the passcode, if necessary.** The *passcode* is a number, usually four or six digits, that must be typed into the phone within about a minute. You have to enter this only once, during the initial pairing process. The idea is to prevent some evildoer sitting nearby in the airport lounge, for example, to secretly pair *his* earpiece with *your* iPhone.

The user's manual for your earpiece should tell you what the passcode is (if one is even required).

When you're using a Bluetooth earpiece, you *dial* using the iPhone itself (unless you're using voice dialing, of course). You usually use the iPhone's own volume controls, too. You generally press a button on the earpiece itself to answer an incoming call, to swap call waiting calls, and to end a call.

If you're having any problems making a particular earpiece work, Google it. Type "iPhone Motorola H800 earpiece," for example. Chances are good that you'll find a writeup by somebody who's worked through the setup and made it work.

Car Kits

The iPhone works beautifully with Bluetooth car kits, too. The pairing procedure generally goes exactly as described above: You make the car discoverable, enter the passcode on the iPhone, and then make the connection.

Once you're paired up, you can answer an incoming call by pressing a button on your steering wheel, for example. You make calls either from the iPhone or, in some cars, by dialing the number on the car's own touchscreen.

 Note When Bluetooth is turned on but the earpiece isn't, or when the earpiece isn't nearby, the ✳ icon appears in gray. And when it's connected and working right, the earpiece's battery gauge appears on the iPhone's status bar.

Of course, studies show that it's the act of driving while conversing that causes accidents—not actually holding a phone. So the hands-free system is less for safety than for convenience and compliance with state laws.

Custom Ringtones

The iPhone comes with 25 creative and intriguing ringing sounds, from an old car horn to a peppy marimba lick. Page 455 shows you how to choose the one you want to hear when your phone rings. You can also buy ready-made pop-music ringtones from the wireless iTunes Store (read on).

But where's the fun in that? Surely you don't want to walk around listening to the same ringtones as the millions of *other* iPhone owners.

Fortunately, you can also make up *custom* ring sounds, either to use as your main iPhone ring or to assign to individual callers in your Contacts list. This section covers the two official ways of going about it—carving 30-second ringtone snippets out of pop songs and recording your own in GarageBand on a Mac—and points you to the two sneakier ways.

iTunes Ringtones

Apple began selling custom ringtones from its iTunes Store in 2007. Using simple audio tools in the iTunes program, you could buy a song for $1, choose a 30-second chunk, pay $1 more for the ringtone, and sync the result to your iPhone. It was a flop (at $1 for 30 seconds, is it any wonder?), and Apple quietly shut down that offering.

You can still buy canned pop-music snippets as ringtones, though—chosen by Apple or the record company, not you—for $1.30 each. See page 455.

GarageBand Ringtones

If you have a Macintosh, then you can also create your own ringtones without paying anything to anyone—by using GarageBand, the music-editing program that comes on every new Mac (version '08 or later).

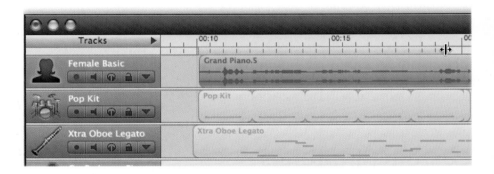

Start by building the ringtone itself. You can use GarageBand's Loops (prerecorded instrumental snippets designed to sound good together), for example, or sound you've recorded with a microphone. (There's nothing like the prerecorded sound of your spouse's voice barking out from the phone: "HONEY! PICK UP! IT'S ME!" every time your beloved calls.)

If you're not especially paranoid about record-company lawyers, you can also import any song at all into GarageBand—an MP3, AIFF, MIDI, or non-copy-protected AAC file, for example—and adapt a piece of it into a ringtone. That's one way for conscientious objectors to escape the $1.30-per-ringtone surcharge.

In any case, once you have your audio laid out in GarageBand tracks, press the letter C key. That turns on the *Cycle strip*—the yellow bar in the ruler shown above. Drag the endpoints of this Cycle strip to determine the length of your ringtone (up to 40 seconds long).

Tip One feature that's blatantly missing on the iPhone is a "vibrate, *then* ring" option. That's where, when a call comes in, the phone first vibrates silently to get your attention and begins to ring out loud only if you still haven't responded after, say, 10 seconds.

GarageBand offers the solution: Create a ringtone that's silent for the first 10 seconds (drag the Cycle strip to the left of the music) and only *then* plays a sound. Then set your iPhone to vibrate and ring. When a call comes in, the phone plays the ringtone immediately as it vibrates—but you won't hear anything until after the silent portion of the ringtone has been "played."

Press the space bar to start and stop playback as you fiddle with your masterpiece.

When everything sounds good, choose Share→Send Ringtone to iTunes. Next time you set up your iPhone sync, click the Ringtones tab in iTunes and schedule your newly minted ringtone for transfer to the phone.

 Tip There are two other, less-official ways to create ringtones. One method lets you snag a piece of any not-copy-protected song in your iTunes library. The process takes several steps, but it's free and doesn't require special software. Details are in the free PDF appendix on this book's "Missing CD" at *www.missingmanuals.com*.

The other is to use a program like Ringtone Recorder Pro, a $1 download from the App Store. It emails you a ringtone (for subsequent syncing from iTunes) from anything you can record with your iPhone's microphone—voices, music, any audio—which is a very cool idea.

Talking Buttons—and Accessibility

If you were told the iPhone was one of the easiest phones in the world for a disabled person to use, you might spew your coffee. The thing has almost no physical keys at all! How would a blind person use it? It's a phone that rings! How would a deaf person use it?

You won't believe the lengths to which Apple has gone to make the iPhone usable for people with vision, hearing, or other physical impairments. If you're deaf, you can have the LED flash to get your attention. If you're blind, you can literally turn the screen off and operate *everything*—do your email, surf the Web, adjust settings, run apps—by tapping and letting the phone speak what you're touching, in whatever language your iPhone uses. It's pretty amazing.

You can also magnify the screen, reverse black for white (for better-contrast reading), set up custom vibrations for each person who might call you, and convert stereo music to mono (great if you're deaf in one ear).

Some of these features are useful even if you're not disabled—in particular, the LED flash, custom vibrations, and zooming. And if you're disabled in the sense of being over 40, you might find the Large Text option especially handy when you can't find your reading glasses.

Finally, if you have an iPhone 4S, don't forget about Siri (Chapter 4). She may be the best friend a blind person's phone ever had.

Here's a rundown of the accessibility features in iOS 5. To turn on any of the features described here, go to the Home screen and tap Settings→General→ Accessibility.

 Tip You can turn the iPhone's accessibility features on and off with a triple-click on the Home button. See page 15 for details.

VoiceOver

VoiceOver is the option that makes the iPhone speak everything you touch—even the little status gauges at the top of the screen.

On the VoiceOver settings pane, tap the On/Off switch to turn VoiceOver on. You can also adjust the Speaking Rate of the synthesized voice.

Now you're ready to start using the iPhone in VoiceOver mode. There's a lot to learn, and practice makes perfect, but here's the overview:

- **Tap something to hear it.** Tap icons, words, even status icons at the top; as you go, the voice tells you what you're tapping. "Messages." "Calendar." "Mail—14 new items." "45 percent battery power." You can tap the dots on the Home screen, and you'll hear, "Page 3 of 9."

  Once you've tapped a screen element, you can also flick your finger left or right—anywhere on the screen—to "walk" through everything on the screen, left to right, top to bottom.

 Tip A little black rectangle appears around whatever the voice is identifying. That's for the benefit of sighted people who might be helping you.

- **Double-tap the screen to "tap" it.** Ordinarily, you tap something on the screen to open it. But since single-tapping now means "speak this," you need a new way to open everything. So: To open something you've just heard identified, double-tap *anywhere on the screen.* (You don't have to wait for the voice to finish talking.)

 Tip Or do a *split tap.* Tap something to hear what it is—and with that finger still down, tap somewhere else with a different finger to open it.

There are all kinds of other special gestures in VoiceOver. Make the voice stop speaking with a *two-finger tap;* read everything, in sequence, from the top of the screen with a *two-finger upward flick;* scroll one page at a time with a *three-finger flick up or down;* go to the next or previous screen (Home, Stocks, and so on) with a *three-finger flick left or right;* and more.

Or try a *three-finger triple tap;* it blacks out the screen, giving you total privacy as well as a heck of a battery boost. (Repeat to turn the screen back on.)

At the bottom of the VoiceOver settings screen, you'll find an expanded wealth of options for using the iPhone sightlessly. For example:

- **Speak Hints** makes the phone give you additional suggestions for operating something you've tapped. For example, instead of just saying "Safari," it says, "Safari. Double-tap to open."

- **Typing Feedback** governs how the phone helps you figure out what you're typing. It can speak the individual letters you're striking, the words you've completed, or both.

- **Use Phonetics** makes the phone even clearer when it's reading letter by letter (it says not just "F," but "F—foxtrot").

- **Use Pitch Change** makes the phone talk in a higher voice when you're entering letters and a lower voice when you're deleting them. It also uses a higher pitch when speaking the first item of a list, and a lower one when speaking the last item of a group. In both cases, this option is a great way to help you understand where you are in a list.

- **Speak Notifications** makes the phone announce, with a spoken voice, when an alert or update message has appeared.

- **The Rotor** is an imaginary dial. You turn it by twisting two fingers on the screen as if you were turning an actual dial; each new position of the "dial" changes the way VoiceOver moves through a document. You can change the dial so that a flick downward moves through text letter by letter instead of word by word, for example.

The rotor is even more important when you're using the Web. It contains the names of Web page elements like pictures, headers, links, text boxes, and so on. Use the rotor to choose, for example, images—then you can flick up and down from one picture to the next on that page.

If you rely on VoiceOver for using your iPhone, then you should visit the more complete user guide at *http://support.apple.com/kb/HT3598*.

 Tip VoiceOver is especially great at reading your iBooks out loud. Details are on page 150.

Zooming

The iPhone may be a neat little computer, but it's a neat *little* computer; it has the smallest screen of any laptop on the market. Every now and then, you might need a little help reading small text or inspecting those tiny graphics.

If you turn on Zoom (in Settings→General→Accessibility), then you can magnify the screen whenever it's convenient, up to 500 percent. Of course, the screen image is now too big to fit the physical glass of the iPhone, so you'll need a way to scroll around on your jumbo virtual screen. Here's the scheme:

• **Turn zooming on or off** by tapping the screen with three fingers.

(That's why you can't use Zoom while VoiceOver is also turned on; the three-finger tap has a different function in each.) The screen is now 200 percent of original size (facing page, left).

• **Pan around the virtual giant screen** by dragging or flicking with three fingers.

 Tip Once you begin a three-finger drag, you can lift two of your fingers. You can slide the remaining finger close to any screen border to continue scrolling in that direction—faster the closer you are to the edge.

• **Zoom in more or less** by double-tap/dragging with three fingers. It's like double-tapping, except that you leave your fingers down on the second tap—and drag them upward to zoom in more (up to 500 percent), or down to zoom out again.

Tip Once again, you can lift two of your three fingers after the dragging has begun. That way, it's easier to see what you're doing.

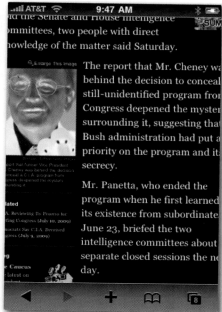

Large Text

This option is a game-changer if you have aging eyes—that is, if you often find the type on the screen too small. You can choose a larger type size, from 20- to 56-point type, for all text the iPhone displays in text messages, email, notes, Contacts, and the Calendar.

White on Black

By reversing the screen's colors black for white, like a film negative, you create a higher-contrast effect that some people find is easier on the eyes (above, right). To try it out, go to Settings→General→Accessibility and turn on White on Black. (The colors reverse, too—red for green, and so on—an interesting effect, to say the least.)

Speak Selection

This convenient option adds a new Speak command to the buttons that appear whenever you highlight text in any app (page 56). Tap that button to make the phone read the selected text out loud. It can be an email message, a Web page, a text message—anything.

Speak Auto-Text

You know how the iPhone suggests a word as you type? This option in Settings→General→Accessibility makes the iPhone *speak* each suggestion. That effect has three benefits. First, of course, it helps blind people know what they're typing. Second, you don't have to take your eyes off the keyboard, which is great for speed and concentration. Third, if you're zoomed in, you may not be able to see the suggested word appear under your typed text— but now you still know what the suggestion is.

Custom Vibrations

How come nobody talks about this new iOS 5 feature? It lets you assign a custom vibration pattern to each person in your Contacts, so that you know by feel who's calling, without even removing the phone from your pocket. It's a surprisingly useful option, whether you're deaf or not.

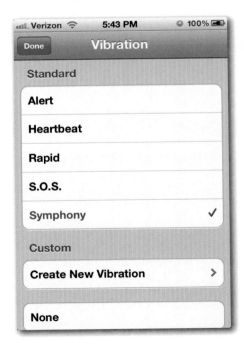

Turn Custom Vibrations to On. Then open your Contacts app. Tap somebody's name, and then tap Vibration. You're offered a choice of canned patterns (Heartbeat, Rapid, S.O.S., and so on—facing page, left). But if you tap Create New Vibration, you can then tap the screen in whatever rhythm you like. It can be diddle diddle dee…or the opening notes the Hallelujah Chorus…or the actual syllables of the person's name. ("Maryanna Beckleheimer." Can you feel it?)

The phone records your pattern, which you can prove to yourself by tapping Play. If you tap Save and name that pattern, then it becomes one of the choices when you choose a vibration pattern for someone in your Contacts.. It's what you'll feel whenever this person calls you. Yes, it's tactile caller ID. Wild.

LED Flash

If you're deaf, you know when the phone is ringing—because it vibrates, of course. But what if it's sitting on the desk, or it's over there charging? This option lets you know when you're getting a call, a text, or a notification by blinking the flash on the back of the phone—the very bright LED light. (This option appears on the iPhone 4 and 4S only.)

Mono Audio/Balance Slider

If you're deaf in one ear, then listening to any music that's a stereo mix can be frustrating; you might be missing half the orchestration or the vocals. When you turn on the Mono Audio option in Settings→General→Accessibility, the iPhone mixes everything down so that the left and right channels contain the same monaural playback. Now you can hear the entire mix in one ear.

 Tip This is also a great feature when you're sharing an earbud with a friend, or when one of your earbuds is broken.

A new balance slider appears here, too—the L/R slider. It lets you adjust the phone's stereo mix, in case one of your ears has better hearing than the other.

AssistiveTouch

The iPhone has always been pretty good at helping out if you're blind or deaf. But until iOS 5 came along, it was "tough rocks" if you had motor-control problems. How are you supposed to shake the phone (a shortcut for "Undo") if you can't even hold the thing? How are you supposed to pinch-to-zoom if you can't move your fingers?

This new feature is Apple's accessibility team at its most creative. When you turn AssistiveTouch on, you get a new, glowing white circle at the bottom of the screen. It stays there all the time (below, lower left).

Tip Actually, it stays *somewhere* all the time. You can drag the white circle to any spot on the right or left edges of the screen.

When you tap it, you get four ways to trigger motions and gestures on the iPhone screen without requiring hand or multiple-finger movement (below, left). All you have to be able to do is tap with a single finger—even a stylus clenched in your teeth or foot:

- **Home.** You can tap this button instead of pressing the physical Home button.

- **Device.** Tap this button to open a palette of six functions that would otherwise require you to grasp the phone or push its tiny physical buttons (above, right). There's Rotate Screen (you can tap this instead of turning the phone 90 degrees), Lock Screen (instead of pressing the Sleep switch), Volume Up and Volume Down (instead of pressing the volume keys), Shake (does the same as shaking the phone to undo typing, and Mute/Unmute (instead of flipping the small Mute switch on the side).

- **Gestures.** Tap here to open up a peculiar palette that depicts a hand holding up two, three, four, or five fingers. When you tap, for example, the three-finger icon, you get three blue circles on the screen. They move together. Drag one of them (with a stylus, for example), and the phone thinks you're dragging three fingers on its surface. Using this technique, you can operate apps that require multiple fingers dragging on the screen.

- **Favorites.** Impressively enough, you can actually define your own gestures. In Settings→General→Accessibility, you can tap Create New Gesture to draw your own gesture right on the screen, using one, two, three, four, or five fingers.

For example, suppose you're frustrated in Google Maps, because you can't do the two-finger double-tap that means "zoom out." On the Create New Gesture screen, get somebody to do the two-finger double-tap for you. Tap Save and give the gesture a name—say, "2 double tap."

From now on, "2 double tap" shows up on the Favorites screen, ready to trigger with a single tap by a single finger or stylus.

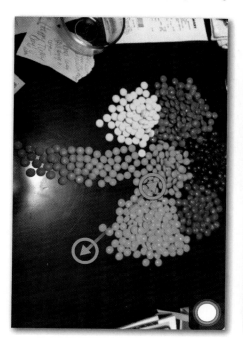

Tip Apple starts you off with one predefined gesture in Favorites: pinch. That's the two-finger pinch or spread gesture you use to zoom in and out of photos, maps, Web pages, PDF documents, and so on. And now you can trigger it with only one finger, as shown on the previous page; just drag either one of the two handles to stretch them apart. Drag the connecting line to move the point of stretchiness.

Incoming Calls

When a call comes in, where do you want it to go? Your headset? Directly to the speakerphone? Or the usual (headset unless there's no headset)? Here's where you make your choice.

Triple-Click Home

Burrowing all the way into the Settings→General→Accessibility screen is quite a slog when all you want to do is flip some feature on or off. Therefore, you get this handy shortcut: a fast triple-press of the Home button.

The options here ask, "What do you want to happen when you triple-press?" Your options are Toggle VoiceOver (meaning, turn it on or off); Toggle White on Black; Toggle Zoom; Toggle AssistiveTouch; and Ask (which means, "Ask me which one of these to turn on or off").

The iPhone as iPod

O f all the iPhone's talents, its iPoddishness may be the most successful. This function, after all, is the only one that doesn't require the participation of your cell network. It works even on planes and in subways. And it gets the most impressive battery life (30 hours of music playback on the 3GS, or 40 hours on the iPhone 4 and 4S).

This chapter assumes that you've already loaded some music or videos onto your iPhone, as described in Chapter 13.

To enter iPod Land, open the Music app. On a new phone, it's at the lower-right corner of the screen. (And why did Apple change the name from iPod to Music? One reason: In iOS 5, Videos is now a separate app.)

Tip A reminder: There's another way to get to the iPod mode. Just double-press the Home button. That opens the task switcher at the bottom of the screen. One swipe to the right, and you're viewing the music playback controls, along with the icon for the Music app itself.

List Land

The Music program begins with lists—lots of lists. The first four icons at the bottom of the screen represent your starter lists. You can rearrange or swap them, but you start out with either Playlists, Artists, Songs, Albums, and More—or, if you've turned on the Genius feature described on page 163, you have Genius, Playlists, Artists, Songs, and More. Here's what they all do.

Playlists

A *playlist* is a group of songs you've placed together, in a sequence that makes sense to you. One might consist of party tunes; another might hold romantic dinnertime music; a third might be drum-heavy workout cuts.

In the olden days, you could create playlists only in the iTunes software. (And you still can. After you sync the iPhone with your computer, the playlists appear here.) These days, however, you can create playlists right on the phone, as described on page 162.

Using Playlists

Scroll the Playlist list by dragging your finger or by flicking. To see what songs or videos are in a playlist, tap its name. (The > symbol in a Music menu always means "Tap to see what's in this list.")

Here, you can use a standard iPhone convention: Anywhere you're asked to drill down from one list to another—from a playlist to the songs inside, for example—you can backtrack by tapping the blue button at the upper-left corner of the screen. Its name changes to tell you what screen you just came from (Playlists, for example).

 Tip If you have a lot of video on your iPhone, you'll like this one. You can create a playlist of *videos* in iTunes. These video playlists show up on the iPhone—not in the Videos app, but in the Music app—and play your shows in sequence, just as you'd hope.

You now arrive at a Playlist details screen, where your tracks are listed for your inspection. To start playing a song once you see it in the Playlist list, tap it.

> **Tip** New in iOS 5: If you hold your finger down on the name of a song or album, its full name and performer name appear in a balloon. It's great for long titles that go off the edge of the screen.

Tap Edit, if you like, to drag the songs into a new sequence or to delete some of them. Tap Clear if you want to choose a different set of songs within this playlist name, or Delete to get rid of the playlist altogether. (Tapping Shuffle starts them playing right now, in a random order.)

Creating Playlists on the Phone

You can make as many new playlists as you want, right on the iPhone. Whatever playlists you create (or edit) here will wind up back on your computer, in iTunes, the next time you sync.

Here's how to make a playlist. In the Music app, on the Playlists screen, tap Add Playlist. Type a name for your new playlist (previous page, left), and then tap Save.

Now you're shown an alphabetical master list of songs. Tap each song you want to add to the new playlist (you don't have to tap the **+** button itself). Tap Done when you've added all the songs you want.

You arrive at the details screen for this playlist (previous page, center), where you can inspect or edit your handiwork. Tap Edit to rearrange the playlist songs or to delete some (previous page, right). Or tap Playlist to back out to the list of playlists, where your newly minted playlist is nestled.

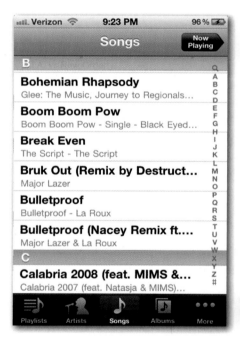
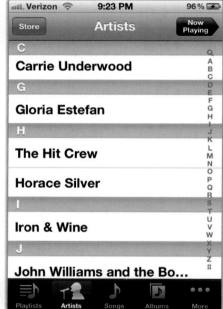

Genius

Apple's Genius playlist feature is supposed to analyze all your music and then, at the click of a button, create a playlist containing other songs from your library that "sound great" with one particular "seed" song. (Basically, it seems to clump songs by their degree of rockiness: soft-rock songs, harder rock, and so on.)

If you've used this feature in iTunes on your Mac or PC, and you've built up a Genius playlist or two, you'll also find those playlists on your iPhone. But you can make a Genius playlist right on the phone.

To do that, start playing the song you want to be the "seed"—the one you want the playlist to sound the most like. Then tap the ✳ button on the Now Playing screen (page 168). The Genius screen appears, displaying the songs it's proposing for your new instant Genius playlist. (That is, *if* you have enough music on the machine. If you don't have quite a lot of music, you may get the "This song does not have enough related songs" error message. Tap OK and then try a different song.)

If the suggestions look fine, then tap Save. The new playlist now appears among your others on the Playlists screen, named after your seed song, bearing the ✳ logo to remind you that the phone created that wicked mix.

Next time you sync, this playlist will return to the mother ship—iTunes.

If you spot a song you can't stand, you can either tap Edit and then delete it from the Genius playlist, or tap Refresh to make the iPhone try again with a different assortment (based on the seed song).

The Genius Icon

Once you've started using the Genius feature, you can add a Genius icon on the bottom row of the Music app, alongside Playlists, Artists, and so on.

When you tap this icon, your first Genius playlist appears and starts to play. You can swipe your finger across the screen to summon the next one, and the next, and so on. Sooner or later, you'll find music that suits even your most finicky mood.

 Tip If you don't see any of this Genius business on your phone, one of two things may be at play. If you haven't turned Genius on in iTunes, then you won't see Genius icons on your phone (except the one on the Now Playing screen). And if you've turned on iTunes Match (page 433), then Genius Mixes and Genius Playlists are turned off on the iPhone. Apple works in strange and mysterious ways.

Artists, Songs, Albums...

The other icons across the bottom of the Music screen go like this:

- **Artists.** This list identifies all the bands, orchestras, or singers in your collection. Even if you have only one song from a certain performer, it shows up here.

  Once again, you drill down to the list of individual songs by tapping an artist's name. At that point, tap any song to begin playing it.

- **Songs.** Here's an alphabetical list of every song on your iPhone. Scroll or flick through it; use the index at the right side of the screen to jump to a letter of the alphabet; or scroll all the way to the top and type a song name, album name, podcast name, or band name into the search box. Tap anything to begin playing it.

- **Albums.** That's right, it's a list of all the CDs or downloaded albums from which your music collection is derived, complete with miniature pictures of the album art. Tap an album's name to see a list of songs that came from it; tap a song to start playing it.

Tip At the bottom of any of these lists, you'll see the total number of items *in* that list: "76 Songs," for example. At the top of the screen, you may see the Now Playing button, which opens up the playback screen of whatever's playing.

Best of all, if you *drag downward* on any list—Music, Podcasts, whatever—you'll see that a search box has been hiding from you, up off the top of the screen. It lets you search your audio stash by name (title, band, or album).

Other Lists

The icons at the bottom of the Music app—usually Playlists (and/or Genius), Artists, Songs, and Albums—are only suggestions. On a *real* iPod, of course, you can slice and dice your music collection in all kinds of other listy ways: by Genre, Composer, and so on.

You can do that on the iPhone, too; there just isn't room across the bottom row to hold more than four list icons at a time.

To view some of the most useful secondary lists, tap the fifth and final icon, labeled More. The More screen appears, listing a bunch of other ways to view your collection.

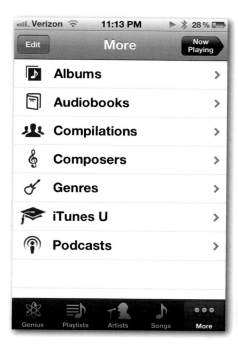

Here are your options:

- **Audiobooks.** One of the great pricey joys of life is listening to digital "books on tape" that you've bought from Audible.com. They show up in this list. (Audiobooks you've ripped from CDs don't show up here—only ones you've downloaded from Audible.)

 Tip In a hurry? You can speed up the playback of audiobooks (or podcasts) without making the narrator sound like a chipmunk—or slow the narrator down if he's talking too fast. Page 172 has the details.

- **Compilations.** A *compilation* is one of those albums that's been put together from many different performers. You know: "Zither Hits of the 1600s," "Kazoo Classics," and so on. You're supposed to turn on the Compilation checkbox manually, in iTunes, to identify songs that belong together in this way. Once you've done that, all songs that belong to compilations you've created show up in this list.

- **Composers.** Here's your whole music collection sorted by composer—a crumb the iPod/iPhone creators have thrown to classical-music fans.

- **Genres.** Tap this item to sort your collection by musical genre: Pop, Rock, World, Podcast, Gospel, or whatever.

- **iTunes U.** Here are the lectures, lab reports, movies, and other educational materials supplied to the world by universities. You can find and subscribe to them using iTunes.

- **Podcasts.** Here are all your podcasts (page 392), listed by creator. A blue dot indicates that you haven't yet listened to some of the podcasts by a certain podcaster. Similarly, if you tap a podcast's name to drill down, you'll see the individual episodes, once again marked by blue "you haven't heard me yet" dots.

- **Genius.** This button is a shortcut that brings up the first Genius playlist.

Customizing List Land

Now you know how to sort your collection by every conceivable criterion. But what if you're a huge podcast nut? Are you really expected to open up the More screen every time you want to see your list of podcasts? Or what if you frequently want access to your audiobooks or composer list?

Fortunately, you can add the icons of these lists to the bottom of the main Music screen, where the four starter categories now appear (Playlists, Artists, Songs, Albums). That is, you can replace or rearrange the icons that show up here so the lists you use most frequently are easier to open.

To renovate the four starter icons, tap More and then Edit (upper-left corner). You arrive at the Configure screen (page 165, right).

Here's the complete list of music-and-video sorting lists: Genius, Playlists, Artists, Songs, Albums, Audiobooks, Compilations, Composers, Genres, iTunes U, and Podcasts.

To replace one of the four starter icons at the bottom, use a finger to drag an icon from the top half of the screen downward, directly onto the *existing* icon you want to replace. It lights up to show the success of your drag.

When you release your finger, you'll see that the new icon has replaced the old one. Tap Done in the upper-right corner.

Oh, and while you're on the Edit screen: You can take this opportunity to *rearrange* the first four icons at the bottom. Drag them around with your finger. Fun for the whole family!

Cover Flow

Anytime you're using the iPhone's Music personality, whether you're playing music or just flipping through your lists, you can rotate the iPhone 90 degrees in either direction—so it's in landscape orientation—to turn on Cover Flow. *Nothing* gets oohs and ahhs from an admiring crowd like Cover Flow.

In Cover Flow, the screen goes dark for a moment—and then it reappears, showing 2-inch-tall album covers floating on a black background. Push or flick with your fingers to make them fly and flip over in 3-D space, as though they're CDs in a record-store rack.

If you tap one (or tap ❸ in the lower-right corner), the album flips around so you can see the "back" of it, containing a list of songs from that album. Tap a song to start playing it; tap the **II** in the lower-left corner to pause. Tap the back (or the ❸ button) again to flip the album cover back to the front and continue browsing.

To turn off Cover Flow, rotate the iPhone upright again.

So what, exactly, is Cover Flow for? You could argue that it's a unique way to browse your collection, to seek musical inspiration without having to stare at scrolling lists of text.

But you could also argue that it's just Apple's engineers showing off.

The Now Playing Screen (Music)

Whenever a song is playing, the Now Playing screen appears, filled with information and controls for your playback pleasure.

Return to list

Songs on this album

Swipe this way to return to the list

Volume slider

For example:

- **Return arrow.** At the top-left corner of the screen, the fat, left-pointing arrow means, "Return to the list whence this song came." It takes you back to the list of songs in this album, playlist, or whatever.

- **Song info.** Center top: the artist name, track name, and album name. If one of those tidbits is too long to fit, it scrolls like a stock ticker.

- **Album list.** At the top-right corner, there's a :≣ icon that seems to say "list." Tap it to view a list of the other songs on *this* song's album.

 Tip You can double-tap the big album art picture to open the track list, too. It's a bigger target.

This track-listing screen offers three enjoyable activities. You can jump directly to another cut by tapping its name. You can check out the durations of the songs in this album.

And you can *rate* a song, ranking it from one to five stars, by tapping its name and then tapping one of the five dots at the top of the screen. If you tap dot number 3, for example, then the first three dots all turn into stars. You've just given that song three stars. When you next sync your iPhone with your computer, the ratings you've applied magically show up on the same songs in iTunes.

To return to the Now Playing screen, tap the upper-right icon once again. (Once you tap, that icon looks like the album cover.) Or, for a bigger target, double-tap any blank part of the screen.

- **Album art.** Most of the screen is filled with a bright, colorful shot of the original CD's album art. (If none is available—if you're listening to a song *you* wrote, for example—you see a big gray generic musical-note picture. You can drag or paste in an album-art graphic—one you found on the Web, for example—in iTunes.)

Controlling Playback (Music)

Once you're on the Now Playing screen, a few controls await your fingertip—some obvious and some not so obvious.

- **Play/Pause button.** The Pause button looks like this ‖ when the music is playing. If you do pause, then the button turns into the Play button (▶).

- **Previous, Next (I◀◀, ▶▶I).** These buttons work exactly as they do on an iPod: Tap I◀◀ to skip to the beginning of this song (or, if you're already at the beginning, to the previous song). Tap ▶▶I to skip to the next song.

If you hold down one of these buttons, you rewind or fast-forward. You hear the music speeding by, without turning the singer into a chipmunk. The rewinding or fast-forwarding accelerates if you keep holding down.

- **Volume.** You can drag the round, white handle of this slider (bottom of the screen) to adjust the volume—or you can use the volume keys on the left side of the phone.

Of course, you probably didn't need a handsome, full-color book to tell you what those basic playback controls are for. But there are also four *secret* controls that don't appear until you tap anywhere on an empty part of the screen (for example, on the album cover):

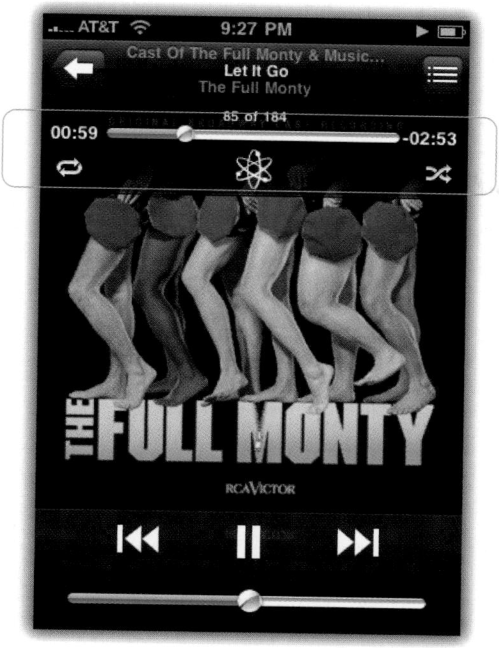

- **Loop button.** If you *really* love a certain album or playlist, you can command the iPhone to play it over and over again, beginning to end. Just tap the Loop button () so it turns blue ().

> **Tip** Tap the Loop button a second time to endlessly loop *just this song.*
>
> A tiny "1" icon appears on the blue loop graphic, like this , to let you know you've entered this mode. Tap a third time to turn off looping.

- **Scroll slider.** This slider (top of the screen) reveals three useful statistics: how much of the song you've heard, in minutes and seconds (at the left end), how much time remains (at the right end), and which slot this song occupies in the current playlist or album.

  To operate the slider, drag the tiny round handle with your finger. (Tapping directly on the spot you want to hear doesn't work.)

- **Genius button ().** Tap the button to create a Genius playlist based on the song you' re listening to. You can read more about Genius playlists on page 163.

- **Shuffle button.** Ordinarily, the iPhone plays the songs in an album sequentially, from beginning to end. But if you love surprises, tap the button so it turns blue. Now you'll hear the songs on the album in random order.

To hide the slider and the Loop, Genius, and Shuffle buttons, tap an empty part of the screen once again.

By the way, there's nothing to stop you from turning on Shuffle *and* Loop, meaning that you'll hear the songs on the album played endlessly, but never in the same order twice.

> **Tip** Shake the whole iPhone to shuffle—that is, to start playing another random song.

Special Podcast/Audiobook Controls

When you're listening to a podcast or an audiobook, tapping any empty part of the screen during playback produces, once again, that ordinarily hidden strip of controls. This time, though, three new buttons replace the Loop, Genius, and Shuffle buttons described above:

- **Email (✉).** This button opens up an outgoing email message containing a link to the podcast's original spot in the iTunes Store, so you can share the goodness.

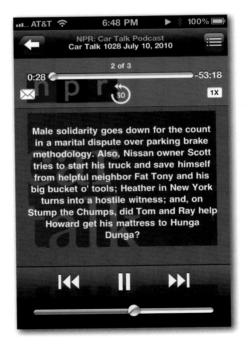

- **30-second repeat ().** This jumps the audio back 30 seconds so you can hear something you missed. Perfect when you've just been interrupted by an inquiry from a spouse, boss, or highway patrolman.

- **Playback speed (½X, 1X, or 2X).** This feature may be God's gift to the audiobook or podcast fan: It changes how fast people are talking.

  Get through a podcast or audiobook faster when you're stuck with a slow droner; slow it down if it's a New York mile-a-minute chatterer. Each time you tap this button, the playback cycles through to the next speed.

> **Tip** Along with the special podcast controls, you also get superimposed white text on the album art when you tap the screen. It displays a description of the episode, if the creators of the podcast bothered to supply one.

Voice Control

There's one more way to control your playback—a way that doesn't involve taking your eyes off the road or leaving whatever app you're using. You can control your music playback by voice command, even if you don't have the iPhone 4S with its Siri feature. See Chapter 4.

Multi(music)tasking

Once you're playing music, it keeps right on playing, even if you press the Home button and move on to do some other work on the iPhone. After all, the only thing more pleasurable than surfing the Web is surfing it with a Beach Boys soundtrack.

A tiny ▶ icon at the top of the screen reminds you that music is still playing. That's handy if the earbuds are plugged in but you're not wearing them.

Music is playing

Tip Even with the screen off, you can still adjust the music volume (use the buttons on the left side of the phone), pause the music (pinch the earbud clicker once), or advance to the next song (pinch it twice).

Or if you've got something else to do—like jogging, driving, or performing surgery—tap the Sleep/Wake switch to turn off the screen. The music keeps playing, but you'll save battery power.

When a phone call comes in, the music fades, and you hear your chosen ringtone—through your earbuds, if you're wearing them. Squeeze the clicker on the earbud cord, or tap the Sleep/Wake switch, to answer the call. When the call ends, the music fades back in, right where it left off.

Bluetooth Stereo Headphones

Bluetooth wireless stereo is a wicked-cool feature that snuck onto the marketplace a few years ago, but practically nobody noticed. That's probably (a) because you had to buy *both* a special set of headphones or speakers capable of receiving Bluetooth stereo signals *and* a Bluetooth transmitter to snap onto your music player, and (b) because the real name for this feature is *Bluetooth A2DP profile.* Yuck.

If you have an iPhone, there's one less thing to buy. You still have to buy some wireless headphones, but at least you don't have to buy the transmitter; it's built right into the iPhone.

Shop for your headphones carefully. You want to make sure the box specifically says "A2DP." (There are lots of Bluetooth *headsets,* used for making office phone calls and so on, that don't play *music* over Bluetooth.) Motorola, Altec Lansing, and Plantronics sell several A2DP headphones, for example. There are also Bluetooth A2DP stereo speakers that broadcast your iPhone's music from as far as 20 or 30 feet away.

Once you've bought your 'phones, you have to introduce them to the iPhone—a process called *pairing.*

From the Home screen, tap Settings→General→Bluetooth. Turn Bluetooth on; you see the Searching ❋ animation as the iPhone wirelessly hunts for your headphones.

Grab them, turn them on, and start the pairing procedure, as described in the manual. Usually, that means holding down a certain button until a tiny light starts flashing. At that point, the headphones' name appears on the iPhone's screen.

 Tip If the headphones or speakers require a one-time passcode—it's usually 0000, but check the manual—the iPhone's keyboard appears automatically, so you can type it in.

A couple of seconds later, it says Connected; at this point, any sound that the iPhone would ordinarily play through its speakers or earbuds now plays through the headphones. Not just music—which, in general, sounds amazing—but chirps, game sounds, and so on.

Furthermore, the Bluetooth symbol now appears at the bottom of the Now Playing screen. When you tap it, the iPhone lets you choose whether to play its sounds through the wireless headphones or through the speaker (or headphones or dock connector, whichever is currently hooked up) as usual.

 Tip For best results, switch the audio back to the iPhone's built-in sources *before* you turn off your headphones. Otherwise, the iPhone can get confused and play nothing at all.

Once you're playing music through your headphones, the iPhone's own volume controls don't do anything; use the controls on the headphones themselves.

If your headset has a microphone, too, you can even answer and make phone calls wirelessly. (There's an Answer button right on the headphones.)

Using Bluetooth wireless stereo does eat up your battery charge faster. But come on: listening to your music without wires, with the iPhone still in your pocket or bag? How cool is that?

Familiar iPod Features

In certain respects, the iPhone is *not* a traditional iPod. It doesn't have a click wheel, it doesn't come with any games, and it doesn't offer disk mode (where the iPod acts as a hard drive for transporting computer files).

 Tip OK, OK—there actually *is* a way to simulate iPod disk mode on the iPhone. Just download an app like PhoneView. You can find it on this book's "Missing CD" page at *www.missingmanuals.com*.

It does have a long list of traditional iPod features, though. You just have to know where to find them. The first six of these options all await in Settings→Music.

Shake to Shuffle

If you turn this option on, then you can give the phone itself a quick shake to shuffle the current playlist, album, or all-music playback. That's great when, for example, you're jogging, but just not feeling much inspiration from some lame ballad that's come on.

Sound Check

This feature smooths out the master volume levels of tracks from different albums, helping to compensate for differences in their recording levels. It doesn't deprive you of peaks and valleys in the music volume, of course—it affects only the baseline level.

EQ (Equalization)

Like any good music player, the iPhone offers an EQ function: a long list of presets, each of which affects your music differently by boosting or throttling back various frequencies. One might bring out the bass to goose up your hip-hop tunes; another might emphasize the midrange for clearer vocals; and so on.

Volume Limit

It's now established fact: Listening to a lot of loud music through earphones can damage your hearing. Pump it up today, pay for it tomorrow.

MP3 players can be sinister that way, because in noisy places like planes and city streets, people turn up the volume much louder than they would in a quiet place, and they don't even realize how high they've cranked it.

That's why Apple created this volume limiter. It lets parents program their children's iPods (and now iPhones) to max out at a certain volume level that can be surpassed only with a password. Set the volume slider, tap Lock Volume Limit, enter the four-digit password twice, and hand it over to the kids.

Lyrics & Podcast Info

If you've pasted lyrics for a song into iTunes on your computer (or used one of the free automated lyrics-fetching programs—search "iTunes lyrics" in Google), you can make them appear on the iPhone screen during playback just by tapping the album art on the playback screen. (Scroll with a flick.) When you're listening to a podcast, its text description appears instead.

Group By Album Artist

Suppose you've bought a movie soundtrack album or compilation album with a different band on each track.

In iTunes, you can see all these songs listed in a group, thanks to a text field called Album Artist. (There you see the unifying title—the movie name, for example.) But until iOS 5 came along, the iPhone couldn't sort by Album Artist.

When you turn on this option, the Music app consolidates all those artist names into a single new album-name entry in your Artists list. For example, you'll see an entry for "Apocalypse Now Soundtrack," which you can tap to see the individual '60s songs within it; the individual bands are no longer scattered alphabetically through the Artists list.

 Tip Many soundtrack albums come with their Album Artist identified only as "Various Artists," and that's how your iPhone will group them. In iTunes, however, you can select all the songs on the album, choose File→Get Info, and change the Album Artist to something more descriptive, like the movie title. When you sync the results back to your phone, the album will show up in the proper spot in the Artists list.

The iTunes Store

It's freaky but true: The iPhone lets you shop Apple's iTunes Store, browsing, buying, and downloading songs and videos wirelessly. Anything you buy gets autosynced back to your computer's copy of iTunes when you get home. Whenever you hear somebody mention a buy-worthy song, for example, you can have it within a minute.

In the bad old days, you could shop the store only when you were on a WiFi network. Now, however, you can also buy songs over the cellular network, for instant gratification that the you of 1995 would never have believed.

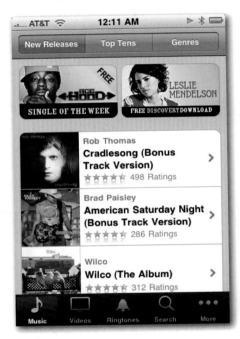
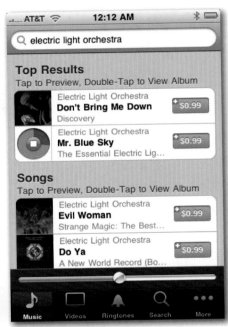

To begin, tap iTunes on the Home screen. The icons at the bottom of the screen include Music, Videos, Search, and Purchased.

When you tap Music or Videos, the top of the screen offers further drilling-down buttons like New Releases, Top Tens (meaning "most popular"), and Genres; under Videos, you get Movies, TV Shows, and Music Videos.

(Beneath each list is a Redeem button, which you can tap if you've been given an iTunes gift certificate or promo code, and your current credit balance.)

Tip In theory, you can even buy *videos* on the cellular network (and not just in WiFi hotspots). In practice, you're limited to certain music videos. If you try to buy a TV show or movie, an error message says: "This item is over 20MB." Which is your cell company's way of saying, "We don't want you jamming up our precious cellular network with your hefty video downloads, bucko."

Note, by the way, that you can *rent* movies from the store instead of buying them outright. You pay only $3, $4, or $5 to rent (instead of $10 to $16 to buy). But once you start watching, you have only 24 hours to finish; after that, the movie deletes itself from your phone. (If you like, you can sync it to your Mac or PC to continue watching in iTunes—within the same 24 hours.)

To search for something in particular, tap Search. The keyboard appears. Type the name of a song, movie, show, performer, or album. At any time, you can stop typing and tap the name of a match to see its details.

All these tools eventually take you to a list of songs or videos. For a song, tap its name to hear an instant 30-second preview (tap again to stop). Tap the price button to buy the song, show, or album (and tap BUY NOW to confirm). Enter your Apple ID password when you're asked.

Downloading a TV show, movie, or music video is similar, except that tapping the name takes you to a details page. It contains a description, a Preview button (it plays the movie's trailer, for example), and other people's ratings. Tap the price button to buy the video. (For movies, you can choose either Buy or Rent, priced accordingly.) Tap a second time to confirm. Enter your Apple ID when you're asked.

At this point, your iPhone downloads the music or video you bought.

Purchased Items

The Purchased button is the gateway to one of the most useful features in the Apple ecosystem. It contains two lists (usually divided onto separate Music and Videos tabs):

- **All.** Here's a list of everything you've bought that's been transferred to your iPhone.

- **Not On This iPhone.** This is the cool part. Here you see not just the files on the iPhone in your hand, but things you've bought on other Apple gadgets—an album you bought on your iPad, for example, or a song you downloaded to your iPod Touch. (This assumes that you're using the same Apple ID on all your gizmos.)

The beauty of this arrangement, of course, is that you can tap the name of something that's Not On This iPhone—and then download it. No extra charge.

> **Tip** If you prefer, you can direct your phone to download those purchases that you made on other gadgets automatically, without your having to tap Not On This iPhone. **Visit** Settings→Store, **and turn on the switches for** Music, Apps, **and/or** Books **under Automatic Downloads. If you also turn on** Use Cellular Data, **then your phone will do this auto-downloading when you're in any 3G cellular Internet area, not just in a WiFi hotspot.**

If you tap More at the bottom of the screen, you get these options:

- **Genius.** Apple offers a list of music, movies, and TV shows for sale that it thinks you'll like, based on stuff you already have.

- **Ping.** Ping is Apple's social network for music fans. Once you've set yourself up (using iTunes on your computer), this screen shows you the posts and news items from the bands and fans you've opted to follow.

- **Tones.** You can buy ready-made ringtones on this page—30-second slices of pop songs. (Don't ask what sense it makes to pay $1.30 for 30 seconds of a song, when you could buy the whole song for the same price.)

- **Podcasts.** Browse for thousands of free, and delightful, podcasts (commercial and homemade downloadable "radio shows" and "TV shows").

- **Audiobooks.** This means you, Audible.com subscribers. Wondered where all your books were? Here they are.

- **iTunes U.** Instant access to free, professionally recorded audio university lectures. It's intended for college kids, of course, but there's all kinds of good stuff here for anyone.

- **Downloads.** Shows you a progress bar for anything you've started to download. Also shows you anything that's queued up to download but hasn't started yet.

> **Tip** If you tap Edit, you'll see that you can replace any of the four iTunes Store bottom-row icons with one of the More buttons (Audiobooks, Downloads, iTunes U, or Podcasts). The procedure is exactly like the one described on page 165.

Now you've done it: downloaded one of the store's millions of songs, podcasts, TV shows, music videos, ringtones, or movies directly to your phone. Next time you sync, that song will swim *upstream* to your Mac or PC, where it will be safely backed up in iTunes. (And if you lost your connection before the iPhone was finished downloading, your Mac or PC will finish the job automatically. Cool.)

The Videos App

It used to be that a single app, called iPod, dished out both music and videos—just like a physical iPod. But in the world of apps, that combination of functions didn't make a lot of sense. So in iOS 5, there's a separate app for playing TV shows, movies, and video podcasts. It's called, of all things, Videos.

If you can't figure out how to operate this app, then you shouldn't be allowed to have an iPhone. It's simply a scrolling list of shows, organized into Movies, TV Shows, and Podcasts. Tap the name of the video or the series you want to watch; tap an episode in that series, if necessary; and begin watching.

When you're playing video, anything else on the screen is distracting, so Apple hides the video playback controls. Tap the screen once to make them appear, and again to make them disappear.

Here's what they do:

- **Done.** Tap this blue button, in the top-left corner, to stop playback and return to the master list of videos.

- **Scroll slider.** This progress indicator (top of the screen) is exactly like the one you see when you're playing music. You see the elapsed time, the remaining time, and a white, round handle that you can drag to jump forward or back in the video.

- **Zoom/Unzoom.** In the top-right corner, a little or button appears. Tap it to adjust the zoom level of the video, as described on the facing page.

- **Play/Pause (▶/II).** These buttons (and the earbud clicker) do the same thing to video as they do to music: alternate playing and pausing.

- **Previous, Next (I◀◀, ▶▶I).** Hold down your finger to rewind or fast-forward the video. The longer you hold, the faster the zipping. (When you fast-forward, you even get to hear the sped-up audio, at least for the first few seconds.)

If you're watching a movie from the iTunes Store, you may be surprised to discover that it comes with predefined chapter markers, just like a DVD. Internally, it's divided up into scenes. You can tap the I◀◀ or ▶▶I button to skip to the previous or next chapter marker—a great way to navigate a long movie quickly.

Tip If you're wearing the earbuds, you can pinch the clicker *twice* to skip to the next chapter, or *three times* to go back a chapter.

- **Volume.** You can drag the round, white handle of this slider (bottom of the screen) to adjust the volume—or you can use the volume keys on the left side of the phone.

- **Language ().** You won't see this button often. But when you do, it summons subtitle and alternate-language soundtrack options, just like a DVD player.

Tip To delete a video, swipe across its name in the Videos list; tap Delete to confirm. (You still have a copy on your computer, of course.)

Zoom/Unzoom

The iPhone's screen is bright, vibrant, and stunningly sharp. (The 3GS has 320 × 480 pixels, crammed so tightly that there are 160 per inch; the iPhone 4 and 4S are four times as sharp.) It's not, however, the right shape for videos.

Standard TV shows are squarish, not rectangular. So when you watch TV shows, you get black letterbox columns on either side of the picture.

Movies have the opposite problem. They're *too* wide for the iPhone screen. So when you watch movies, you wind up with *horizontal* letterbox bars above and below the picture.

Some people are fine with that. After all, HDTVs have the same problem. At least when letterbox bars are onscreen, you know you're seeing the complete composition of the scene the director intended.

Other people can't stand letterbox bars. You're already watching on a pretty small screen; why sacrifice some of that precious area to black bars?

Fortunately, the iPhone gives you a choice. If you double-tap the video as it plays, you zoom in, magnifying the image so it fills the entire screen. Or, if the playback controls are visible, you can also tap ■ or ■.

Of course, now you're not seeing the entire original composition. You lose the top and bottom of TV scenes, or the left and right edges of movie scenes.

Fortunately, if this effect chops off something important—some text, for example—the original letterbox view is just another double-tap away.

 In many Starbucks shops and a few other places (hotels, bookstores, and so on), your iPhone (and laptop) get a free WiFi connection to iTunes. Cool.

When you're in a Starbucks, another slick feature awaits: On the iPhone, a Starbucks button appears at the bottom of the screen automatically, leading to a Now Playing display that identifies what's playing in the store right now.

TV Output

When you crave a screen bigger than 3½ inches, you can play your iPhone's videos on a regular TV. All you need is the right cable.

If you have an iPhone 3GS or 4, you can use Apple's Composite AV Cable or Component AV Cable ($40 each), depending on the kind of TV you have.

If you have the iPhone 4S, you have an even nicer option: the Apple Digital AV Adapter. It's better for three reasons. First, it carries both audio and video over a single cable (an HDMI cable). Second, the picture quality is the highest possible.

Third, this is the only way to *mirror* what's on the phone. With the Composite or Component cables, your phone sends only videos, photo slideshows, and Keynote presentations to the TV—not your Home screen, email, Safari, and everything else. But the Digital AV Adapter can put *everything* you see on your iPhone 4S screen onto your TV.

(The exceptions: Photos and presentations still appear on your TV in pure, "video outputted" form, without any controls or other window clutter.)

AirPlay

Actually, if you have an iPhone 4S, you have an even juicier option available to you: wireless projection, thanks to a feature called AirPlay. It transmits music or hi-def video from your iPhone to an AirPlay-equipped receiver across the room. It's a fantastic way to send slideshows, movies, presentations, games, FaceTime calls, and Web sites to your TV for a larger audience to enjoy. Whatever's on the screen gets sent to your Apple TV, even if you rotate the phone partway through.

AirPlay receivers include the Apple TV (version 2 or later), as well as speakers, stereos, and audio receivers from Denon, Marantz, JBL, iHome, and other companies.

To make AirPlay work, make sure the phone and the AirPlay receiver are on the same WiFi network. Then double-press the Home button to open the task switcher (page 13). Swipe all the way to the right until you see the ◻ icon.

When you tap it, you get a list of available AirPlay receivers. If you have an Apple TV, turn its Mirroring switch On. That's it! Everything on the iPhone screen now appears on the TV or sound system. (The phone's status bar turns blue and displays the ◻ icon, so you don't wander off and forget that every move you make is visible to the entire crowd in the living room.)

7 Taking Photos, Shooting Video

This chapter is all about the iPhone's ability to display photos copied over from your computer, to take new pictures with its built-in camera, and to capture videos. You've probably never seen pictures and movies look this good on a pocket gadget. The iPhone screen is bright, the colors are vivid, and the super-high pixel density makes every shot of your life look cracklin' sharp.

With each new version of the iPhone, Apple improves its camera—and on the iPhone 4S, it's unbelievably good. There's no optical zoom, but otherwise, the photos *can* look every bit as good as what you'd get from a dedicated camera. And the hi-def videos are nearly indistinguishable from what you'd get out of a camcorder. They're even auto-stabilized!

Taking Still Photos

The little hole on the back of the iPhone, in the upper-left corner, is its camera.

On the latest iPhones, it's pretty impressive, at least for a cellphone cam. The iPhone 4S, for example, has an LED flash, takes excellent 8-megapixel photos, and does amazingly well in low light.

The earlier iPhone models' cameras aren't quite as good, but they're still fine as long as your subject is still and well lit. Action shots may come out blurry, and dim-light shots come out rather grainy.

Now that you know what you're in for, here's how it works.

Firing Up the Camera

For years, the usual ritual for opening up the Camera app has been tapping its icon on the Home screen.

And that still works. Unfortunately, photographic opportunities are frequently fleeting; by the time you fish the phone from your pocket, wake it up, slide your finger to unlock it, press the Home button, find the Camera app, and wait for it to load, the magic moment may be gone forever.

That's why, in iOS 5, Apple added a much quicker way to get to the Camera app when the phone is asleep:

❶ Double-press the Home button to wake the phone—and make the new button appear next to the slider.

❷ Tap the button.

The Camera app opens directly. This new trick shaves an unbelievable amount of time off of the old get-to-the-camera method.

Note Of course, this new Camera shortcut bypasses the "enter password" screen (if you've put a password on your phone). Any random stranger who picks up your phone would be able to jump directly into picture-taking mode.

Said stranger couldn't do much damage, though. She could take new photos, or delete the new photos taken during this session—but the photos you've already taken are off limits, and the features that could damage your reputation (editing, emailing, and posting photos) are unavailable in the Camera app. You have to open the Photos app to get to those—and that requires the phone password.

During the 2 seconds it takes the Camera program to warm up, you see a very cool iris shutter–opening effect.

The first time you use the camera, you're asked if it's OK to *geotag* your shots (record where you were when you took them). Unless you're a burglar or are having an affair, tap OK.

Set the Focus and Exposure Point

Now frame up the shot, using the iPhone screen as your viewfinder. At 3½ inches, it's most likely the largest digital-camera viewfinder you've ever used. You can turn it 90 degrees for a wider shot, if you like.

Now then: See the white box that appears briefly on the screen?

It's telling you where the iPhone thinks the most important part of the photo is. That's where it will focus, that's the area it examines to calculate the overall brightness of the photo (exposure), and that's the portion that will determine the overall *white balance* of the scene (that is, the color cast).

But often, dead center is not the most important part of the photo. The cool thing is that you can *tap* somewhere else in the scene to move that white square—to make the camera recalculate the focus, exposure, and white balance.

Here's when you might want to do this tapping:

- **When the whole image looks too dark or too bright.** If you tap a *dark* part of the scene, you'll see the whole photo brighten up; if you tap a *bright* part, the whole photo will darken a bit. You're telling the camera, "Redo your calculations so *this* part has the best exposure; I don't really care if the rest of the picture gets brighter or darker."

Tap here; this spot is correctly exposed, but the rest is too dark.

Tap here; everything brightens up accordingly.

- **When the scene has a color cast.** If the photo looks, for example, a little bluish or yellowish, tap a different spot in the scene—the one you care most about. The iPhone recomputes its assessment of the white balance.

- **When you're in macro mode.** If the foreground object is very close to the lens—4 to 8 inches away—the iPhone automatically goes into *macro* (super closeup) mode. In this mode, you can do something really cool: You can *defocus the background.* The background goes soft, slightly blurry, just like the professional photos you see in magazines. Just make sure you tap the foreground object.

Locking Focus and Exposure

The iPhone likes to focus and calculate the exposure before it shoots. Yeah—cameras are funny that way.

That tendency, however, can get in your way when you're shooting something that moves fast. Horse races, divers. Pets. Kids on merry-go-rounds, kids on slides, kids in your house. By the time the camera has calculated the focus and exposure, which takes about a second, you've lost the shot.

In iOS 5, therefore, Apple has added an advanced feature that's common on professional cameras but very rare on phones: Auto-Exposure Lock and Autofocus Lock. They let you set up the focus and exposure in advance, so that there's zero lag when you finally snap the shot.

To use this feature on your iPhone, point the camera at something that has the *same distance and lighting* as the subject-to-be. For example, focus at the base of the merry-go-round that's directly below where your daughter's horse will be. Or point at the bottom of the water slide before your son is ready to go.

Now hold down your finger on that spot on the iPhone's screen until you see the blue square blink twice. At the bottom of the screen, the phrase "AE/AF Lock" appears to tell you that you've now locked in exposure and autofocus.

Now you can snap photos, rapid-fire, without ever having to wait while your iPhone rethinks focus and exposure.

To turn off the lock, tap anywhere on the screen.

The Flash

The iPhone 4 and 4S have what, in the cellphone industry, is called a flash. It's actually just a very bright LED light on the back of the phone. You can make it turn on momentarily, providing a small boost of illumination when the lights are low. (That's a *small* boost—it won't do anything for subjects more than a few feet away.)

Ordinarily, the flash is set to Auto. It will turn on automatically when the scene is too dark, in the iPhone's opinion. But if you tap the ⚡Auto icon, two other options pop out: On (the flash will turn on no matter what the lighting conditions) and Off (the flash will not fire, no matter what).

 Tip It took all of about 11 seconds before iPhone apps appeared that can control the flash even when you're not taking pictures. Free apps like Flashlight and LED Light, for example, let you turn it on and leave it on, so you can see your key in the lock or read the tiny type in a program. They can also turn the flash into a blinking strobe light.

Zooming In

The iPhone has a zoom, which can help bring you "closer" to the subject—but it's a *digital* zoom. It doesn't work like a real camera's zoom (which actually moves lenses to blow up the scene). Instead, it basically just blows up the image, making everything bigger, and slightly degrading the picture quality in the process.

If you're still interested, there's a new way to zoom in: *Spread two fingers.* That's right: In iOS 5, simply using the traditional two-finger-spreading "zoom in" gesture works on the live camera preview. As you spread, a zoom slider appears on the screen; you can also drag the handle in the slider, or tap **+** or **−**, for more precise zooming.

Sometimes, getting closer to the action is worth some image-quality sacrifice.

The "Rule of Thirds" Grid

The Rule of Thirds, long held as gospel by painters and photographers, suggests that you imagine a tic-tac-toe grid superimposed on your frame. Now, as you frame the shot, position the important parts of the photo on those lines, or better yet, at their intersections.

According to the Rule of Thirds, this setup creates a stronger composition than putting everything in dead center, which is most people's instinct.

Now, it's really a *Guideline* of Thirds, or a *Consideration* of Thirds; plenty of photographs are, in fact, strongest when the subject is centered.

But if you want to know where those magic intersections are so that you can at least *consider* the Rule of Thirds, tap the Options button on the screen, turn the Grid option On, and then tap Done. The phone displays the tic-tac-toe grid on your viewfinder, for your composition pleasure. (It's not part of the photo. You turn it off the same way.)

High Dynamic Range (HDR)

Digital cameras have come a long way, but in one regard, they're still pathetic: Compared with the human eye, they still have terrible *dynamic range.*

That's a reference to the scale of bright and dark spots in a single scene. If you see someone standing in front of a bright window, you can probably make out who it is. But in a photo, that person will be a solid black silhouette. The camera doesn't have enough dynamic range to handle both the bright background and the person standing in front of it.

Sure, you could adjust the exposure so that the person's face is lit—but in the process, you'd brighten the background into a nuclear-white rectangle.

Until the world's cameras are as sensitive as our eyes, we can make do with HDR (high dynamic range) photography. That's when the camera takes three photos (or even more)—one each at dark, medium, and light exposure settings. Then software combines the best parts of all three, bringing details to both the shadows and the highlights.

Believe it or not, your iPhone has a built-in HDR feature. It's not as amazing as what an HDR guru can do in Photoshop—for one thing, you have zero control over how the images are combined, how many are combined, or how much of each is combined. And sometimes, the HDR version of the photo looks worse than the original.

But often, an iPhone HDR photo does indeed show more detail in both bright and dark areas than a single shot would.

To use HDR, tap Options, turn HDR to On (you can see it on the facing page at left), and tap Done. Take your best shot.

When you inspect your photos later in the Photos app, you'll know which ones were taken with HDR turned on; when you tap the photo, you'll see the faint superimposed HDR logo at the upper-left corner. In this example, you can see how much more detail the HDR shot (right) maintained in the background, which was too bright for a regular shot (left).

Taking the Shot

All right. You've opened the Camera app. You've set up the focus, exposure, flash, grid, HDR, and zoom. If, in fact, your subject hasn't already left the scene, you can now take the picture.

You can do that in either of two ways:

- Tap the ⊙ button.

- Press the Volume Up button. (It's the center button on the left edge of the phone.)

  This is a new option in iOS 5, and it's fantastic. If you hold the phone with the volume buttons at the top, that little + button is right where the shutter button would be on a real camera. Pressing it feels more natural than, and doesn't shake the camera as much as, tapping the onscreen button.

Note The iPhone knows which way you're holding the phone, thanks to its built-in gyroscope. The "which way is up" information accompanies the photo; any Apple photo-viewing app (like iPhoto, Aperture, or the iPhone's own Photos app) will therefore display your photo right-side up. If you use the volume key as a shutter button, that's lucky, because technically, you're holding the phone upside-down.

Unfortunately, Windows photo software isn't so lucky. Photos you take with the volume keys up will appear upside-down on a PC. Of course, you can always flip a photo right-side up before you send it, right on the phone, using the new Edit controls described below.

Either way, if the phone isn't muted, you hear the *snap!* sound of a picture successfully taken.

You get to admire your work for only about half a second—and then the photo slurps itself into the ⬚ thumbnail icon at the corner of the screen.

There are two ways to review the photo you just took, too:

- Tap that ⬚ thumbnail icon at the corner of the screen.

- Swipe across the screen, left to right. This option is new in iOS 5, and, here again, it's a great improvement. The entire screen offers a much bigger finger target than the ⬚ button.

Tip To return to taking pictures, you can swipe the other way, right to left, until the live viewfinder comes back. Of course, tapping the blue button performs the same job.

To look at other pictures you've taken, tap Camera Roll at the top of the screen. (Camera Roll refers to pictures you've shot with the iPhone, as opposed to pictures from your computer.)

Here again, you see the table of contents showing your iPhone shots. You might notice, in fact, that this view of your Camera Roll has three tabs at the top: All, Photos, and Videos. These new buttons let you isolate just the still photos or just the movies you've shot with the phone.

 Tip For details on copying your iPhone photography and videos back to your Mac or PC, see page 414.

Self-Portraits (the Front Camera)

Until the iPhone 4 came along, self-portraits were tricky. The chrome Apple logo on the back is not a self-portrait mirror, unless all you care about is how your nostril looks.

Everything's different now. The iPhone 4 and 4S have a second camera, right there on the front, above the screen. The point, of course, is that you can now use the screen itself as a viewfinder to frame yourself, experiment with your expression, and check your teeth.

To activate the front camera, open the Camera app, and then tap the ⟲ icon. Suddenly, you see yourself on the screen. Frame the shot, and then tap the ⦿ button to take the photo.

Now, don't get your expectations too high. The front camera is not the back camera. It's much lower resolution (640 × 480 pixels—not even enough for a small print). There's no flash. You can't zoom.

But when your goal is a well-framed self-portrait that you'll use on the screen— in an email or on a Web page, for example, where high resolution isn't very important—having the front-camera option is better than not having it.

Recording Video

You can record video as well as still photos. And not just crummy, jerky, microscopic cellphone video, either—it's smooth (30 frames per second), sharp, colorful video that does surprisingly well in low light. It's probably the best-looking video a cellphone can take.

On the iPhone 4S, the video is the best flavor of high definition (1080p)—and it's even stabilized to prevent hand jerkiness, just like a real camcorder is.

Using video is almost exactly like taking stills. Pop into the Camera mode. Then tap the ⬛/◼◀ switch so that the ◼◀ is selected. You can hold the iPhone either vertically or horizontally; it doesn't care if your video is tall and thin or wide and squat.

 Tip When you switch from still-photo mode to video, you may notice that the video image on the screen suddenly jumps bigger, as though it's zooming in. And it's true: The iPhone is oddly more "zoomed in" in camcorder mode than in camera mode. Still, you can mitigate the problem by double-tapping the screen so the video preview is a true widescreen image, no longer chopping off the edges.

Tap to compute focus, exposure, and white balance, as described on the previous pages. (You can even hold your finger down to trigger the exposure and focus locks, as described earlier.)

Then tap the Start/Stop button in the middle (⊙)—or press the Volume Up button on the edge of the phone—and you're rolling! As you film, the button blinks red and a time counter ticks away in the corner.

 Tip You can change focus while you're filming, too, which is great when you're panning from a nearby object to a distant one. It's not automatic, as it is on regular camcorders. Still, you can tap somewhere in your "viewfinder" to specify a new focus point. The iPhone recalculates the focus, white balance, and exposure at that point, just as it does when you're taking stills.

You can't zoom in or out (except by walking). But look at the bright side: There's no easier-to-use camcorder on earth. And man, what a lot of capacity! Each individual shot can be one hour long—and on the 64-gigabyte iPhone, you can record *34 hours* of video. Which ought to be just about long enough to capture the entire elementary-school talent show.

When you're finished recording, tap the ⊙ button again. The iPhone stops recording and plays a couple of notes; it's ready to record another shot.

The Front Camera

You can film yourself, too. Just tap the icon before you film to make the iPhone use its front-mounted camera, so that the screen shows you. Be aware that videos you capture this way aren't hi-def—they're the standard 640 × 480–pixel quality of iPhones gone by.

The Video Light

You know the LED "flash" on the back of the phone? You can use it as a video light, too, supplying some illumination to subjects within about 5 feet or so. Just tap the (⚡ Auto) icon, and then tap On. The light remains on until you tap to turn it off (or you exit the Camera app).

> **Tip** You can turn the video light on and off even in the middle of a shot. In fact, you can turn the video light on even when you're not filming—great when you need a little help reading a restaurant menu in tiny type by candlelight. (Download a free app like LED Light for quicker access to turning on that light.)

Editing Video

To review what you just shot, tap the ⎐ thumbnail icon at the lower corner of the screen—or swipe your finger right to left. You've just opened up the video playback screen. Tap the big ▶ button to play back the video you just shot.

What's really cool, though, is that you can *edit* this video right on the phone. You can trim off the dead air at the beginning and the end.

To do that, tap the screen to make the scroll bar appear at the top (if you don't already see it). Then drag the vertical trim marks inward, so that they turn yellow. Adjust them, hitting ▶ to see the effect as you go.

Tip You can drag the playback cursor—the vertical bar that indicates your position in the clip—with your finger. That's the closest thing you get to Rewind and Fast-Forward buttons.

When you've positioned the handles so that they isolate the good stuff, tap Trim.

Finally, tap either Trim Original (meaning "shorten the original clip permanently") or Save as New Clip (meaning "leave the original untouched, and spin out the shortened version as a separate video").

iMovie for iPhone

Now, depending on your creative sophistication, you might be scoffing at the heading for the previous section. "Editing video? You call trimming the ends editing?"

It's true—there's more to editing than just snipping dead air from the ends of a clip. That's why Apple made iMovie for iPhone. This little $5 app lets you trim and rearrange video clips, add music and credits, drop in photos with zooming and crossfades, and then post the whole thing directly to YouTube.

Sure, the whole concept sounds a little ridiculous; video editing on a phone? You might as well introduce Microsoft Excel for Toaster Ovens.

But you watch. The way life goes, some iPhone production will win at Cannes next year.

If the idea appeals to you, you can buy the app from the App Store—and you can get instructions for using it in the free downloadable PDF appendix to this chapter, "iMovie for iPhone." It's available on this book's "Missing CD" at *www. missingmanuals.com.*

Uploading Your Video to YouTube, MMS, or Email

Now, here's something not every cellphone can do: film a movie, edit out the boring parts, and then upload it to YouTube—right from the phone!

Call up the video, if it's not already on the screen before you. Tap the 📤 button. You get three choices:

- **Email Video.** The iPhone compresses the video so that it's small enough to send as an email attachment (smaller dimensions, lower picture quality). Then it opens an outgoing email message with the video attached, ready for you to address and send.

- **Message.** Here again, the iPhone compresses the video and then attaches it to an outgoing text message. Fill in the address; if the phone realizes that the recipient has an iPhone, iPad, or iPod Touch running iOS 5, then it automatically sends the video as an iMessage. Otherwise, it sends the video as an MMS message. Both are described in Chapter 5.

- **Send to YouTube.** The iPhone asks for your YouTube account name and password. Next it wants a title, description, and *tags* (searchable keywords like "funny" or "babies").

  It also wants to know if the video will be in standard definition or high definition (and it gives the approximate size of the file). You should also pick a Category (Autos & Vehicles, Comedy, Education, or whatever).

  Finally, choose from Public (anyone online can search for and view your video), Unlisted (only people who have the link can view this video), or Private (only specific YouTube users can view). When everything looks good, tap Publish.

  After the upload is complete, you're offered the chance to see the video as it now appears on YouTube, or to Tell a Friend (that is, email the YouTube link to a pal). Both are excellent ways to admire your masterful cinematography.

Capturing the Screen

Let's say you want to write a book about the iPhone. (Hey, it could happen.) How on earth are you supposed to illustrate that book? How can you take pictures of what's on the screen?

The trick is very simple: Start by getting the screen just the way you want it, even if that means holding your finger down on an onscreen button or a keyboard key. Now hold down the Home button, and while it's down, press the Sleep switch at the top of the phone. (Yes, you may need to invite some friends over to help you execute this multiple-finger move.)

But that's all there is to it. The screen flashes white. Now, if you go to the Photos program and open up the Camera Roll, you see a crisp, colorful pixel image, in PNG format, of whatever was on the screen. (Its resolution matches the screen: 480 × 320 pixels on the iPhone 3GS, or 960 × 480 on the iPhone 4 or 4S.)

At this point, you can send it by email (to illustrate a request for help, for example, or to send a screen from Maps to a friend who's driving your way); sync it with your computer (to add it to your Mac or Windows photo collection); or designate it as the iPhone's wallpaper (to confuse the heck out of its owner).

Photo Stream

iCloud is Apple's free suite of online services. It's described in Chapter 14—but for the iPhone shutterbug, its most interesting feature by far is Photo Stream.

The concept is simple: Every time a new photo enters your life—when you take a picture with your iPhone, for example, or import one onto your computer—it gets added to your Photo Stream. From there, it appears automatically on all your other iCloud machines.

 Note Photo Stream doesn't sync over the cellular airwaves. It sends photos around only when you're in a WiFi hotspot or connected to a wired network.

Using Photo Stream means all kinds of good things:

- Your photos are always backed up. Lose your iPhone? Get a new one? No biggie—your latest 1,000 photos appear on it automatically.

- Any pictures you take with your iPhone appear automatically on your computer. You don't have to connect any cables or sync anything yourself.

 Tip Actually, there's one exception. Suppose you take a photo, and then look it over while you're still in the Camera app. You hate it. You delete it.

In that case, the photo will never become part of your Photo Stream, because you deleted it while you were still in the Camera mode.

A similar rule holds true with edits: If you edit a photo you've just taken, those edits become part of the Photo Stream copy. But if you take a photo, leave the Camera app, and *later* edit it, the Photo Stream gets the original copy only.

Here's a sneaky one: You can drag favorite photos into your Photo Stream from your computer's photo stash—a quick, easy way to get pictures from your computer onto your iPhone.

To get started with Photo Stream on your iPhone, you need an iCloud account (Chapter 14). You also have to turn *on* Photo Stream, which you do in Settings→iCloud. (You should also turn it on using the iCloud control panel on your computers. That's in System Preferences on your Mac, or in the

Control Panel of Windows.) Give your phone some time in a WiFi hotspot to form its initial slurping-in of all your most recent photos.

Once Photo Stream is up and running, here's how to use it.

On the iPhone (or iPad or iPod Touch)

Open your Photos app. There it is: a new "album" called Photo Stream. It shows the most recent photos that have entered your life, either by taking them with any i-gadget, or by importing them into your computer from a scanner or a digital camera.

Now, Apple realizes that your i-gadget doesn't have nearly as much storage available as your Mac or PC; you can't yet buy an iPhone with 750 gigabytes of storage. That's why, on your iPhone/iPad/iPod, your Photo Stream consists of just the last 1,000 photos. (There's another limitation, too: The iCloud servers store your photos for 30 days. As long as your gadgets go online at least once a month, they'll remain current with the Photo Stream.)

Ordinarily, the oldest of the 1,000 photos in your Photo Stream scroll away forever as new photos come in. But you can rescue the best ones from that fate—by saving them into your Camera Roll, where they're free from the risk of automatic deletion.

To do that, open Photos, and then open the Photo Stream. Tap the button, and then tap the thumbnails of the photos you want to preserve (shown here at left). Once they're selected, tap Save in the lower-right corner.

Tip To save a photo you've already opened, tap the button. On the resulting screen, tap Save to Camera Roll (below, right).

That's it. Now the photos you rescued appear in *both* your Photo Stream, where they will eventually disappear, *and* in your Camera Roll, where they're safe until you delete them manually.

On the Mac or PC

In iPhoto or Aperture (Mac), your Photo Stream photos appear in a new album called, of course, Photo Stream. On a Windows PC, you get a Photo Stream folder in your Pictures folder.

On the computer, you don't have to worry about that 30-day, 1,000-photo business. Once pictures appear here, they're here until you delete them.

This, in its way, is one of the best features in all of iCloudland, because it means you don't have to sync your iPhone over a USB cable to get your photos onto your computer. It all happens automatically, wirelessly over WiFi.

 Tip You can also drag photos *into* your Photo Stream from your computer. That's a quick, easy way to get them onto your iPhone wirelessly. On the Mac, drag the photos into the Photo Stream album (within iPhoto or Aperture). In Windows, drag them into the Photo Stream Uploads folder, which you designate in the iCloud Control Panel.

On the Apple TV

When you're viewing your photos on an Apple TV, a new album appears there called Photo Stream. There they are, ready for showing on the big plasma. You can use your Photo Stream in an Apple TV screensaver, too.

If you bought your gadget/photo software/Apple TV before iCloud's debut, of course, you'll need a software update to add the Photo Stream feature.

Photo Stream Permanence—and Emergency Reset

You can't choose what photos go into the Photo Stream. *Every* picture you take with the iPhone goes into it. *Every* photo you bring into your computer goes into it. Every photo you save on your iPhone from an app like Twitter goes into it. Every screenshot you make goes into it. And you can't delete individual photos from it.

And remember, the same 1,000 photos appear on all your Apple gadgets (assuming you've turned on Photo Stream on each one). You might think you're taking a private picture with your phone, forgetting that your spouse or parent will see it seconds later on the iPad. It's only a matter of time before Photo Stream gets some politician in big trouble.

Even if you delete a photo from your iPhone's Camera Roll, it's too late. The Photo Stream version is already out there, replicated across all your i-gadgets and computers.

If you run into an emergency, though—if a photo gets into your stream that you really, really don't want floating around to other machines—you can resort to the Nuclear Option: resetting your Photo Stream.

Here's how. Log into *www.icloud.com*. Click the ☁ button in the corner of the screen, if necessary, so that you see the main iCloud screen shown here:

Click your name in the upper-right corner. Click Advanced, and then click Reset Photo Stream. Click Done.

Now, this maneuver does wipe out the last 30 days' worth of photos that have entered your Photo Stream. It does not, however, touch the copy of the Photo Stream that's already been synced to your i-gadgets and computers. Those previously synced photos are still there.

To get rid of those, you should now go turn off Photo Stream on each machine (iPhone, iPad, Mac, PC…) and then turn it back on again. Now every copy of Photo Stream is empty. Take a deep breath—and be more careful next time.

> **Tip** If you use iPhoto or Aperture, don't forget that these programs offer an Auto-Import feature in their Preferences. That is, any photo that appears in the Photo Stream album automatically gets imported into the program's permanent collection. In the event of an Embarrassing Photo Stream Mistake, don't forget to delete that auto-imported copy of the incriminating photos, too.

Opening Photos

Once you've taken some photos, or copied them to your phone from your computer (see Chapter 13), you'll have some pictures ready to view. You can drill down to a certain set of photos as follows.

 Tip The Photos app is fully rotational. That is, you can turn the phone 90 degrees. Whether you're viewing a list, a screen full of thumbnails, or an individual photo, the image on the screen rotates, too, for easier admiring. (Unless, of course, you've turned on the screen-rotation lock.)

❶ **On the Home screen, tap Photos.**

The Photo Albums screen appears (shown at left on the facing page). First on the list is Camera Roll, which means "pictures you've taken with the iPhone."

Next in the list, you may see Photo Stream, described in the previous pages. Then comes Photo Library, which means *all* the photos you've selected to copy from your Mac or PC.

After that is the list of *albums* you've brought over from the computer. (An album is the photo equivalent of a playlist. It's a subset of photos, in a sequence you've selected.)

❷ **Tap one of the rolls or albums.**

Now the screen fills with 18 or 20 postage-stamp-sized thumbnails of the photos in this roll or album. You can scroll this list by flicking.

❸ **Tap the photo you want to see.**

It fills the screen, in all its glory.

 Tip If you hold your finger down on the photo, a Copy button appears. That's the first step if you want to paste a single photo into an email message, an MMS (picture or video) message to another phone, and so on.

Faces and Places

The Albums list may not be the only way to burrow into your photo collection. If you use iPhoto or Aperture (Apple's photo-editing programs for the Mac), a special treat awaits you: You can browse your photos according to who's in them or where they were taken. This is the intriguing world of what Apple calls *Faces* and *Places* data.

- **Faces.** Both iPhoto and Aperture have features that let you identify, by name, the people whose faces are in your photos. Once you've given the software a running start, it can find those people in the rest of your photo collection automatically. That's handy every now and then—when you need a photo of your kid for a school project, for example.

- **Places.** The iPhone can also show you, on a map, where you took your pictures. Not all your photos—just the ones that your camera or you have geotagged (flagged with invisible latitude and longitude coordinates for reference later). You can read about geotagging on page 226; for now, it's enough to note that you can now see the locations of your geotagged photos right on a map, represented by pushpins. Zoom into the map to get a more precise idea of where these photos were taken.

 Note In theory, all the pictures you take with the iPhone itself show up in Places, because the iPhone geotags every picture you take (unless you've turned off the camera location feature in Settings→Location Services).

If any of your photos do, in fact, have face or geotagging information stored with them, then additional buttons show up at the bottom of the Photos screen. Tap Faces (below, left) to see a list of the people you identified in iPhoto or Aperture; tap Places (below, right) to see a map with pushpins showing where you took the photos. From here, you can drill down; tap a face to see thumbnails of all the pictures that person is in (even if they come from different albums); tap a pushpin to see a little flag telling you how many photos were taken there, and then tap the ⊙ button to see the thumbnails of those shots.

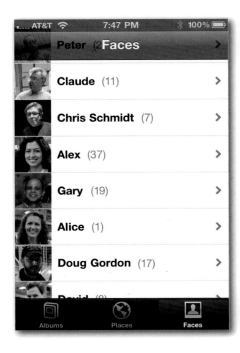

Flicking, Rotating, Zooming, Panning

Once a photo is open at full size, you have your chance to perform the four most famous and most dazzling tricks of the iPhone: flicking, rotating, zooming, and panning a photo.

- **Flicking** right to left is how you advance to the next picture or movie in the batch. (Flick from left to right to view the *previous* photo.)

- **Rotating** is what you do when a horizontal photo or video appears on the upright iPhone, which makes the photo look small and fills most of the screen with blackness.

  Just turn the iPhone 90 degrees in either direction. Like magic, the photo itself rotates and enlarges to fill its new, wider canvas. No taps required. (This doesn't work when the phone is flat on its back—on a table, for example. It has to be more or less upright. It also doesn't work when Portrait Orientation is locked.)

  This trick also works the other way—that is, you can also make a *vertical* photo or video fit better when you're holding the iPhone horizontally. Just rotate the iPhone upright.

- **Zooming** a photo means magnifying it, and it's a blast. One quick way is to double-tap the photo; the iPhone zooms in on the portion you tapped, doubling its size.

  Another way is to use the two-finger spread technique. That technique gives you more control over what gets magnified and by how much.

  (Remember, the iPhone doesn't actually store the giganto 20-megapixel originals of pictures you took with your fancy digital camera—only scaled-down, iPhone-appropriate versions—so you can't zoom in more than about three times the original size.)

  Once you've spread a photo bigger, you can then pinch the screen to scale it down again. Or just double-tap a zoomed photo to restore its original size. (You don't have to restore a photo to original size before advancing to the next one, though; if you flick enough times, you'll pull the next photo onto the screen.)

- **Panning** means moving a photo around on the screen after you've zoomed in. Just drag your finger to do that; no scroll bars are necessary.

 Tip When the iPhone is rotated, all the controls and gestures reorient themselves. For example, flicking right to left still brings on the next photo, even if you're now holding the iPhone the wide way.

Deleting Photos

If some photo no longer meets your exacting standards, you can delete it. But this action is trickier than you may think.

- **If you took the picture using the iPhone,** no sweat. Open the photo; tap the 🗑 button. When you tap Delete Photo, that picture is gone.

- **If the photo was synced to the iPhone from your computer,** well, that's life. The iPhone remains a *mirror* of what's on the computer. In other words, you can't delete the photo right on the phone. Delete it from the original album on your computer (which does *not* mean deleting it from the computer altogether). The next time you sync the iPhone, the photo disappears from it, too.

 Tip Aannnnd, just one more reminder: You can't delete a single photo from your Photo Stream.

Photo Controls

If you tap the screen once, some useful controls appear. They remain on the screen for only a couple of seconds, so as not to ruin the majesty of your photo, so act now.

- **Album name.** You can return to the thumbnails page by tapping the screen once, which summons the playback controls, and then tapping the album name in the upper-left corner.

- **Photo number.** The top of the screen says, "88 of 405," for example, meaning that this is the 88th photo out of 405 in the set.

- **Edit.** This button is the gateway to iOS 5's new photo-editing features, described later in this chapter.

- **Share icon.** Tap the 📤 button in the lower left if you want to do something more with this photo than just stare at it. You can use it as your iPhone's wallpaper, send it by email, use it as somebody's headshot in your Contacts list, send it to another cellphone, print it, or post it on Twitter. All four of these options are described in the next sections.

- ▶. Tap this button to begin a slideshow, as described next.

Slideshows

A slideshow is a great way to show off your photos and videos. You can turn any album, or the Camera Roll itself, into a slideshow by tapping the ▶ button.

You have a surprising amount of control over your slideshow, too. But beware: The controls are split up between two locations. Some of them appear when you first tap the ▶ button, as shown here:

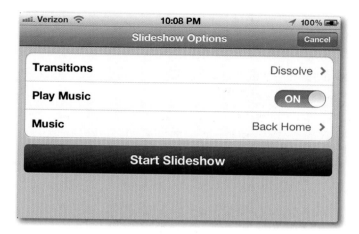

- **Transitions.** What kind of crossfade or special effect do you want the phone to create in the blend from one photo to the next? You're offered five choices—Dissolve, Cube, Ripple, Wipe Across, Wipe Down. (Dissolve is the least tacky one.)

- **Play Music.** Would you like tunes with that? If you want background music, turn this switch on.

- **Music.** Finally, tap the new Music pop-up menu to choose a song from your music collection.

The other set of controls is buried in Settings→Photos:

- **Play Each Slide For.** You can specify how many seconds each photo hangs around.

- **Repeat.** Makes the slideshow play over and over again until you stop it manually.

- **Shuffle.** Randomizes the sequence of photos within the chosen album.

While the slideshow is going on, tapping the screen stops the show, freezing it on the current photo. You can tap the ▶ button to resume the slideshow from the photo where you stopped.

And remember that you must let each video play to its conclusion if you want the show to continue. (Or tap to interrupt a particularly boring video; swipe to the next photo or video; and tap the ▶ button to pick up the slideshow from there.)

Feel free to turn the iPhone 90 degrees to accommodate landscape-orientation photos as they come up; the slideshow keeps right on going.

Copying/Sending/Deleting in Batches

You can select batches of photos at once, which is great for sending several pictures in a single email (up to five); for pasting them as a group into another program; for pasting them into an outgoing MMS message; or for deleting a bunch of pictures in one fell swoop.

The fun begins on the page of thumbnails that appears when you tap an album, a face, a Place thumbtack, the Photo Stream, or the Camera Roll. Tap the 📤 button.

A new button row sprouts across the bottom. First, however, tap the thumbnails of the photos or videos you want to manipulate. With each tap, a checkmark appears, meaning, "OK, this one will be included." (Tap again to remove the checkmark.)

Now you can tap one of the bottom-row buttons:

- **Share.** When you tap Share, you're offered a new choice of buttons: Email, meaning "send as email attachments"; Message, meaning "send as either MMS text messages or free iMessages, if possible (Chapter 4); Tweet to post the photo on Twitter (page 336); and Print (see page 251).

 The Email option doesn't appear if you've chosen more than five photos. That's because five is the maximum for sending as email attachments. More than that, and the attachment will be too big for most email systems.

- **Copy.** Tapping this one copies the indicated number of photos to the invisible iPhone Clipboard (maximum: five photos). Now you can switch to another program—like Messages or Mail—and paste the selected photos or videos. (You may be able to paste them into non-Apple apps, too.)

- **Add To.** In iOS 5, for the first time, you can subdivide a bunch of photos into several albums. That's a great way to organize a huge batch you've shot on vacation, for example.

  Once you've selected the photos you want to move, tap Add To. If you've already created new albums on the phone, you're now offered an Add to Existing Album button; tap it to see a list of albums you've created on the phone; tap the one you want. (You can't, in other words, move photos into albums that were created on the computer and then synced over to the phone.)

  Either way, you also get an Add to New Album button; you're asked to type out the name you want for the new album and then tap Save.

 These buttons don't actually move photos out of their original albums. You're creating *aliases* of them—pointers to the original photos. If you edit or delete a photo from one album, it's edited or deleted from all of them.

You can even *delete* albums on the phone now—but only the ones you *created* on the phone. To do that, on the main Photos screen, tap Edit, and then tap the button next to the album you want to delete.

- **Delete.** Here's where you can delete a bunch of photos at once. (Here again, you can delete only photos or videos you've taken *with the iPhone*—not ones you transferred from your computer.)

Editing Photos

Yes, kids, it's one of the most eagerly anticipated new iOS 5 features: You can now crop and edit your pictures right on the phone. The tools Apple gives you aren't exactly Photoshop, but at least you don't need to download some app just to touch up a promising picture.

To edit a photo, tap its thumbnail (from the Camera Roll, Photo Stream, or any album) to open it. Tap Edit in the upper right.

Now you get four buttons across the bottom: Rotate, Auto-Enhance, Remove Red-Eye, and Crop; read on.

The Rotate button ( )

Tap this button to rotate the photo 90 degrees.

> **Tip** You can rotate the photo in smaller amounts when you enter Crop mode, as described below—straightening a tilted horizon, for example.

Auto-Enhance ()

When you tap this magical, do-it-all button, the iPhone analyzes the relative brightness of all the pixels in your photo and attempts to "balance" it. After a moment, the app adjusts the brightness and contrast and intensifies dull or grayish-looking areas. Usually, the pictures look richer and more vivid as a result.

You may find that Auto-Enhance has little effect on some photos, only minimally improves others, and totally rescues a few. In any case, if you don't care for the result, you can tap the button again to turn Auto-Enhance off.

Remove Red-Eye (⌀)

Red eye is a common problem in flash photography. This creepy, possessed look—devilish, glowing-red pupils in your subjects' eyes—has ruined many an otherwise great photo.

Red eye is caused by light reflected back from eyes. The bright light of your flash illuminates the blood-red retinal tissue at the back of the eyes. That's why red-eye problems are worse when you shoot pictures in a dim room: Your subjects' pupils are dilated, allowing even *more* light from your flash to reach their retinas.

When you tap this button, a message says, "Tap each red-eye." Do what it says: Tap with your finger inside each eye that has the problem. The app turns the red in each eye to black.

 Tip It usually helps to zoom in first. Use the usual two-finger spread technique.

Crop ()

Cropping means shaving off unnecessary portions of a photo. Usually, you crop a photo to improve its composition—adjusting where the subject appears within the frame of the picture. Often, a photo has more impact if it's cropped tightly around the subject, especially in portraits. Or maybe you want to crop out wasted space, like big expanses of background sky. You can even chop a former romantic interest out of an otherwise perfect family portrait.

Cropping is also very useful if your photo needs to have a certain *aspect ratio* (length-to-width proportion), like 8 × 10 or 5 × 7.

To crop a photo you've opened, tap the ⊡ button. A white tic-tac-toe grid appears on your photo, just in case you want to crop according to the Rule of Thirds (page 190).

Drag inward on any edge or corner. The part of the photo that iPhoto will eventually trim away is dimmed out. You can re-center the photo within your cropping frame by dragging any part of the photo, inside or outside of the white grid. Adjust the frame and drag the photo until everything looks just right.

 Tip In Cropping mode, you can also straighten or fine-tune the rotation of a picture. Place two fingers on the screen and twist them. Who knew?

Ordinarily, you can draw a cropping rectangle of any size and proportions, freehand. But if you tap the Constrain button, you get a choice of nine canned proportions: Square, 3 × 2, 3 × 5, 4 × 3, and so on. They make the app limit the cropping frame to preset proportions.

The Constrain feature is especially important if you plan to order prints of your photos. Prints come only in standard photo sizes: 4 × 6, 5 × 7, 8 × 10, and so on. But unless you crop them, the iPhone's photos are all 3 × 2, which doesn't divide evenly into standard print photograph sizes. Limiting your cropping to one of these standard sizes guarantees that your cropped photos will fit perfectly into Kodak prints. (If you don't constrain your cropping this way, Kodak—not you—will decide how to crop them to fit.)

 Tip The Original option here maintains the proportions of the original photo even as you make the grid smaller.

The iPhone's Constrain feature doesn't work like the one in iPhoto, Picasa, Photoshop, or any other app. When you tap one of the preset sizes, the cropping frame jumps to those proportions—but it doesn't *stay* that way. If you start to drag the frame edges again, you're back to freehand.

In other words, the trick is to get the frame *almost* the way you want it, and *then* tap the Constrain button. If your cropping frame is a little too big or small, you'll have to drag to adjust it and then use the Constrain button again.

Saving Your Changes

Once you've rotated, cropped, auto-enhanced, or de-red-eyed a photo, tap the Save button in the upper-right corner of the screen. You've just immortalized your changes to the photo. If you send the picture off your phone—send it by email or text message, or sync it to your Mac or PC—it arrives in its edited condition.

What's especially convenient, though, is that the Photos app never forgets the original photo. At any time, hours or years later, you can return to the Edit screen and undo the changes you've made. You can recrop the photo back to its original size, for example, or turn off the Auto-Enhance button. In other words, your changes are never really permanent.

> **Tip** If you sync your photos to iPhoto or Aperture on the Mac, they show up in their edited condition. Yet the amazing thing is, you can undo or modify the edits there! The original photo is still lurking behind the edited version. You can use your Mac's Crop tool to adjust the crop, for example. Or you can use the iPhone's Revert to Original command to throw away *all* the edits you made to the original photo while it was on the iPhone.

Printing Photos

You can print a photo easily enough, provided that you've hooked up your iPhone to a compatible printer. Once you've opened the photo, tap the 🔁 button, and then tap Print.

The rest goes down as described on page 251.

Photo Wallpaper

Wallpaper, in the world of iOS, can refer to the background photo that appears in either of two places: the Home screen (plastered behind your app icons) or the Unlock screen (which appears every time you wake the iPhone).

You can replace Apple's standard photos with one of your photos or with a different one of Apple's. You go at this task in either of two ways.

Start in Settings

From the Home screen, tap Settings→Wallpaper.

Now you see miniatures of the two places you can install wallpaper—the Lock screen and the Home screen (facing page, left). (Each shows what you've got installed there as wallpaper at the moment.) These aren't separate buttons; that is, this isn't the place to indicate which screen (Lock or Home) you're redecorating. Just tap once on the whole thing to move on.

When you tap that picture, you're shown a list of photo sources you can use as backgrounds. They include these choices:

- **Wallpaper.** Apple has supplied 27 professional, presized photos and textures that you can use as your wallpaper until you get your own photographic skills in shape (above, right).

- **Camera Roll, Photo Stream, Albums.** These are your own photos, as described earlier in this chapter.

All these pictures show up as thumbnail miniatures; tap one to see what it looks like at full size. If it looks good, tap Set. (Sadly, the Mona Lisa is no longer one of your choices. Leonardo da Vinci's lawyers must have sued.)

Now the iPhone wants to know which of the two places you want to use this wallpaper; tap Set Lock Screen, Set Home Screen, or Set Both (if you want the same picture in both places).

Start in the Photos App

The task of applying one of your own photos to your Home or Lock screen can also begin in the Photos app. Open one of your photos, as described in the previous pages. Tap the 🔄 button, and then tap Use as Wallpaper.

You're now offered the Move and Scale screen so you can fit your rectangular photo within the square wallpaper "frame." Pinch or spread to enlarge the shot; drag your finger on the screen to scroll and center it.

Finally, tap Set. Here again, you specify where you want to use this wallpaper; tap Set Lock Screen, Set Home Screen, or Set Both (if you want the same picture in both places).

Three Ways to Send Photos or Videos

You can send a photo or video by email; by picture message to another cellphone, iPad, or iPod Touch; or to Twitter—all right from the iPhone.

That's useful when you're out shopping and want to seek your spouse's opinion on something you're about to buy. It's handy when you want to remember the parking-garage section where you parked ("4 South"). It's great when you want to give your Twitter fans a glimpse of whatever hell or heaven you're experiencing at the moment.

Start in the Photos app. Tap your way to the photo or video you want to send. Once it's on the screen before you, tap the 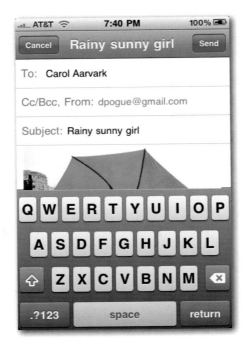 button. Now you have a bunch of options:

- **Email Photo (Email Video).** The iPhone automatically compresses, rotates, and attaches the photo or video clip to a new outgoing message. All you have to do is address it and hit Send.

  At that point, you're asked how much you want the photo *scaled down* from its original size. Tap Small, Medium, Large, or Actual Size, using the megabyte indicator as a guide.

 This size choice doesn't appear when you're emailing low-resolution images, like a screenshot (an image you captured from the iPhone's own screen). The iPhone figures it's not big enough to cause anyone any trouble.

Why is this necessary? Because many email systems won't accept attachments larger than 5 megabytes; even four "actual size" photos taken with the iPhone 4 or 4S would be too big to send by email. The iPhone used to scale your photos down automatically, without offering any control over how much; be grateful that iOS 5 lets you choose. The Size button you tap controls how big the photo will be on the receiving end—and how long the message will take to send.

In general, when you send Small, the photo will arrive in the recipient's message window about the size of a brownie. A Medium image will fill the email window. Large will fill your recipient's computer screen. And Actual Size is intended for making printouts. It sends the full, multimegabyte originals (2048 × 1536 on the iPhone 3GS; 2592 × 1936 on the iPhone 4 and 4S).

 Using the steps on page 214, you can send up to five photos at once.

- **Message.** You can also send a photo or video as a *picture or video message.* It winds up on the screen of the other guy's cellphone.

 If you're sending to another iOS gadget, like an iPhone, iPad, or iPod Touch, it will be sent as a free iMessage; your cellphone carrier won't even be involved. If you're sending to a non-Apple cellphone, it will be a regular MMS message. All of this is described in Chapter 5.

That's a delicious feature, almost handier than sending a photo by email. After all, your friends and relatives don't sit in front of their computers all day and all night (unless they're serious geeks).

Tap Message and then specify the phone number of the recipient—or, to send by iMessage to an iPod Touch or iPad, type in the email address. Or choose someone from your Contacts list. Then type a little note, tap Send, and off it goes.

 Tip Free photo-sharing sites like Flickr and Snapfish let you upload photos from your phone, too. For example, Flickr gives you a private email address for this purpose (visit *www.flickr.com/account/uploadbyemail* to find out what it is). The big ones, including Flickr, also offer special iPhone apps (from the App Store) that make uploading easier.

- **Tweet.** If you've told your iPhone what your Twitter name and password are (in Settings→Twitter), then posting a photo from your phone to your Twitter feed is ridiculously simple.

Open the photo; tap the button; tap Tweet. You're offered the chance to type a message that accompanies your photo. (As usual with Twitter, you have a maximum of 140 characters for your message. Less, actually, because some of your characters are eaten up by the link to the photo.) You can also tap Add Location if you want Twitterites to know where the photo was taken.

Note The Add Location option is available only if you've permitted Twitter to use your location information, which you set up in Settings→Location Services→Twitter.

When you tap Send, your photo, and your accompanying tweet, zoom off straight to Twitter, for all to enjoy.

Headshots for Contacts

If you're viewing a photo of somebody who's listed in Contacts, then you can use it (or part of it) as her headshot. After that, her photo appears on your screen every time she calls.

You can add a photo to a contact from either direction: starting with the photo, or starting with the person's "card" open in Contacts.

Starting with the Photo

In the Photos app, open a picture that you want to assign to someone in your address book. Tap the 📤 button, and then tap Assign to Contact (below, left).

Your address book list pops up. Tap the right person's name.

Now you see a preview of what the photo will look like when that person calls. This is the Move and Scale screen (above, right). It works just as it does when you set wallpaper, as described earlier. But when choosing a headshot for a contact, it's even more important. You'll want to crop the photo and shift it in the frame so only *that person* is visible. It's a great way to isolate one person in a group shot, for example.

Start by enlarging the photo: Spread your thumb and forefinger against the glass. As you go, *shift* the photo's placement in the frame with a one-finger drag. When you've got the person correctly enlarged and centered, tap Set Photo.

Starting with the Contact

You can also assign a photo to somebody's Contacts card right from the card itself; you don't have to begin the process from the photo.

Just open the card, tap Edit, and then tap Add Photo. Now you can hunt through your photo collection until you find a good one. Tap it, do your thing on the Move and Scale screen, and off you go.

Geotagging

Mention to a geek that a gadget has both GPS and a camera, and there's only one possible reaction: "Does it do *geotagging?*"

Geotagging means "embedding your latitude and longitude information into a photo or video when you take it." After all, every digital picture you've ever taken comes with its time and date embedded in its file; why not its location?

The good news is that the iPhone can geotag every photo and movie you take. How you use this information, however, is a bit trickier. The iPhone doesn't geotag unless all the following conditions are true:

- **The location feature on your phone is turned on.** On the Home screen, tap Settings→Location Services. Make sure Camera is turned On.

- **The phone knows where it is.** If you're indoors, the GPS chip in the iPhone probably can't get a fix on the satellites overhead. And if you're not near cellular towers or WiFi base stations, then even the pseudo-GPS may not be able to triangulate your location.

- **You've given permission.** The first time you use the iPhone's camera, a peculiar message appears (shown on page 187). It's asking, "Do you want to geotag your pictures?" If you tap OK, then the iPhone's geographical coordinates will be embedded in each photo you take.

OK, so suppose all of this is true, and the geotagging feature is working. How will you know? Well, thanks to the Places feature described on page 207, you can put geotagging to work right on the phone. You can tap a pushpin on a map and see all the photos you took in that spot.

iPhoto (Get Info)   *Preview (Inspector window)*

You can also transfer the photos to your computer, where your likelihood of being able to see the geotag information depends on what photo-viewing software you're using. For example:

- When you've selected a photo in iPhoto (on the Mac), you can press ⌘-I to view the Photo Info panel. At the very bottom, you'll see the GPS coordinates, expressed as latitude and longitude.

- If you export a photo and open it in Preview (on the Mac), then you can choose Tools→Inspector to open the Inspector panel. Its center tab offers a world map that pinpoints the photo's location.

- If you click Locate (on the Preview panel shown above), you pop into Google Maps online, where you get to see an aerial photo of the spot where you snapped the picture.

- Once you've posted your geotagged photos on Flickr.com (the world's largest photo-sharing site), people can use the Explore menu to search for them by location, or even see them clustered on a world map.

- If you import your photos into Picasa (for Windows), then you can choose Tools→Geotag→View in Google Earth to see a picture's location on the map (if the free Google Earth program is installed on your computer, that is).

Or choose Tools→Geotag→Export to Google Earth File to create a .kmz file, which you can send to a friend. When opened, this file opens Google Earth (if it's on your friend's computer) and displays a miniature of the picture in the right place on the map.

8 All About Apps

When you get right down to it, the iPhone is a computer. It's got memory, a screen, a processor, WiFi; It runs a variant of Mac OS X. But during the first year of its existence, people couldn't write new programs (apps) for it. Apple didn't allow it.

Apple said it was only trying to preserve the stability of the phone and of the AT&T network. It needed time to redesign the iPhone operating system, to create a digital sandbox where all those loose-cannon non-Apple programs could run without interfering with the iPhone's "real" functions.

During that year of preparation, new programs appeared on the iPhone, all right—but in forms that most ordinary iPhone fans didn't bother with. There were the semi-lame "Web apps," which were little more than iPhone-shaped Web pages, and there were hacks.

That's right, hacks. The hacking community learned to "jailbreak" the iPhone, using special software tools to open it up (metaphorically speaking) and shoehorn their own programs onto it, violating their warranties in the process.

Finally, though, Apple threw open its doors to independent programmers by the tens of thousands, and in July 2008, it offered a simple way for you to get the new iPhone programs they wrote: the iPhone App Store.

Welcome to App Heaven

"App" is short for *application,* meaning software program, and the App Store is a single, centralized catalog of every authorized iPhone add-on program in the world.

Nothing like the App Store had ever been attempted before. Oh, sure, there were thousands of programs for the Mac, Windows, Palm organizers, Treos,

BlackBerries, and Windows Mobile phones—but there was never a *single* source of software for those platforms.

In the iPhone's case, there's only one place where you can get new programs (at least without hacking your phone): the App Store.

You hear people talking about downsides to this approach: Apple's stifling the competition, Apple's taking a 30 percent cut of every program sold, Apple's maintaining veto power over programs it doesn't like (or that may compete with its products and services).

But there are some enormous benefits to this setup, too. First, the whole universe of software programs is all in one place. Second, Apple checks out every program to make sure it's decent and runs decently. Third, the store is beautifully integrated with the iPhone itself, making it fast, simple, and idiotproof to download and install new software morsels.

There's an incredible wealth of software in the App Store. These programs can turn the iPhone into an instant-message tool, a pocket Internet radio, an eBay auction tracker, a medical reference, a musical keyboard, a time and expense tracker, a home-automation remote control, a photo editor, an Etch-a-Sketch, a recipe box, a tip calculator, a currency converter, an ebook reader, a restaurant finder, a friend finder, a teleprompter, a parenting handbook, and so on. The best of them exploit the iPhone's motion sensor, WiFi, Bluetooth, GPS, and other features.

Above all, the iPhone is a dazzling handheld game machine. There are arcade games, classic video games, casino and card games, multiplayer games, puzzles, strategy games, and on and on. Some of them feature smooth 3-D graphics and tilt control. Watch out, Game Boy.

It's so much stuff—500,000 apps in four years, 15 billion downloads—that the challenge now is just finding your way through it. Thank goodness for those Most Popular lists.

Two Ways to the App Store

You can get to the App Store in two ways: from the phone itself, or from your computer's copy of the iTunes software.

Using iTunes offers a much easier browsing and shopping experience, of course, because you've got a mouse, a keyboard, and that big screen. But downloading straight to the iPhone, without ever involving the computer, is also wicked cool—and it's your only option when you're out and about.

Shopping from the Phone

To check out the App Store from your iPhone, tap the App Store icon. You arrive at the colorful, scrolling wonder of the store itself.

Across the bottom, you see the now-familiar lineup of iPhone buttons that control your view of the store:

- **Featured.** Here are the programs Apple is recommending this week. (If you tap the Genius button, you're shown a list of apps you might enjoy, based on the apps you've already downloaded.)

- **Categories.** This list shows the entire catalog, organized by category: Books, Business, Education, Entertainment, Finance, Games, and so on. Tap a category to see what's in it.

- **Top 25.** Tap this button to reveal a list of the 25 most popular programs at the moment, ranked by how many people have downloaded them. You can also tap the Top Free button at the top of the screen to see the most popular *free* programs. There are lots of them, and they're one of the great joys of the App Store. And Top Grossing shows which apps have made the most money, even if they haven't sold the most copies.

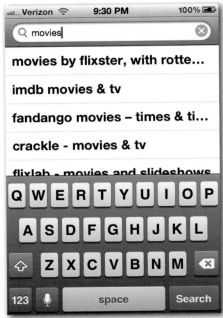

- **Search.** Scrolling through those massive lists is a fun way to stumble onto cool things. But as the number of iPhone programs grows into the hundreds of thousands, viewing by list begins to get awfully unwieldy.

  Fortunately, you can also *search* the catalog, which is a very efficient way to go if you know what you're looking for (either the name of a program, the kind of program, or the software company that made it). Tap in the search box to make the keyboard appear. As you type, the list shrinks so that it's showing you only the matches. You might type *tetris,* or *piano,* or *Disney,* or whatever. Tap anything in the results list to see a more refined summary list of matching apps.

- **Updates.** Unlike its buddies, this button isn't intended to help you navigate the catalog. Instead, it lets you know when one of the programs you've *already* installed is available in a newer version. Details in a moment.

Once you're looking at the scrolling list of programs—no matter which button was your starting point—the next steps are the same. Each listing shows you the program's name, its icon, and its price. About a third of the App Store's programs are free; the rest are usually under $10, although a few, intended for professionals (pilots, for example), can cost a lot more.

Best of all, this listing shows each program's star rating, which may be the most important statistic of all. You can think of it as a letter grade, given to this program by everyone who's tried it out so far and expressed as an average. (In small type, you can even see how *many* people's opinions are included in this score. You can also see the average rating for *this version* of the program; these apps are constantly being revised and updated.)

Why is it so important? Because the App Store's goodies aren't equally good. Remember, these programs come from a huge variety of people—teenagers in Hungary, professional firms in Silicon Valley, college kids goofing around on weekends—and just because they made it into the store doesn't mean they're worth the money (or even the time to download).

Sometimes a program has a low score because it's just not designed well or it doesn't do what it's advertised to do. And sometimes, of course, it's a little buggy.

The App Details Screen

When you tap a program's name, you wind up at a screen that contains even more detail. There's a description, a horizontally scrolling set of screenshots, details about the author, the date posted, the version number, and so on. You can also tap the Reviews link to dig beyond the average star rating into the *actual* written reviews from people who've already tried the thing.

If you decide something is worth getting, scroll back to the top of the page and tap its price button. That button changes to say Install, and it does just what it says. Once you tap Install, you've committed to downloading the program. There are only a few things that may stand in your way:

- **A request for your iTunes account info.** You can't use the App Store without an iTunes account—even if you're just downloading free stuff. If you've ever bought anything from the iTunes Store, signed up for an iCloud account, or bought anything from Apple online, then you already have an iTunes account (an Apple ID).

  The iPhone asks you to enter your iTunes account name and password the first time you access the App Store and every so often thereafter, just to make sure some marauding child in your household can't run up your bill without your knowledge.

- **A file size over 20 megabytes.** Most iPhone apps are pretty small— small enough to download directly to the phone, even over a cellular connection. If a program is bigger than 20 MB, though, you can't download it over the cellular airwaves, a policy no doubt intended to soothe nerves at AT&T, Sprint, and Verizon, whose networks could be choked with 100 million iPhoners downloading huge files.

  Instead, over-20-meg files are available only when you're on a WiFi connection. Of course, you can also download them to your computer and sync them from there, as described later in this chapter.

Once you begin downloading a file, the iPhone automatically switches back to the Home screen, where you can see the new icon appear; a tiny progress bar inches across it to indicate the download's progress.

 Tip You don't have to sit there and stare at the progress bar. You can go on working on the iPhone. In fact, you can even go back to the App Store and start downloading something else simultaneously.

Two Welcome Notes about Backups

Especially when you've paid good money for your iPhone apps, you might worry about what would happen if your phone gets lost or stolen, or if someone (maybe you) accidentally deleted one of your precious downloads.

You don't actually have to worry, for two reasons.

First, the next time you sync your iPhone with iTunes, iTunes asks if you want the newly purchased apps backed up onto your computer. If you click Transfer, then the programs eventually show up on the Applications tab in iTunes.

Second, here's a handy little fact about the App Store: It remembers your phone and what you've already bought. You can redownload a purchased program at any time, on any of your iPhones, iPads, or iPod Touches, without having to pay for it again.

 Tip If some program doesn't download properly on the iPhone, don't sweat it. Go into iTunes and choose Store→Check for Purchases. And if a program does download to the phone but doesn't transfer to iTunes, choose File→Transfer Purchases from "iPhone". These two commands straighten things out, clear up the accounting, and make all well with your two copies of each program (iPhone + computer).

Shopping in iTunes

You can also download new programs to your computer using iTunes and then sync them over to the phone. By all means use this method whenever you can. It's much more efficient to use a mouse, a keyboard, and a full screen.

In iTunes, click Store (in the Source list). In the iTunes Store box, click App Store.

Now the screen fills with starting points for your quest. There are Top 10 lists (meaning most popular), a Categories list, What's New and What's Hot listings, and so on. Start clicking away to browse the store.

Or use the search box at top right. Be aware, though, that whatever you type here winds up searching the *entire* App Store, complete with pop songs, TV shows, movies, and so on. The results are grouped by category, but you can click Apps (in the Filter box at left) to hide everything except actual apps. Or click Power Search, where you can limit the search to iPhone apps, to free ones, to iPhone-only programs (as opposed to ones that also work on the iPod Touch or iPad), and so on.

From here, the experience is the same as it is on the phone. Drill down to the Details page for a program, read its description and reviews, look at its photos, and so on. Click Buy App to download and, at the next sync, install it.

 Tip The little numbers next to the app names in the iTunes listings (like "4+") are age recommendations. Now you know.

Organizing Your Apps

As you add new apps to your iPhone, it sprouts new Home screens as necessary to accommodate them all, up to a grand total of 11 screens. That's 180 icons—and yet you can actually go all the way up to 2,160 apps, thanks to the miracle of *folders.*

That multiple–Home screen business can get a little unwieldy, but a couple of tools can help you manage. First, the Spotlight search feature can pluck the program you want out of your haystack, as described on page 58.

Second, you can organize your apps into folders, which greatly alleviates the agony of TMHSS (Too Many Home-Screens Syndrome).

It's well worth taking a moment to arrange the icons on your Home screens into logical categories, tidy folders, or at least a sensible sequence.

You can do that either on the phone itself or in iTunes on your computer. (That's a far quicker and easier method, but of course it works only when your phone is actually connected to the Mac or PC.)

Rearranging/Deleting Apps Using iTunes

To fiddle with the layout of your Home screens with the least amount of hassle, connect the iPhone to your computer using the white charging cable or over WiFi. Open iTunes.

Click your iPhone's icon in the left-side list, and then click the Apps tab at the top of the screen. You see the display on the next page.

From here, it's all mouse power:

- Turn on Sync Apps, if necessary, and then turn on the checkboxes of the apps you want on your phone. In other words, you can store hundreds of apps in iTunes but load only some of them onto your iPhone.

- Click one of the Home-screen thumbnails in the scrolling far-right list to indicate which screen you want to edit. Then drag the app icons to rearrange them on that page.

- It's totally fine to drag an app onto a different page thumbnail. You can organize your icons on these Home screens by category, frequency of use, color, or whatever tickles your fancy. (The empty gray thumbnail at the bottom of the thumbnails list means, "Drag an app here to install an additional Home screen.")

 Tip You can select several app icons simultaneously by ⌘-clicking them (or Ctrl-clicking in Windows); that way, you can move a bunch of them at once.

- You can drag the page thumbnails up or down to rearrange *them*, too.

- To delete an app from the iPhone, point to its icon and click the ✖ that appears. (You can't delete the original iPhone apps like Safari and Mail.)

- Create a folder by dragging one app's icon on top of another (see page 240 for more on folders).

When your design spurt is complete, click Apply in the lower-right corner of the screen.

Rearranging/Deleting Apps Right on the Phone

If you're out and about, it may not be practicable to connect to iTunes. Fortunately, you can also redesign your Home screens right on the iPhone.

To enter this Home-screen editing mode, hold your finger down on any icon until, after about a second, the icons begin to—what's the correct term?— *wiggle.* (That's got to be a first in user-interface history.)

 Tip You can even move an icon onto the Dock. Just make room for it by first dragging an *existing* Dock icon to another spot on the screen.

At this point, you can rearrange your icons by dragging them around the glass into new spots; the other icons scoot aside to make room.

Tip You can drag a single icon across multiple Home screens without ever having to lift your finger. Just drag the icon against the right or left margin of the screen to "turn the page."

To create an additional Home screen, drag a wiggling icon to the right edge of the screen; keep your finger down. The first Home screen slides off to the left, leaving you on a new, blank one, where you can deposit the icon. You can create up to 11 Home screens in this way.

You may have noticed that, while your icons are wiggling, most of them also sprout little ⊗'s. That's how you *delete* a program you don't need anymore: Tap that ⊗. You'll be asked if you're sure; if so, it says bye-bye.

(You can't delete one of Apple's preinstalled apps, so no ⊗ appears on those icons. If they really bug you, you can drag the little-used Apple apps into a folder somewhere.)

When everything looks good, press the Home button to stop the wiggling.

Restoring the Home Screen

If you ever need to undo all the damage you've done, tap Settings→General→ Reset→Reset Home Screen Layout. That function preserves any new programs you've installed, but it consolidates them. If you'd put 10 programs on each of four Home screens, you wind up with only two screens, each packed with 20 icons. Any leftover blank pages are eliminated. This function also places all your downloaded apps in alphabetical order.

Folders

Folders. Such a simple concept. So useful on your Mac or PC. But so, so missing during the first three years of the iPhone era.

Now, they're here. Folders let you organize your apps, de-emphasize the ones you don't use often, and restore order to that horribly flat, multipage display of icons.

Setting Up Folders in iTunes

As usual, it's fastest and easiest to set up your folders within iTunes, on your Mac or PC, where you have a mouse and a big screen to help you. Connect your iPhone to your computer (by cable or WiFi), open iTunes, click the iPhone's icon in the list at left, and then click the Apps tab at the top. You see something like the illustration on page 238.

To create a folder, drag one app's icon on top of another. The software puts both of them into a single new folder. If they're the same kind of app, iOS 5 even tries to figure out what category they both belong to—and names the new folder accordingly ("Music," "Photos," "Kid Games," or whatever). As on the iPhone, this new name is only a proposal; an editing window also appears so that you can type a custom name you prefer.

Once you've got a folder, you can open it just by double-clicking. A special black panel sprouts from the folder icon, revealing its contents; the rest of the screen goes dim. Now you can edit the folder's name, drag the icons around inside it, or drag an app right out of the black strip to remove it from the folder.

If you remove all the apps from a folder, the folder disappears.

Setting Up Folders on the iPhone

iTunes is efficient for working with folders, but let's face it: You're not always seated at your computer. (If you were, you wouldn't have bought a pocket computer.)

To create and edit folders right on the phone, you must always begin by entering Home-screen editing mode. That is, hold your finger down on any icon until all the icons begin to wiggle.

At this point, to create a folder, drag one app's icon on top of another. Just like in iTunes, the software puts both of them into a new folder and gives it a proposed name, as shown here.

Drag one app onto another...

...and a new folder is born.

Drop more apps onto the folder to put them inside. In wiggling-icon mode, you can also rename the folder.

Note You can fit up to 12 apps in each folder. And you can have 16 folders on each of your 11 Home screens. And you can have four more folders on the Dock that's always at the bottom of the Home screen. So let's see: 12 apps × 16 folders × 11 Home screens + (4 Dock folders × 12 apps) = 2,160 apps. Apple says you can therefore cram 2,160 apps onto an iPhone!

But wait a minute. Once you've got 15 folder icons on the last page, the 16th icon would have to be a single app icon, and there'd be no way to create a final folder!

Did Apple lie to us? Not exactly. You can't set up 2,160 apps on the iPhone. But remember that you can also organize your Home screens in iTunes. There, you can drag apps around with the mouse—including dragging them from your list of apps in iTunes, freeing you from the "drop an app on an app" limitation. So, yes, by using iTunes, you can create 11 Home screens full of folders, and therefore accommodate 2,160 apps.

(Actually, 2,160 is not the limit even then. That's only how many *icons* show up on the Home screens—but you can keep downloading and downloading, hundreds or thousands more. You can keep going until the iPhone is out of memory. Only 2,160 icons show up—but you can still find and open the others by using Spotlight.)

Once you've created a folder or two, they're easy to rename, move, delete, and so on. (Again, you can do all of the following *only in icon-wiggling editing mode.*) Like this:

- **Take an app out of a folder** by dragging its icon anywhere else on the Home screen. The other icons scoot aside to make room, just as they do when you move them from one Home screen to another.

- **Move a folder around** by dragging, as you would any other icon.

Tip You can drag a folder icon onto the Dock, too, just as you would any app (page 34). Now you've got a popup subfolder full of your favorite apps—on the Dock, which is present on every Home screen. That's a very useful feature; it multiplies the handiness of the Dock itself.

- **Rename a folder** by opening it (tapping it). At this point, the folder's name box is ready for editing.

- **Delete a folder** by removing all of its contents. The folder disappears automatically.

When you're finished manipulating your folders, press the Home button to exit Home-screen editing mode—and stop all the wiggling madness.

App Preferences

If you're wondering where you can change an iPhone app's settings, consider backing out to the Home screen and then tapping Settings. Believe it or not, Apple encourages programmers to add their programs' settings *here,* way down below the bottom of the iPhone's own Settings screen.

Some programmers ignore the advice and build the settings right into their apps, where they're a little easier to find. But if you don't see them there, now you know where else to look.

App Updates

When a circled number appears on the App Store's icon (on the Home screen), or when one appears on the Updates icon within the App Store program, that's Apple's way of letting you know that a program you already own has been updated. The beauty of a single-source catalog like the App Store is that Apple knows which programs you've bought—and notifies you automatically when new, improved versions are released.

When you tap Updates, you're shown a list of the programs with waiting updates. And when you tap a program's name, a details screen tells you precisely what the changes are—new features, perhaps, or some bug fixes.

You can download the update, or all the updates, with a single tap...no charge.

 Note You can also download your updates from iTunes. Click Applications in the Source list (under the Library heading); the lower edge of the window lets you know if there are updated versions of your programs waiting and offers buttons that let you download the updates individually or all at once.

How to Find Good Apps

If the Recommended, What's Hot, and Top 25 lists aren't getting you inspired, there are all kinds of Web sites dedicated to reviewing and recommending iPhone apps. There's *appcraver.com*, for example, and *iphoneappreviews.net*, *whatsoniphone.com*, and on and on.

But if you've never dug into iPhone apps before, you should at the very least try out some of the superstars, the big dogs that almost everybody has.

Here are a few—a very few, a drop in the bucket at the tip of the iceberg—meant only to suggest the infinite variety that's available from the App Store:

- **Dragon Dictation (free).** Speak to type, just like on the iPhone 4S—except it works on older iPhone models, too. After the transcription appears, one tap slaps the text into an outgoing email message, text message, Tweet, or Facebook update. Much faster than typing with your finger.

- **Ocarina ($1).** A bona fide wind instrument. Blow into the microphone, learn the fingerings of the four "holes" on the glass screen…beautiful music.

- **Google Mobile (free).** Speak to search Google's maps. Includes Google Goggles: Point the phone's camera at a book, DVD, wine bottle, logo, painting, landmark or bit of text, and the hyper-intelligent app recognizes it and displays information about it from the Web.

- **LED Light (free).** The powerful LED "flash" on the iPhone 4 and 4S is fantastic for reading menus and show programs in dim light, for inspecting plumbing and car parts in narrow spaces, and for removing splinters. Unfortunately, turning it on involves opening the Camera app, switching to video and turning on the video light. Right? Not anymore. Just open this app to activate the LED instantly—bright and easy.

- **FlightTrack Pro ($10).** Incredible. Shows every detail of every flight: gate, time delayed, airline phone number, where the flight is on the map, and more. Knows more—and knows it sooner—than the actual airlines do.

- **Fake Calls ($1).** When you tap this icon on your Home screen, in about 10 seconds, your phone rings. It's a fake call—from anyone you've selected in advance. The simulation of the iPhone's traditional incoming-call screen is perfect—ring tone, contact info, Mute and Hold buttons, the works. Ideal for extricating yourself from difficult situations, like meetings or bad dates.

- **Line2 (free).** Gives your iPhone a second phone line with its own number—one that makes or receives calls over WiFi when you're in a hotspot (no cellular minutes!), or over your regular carrier when you're not. Unlimited texting, unlimited calling, $10 a month.

- **Twitter (free).** Most free Twitter apps are a bit on the baffling side. This one is the official app from Twitter, Inc., and it's simple and clean; you can download it, in fact, directly from Settings→Twitter.

- **SoundHound (free).** Beats Shazam at its own game. Hold this app up to a song that's playing on the radio, or even hum or sing the song, and the app miraculously identifies the song and offers you lyrics. It's faster than Shazam, too.

- **Bump (free).** If you and another iPhone owner both have this app, you just bump your phones together to exchange business cards (or photos, or other files).

- **MapQuest (free).** Your iPhone has built-in GPS and maps, but it doesn't give you spoken turn-by-turn directions, as a real GPS unit does. Unless, that is, you get this app.

- **Hipstamatic ($2)** turns the screen of the iPhone into a perfect replica of a cheap plastic toy camera of days gone by; by swiping your finger across the lens or the flash or the film window, you can choose different lenses, flashes or film types. It's just a glorified effects picker, and you have to pay extra for additional options. Still, it's cool and creative and really fun.

- **Instagram (free)** is the other buzz of the photo-app world. Yes, it has a bunch of filter effects. But the real magic is in the way it's designed to share your photos. You sign up to receive Instagrams from Facebook

or Twitter folk. They (the photos, not the folk) show up right in the app, scrolling up like a photographic Twitter feed. Seeing what other people are doing every day with their cameraphones and creative urges is really inspirational.

Other essentials: Angry Birds. Skype. Kayak (finds flights). The New York Times, of course. The Amazon Kindle book reader, B&N eReader. Dictionary. Facebook. TEDPlayer. Mint.com. Scrabble. Keynote Remote (controls your Keynote presentations from the phone). Remote (yes, another one, also from Apple—turns the iPhone into a WiFi, whole-house *remote control* for your Mac or PC's music playback).

Foursquare. Pandora. Yelp. Flickr. Instant-messaging apps like AIM and Yahoo Messenger—or apps that connect to multiple networks at once (like IM+ or Beejive IM).

Happy apping!

Multitasking

You don't have to exit one program before opening the next. The iPhone is, more or less, a multitasking phone now.

The big benefit here is speed. You can duck out of what you're doing, check some other app, and return to where you left off—without having to wait for your apps to close and then reopen (which often takes several seconds), and without having to reconstruct how you had things when you left.

Switching out of a program doesn't actually close it. Instead, it's just suspended—frozen in the middle of whatever it was doing—and therefore not using up any battery power or slowing down your little i-computer.

That, of course, is not real multitasking. Just freezing a background program isn't the same as letting it run.

That, however, is just how Apple wants it. If you always left a bunch of apps running in the background, they'd run down your battery in no time (see also: Android phones).

There are some exceptions, however, special cases when Apple permits actual multitasking to take place, where programs are allowed to keep processing away, even in the background. These happy, authorized exceptions:

- **Internet audio.** At long last, you can keep listening to an Internet music service like Pandora or Last.fm, or listen to the game on an Internet radio station, while you tap out some email, surf the Web, or whatever. Just start the radio app playing, and then switch into a different program.

- **GPS apps.** GPS programs are allowed to keep going in the background, too. For navigation apps, that means they'll continue tracking your position, and even speaking the turn-by-turn directions, while you work in other programs. (But not while you're driving, of course…right?)

  Nice touch: If you're listening to music in one app while your GPS app continues to direct you, the iPhone automatically lowers the music volume each time the GPS program speaks an instruction.

  Social-networking apps like Foursquare, which also rely on GPS, can work in the background, too. That is, your friends can track your location even when Foursquare isn't the frontmost app.

- **Internet phone apps.** Apps that let you make calls over WiFi networks, thereby avoiding using up any of your monthly cellular minutes, are one of the greatest joys of iPhonedom. But these programs, like Skype and Line2, always had one huge downside: You couldn't *receive* calls unless the Phone app was open and running. Kind of a bummer, really.

  But now, thanks to multitasking, they can answer incoming calls (and make your iPhone ring) even when they're in the background—and even when the phone is asleep. And once you've answered, you can switch to another app without losing the call—great when you want to consult your calendar, get Google Maps driving instructions, or look up someone's phone number, without having to hang up.

- **Notifications.** Background apps may not be allowed to run in all their glory. They are, however, allowed to send notices to you from the background. They can send you little alert messages, which pop up on the screen much like text messages do. You might get news headlines, requests to play online games, reminders, and other notices, without having to open the relevant program.

The Task Switcher

If you hadn't read about it, you might not even realize that your iPhone can do this multitasking thing. The key to the whole feature is the *task switcher,* the row of icons that appears at the bottom of the screen when you double-press the Home button.

The task switcher is introduced on page 13, but here are the basics:

- **It slides to the left (older apps).** When you double-press the Home button, whatever's on the screen gracefully slides upward to reveal the first segment of the task switcher: the icons of the four apps you've used most recently (shown here at top left). This is awesome; it's amazing how often those are what you want when you need to duck out of what you're doing. You can tap one to open it without having to return to the Home screen or hunt through *multiple* Home screens.

Rotation lock   *Playback controls*   *Current music app*

But if you swipe your finger to the left, you pull into view the next four most recent apps you had open. Swipe again for the *next* four. And so on, and so on, until you're 10 or 12 swipes deep, and you've just wasted a lot of time. (If you had to go that far, you might as well have just used Spotlight!)

When you tap an icon on the task switcher, you open that app. A cool, carousellish animation makes it look like the incoming app is a card flipping out from behind the outgoing one.

- **It slides to the right (Widget bar).** If you double-press the Home button and then swipe to the *right,* you reveal five handy buttons, as shown on the previous page. The first one is Rotation Lock (page 14). The next three are playback controls for your iPod music; the last is the Music app's icon.

  The thought here is that these are functions you need often, so they've been installed on the task switcher, where they're always a couple of swipes and taps away.

- **You can force quit an app.** The task switcher lets you manually exit an app that's misbehaving or frozen. To do that, open the task switcher. Hold your finger down on any one of the apps there until they all start to wiggle (sound familiar)? At this point, a little ⊖ icon appears in the corner of each icon; tap that button to delete the icon. The ones to its right slide in to take its place.

  (The app will return to the lineup the next time you open it from the Home screen; it's not really gone.)

AirPrint: Printing from the Phone

The very phrase "printing from the phone" might seem a little peculiar. How do you print from a gadget that's smaller than a Hershey bar—a gadget without any jacks for connecting a printer?

Wirelessly, of course.

You can send printouts from your phone to any printer that's connected to your Mac or PC on the same WiFi network if you have a piece of software like Printopia ($20).

Or you can use the iPhone's built-in AirPrint technology, which can send printouts directly to a WiFi printer without requiring a Mac or PC.

Not just any WiFi printer, though—only those that recognize AirPrint. A lot of recent Canon, Epson, HP, and Lexmark printers work with AirPrint; you can see a list of them on Apple's Web site, here: *http://support.apple.com/kb/HT4356*.

Not all apps can print. Of the built-in Apple programs, only iBooks, Mail, Photos, and Safari offer Print commands. Those apps contain what most people want to print most of the time: PDF documents (iBooks), email messages, driving directions from the Web, and so on. Plenty of non-Apple apps work with AirPrint, too.

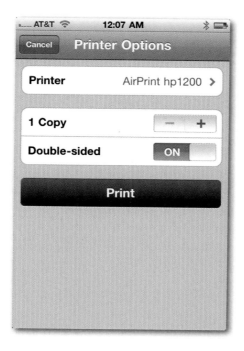

To use Printopia or AirPrint, start by tapping the button. A bunch of sharing-option buttons appear—and one of them says Print. When you tap it, you're offered a few printing options (number of copies and so on)—and when you finally tap Print, your printout shoots wirelessly to the printer, exactly as though your phone and printer were wired together.

> **Tip** While the printing is going on, you can view the Print Queue—the list of printouts-in-waiting. To do that, double-press the Home button to open the task switcher; tap Print Center.

Troubleshooting Apps

Let's face it: Little freebie apps created by amateur programmers aren't always as stable and well-designed as, say, Apple's programs. Plenty of them are glitchy around the edges.

If a program is acting up—opening it returns you immediately to the Home screen, for example, or even restarts the iPhone—follow these steps, in sequence:

- **Open the program again.** Sometimes, second time's the charm.

- **Force quit the program.** Use the task switcher, as described on page 250.

- **Restart the iPhone.** That is, hold down the Sleep switch on the top until the slide to power off note appears. Slide your finger to turn off the iPhone, and then turn it back on again. In many cases, that little micro-nap is all the iPhone needs to get its memory straight again.

- **Reinstall the annoying program.** This one could take several steps. It involves deleting the program from the iPhone and then re-downloading it from the App Store. You'll get a message that says, "You have already purchased this item," which you already knew. Just tap OK. (You won't be charged again.)

- **Reset the iPhone.** If the iPhone is actually *frozen*—nonresponsive—then *reset* it instead. Follow the sequence described on page 504.

Finally, if you're feeling goodwill toward your fellow iPhone-lovers, consider reporting the problem so other people might be spared the headache you've just endured.

To do that, open the App Store on your iPhone. Navigate back to the program as though you were going to download it again. But on its info screen, scroll down and then tap Report a Problem.

Here you can specify what kind of problem you're having (technical or cultural) and type in the specifics.

When you tap Report and then tap OK in the confirmation box, your bug report gets sent along—not to Apple, but to the author of the program, who may or may not be moved to do something about it.

9 The Built-In Apps

Your Home screen comes already loaded with the icons of about 25 programs. These are the essentials, the starting points; eventually, of course, you'll fill that Home screen, and many overflow screens, with additional apps you install yourself. The starter apps include major gateways to the Internet (Safari), critical communications tools (Phone, Messages, Mail, Contacts), visual records of your life (Photos, Camera), Apple shopping centers (iTunes, the App Store), and a well-stocked entertainment center (Music, Videos).

Those essential apps get special treatment in the other chapters in this book. This chapter covers all the rest—the secondary programs, in alphabetical order: Calculator, Calendar, Clock, Compass, Find My Friends, Game Center, iBooks, Maps, Newsstand, Notes, Reminders, Stocks, Voice Memos, Weather, and YouTube.

Calculator

The iPhone wouldn't be much of a computer without a calculator, now would it? And here it is, your everyday memory calculator—with a secret twist.

 Note On a new iPhone, the Calculator sits in a folder called Utilities on the first Home screen.

In its basic four-function mode, you can tap out equations (like *15.4 × 300 =*) to see the answer at the top. (You can *paste* things you've copied into here, too; just hold your finger down until the Paste button appears.)

 Tip When you tap one of the operators (like ×, +, −, or ÷) it sprouts a white outline to help you remember which operation is in progress. Let's see an ordinary calculator do *that!*

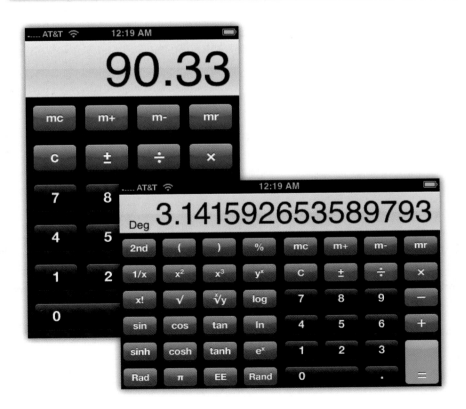

The Memory function works like a short-term storage area that retains numbers temporarily, making it easier to work on complicated problems. When you tap m+, whatever number is on the screen gets added to the number already in the memory; the mr button glows with a white ring to let you know you've stored something there. Press m- to *subtract* the currently displayed number from the number in memory.

And what *is* the number in memory? Press mr to display it—to use it in a subsequent calculation, for example. Finally, tap mc to clear the memory and do away with the white ring.

Now the twist: If you rotate the iPhone 90 degrees in either direction, the Calculator morphs into a full-blown HP *scientific* calculator, complete with trigonometry, logarithmic functions, exponents, roots beyond the square root, and so on. Go wild, ye engineers and physicists!

Calendar

What kind of digital companion would the iPhone be if it didn't have a calendar program? In fact, not only does it have a calendar—but it even has one that syncs with your computer.

If you maintain your life's schedule on a Mac (in iCal or Entourage) or a PC (in Outlook), then you already have your calendar on your iPhone. Make a change in one place, and it changes in the other, every time you sync over the USB cable.

Better yet, if you have an iCloud account or work for a company with an Exchange server (Chapters 14 and 15), then your calendar can be synchronized with your computer *automatically,* wirelessly, over the air.

Or you can use Calendar all by itself.

 Tip The Calendar icon on the Home screen shows what looks like one of those paper Page-a-Day calendar pads. But if you look closely, you'll see a sweet touch: It actually shows *today's* day and date.

Working with Views

By clicking one of the view buttons at the bottom of the screen, you can switch among these views:

- **List** view offers you a tidy chronological list of everything you've got going on, from today forward. Flick or drag your finger to scroll through it.

> **Tip** List view also houses the Spotlight box, which can search your whole calendar. Type a few letters of the appointment's name, and then tap the result in the list to open its Details page.

- **Day** shows a single day's events, broken down by time slot. You can tap the ◀ and ▶ buttons to move backward and forward a day at a time. That's how the suckers do it, though. There's a much better iOS 5 method: *Swipe your finger* across the Day screen.

 Tip Hold down the ◀ or ▶ buttons to zoom through the dates quickly. You can skip into a date next month in just a few seconds.

- **Month** shows the entire month. Dots on the date squares show you when you're busy. Tap a date square to read, in the bottom part of the screen, what you've got going on that day. (You can flick or drag that list to scroll it, although this list isn't what you'd call roomy.)

In all three views, you can tap Today (bottom left) to return to today's date.

There's also a fourth view in iOS 5, which may be the most useful yet: a scrolling Week view, like the one shown here:

No button opens this view; instead, turn the phone 90 degrees, so that it's in landscape mode. Here, you can swipe sideways to move to earlier or later dates. (A "time ruler" column separates one week from the next.) Swipe up or down to move through the hours of the day.

 Note OK, OK—what Apple calls "Week" view shows only three days at a time. Whatever it's called, though, it's very nice to have.

Making an Appointment (List, Day, Month View)

The basic calendar is easy to figure out. After all, with the exception of one unfortunate Gregorian incident, we've been using calendars successfully for centuries.

Even so, recording an event on this calendar is quite a bit more flexible than entering one on, say, one of those "Hunks of the Midwest Police Stations" paper calendars.

Start by tapping the ✚ button (top-right corner of the screen). The Add Event screen pops up, filled with tappable lines of information. Tap one (like Starts/ Ends or Repeat) to open a configuration screen for that element.

 Tip In Month view, here's a great shortcut: You can hold your finger down on one of the tiny date squares to open the Add Event screen. It comes all ready to create an all-day event. That is, you have no option to add specific start and end times; it's better suited for things like "Chris's birthday" or "Last day of school."

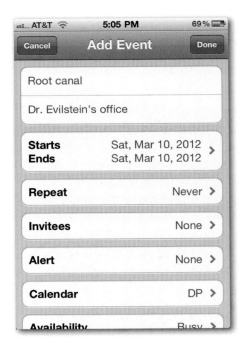

For example:

- **Title/Location.** Name your appointment here. For example, you might type *Fly to Phoenix.*

The second line, called Location, makes a lot of sense. If you think about it, almost everyone needs to record *where* a meeting is to take place. You might type a reminder for yourself like *My place,* a specific address like *212 East 23rd*, a contact phone number, or a flight number.

Use the keyboard as usual. When you're finished, tap Save.

- **Starts/Ends.** On this screen, tap Starts, and then indicate the starting time for this appointment, using the four spinning dials at the bottom of the screen. The first sets the date; the second, the hour; the third, the minute; the fourth, AM or PM. If only real alarm clocks were so much fun!

Then tap Ends, and repeat the process to schedule the ending time. (The iPhone helpfully presets the Ends time to one hour later.)

Appointment, with times

All-day event

An All-day event, of course, has no specific time of day: a holiday, a birthday, a book deadline. When you turn this option on, the Starts and Ends times disappear. The event appears at the top of the list for that day.

Tip Calendar can handle multiday appointments, too, like trips away. Turn on All-day—and then use the Starts and Ends controls to specify beginning and ending *dates*. On the iPhone, you'll see it as a list item that repeats on every day's square. Back on your computer, you'll see it as a banner stretching across the Month view.

Tap Save when you're done.

- **Repeat.** The screen here contains common options for recurring events: every day, every week, and so on. It starts out saying None.

  Once you've tapped a selection, you return to the Edit screen. Now you can tap the End Repeat button to specify when this event should *stop* repeating. If you leave the setting at Repeat Forever, you're stuck seeing this event repeating on your calendar until the end of time (a good choice for recording, say, your anniversary, especially if your spouse might be consulting the same calendar).

  In other situations, you may prefer to spin the three dials (month, day, year) to specify an ending date, which is useful for car and mortgage payments.

- **Invitees.** This new iOS 5 feature lets you invite people to an event—a meeting, a party, whatever—and track their responses, right there on your phone (or any iCloud gadget). When you tap Invitees, you get an Add Invitees screen, where you can type in the email addresses of your lucky guests. (Or tap the ⊕ button to choose them from your Contacts list.)

  When you tap Done, the phone fires off email invitations to those guests. It contains buttons for them to click: Accept, Decline, and Maybe. You get to see their responses right here in the Details of your calendar event.

  As icing on the cake, your guests (at least those hip enough to be using iOS 5) will see a pop-up reminder on their phones when the time comes for the party to get started.

- **Alert.** This screen tells Calendar how to notify you when a certain appointment is about to begin. Calendar can send any of four kinds of flags to get your attention. Tap how much notice you want: 5, 15, or 30 minutes before the big moment; an hour or two before; a day or two before; or on the day of the event.

When you tap Save and return to the main Add Event screen, you see that a new line, called Second Alert, has sprouted up beneath the first Alert line. This line lets you schedule a *second* warning for your appointment, which can occur either before or after the first one. Think of it as a backup alarm for events of extra urgency. Tap Save.

Once you've scheduled these alerts, you'll see a message appear on the screen at the appointed time(s). (Even if the phone was asleep, it appears briefly.) You'll also hear a chirpy alarm sound.

- **Calendar.** Tap here to specify which color-coded *calendar* (category, like Home, Kids, or Work) this appointment belongs to. Turn to page 265 for details on the calendar concept.

- **URL.** Here's a spot where you can record the Web address of some online site that provides more information about this event.

- **Notes.** Here's your chance to customize your calendar event. You can type any text you want in the Notes area—driving directions, contact phone numbers, a call history, or whatever. Tap Save when you're finished.

When you've completed filling in all these blanks, tap Done. Your newly scheduled event now shows up on the calendar.

Making an Appointment (Day View, Week View)

As noted earlier, turning the phone 90 degrees opens up a new, widescreen, scrolling Week view of your life.

In both Day view and this new Week view, you can *hold your finger down on a time slot* to add a new, one-hour appointment right there. You're asked to enter a name and, if you like, location for this new appointment. Tap Done.

You can always edit this appointment's details or duration later, as described next—but this quick-and-dirty technique saves the effort of tapping in Start and End times.

Editing, Rescheduling, and Deleting Events (Long Way)

To examine the details of an appointment in the calendar, tap it once. The Event Details screen appears, filled with the details you previously established.

To edit any of these characteristics, tap Edit. You return to what looks like a clone of the New Event screen shown on page 260.

Here you can change the name, time, alarm, repeat schedule, calendar category, or any other detail of the event, just the way you set them up to begin with.

This time, there's a big red Delete Event button at the bottom. That's the only way to erase an appointment from your calendar.

Editing and Rescheduling Events (Fun Way)

In Day or Week views, you can *drag an appointment's block* to another time slot or even another day. Just hold your finger down on the appointment's bubble for about a second—until a shadow appears around it—before you start to drag. It's a lot quicker and more fluid than having to edit in a dialog box.

You can also change the *duration* of an appointment in Day and Week views. Hold your finger down on its colored block for about 1 second; when you let go, small, round handles appear:

You can drag those tiny handles up or down to make the block taller or shorter, in effect making it start or end at a different time.

Whether you drag the whole block, the top edge, or the bottom edge, the iPhone thoughtfully displays ":15," ":30," or ":45" on the left-side time ruler to let you know where you'll be when you let go.

The Calendar (Category) Concept

A *calendar,* in Apple's somewhat confusing terminology, is a color-coded sub-set—a *category*—into which you can place various appointments. They can be anything you like. One person might have calendars called Home, Work, and TV Reminders. Another might have Me, Spouse 'n' Me, and The Kidz. A small business could have categories called Deductible Travel, R&D, and R&R.

In iOS 5, for the first, time, you can create and edit calendar categories right on the iPhone—not just in your desktop calendar program. Or, if you're an iCloud member, you can also set up your categories at *www.icloud.com* when you're at your computer; all your categories and color-codings show up on the iPhone automatically.

At any time, on the iPhone, you can choose which subset of categories you want to see. Just tap Calendars at the top of any calendar view. You arrive at the big color-coded list of your categories (below, left).

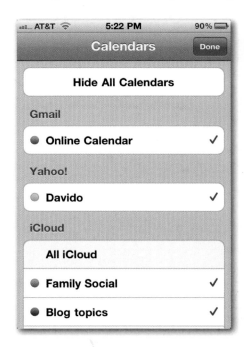 

This screen exists partly as a reference, a cheat sheet to help you remember what color goes with which category, and partly as a tappable subset-chooser. That is, you can tap a category's name to hide or show all of its appointments on the calendar. A checkmark means that you're seeing its appointments.

If you tap Edit, a little > appears next to each calendar's name. If you tap it, you're offered a screen where you can change the calendar's name or color—or scroll all the way down to see the Delete Calendar button.

The Edit Calendars screen also offers an Add Calendar button. It's the key to creating, naming, and colorizing a new calendar on the phone. (Whatever changes you make to your calendar categories on the phone will be synced back to your Mac or PC.)

You can set up real-time, wireless connections to calendars published on the Web in the CalDAV format—notably your Yahoo or Google calendar. Just tap your way to Settings→Mail, Contacts, Calendars→Add Account. Here, you can tap iCloud, Microsoft Exchange, Gmail, Yahoo, AOL, or Hotmail to set up your account. (You can also tap Other→Add CalDAV Account to fill in the details of a less well-known calendar server.)

Now you have a two-way synced calendar between your iPhone and (in this case) your online calendar. To read about other ways of syncing the iPhone with online calendars, including read-only .ics files (like sports-team schedules), download the PDF appendix called "Syncing Calendar with .ics Files" from this book's "Missing CD" page at *www.missingmanuals.com*.

Clock

It's not just a clock—it's more like a time factory. Hiding behind this single icon on the Home screen are four programs: a world clock, an alarm clock, a stopwatch, and a countdown timer.

 On a new iPhone, the Clock comes stored in a folder called Utilities on the first Home screen.

World Clock

When you tap World Clock on the Clock screen, you start out with only one clock, showing the current time in Apple's own Cupertino, California.

The neat part is that you can open up *several* of these clocks and set each one up to show the time in a different city. The result looks like the row of clocks in a hotel lobby, making you seem Swiss and precise.

By checking these clocks, you'll know what time it is in some remote city, so you don't wake somebody up at what turns out to be 3 a.m.

To specify which city's time appears on the clock, tap the **+** button at the upper-right corner. The keyboard pops up so you can type the name of a major city. As you type, a scrolling list of matching city names appears above the keyboard; tap the one whose time you want to track.

As soon as you tap a city name, you return to the World Clock display. The color of the clock indicates whether it's daytime (white) or night (black). Note, too, that you can scroll the list of clocks. You're not limited to four, although only four fit on the screen at once.

Tip Only the world's major cities are in the iPhone's database. If you're trying to track the time in Squirrel Cheeks, New Mexico, consider adding a major city in the same time zone instead—like Albuquerque.

To edit the list of clocks, tap Edit. Delete a city clock by tapping ⊖ and then Delete, or drag clocks up or down using the ☰ as a handle. Then tap Done.

Alarm

If you travel much, this feature could turn out to be one of your iPhone's most useful functions. It's reliable, it's programmable, and it even wakes *the phone* first, if necessary, to wake *you.*

To set an alarm, tap Alarm at the bottom of the Clock program's screen. You're shown the list of alarms you've already created, even if none are currently set to go off (facing page, right). For example, you might create a 6:30 a.m. alarm for weekdays, and an 11:30 a.m. alarm for weekends.

To create a new alarm, tap the **+** button at the upper-right corner to open the Add Alarm screen (below, right).

You have several options here:

- **Repeat.** Tap to specify what days this alarm rings. You can specify, for example, Mondays, Wednesdays, and Fridays by tapping those three buttons. (Tap a day-of-the-week button again to turn off its checkmark.) Tap Back when you're done.

- **Sound.** Here's where you specify what sound you want to ring when the time comes. You can choose from any of the iPhone's 25 ringtone sounds, or any you've added yourself. Tap Back.

- **Snooze.** If this option is on, then at the appointed time, the alarm message on the screen offers you a Snooze button. Tap it for 10 more minutes of sleep, at which point the iPhone tries again to get your attention.

- **Label.** Tap to give this alarm a description, like "Get dressed for wedding." That message appears on the screen when the alarm goes off.

- **Time dials.** Spin these three vertical wheels—hour, minute, AM/PM—to specify the time you want the alarm to go off.

When you finally tap Save, you return to the Alarm screen, which lists your new alarm. Just tap the On/Off switch to cancel an alarm. It stays in the list, though, so you can quickly reactivate it another day, without having to redo the whole thing. You can tap the ✚ button to set another alarm, if you like.

Note, too, that the ● icon appears in the status bar at the top of the iPhone screen. That's your indicator that the alarm is set.

To delete or edit an alarm, tap Edit. Tap ⊖ and then Delete to get rid of an alarm completely, or tap the alarm's name to return to the setup screen, where you can make changes to the time, name, sound, and so on.

So what happens when the alarm goes off? The iPhone wakes itself up, if it was asleep. A message appears on the screen, identifying the alarm and the time.

And, of course, the sound rings. This alarm is one of the only iPhone sounds that you'll hear *even if the silencer switch is turned on.* Apple figures that if you've gone to the trouble of setting an alarm, you probably *really* want to know about it, even if you forget to turn the ringer back on.

In that case, the screen says, slide to stop alarm.

To cut the ringing short, tap OK or Snooze, or press the Sleep switch, or tap a volume button. After the alarm plays (or you cut it short), its On/Off switch goes to Off (on the Alarm screen).

 Tip Oddly enough, however, flipping the silencer switch isn't the same thing as turning the volume all the way down to zero.

If you just turn on the iPhone's silencer switch, then the alarm will ring *and* vibrate. If you choose None as the alarm sound, it won't ring *or* vibrate.

But if you press the Volume Down key all the way to zero, whatever alarm you've set becomes a silent, *vibrating* alarm. It can be a subtle cue that it's time to wrap up your speech, conclude a meeting, or end a date so you can get home to watch *American Idol.*

Stopwatch

You've never met a more beautiful stopwatch than this one. Tap Start to begin timing something: a runner, a train, a long-winded person who's arguing with you.

While the digits are flying by, you can tap Lap as often as you like. Each time, the list at the bottom identifies how much time elapsed since the *last* time you tapped Lap. It's a way for you to compare, for example, how much time a runner is spending on each lap around a track.

(The tiny digits at the *very* top measure the *current* lap.)

You can do other things on the iPhone while the stopwatch is counting, by the way. In fact, the timer keeps ticking away even when the iPhone is asleep! As a result, you can time long-term events, like how long it takes an ice sculpture to melt, the time it takes for a bean seed to sprout, or the length of a Michael Bay movie.

Tap Stop to freeze the counter; tap Start to resume the timing. If you tap Reset, you reset the counter to zero and erase all the lap times.

Timer

The fourth Clock mini-app is a countdown timer. You input a starting time, and it counts down to zero.

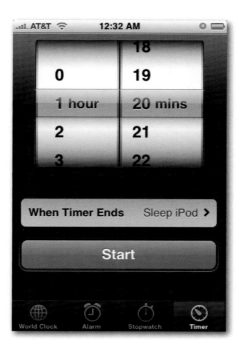

Countdown timers are everywhere in life. They measure the periods in sports and games, of cooking times in the kitchen, of penalties on *The Amazing Race*. But on the iPhone, the timer has an especially handy function: It can turn off the music or video after a specified amount of time. In short, it's a Sleep timer that plays you to sleep and then shuts off to save power.

To set the timer, open the Clock app and then tap Timer. Spin the two dials to specify the number of hours and minutes you want to count down.

Then tap the When Timer Ends control to set up what happens when the timer reaches 0:00. Most of the options here are ringtone sounds, so you'll have an audible cue that the time's up. The top one, though, Sleep iPod, is the aforementioned sleep timer. It stops audio and video playback at the appointed time, so that you (and the iPhone) can go to sleep. Tap Set.

Finally, tap Start. Big clock digits count down toward zero. While it's in progress, you can do other things on the iPhone, change the When Timer Ends settings, or just hit Cancel to forget the whole thing.

> On the iPhone 4S, it's much faster and simpler to use Siri to start, pause, and resume the Timer. See page 106.

Compass

Yeah, yeah: WiFi, camera, Bluetooth, music, touchscreen, tilt sensor—all phones have that stuff these days. But the iPhone still has something the also-rans lack: a magnetic-field sensor known as a magnetometer, which is even better known as a compass.

> On a new iPhone, the Compass comes stored in a folder called Utilities on the first Home screen.

When you open the Compass app, you get exactly what you'd expect: a classic Boy Scout wilderness compass that always points north.

Except it does a few things the Boy Scout compasses never did. Like displaying a digital readout of your heading (shown on the facing page, right) or displaying your precise geographic coordinates at the bottom, or offering a choice of *true* north (the "top" point of the Earth's rotational axis) or *magnetic* north (the spot traditional compasses point to, which is about 11 degrees away from true north). (Tap the ⓘ to specify which north you prefer.)

The very first time you use the Compass app (or anytime you're standing near something big and metal—or magnetic, like stereo speakers), you get the little message shown above at left. It's telling you to move away from the big metal thing, and to de-confuse the compass by moving it through 3-D space in a big figure 8. (Yes, you look like a deranged person, but it's good exercise.)

Once the compass is working, hold it roughly parallel to the ground, and then read it like…a compass.

For many people, the real power of the compass isn't even on display here. It's when you're using the Maps program. (You can jump directly from Compass to Maps by tapping the ◤ button in the lower-left corner.)

The compass powers the map-orientation feature—the one that shows you not just where you are on the map, but which way you're facing. That's a rather critical detail when you're lost in a city, trying to find a new address, or emerging from the subway with no idea which way to walk.

But there's more magic yet. People who write iPhone programs can tap into the compass's information, too, and use it in clever new ways. There's an "augmented reality" app called New York Nearest Subway, for example. By using the compass, GPS, and tilt-sensor information, it knows exactly where you are, which way you're facing, and how you're holding the phone—and so it superimposes, in real time, arrows that show you where to find the nearest New York subway stop and which line it's on. Freaky.

Find My Friends

Thanks to components like the compass and the GPS, the iPhone knows where you are at all times. And thanks to the Internet, it's capable of transmitting this information.

That's the secret behind Find My Friends, a free iOS 5 app from Apple that lets you see, on a map, where your friends and family are right now. It's not a tool for spying; your friends have to *want* to be tracked. They have to share their location-tracking data with you in particular. But if it's Saturday night and you're wondering where the gang is hanging out, or if you're on a trip and wonder where your parents are, or if you've provided your teenager with an iPhone on the condition that she allow you to see where she is when she's out, Find My Friends can be very convenient indeed.

 Note Find My Friends doesn't come preinstalled. You have to get it from the App Store—a quick, free download. It also requires an iCloud account.

It's pretty clear that Find My Friends could, if it falls into the wrong hands, pose an invasion of your privacy; that's why privacy controls are baked in all the way through, as you'll soon see.

 Tip Life with Find My Friends is simpler if you've protected your iPhone with a password, because you're always automatically logged into Find My Friends.

If not, you have to enter your Apple ID each time you want to use the app, which is something of a hassle.

In either case, Apple just wants to make sure there's at least *some* way to prevent evil passersby from picking up your phone and tracking your friends and family.

Setting Up Stalking

Find My Friends (or Find Friends, as its iPhone icon says) does nothing for you unless you've done one of these things:

- **Ask to track someone forever.** Tap the All tab at the bottom of the screen, and then tap the ✚ button in the top-right corner. You're asked for your friend's email address, or you can tap the ⊕ button and choose his name from your Contacts list. You're also given the chance to enter a message ("Hi! I'd like to stalk you now!" works fine). When you tap Send, your request lands on the Requests tab of Find My Friends on *his* iOS 5 gadget.

 Note If the person isn't using the Find My Friends app yet, or isn't logged into it using the email address you used, then your invitation takes the form of an email message. It explains how to get the app and set it up.

If he approves your request, then whenever he's logged into Find My Friends, you get to see his position on a Google map, as described in the next section. (He can't see *your* location, though, until he sends *you* an invitation that you accept.)

- **Track a bunch of people temporarily.** One of the app's primary missions is helping a bunch of you get together—for a show, drinks, dinner, a party, whatever. That's the purpose of the Temporary tab: to quickly turn on tracking for a group of pals simultaneously, so everybody can see where everybody else is as you assemble.

Tap it, add the email addresses of the people who'll be joining you (or tap the ⊕ button and choose them from Contacts), type a name for the event, and specify when this universal-stalking period should end (for example, 30 minutes after the party starts). Tap Send. Everybody who accepts the invitation can see everybody else's locations until the time period expires.

On the details page for the event, you can edit the event's name or time whenever you like (everyone else will be notified). You can also invite someone new to the group (tap Add Friends) or uninvite somebody who's just irritated you (swipe across that person's name and tap Remove).

 Note To delete an event that you created, tap Temporary, tap the event's name, and then tap Delete. The event disappears from everybody's screen at once, and you can no longer follow one another.

You can also remove yourself from an event that somebody else created. Tap Temporary, tap the event's name, and then tap Leave Bowling Gang (or whatever it's called).

- **Publish your own location.** If you tap the Temporary tab, you can invite somebody to see where you are for a limited time only.

Accepting an Invitation

Now turn the tables. Suppose somebody has asked *you* to share *your* location.

If that person invited you using the same email address you've used to sign into Find My Friends, then a little number appear on your Requests inbox (lower right). Tap to see who's asking. If the invite came to a different address, it shows up as an email message. Click View Request to accept or decline.

If you tap Accept, then this person will be able to see your location anytime she wants. Actually, that's not true: You're not visible unless you've opened the app and signed in with your password.

 Tip: If you need to disappear from view for a while—you don't think the world needs to know about your visit to Billy Bob's Discount Teeth Whitening, for example—tap the Me tab, and then turn on Hide from Followers.

If you tap Decline—and you should, if it's somebody you don't know—then that person can't see where you are. (He also doesn't get any notification that you've tapped Decline.)

 Note: If you change your mind about allowing someone to follow you, tap the Me tab. Swipe your finger across that person's name, and then tap Remove.

Parental Controls

If you'd sleep better knowing that your kid can't be followed by anybody except people you've approved, or can't follow anybody without your permission, Apple is ready for you.

First, get your kid's stalkers and stalkees set up the way you want, as described above. Then open Settings→General→Restrictions→Find My Friends. Make up a numeric password (not the one that unlocks the iPhone) and tap Don't Allow Changes. From now on, nobody can change the following/follower setup without that password.

Using the Map

Once somebody has approved your invitation, or once you're part of a temporary group, you're now following them. Tap the All tab to see a list of everybody you're now following, temporarily or not; or tap Temporary to see only the people who've been invited to see one another en route to a gathering.

If the location features of your phone and theirs are working, little mileage signs let you know how far away they are. ("99+" means "99 miles away or more," also known as "not available for dinner in half an hour.") You also get to see the last time the app was able to get a fix on each person's location.

 They're sorted by distance from you. Scroll up, above the All Friends **heading, to see a** Name **button that lets you sort alphabetically instead.**

Tap someone's name to open an Info page showing her current location, address, and other contact information. Tap the address to see her current location on Google Maps. (The purple dot represents her; the blue dot is you; the circle indicates the margin of error in the location calculation.)

All the usual Google Maps tricks apply, as described later in this chapter. You can spread two fingers to zoom in, tap the ▰ button to switch in or out of aerial-photo view, and so on. Tap All Friends to see colored dots representing all your friends, or tap the ◤ button to see *you* on the map.

Tap someone's map dot to see her current address, send a text message, call her via FaceTime, or get directions to her spot. (On the Temporary tab, you can also tap Send iMessage, which broadcasts a message to everybody in your invited gang simultaneously.)

 To remove someone from the list of people you follow, tap the All **tab. Swipe across the person's name, and then tap** Remove.

Labeling Locations

If you and your buddies frequent certain addresses often—homes and work-places come to mind—you can label them for easier recognition on the map and in the follower lists.

To change your own location's label, tap the Me tab; to change a friend's location label, tap All, and then tap the person's name.

Now you see a label. It's probably just a city and state name. Tap it for a choice of None (just the city and state will appear), a canned label like Home or School, or Custom (you can type whatever label you want).

Tip: If you can't seem to change the label, it's probably because the other guy is in a place with lousy cell coverage.

A Word about Email Addresses

If you have multiple email addresses, things can get very complicated. If you sign into one of them in Find My Friends, but someone invites you using a different address, you won't get the message in your Requests box. If you can't seem to exchange iMessages with your followers, it's probably because you've signed into iMessage with one address and Find My Friends with another. And so on.

There are ways out of all of these messes. To read about them, open the little-known Help screens for Find My Friends. Tap the Me tab, tap Account, and then tap Find My Friends Help. There's good troubleshooting help in there, too—check it if you can't seem to see friends' locations, or if they can't seem to see yours.

 Note: In related news: Find My Friends identifies you by your Apple ID. So it's not much good for tracking your spouse or your kids if you're sharing the same iCloud account (that is, the same Apple ID). The solution: Create a different iCloud account for each person.

Game Center

Although not everyone realizes it, the iPhone is an accomplished gaming device, the equal of Sony's PlayStation Portable or Nintendo's DS. iPhone features like the accelerometer and touchscreen are perfect for a multitude of games, from first-person shoot-'em-ups to causal games that require nothing more complicated than dragging a tile across the iPhone's screen. Game makers have responded to the iPhone—on the App Store, the Games category is one of the most active sections, with tens of thousands of games available.

To help fan the flames of iPhone gaming, Apple created Game Center in 2010 as a way for iOS device owners to compare scores with their friends and to challenge buddies to games. In iOS 5, Apple added features aimed at making it easier to find both friends and games.

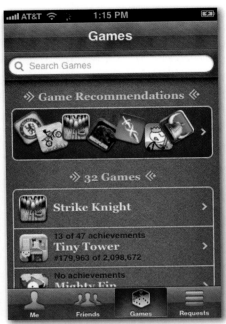

Here's what you can expect when you launch Game Center.

Getting Started

You have to sign up for Game Center before you can use it, but the process is simple: Just enter your Apple ID and password (page 490).

You'll be asked to create a nickname—"AngriestBird" or "BobSmith2000," for example. This nickname is public and can appear on the leaderboards (scoreboards that show the highest point winners) for iOS games; you can also use this nickname when you play multiplayer apps like Super Stickman Golf against other people. You can also turn two settings on and off: One lets friends invite you to play games; the other makes your public profile visible to other Game Center members.

That public profile includes a photo of yourself; you can grab one from your photo library or shoot it from within Game Center itself using the iPhone's front-facing camera. You also have space to write a short little description of yourself, like the bio line in Twitter.

Once all that's in place, the Me tab in Game Center displays your nickname, that clever little phrase you wrote, and your picture. Beneath that, multicol-ored banners display the number of Game Center-compatible games you own, the number of Game Center friends you have, and—perhaps most sig-nificantly—the number of points you've accrued from your gaming activities.

Points and Achievements

Points play a leading role in Game Center. They're what you earn from racking up achievements in Game Center-compatible apps. Smash enough blocks in Angry Birds Seasons, or build a certain number of floors in Tiny Tower, and you unlock achievements in those games; those achievements translate to points, which show up in your Game Center profile.

Those points also provide a way to measure yourself against your friends. On Game Center's Friends tab, you can tap the name of one of your friends. You get a choice of three views: the games your friends play, the names of *their* friends, and the number of points they've tallied. That points view features a side-by-side comparison showing your respective accomplishments in commonly played games, so you can settle once and for all who's tops at Tiny Wings. (Game Center also shows the points your friends have racked up in games you *don't* own, which is Apple's way of suggesting that maybe you should download more games.)

Making Friends

Of course, before you can compare your scores with your friends, you have to *have* some friends. Tap the **+** button in the upper-left corner of the Friends screen to open the Friend Request page, where you can invite someone to be your Game Center buddy using either his nickname or his email address. (Email is probably the better choice, as you may not know your friend's Game Center nickname or he may not be signed up to the service anyhow.) You don't even have to come up with a message—Game Center helpfully proposes a boilerplate friend request in the body of your email (you can edit it).

But what if you don't have any existing friends, or at least none that you know are on Game Center? At the top of the Friends tab, you can tap Recommendations to see a list of potential buddies. They're strangers, of course, but they're based on friends and games you have in common. Tapping one of those names takes you to a page that shows common friends, if any, and a Send Friend Request button.

You can also find gaming companions through your other Game Center friends. Just tap on a name in the list of your current friends, and then select the Friends view on their page to see who *they* hang out with in Game Center when they're not matching scores with you.

Finding Games

Game Center can also help you find games to play—specifically, games that are designed to tie in with Game Center. The Recommendations button at the top of the Games tab takes you to a list of suggested games. Game Center bases these recommendations on what you already own, what your friends play, and popular App Store downloads. Selecting a game in the Recommendations list shows you leaderboards, achievements you can unlock, and which of your friends are playing the game. You can download the app right from this screen.

You can also buy games directly from the list of games your friends play within the Friends tab. Tap a game name to see your friends' rankings, or tap the price tag to download the game directly.

Finally, the Games tab features a list of all the Game Center-compatible games you've installed on your iPhone, in order of the last time you played them. At the bottom of that list is a Find Game Center Games button; tap that, and you'll leave Game Center, launching the App Store application on your iPhone.

iBooks

iBooks is Apple's ebook reading program. It's a free download from the App Store, and it turns the iPhone into a sort of pocket-sized Kindle. With iBooks, you can carry around dozens or hundreds of books in your pocket, which, in the pre-ebook days, would have drawn some funny looks in public.

Most people think of iBooks as a reader for books that Apple sells on its iTunes bookstore—bestsellers and current fiction, for example—and it does that very well. But you can also load it up with your own PDF documents, as well as thousands of free, older, out-of-copyright books.

 Tip iBooks is very cool and all. But in the interest of fairness, it's worth noting that Amazon's free Kindle app, and Barnes & Noble's free B&N eReader app, are much the same thing—but offer much bigger book libraries at lower prices than Apple's.

Downloading Books

To shop the iBooks bookstore, open the iBooks app. Tap Store in the upper-right corner. Here's the literary equivalent of the App Store, complete with

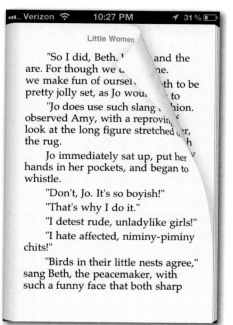

the icons across the bottom. Tap Featured to see what Apple's plugging this week; Charts to see this week's bestsellers, including what's on the *New York Times* Best Seller list; Browse to view the most popular iBook titles—note that there's a special tab for *free* books; Search to search by name; and Purchased to see what you've bought.

 Tip Once you've bought a book from Apple, you can download it again on other iPhones, iPod Touches, iPads, and (someday, when Apple releases the necessary reader software), Macs and PCs. Buy once, read many times. That's the purpose of the Not On This iPhone **tab, which appears when you tap** Purchased.

Once you find a book that looks good, you can tap Get Sample to download a free chapter, read ratings and reviews, or tap the price itself to buy the book and download it straight to the phone.

PDFs and ePub Files

Apple's bookstore isn't the only way to get books. You can also load up your ebook reader from your computer, feeding it with PDF documents and ePub files.

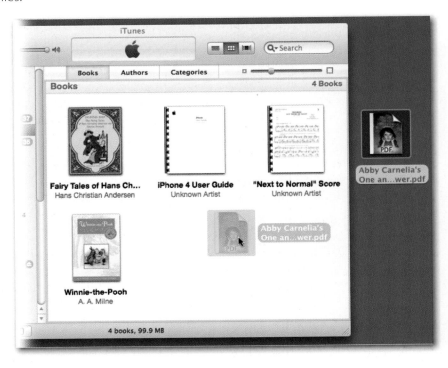

As usual, iTunes is the most convenient loading dock for files bound for your iPhone. Open the program on your Mac or PC. Click Books in the Library list at the left side. Here you'll see all the books, PDF documents, and ePub files that you've slated for transfer.

To add to this set, just drag files off of your desktop and directly into this window, as shown on the facing page.

And where are you supposed to get all these files? Well, PDF documents are everywhere—people send them as attachments, and you can turn any document into a PDF file. (For example, on the Mac, in any program, choose File→Print; in the resulting dialog box, click PDF→Save as PDF.)

 If you get a PDF document as an email attachment, adding it to iBooks is even easier. Tap the attachment to open it; now tap Open in iBooks in the corner of the page. (The iPhone may not be able to open really huge PDFs, though.)

But free ebooks in ePub format are everywhere, too. There are 33,000 free downloadable books at *gutenberg.org*, for example, and over a million at *books.google.com*—oldies, but classic oldies, with lots of Mark Twain, Agatha Christie, Herman Melville, H.G. Wells, and so on. (Lots of these are available in the Free pages of Apple's own iBook store, too.)

 You'll discover that these freebie books usually come with generic-looking covers. But once you've dragged them into iTunes, it's easy to add a good-looking cover. Use *images.google.com* to search for the book's title. Right-click (or Control-click) the cover image in your Web browser; from the shortcut menu, choose Copy Image. In iTunes, right-click (or Control-click) the generic book; choose Get Info; click Artwork; and paste the cover you copied. Now that cover will sync over to the iPhone along with the book.

Once you've got some books loaded up in iTunes, you specify which ones you want synced to the phone by connecting the iPhone, clicking its icon in the list at left, clicking the Books tab at top, and turning on the checkboxes of the books you want to transfer.

Your Library

Once you've supplied your iBooks app with some reading material, the fun begins. When you open the app, you see a handsome wooden bookshelf, with your own personal library represented as little book covers. Mostly what you'll do here is tap a book to open it. But there are all kinds of other activities waiting for you:

- You can reorganize your bookshelf. Hold down your finger on a book until it swells with pride, and then drag it into a new spot.

- If you've loaded some PDF documents, you can switch between the Books and PDFs bookshelves by tapping the buttons at top.

- If you drag your finger down, you reveal a ☰ icon, which switches the book-cover view to a much more boring (but more compact) list view. (Buttons at the bottom let you sort the list by author, title, category, and so on.) And there's a search box, too, which lets you search your books' titles—helpful if you have an enormous library.

- Tap Edit if you want to delete a book, or a bunch of them. To do that, tap each book thumbnail that you want to target for termination; observe how they sprout C marks. Then tap Delete. Of course, deleting a book from the phone doesn't delete your safety copy in iTunes or online.

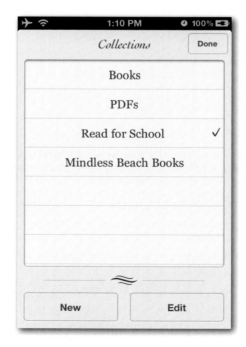

In Edit mode, once you've tapped a book to select it (or several), the Move button becomes available. When you tap it, you get the Collections screen shown here. The idea is that you can create subfolders for your books, called **collections.** You might have one for school, one for work, and a third for somebody who shares your phone, for example. Tap an existing collection to move the selected titles, or tap New to create and name a new collection.

 Tip To switch your bookshelf view among collections, tap the collection's name. It's the top-center button, which starts out saying Books or PDFs.

Reading

But come on—you're a reader, not a librarian. Here's how you read an ebook.

Open the book or PDF by tapping the book cover. Now the book opens, ready for you to read. Looks great, doesn't it? (If you're returning to a book you've been reading, iBooks remembers your place.)

 Tip Turn the phone 90 degrees for a wider column of text. The whole page image rotates with you.

In general, reading is simple: Just read. Turn the page by tapping the edge of the page—or swiping your finger across the page. (If you swipe slowly, you can actually see the "paper" bending over—in fact, you can see through to the "ink" on the other side of the page! Amaze your friends.) You can tap or swipe the left edge (to go back a page) or the right edge (forward).

 Tip This, incidentally, is Rotation Lock's big moment. When you want to read lying down, you can prevent the text from rotating 90 degrees using Rotation Lock (page 14).

But if you tap a page, a row of additional controls appears:

- Library takes you back to the bookshelf view.

- ☰ opens the Table of Contents. The chapter or page names are "live"— you can tap one to jump there.

- ☼ opens a screen-brightness slider (next page). That's a nice touch, because the brightness of the screen makes a big difference in the comfort of your reading—and going all the way to Settings to make the change is a real pain. (The brightness you set here doesn't affect the brightness level of all the other apps—only iBooks.)

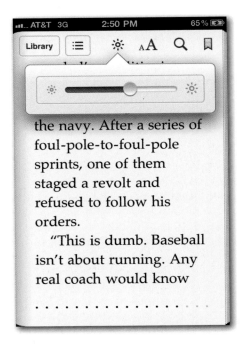

- $_A$A lets you change the type size. That's a huge feature for people with tired or over-40 eyes. And it's something paper books definitely can't do.

  The same pop-out panel offers a Fonts button, where you can choose from five different typefaces for your book, as well as a Sepia On/Off button, which lets you specify whether the page itself is white or off-white.

- Q opens the Search box. It lets you search for text within the book you're reading, which can be extremely useful. As a bonus, there are also Search Google and Search Wikipedia buttons, so that you can hop online to learn more about something you've just read.

- ▤ adds a bookmark to the current page. This isn't like a physical bookmark, where there's only one in the whole book; you can use it to flag as many pages, for as many reasons, as you like.

- **Page dots.** At the bottom of the screen, the horizontal dots represent the chapters of your book. Tap or drag the slider to jump around in the book; as you drag, a pop-up indicator shows you what page number you're scrolling to. (If you've magnified the font size, of course, your book suddenly consumes more pages.)

 Tip An iBook can include pictures and even videos. Double-tap a picture in a book to zoom in on it.

When you're reading a PDF document, by the way, you can do something you can't do when reading regular books: zoom in and out using the usual two-finger pinch-and-spread gestures. Very handy indeed.

 Tip On the other hand, here are some features that *don't* work in PDF files (only ebooks): font and type-size changes, page-turn animations, sepia background on/off, the dictionary, highlighting, and notes.

Notes, Bookmarks, Highlighting, Dictionary

Here are some more stunts that you'd have trouble pulling off in a printed book. If you *double-tap* a word, or *hold your finger down* on a word, you get a bar that offers these options:

- **Copy.** You're all set to copy the selected text to the iPhone's Clipboard, so you can email a juicy quote to somebody who needs a point proven.

- **Dictionary.** Opens up a graceful, elegant page from iBooks' built-in dictionary. You know—in the unlikely event that you encounter a word you don't know.

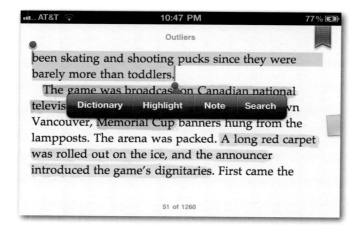

- **Highlight.** Adds yellow transparent highlighting to the word you tapped. For best results, don't tap the Highlight button until you've first grabbed the blue dot handles and dragged them to enclose the entire passage you want highlighted.

 Tip Once you've highlighted some text, you can tap it to open another row of tappable buttons. Colors lets you change the highlighting hue (five choices); Note lets you add a note, as described next; and Remove Highlight does just what it says.

- **Note.** This feature creates highlighting on the selected passage *and* opens an empty yellow sticky note, complete with keyboard, so you can type in your own annotations. When you tap Done, your note collapses down to a tiny yellow Post-it peeking out from the right edge of the margin. Tap it to reopen it.

  To delete a note, tap the highlighted text. Tap Remove Note.

- **Search** opens the same search box that you'd get by tapping the Q icon—except this time, the highlighted word is already filled in, saving you a bit of typing.

There are a couple of cool things going on with your bookmarks, notes, and highlighting, by the way. Once you've added them to your book, they're magically and wirelessly synced to any other copies of that book—on other gadgets, like the iPad or iPod Touch (or other iPhones). Very handy indeed.

Furthermore, if you tap the ☰ button to open the Table of Contents, you'll see a Bookmarks tab. It presents a tidy list of all your bookmarked pages, notes, and highlighted passages. As usual, tap a page to jump there.

 Tip iBooks can actually read to you! Just turn on VoiceOver (see page 150, which also explains some of the other changes in your lifestyle that are required when VoiceOver is turned on).

Then open a book. Tap the first line (to get the highlighting off the buttons at the top).

Now swipe down the page with two fingers to make the iPhone start reading the book to you, out loud, with a synthesized voice. It even turns the pages automatically and keeps going until you tap with two fingers to stop it.

Yes, this is exactly the feature that debuted in the Amazon Kindle and was then removed when publishers screamed bloody murder—but somehow, so far, Apple has gotten away with it.

Maps

Google Maps on the Web is awesome already. It lets you type in any address or point of interest in the U.S. or many other countries—and see it plotted on a map. You have a choice of a street-map diagram or an actual aerial photo, taken by satellite. Google Maps is an incredible resource for planning a drive, scoping out a new city before you travel there, investigating the proximity of a new house to schools and stores, seeing how far a hotel is from the beach, or just generally blowing your mind with a new view of the world.

And now you've got Google Maps on the iPhone, with even more features—like turn-by-turn driving directions, a live national Yellow Pages business directory, GPS that pinpoints your current location, and real-time traffic-jam alerts, represented by color-coding on the roads shown on the map.

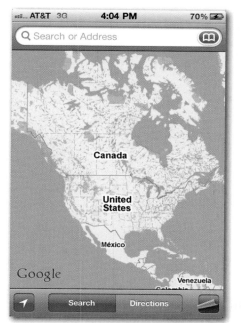 

Browsing the Maps

The very first time you open Maps, you see a miniature U.S. map. Double-tap to zoom in, over and over again, until you're seeing actual city blocks. You can also pinch or spread two fingers to magnify or shrink the view. Drag or flick to scroll around the map.

To zoom *out* again, use the rare *two-finger tap.* So—zoom in with *two* taps using one finger; zoom out with *one* tap using two fingers.

At any time, you can tap the curling-page button in the corner of the screen (◢) to open a secret panel of options. Here you can tap your choice of amazing map views: Map (street-map illustration), Satellite (stunning aerial photos), or Hybrid (photos superimposed with street names).

There's no guarantee that the Satellite view provides a very *recent* photo—different parts of the Google Maps database use photography taken at different times—but it's still very cool.

 You'll know when you've zoomed in to the resolution limits of Google's satellite imagery; it will just stop zooming. Do some two-finger taps to back out again.

Location, Location, Location

If any phone can tell you where you are, it's the iPhone. It has not one, not two, but *three* ways to determine your location.

- **GPS.** First, the iPhone contains a traditional GPS chip, of the sort that's found in automotive navigation units from Garmin, TomTom, and other companies.

  Don't expect it to work as well as those car units, though. This is a cell-phone, for goodness' sake—not some much bigger, single-purpose, dedicated-GPS car unit.

  Still, Apple's designers used every trick in the book to maximize the iPhone's sensitivity. If the iPhone has a good view of the sky, and isn't confounded by skyscrapers or the metal of your car, then it can do a decent job of consulting the 24 satellites that make up the Global Positioning System and determining its own location.

  But what if it can't see the sky? Or what if you have an original iPhone, which has no GPS chip? Fortunately, all iPhones have two other fallback location features.

- **Wi-Fi Positioning System.** Metropolitan areas today are blanketed by overlapping WiFi signals. At a typical Manhattan intersection, you might be in range of 20 base stations. Each one broadcasts its own name and unique network address (its *MAC address*—nothing to do with Mac computers) once every second. Although you'd need to be within 150 feet or so to actually get onto the Internet, a laptop or phone can detect this beacon signal from up to 1,500 feet away.

  Imagine if you could correlate all those beacon signals with their physical locations. Why, you'd be able to simulate GPS—without the GPS!

  So for years, all those millions of iPhones have been quietly logging all those WiFi signals, noting their network addresses and locations. (The iPhone never has to *connect* to these base stations. It's just reading the one-way beacon signals.)

  At this point, Apple's database knows about millions of hotspots—and the precise longitude and latitude of each.

  If the iPhone can't get a fix on GPS, then it sniffs around for WiFi base stations. If it finds any, it transmits their IDs back to Apple (via cellular network), which looks up those network addresses—and sends coordinates back to the phone.

  That accuracy is good only to within 100 feet at best, and of course the system fails completely once you're out of populated areas. On the other hand, it works indoors, which GPS definitely doesn't.

- **Google's cellular triangulation system.** Finally, as a last resort, any iPhone can turn to a system of location-guessing based on your proximity to the cellphone towers around you. Software provided from Google works a lot like the WiFi location system, but it relies upon its knowledge of cellular towers' locations rather than WiFi base stations. The accuracy isn't as good as GPS—you're lucky if it puts you within a block or two of your actual location—but it's something.

 The iPhone's location circuits eat into battery power. To shut them down when you're not using them, use the Settings switches described on page 452.

Finding Yourself

All right—now that you know how the iPhone gets its location information, here's how you can use it. It does *not* give you GPS-like navigation instructions, with a voice saying, "Turn left on Elm Street"—at least not unless you get an app that does that from the App Store. (Most require a monthly fee, but not all; try MapQuest 4 Mobile, for example.)

What it can do, though, is show you where you are. Tap the Locate button (⏻) at the bottom of the Maps screen. The button turns blue, indicating that the iPhone is consulting its various references—GPS, WiFi network, cellular network—to try to figure out where you are.

What you see now depends on what kind of luck the phone is having (read the illustration on the facing page from right to left):

- **Good: The Location circle pulsates.** The first thing that usually happens when you tap the ⏻ button is that a big, crosshairs-like circle appears on the map. That's the iPhone's first guess, a quick stab based on triangulation of the local cell towers. As long as it's bouncing inward and outward, it's saying: "I think you're around here. But hold on—let me see if I can be a little more specific."

 Actually, the *first* thing that may happen is you may be informed: "Maps would like to use your current location." (A similar query appears the first time you use *any* program that uses the iPhone's location info.) It's just a little heads-up for the privacy-conscious. Unless you're paranoid, tap OK.

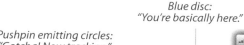

Pushpin emitting circles:
"Gotcha! Now tracking."

Blue disc:
"You're basically here."

Bouncing ring:
"Trying to get a fix on you."

- **Better: The circle sits still.** The blue circle stops pulsing when it's exhausted all the iPhone's location technologies. It's saying: "You're in here somewhere, mate, but I'm afraid this is the best I can do."

- **Best: The blue pushpin appears—and moves with you.** If you're outdoors (so that the GPS can work), or indoors in a big city (so that the WiFi location circuit works), the iPhone may drop a blue pushpin onto the map. That's it saying, "OK, pal, I've got you. You're *here.*"

The iPhone is now tracking you, moving along the map *with* you as you drive, ride, or walk. (The smoothness of the animation depends on the iPhone's success at getting a good location signal.)

The iPhone keeps tracking you until you push the ◀ button again.

Sometimes a blue, see-through disc appears around the pushpin, indicating the iPhone's degree of uncertainty. Still, in times of navigational confusion, that guidance can be extremely useful. It's not just seeing where you are on a map—it's seeing which way you're *going* on the map.

Once you've found something on the map—your current position, say, or something you've searched for—you can drop a pin there for future reference. Tap the ▣ button; when the page curls up, tap Drop Pin. A blue pushpin appears on the map.

You can drag the pin to move it, or tap ◉ to add it to your Bookmarks (described in a moment), use it as a starting point for directions, add it to your Contacts app, or send it to somebody else. And if you tap Directions, the iPhone lists "Dropped Pin" as your starting point—usually a good guess.

Orienting the Map

It's great to see a blue pin on the map, and all—but how do you know which way you're facing? Legions of iPhone fans have developed a peculiar ritual known as the iPhone Circle, in which they run the perimeter of an imaginary 50-yard circle, holding out the iPhone before them, in an attempt to figure out which way is up on the map.

Truth is, you don't have to bother. Thanks to the built-in magnetometer (compass), the map can orient itself for you.

Just tap the ✦ button twice. The map spins so that the direction you're facing is upward. A "flashlight beam" emanates from your blue dot; its width indicates the iPhone's degree of confidence. (The narrower the beam, the surer it is.)

Searching the Maps

You're not always interested in finding out where you are; often enough, you know that much perfectly well. Instead, you want to see where something *else* is. That's where the Search button comes in.

Tap it to summon the search box and the iPhone keyboard. (If there's already something in the search box, tap the ✖ button to clear it out.)

 Tip If you have an iPhone 4S, it's *much* quicker to use Siri to specify what you want to find. You can say, for example, "Show me the map of Detroit" or "Show me the closest Starbucks" or "Red Roof Inn, San Francisco." Siri shows you that spot on a map, which you can tap to jump right into the Maps app.

Here's what Maps can find for you:

- **An address.** You can skip the periods (and usually the commas, too). And you can use abbreviations. Typing *710 w end ave ny ny* will find 710 West End Avenue, New York, New York. (In this and any of the other examples, you can type a Zip code instead of a city and a state.)

- **An intersection.** Type *57th and lexington, ny ny*. Maps will find the spot where East 57th Street crosses Lexington Avenue in New York City.

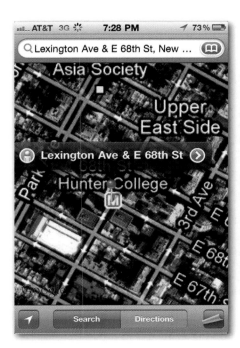 

- **A city.** Type *chicago il* to see a map of the city. You can zoom in from there.

- **A Zip code.** Type *10024* to see that region.

- **A point of interest.** Type *washington monument* or *niagara falls*.

When Maps finds a specific address, an animated, red-topped pushpin comes flying down onto its precise spot on the map. A translucent bubble identifies the location by name.

 Tip Tap the bubble to hide it. Tap the map pin to bring the bubble back. Tap the ◉ to bookmark the spot, to get directions, to add it to Contacts, or to share it with other people (via email, text message, or Twitter).

Finding Friends and Businesses

Maps is also plugged into your Contacts list, which makes it especially easy to find a friend's house (or just to see how ritzy his neighborhood is).

Instead of typing an address into the empty search bar, tap the 📖 button at the right end of it. You arrive at the Bookmarks/Recents/Contacts screen, containing three lists that can save you a lot of typing.

Two of them are described in the next section. But if you tap Contacts, you see your master address book (Chapter 3). Tap the name of someone you want to find. In a flash, Maps drops a red, animated pushpin onto the map to identify that address.

 Tip If you're handy with the iPhone keyboard, then you can save a few taps. Type part of a person's name into the search bar. As you go, the iPhone displays a list of matching names. Tap the one you want to find on the map.

That pushpin business also comes into play when you use Maps as a glorified national Yellow Pages. If you type, for example, *pharmacy 60609*, those red pushpins show you all the drugstores in that Chicago Zip code. It's a great way to find a gas station, a cash machine, or a hospital in a pinch. Tap a pushpin to see the name of the corresponding business.

As usual, you can tap the ◉ button in the map pin's label bubble to open a details screen. If you've searched for a friend, then you see the corresponding Contacts card. If you've searched for a business, then you get a screen containing its phone number, address, Web site, and so on. Remember that you can tap a Web address to open it, or tap a phone number to dial it. ("Hello, what time do you close today?")

Tip If the cluster of map pins makes it hard to see what you're doing, then tap List. You see a neat text list of the same businesses. Tap one to see it alone on the map, or tap ⊙ to see its details card.

In both cases, you get two useful buttons, labeled Directions To Here and Directions From Here. Turn the page for details.

You also get buttons like Add to Bookmarks and Create New Contact, which save this address for instant recall (read on).

Bookmarks and Recents

Let's face it: The iPhone's tiny keyboard can be a little fussy. One nice thing about Maps is the way it tries to eliminate typing at every step.

If you tap the ☐ button at the right end of the search bar, for example, you get the Bookmarks/Recents/Contacts screen—three lists that spare you from having to type stuff.

- **Bookmarks** are addresses you've flagged for later use by tapping Add to Bookmarks, an option that appears whenever you tap the ⊙ in a push-pin's label. For sure, you should bookmark your home and workplace. They'll make it much easier to request driving directions.

- **Recents** are searches you've conducted. You'd be surprised at how often you want to call up the same spot again later—and now you can, just by tapping its name in this list. You can also tap Clear to empty the list (if, for example, you intend to elope and don't want your parents to find out).

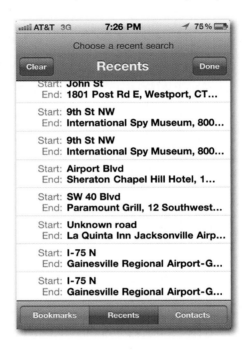

- **Contacts** is your iPhone address book. One tap maps out where some-one lives.

Directions

If you tap Directions, the search bar turns into *two* search bars: one labeled Start and the other, End. Plug in two addresses—if you've used the Location function, the Start address already says "Current Location"—and let Google Maps guide you from the first to the second.

The iPhone *does* give you turn-by-turn directions—but only as written instruc-tions on the screen, not as a spoken voice. Also, you have to *ask* for each successive instruction; this app doesn't display them automatically based on your current position. It's not a Garmin, in other words.

Still, for a phone, it's not bad.

Begin by filling in the Start and End boxes. You can use any of the address shortcuts on pages 297-298, or you can tap 🔖 to specify a bookmark, a recent search, or a name in Contacts. (Or, after performing any search that produces a pushpin, you can tap the ❯ button in its label bubble and then tap Directions To Here or Directions From Here on the details screen.)

Then tap Route. In just a moment, Maps displays an overview of the route you're about to drive. In fact, in iOS 5, it usually proposes several different routes. They're labeled with little tags: Route 1, Route 2, Route 3, for example.

If you tap one of these tags, the top of the screen lets you know the distance and estimated time for that option and identifies the main roads you'll be on. Feel free to zoom in for more detail.

Amazingly, you also see buttons for 🚌 (public transportation) and 🚶 (walking) directions. These usually take you longer, and public transport isn't always available, but it's amazing that they're even an option.

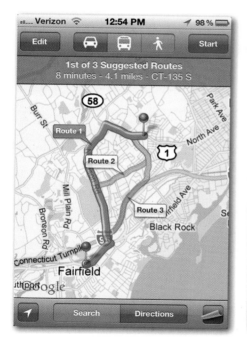

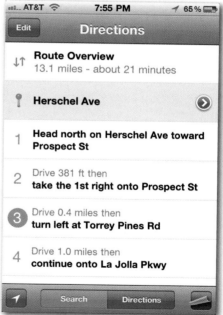

Tip Even more amazingly, in big cities, Maps can display the arrival time of the next bus! Tap the clock icon to see today's remaining bus arrival times.

Tap the Route label you want, and then tap Start to see the first driving instruction. The map also zooms into the actual road you'll be traveling, which looks like it's been drawn in with purple highlighter. It's just like having a printout from MapQuest—the directions at the top of the screen say, for example, "Head east on Canterbury Ln toward Blackbird Ave – go .5 mi." Unlike MapQuest, though, you see only one instruction at a time (the current step)—and you don't have to clutch and peer at a crumpled piece of paper while you're driving.

Tap the ← or → buttons to see the previous or next driving instruction. At any time, you can also tap ☰ and then List to see the master list of turns (previous page, righ). Tap an instruction to see a closeup of that turn on the map.

To adjust one of the addresses, tap the current driving instruction; the search boxes reappear. And to exit the driving mode, tap the ⚷ button again.

 Tip If you tap the ⊍ button, you swap the Start and End points. That's a great way to find your way back after your trip.

Traffic

How's this for a cool feature? Free, real-time traffic reporting—the same information you'd have to pay Sirius XM Satellite Radio $10 a month for. Just tap ☰ (lower-right corner), and then tap Show Traffic. Now the stretches of road change color to indicate how bad the traffic is.

- **Green** means the traffic is moving at more than 50 miles an hour.

- **Yellow** indicates speeds from 25 to 50 mph.

- **Red** means the road is like a parking lot. The traffic is moving under 25 mph. Time to start up the iPod mode and entertain yourself.

If you don't see any color-coding, it's because Google doesn't have any information for those roads. Usually, the color-coding appears only on highways, and only in metropolitan areas.

 Tip If you turn on Traffic on the very first screen of driving directions, the total-driving-time estimate updates itself to reflect what it knows about traffic speeds.

Street View

OK, if your brain isn't already boggled by the iPhone, this'll do it.

Most people think of Google Maps as an overhead view, like any other map. But these days, there's more to it than that. And it's all lurking in the little 🅰 icon. Look for him on the red pushpin label after any search. He's likely to appear whenever you search for a street address in a suburb or city (or when you search for the city itself).

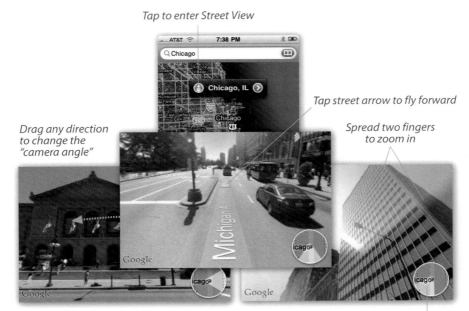

Tap to enter Street View

Drag any direction
to change the
"camera angle"

Tap street arrow to fly forward

Spread two fingers
to zoom in

Tap to return to Map View

When you tap this guy, you open up Street View. It's a 360-degree photographic view of the entire area at street level. You can actually perform a virtual walk-through of an entire city this way! The illustration above tells you all you need to know.

What a great way to check out a neighborhood before you visit, shop—or move—there.

Newsstand

In iOS 5, for the first time, you can subscribe to magazines and newspapers digitally. Just about every major magazine and newspaper now offers downloadable electronic versions; your phone can download and "deliver" them in the background, automatically. They show up right here, in Newsstand. In fact, you can't move their icons anywhere else. (Some magazines and newspapers have yet to be adapted to be Newsstand-compatible, but it won't take long.)

Each magazine or newspaper has its own on/off switch for the automatic-background-downloading feature. It's in Settings→Store. Downloading takes place only when you're in a WiFi hotspot—it doesn't eat up your cellular data each month—so there's no good reason to turn off auto-downloading. But the switch is here if you need it.

Newsstand is the mutant love child of an app and a folder. Like an app, it shows up in the task switcher when you double-press the Home button. Like a folder, when you tap it, you don't leave the Home screen. Instead, a wooden bookshelf version of a folder opens, showing the icons of your subscriptions. (If you had subscribed to some publications before, you'll find them missing from their usual Home-screen positions—they're in here now.)

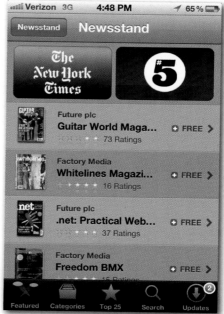

Tap one of these magazine or newspaper icons to open it.

Why is Newsstand a pseudo-folder? Because each magazine or newspaper is different. Some are self-contained apps. Others are just glorified PDF files. Some are nothing more than links to other apps elsewhere on your phone (like *The New York Times,* for example).

At least you know where to find them all.

To subscribe to something, tap Store in the upper-right corner. You arrive at what should look familiar by now: the usual App Store screen. You're looking at a special corner of the store that's dedicated to e-publications. Tap the name of one to see sample pages, read a description, peruse reviews from other readers—and, if you like what you see, download it.

 Tip When you tap Store in Newsstand, the resulting list of periodicals doesn't offer buttons at the top like Top Paid and Top Free. But there's a side door into the Newsstand store that does. Once you're viewing the store, tap Categories and then Newsstand. You arrive at the same list of publications—but now those helpful buttons appear at the top: Top Paid, Top Free, and Release Date.

Many big-name magazines, by the way, *appear* to be free. You can download them, view them in your Newsstand "folder," and so on. But you're really downloading only a shell—a mini-store just for that magazine. When you actually open it, you're asked to pay $4 or $5 to buy issues within that app.

In the same vein, you don't see individual issues on your Newsstand bookshelf. You see *one* cover for each magazine; other issues are inside it. A "NEW" banner appears across the cover to let you know that a new issue has arrived.

 Tip If you don't use Newsstand, you're stuck with it. You can't remove its empty icon from the Home screen, and you can't shove it into a folder to hide it. Or can you?

You can, at least in iOS 5.0.1. Hold down your finger on any app icon until all your apps start wiggling. Drag Newsstand's icon right next to two other apps' icons. Drag one of those apps' icon onto the other to create a new folder. Quickly, during the animation of those two apps merging, drag Newsstand's icon into the new folder.

Later, you can drag the other icons out of the new folder, add new icons, and so on. (Note: Newsstand crashes if you try to open it from within the folder. Presumably you've performed this exercise only because you *don't* intend to use it.)

Notes

The Notes app is the iPhone's answer to a word processor. It's simple in the extreme—there's no option to vary the font, for example, or to apply text formatting to individual words. Still, it's nice to be able to jot down lists, reminders, and brainstorms. (You can email them to yourself when you're finished—or sync them right to your Mac or PC's email program.)

 Tip You have a choice of three typefaces in Notes; tap Settings→Notes to see them. (Your selection here applies to all text in all notes.) You can also change the font *size*. See page 153.

The first time you open Notes, you see what looks like a yellow, lined legal pad. Tap on the lines to make the keyboard appear so you can begin typing.

 Tip This is one of the apps where you can get a much larger, widescreen keyboard by rotating the phone 90 degrees.

When you're finished with a note for now, tap Done. The keyboard goes away, and a **+** button appears at the top right. It opens a new note.

Whenever you put away the keyboard by tapping Done, a handy row of icons appears at the bottom of your Notes page. The rundown:

- **← →**. These buttons let you skip to the previous or next page without requiring a detour to the master Notes list.

- **↪**. Tap to print your note or send it to someone by email. If you tap Print, the note prints (page 220). If you tap Mail, the iPhone creates a new outgoing message, pastes the first line of the note into the subject line, and then pastes the note's text into the body. All you have to do is address the note, edit the body if necessary, and hit Send. Afterward, the iPhone politely returns you to the note you were editing.

- **🗑**. Tap to delete the current note. After you confirm your decision, the Trash's lid opens, the note folds itself up and flies in, and then the lid closes up again. Cute—real cute.

As you create more pages, the Notes button (top left) becomes more useful. It's your table of contents for the Notes pad. It displays the first lines of your notes (most recent at the top), along with the time or date you last edited them. (The **+** button appears here, too.) To open a note, tap its name.

There's a search box hiding here, too. Drag down on the Notes list to bring the Spotlight box into view. Tap it to open the keyboard. You can now search all your notes instantly—not just their titles, but also the text inside them.

Syncing Notes

The iPhone can synchronize your collection of notes with all kinds of other note sources, so the same notes are waiting for you everywhere you look.

For example, most email programs let you create notes. To that end, you can set up iTunes to sync your iPhone notes with Mail (Apple's email program for the Mac) or with Microsoft Outlook 2003, 2007, or 2010 on a PC. Chapter 13 has the details.

Your notes can also sync *wirelessly* with the Notes modules on iCloud, Google, Yahoo, AOL, or another IMAP email account. To set this up, open Settings→Mail, Contacts, Calendars. Tap the account you want (iCloud, Gmail, Yahoo, AOL, or whatever); finally, turn the Notes switch On.

That should do it. Now your notes are synced, both ways, with Mail or Outlook when you connect the iPhone to your computer with the cable. With an iCloud account, notes are synced nearly instantly, wirelessly, both directions.

 One catch: Notes you create at *gmail.com*, *aol.com*, or *yahoo.com* don't wind up on the phone. Those accounts sync wirelessly in one direction only: *from* the iPhone to the Web site, where the notes arrive in a Notes folder. (There's no problem, however, if you get your AOL or Gmail mail in an email *program* like Outlook, Entourage, or Apple Mail. Then it's two-way syncing as usual.)

All of this makes life a little more complex, of course. For example, when you create a note, you have to worry about which account it's about to go into. To do that, be sure to specify an account *before* you create the new note. Do that by tapping Accounts (top-left corner) to see a list of all the Notes-compatible accounts you've set up.

 In Settings→Notes, you can also specify which of your different Notes accounts you want to be the main one—the one that new notes fall into if you haven't specified otherwise.

You'll also see an account called On My Phone. That's where you should store notes that you don't want synced anywhere; they're private ones you want to stay right there on the phone.

Reminders

For years, iPhone fans have grumbled about its lack of a to-do list. What kind of smartphone has a calendar, an email program, an address book—but no to-do list?

Apple has emphatically retired that complaint. In iOS 5, you have Reminders: a program that not only records your life's little tasks, but also reminds you about them, either when the right time comes or when you come to the right place. For example, it can remind you to water the plants as soon as you get home.

If you have an iCloud account, your reminders sync across all of your gadgets. Create or check off a task on your iPhone, and you'll also find it created or checked off on your iPad, iPod Touch, Mac (thanks to iCal), PC (thanks to Outlook or Exchange), and so on.

And on the iPhone 4S—oh, wow. Siri and Reminders are a match made in heaven. "Remind me to file the Jenkins report when I get to work." "Remind me to set the TiVo for tonight at 8." "Remind me about Timmy's soccer game a week from Saturday." "Add waffles to my Groceries list."

> **Tip** Reminders sync wirelessly with anything your iCloud account knows about: the iCal or BusyCal program on your Mac, Outlook on the PC, and so on.

To record a new task the manual way, click the big ✚ button in the upper right. A new blank line appears in your list. Type your reminder (or dictate it, if you have an iPhone 4S). Tap Done when you're finished.

As you go through life completing tasks, tap the checkbox next to each one. A checked-off to-do remains in place until the next time you visit its list. At that point, it disappears. It's moved into a separate list called Completed.

You can move back and forth between the Completed list and the Reminders list by swiping your finger across the screen. As you'll see below, you can create additional lists—one for Groceries, one for Homework, whatever; this

same swiping action lets you move among the different lists. Dots below the screen let you know how many more lists are available.

Tip If you tap Date at the top of the screen, then this swiping action moves between each day's to-do items, rather than your different lists. That's a good way to set things up if you diligently assign due dates to your to-dos. (In this view, you get a date slider at the bottom, a Month view calendar button at top left—with a search box, by the way—and a Today button at top right. These are all tools that let you jump around to different dates.)

The Details Screen

If you tap an item's name, you arrive at the Details screen. Here you can set up a reminder that will pop up at a certain time or place, create an auto-repeating schedule, file this item into a different to-do list with its own name, add notes to this item, or delete it. Here are your options, one by one.

- **Timed reminders.** On the Details screen, tap Remind Me; on the *next* screen, tap On a Day. The proposed time is the next "o'clock"—if it's 12:15 now, the phone suggests 1:00. But you can tap it to bring up the "time wheel" shown above.

When you've dialed in the appropriate time, tap Done to return to the Details screen.

- **Location-based reminders.** If you tap At a Location, then the phone will use its location circuits (GPS, WiFi triangulation, and so on) to remind you of this item when you arrive at a certain place or leave a certain place. The phone proposes "Current Location"—wherever you are at the moment. That's handy if, for example, you're dropping off your dry cleaning and want to remember to pick it up the next time you're driving by.

  But you can tap that line to select either Home (your home address, as you've set it up in Contacts) or Choose Address (which opens up Contacts and lets you choose a person from the list).

 If you choose somebody whose Contacts card doesn't list an address, a message says "No Street Addresses." If you choose someone with *multiple* addresses, you're shown all of them; tap the one you want.

Once you've specified an address, tap Remind Me in the top-left corner to return to the Remind Me screen. The final step here is to tap either When I Leave or When I Arrive. Then tap Done to return to the Details screen.

Later, the phone will remind you at the appointed time or as you approach (or leave) the appointed address, which is fairly mind-blowing the first few times it happens.

 If you set up *both* a time reminder *and* a location reminder, your iPhone uses whichever event happens first. That is, if you ask to be reminded at 3 p.m. today and "When I arrive at the office," you'll get the reminder when you get to the office—or at 3 p.m., if that time rolls around before you make it to work.

- **Repeat.** Reminders can remind you about things that recur in your life, like quarterly tax payments, haircuts, and anniversaries. Tap Repeat if you want this reminder to appear every day, week, two weeks, month, or year.

- **Priority.** If you tap Show More on the Details screen, you get a few additional options. One of them is Priority. Tap here to specify whether this item has High, Medium, or Low priority—or None. In some of the calendar programs that sync with Reminders, you can sort your task list by priority.

- **List.** Tap here to assign this to-do to a different reminder list (read on).

- **Notes.** Here's a handy box where you can record freehand notes about this item: an address, a phone number, details of any kind.

- **Delete.** Tap to remove this to-do altogether. (That's different from marking it as done, of course.)

Lists

Believe it or not, you can create *more than one* to-do list, each with its own name: a Groceries list, Kids' Chores, a running tally of expenses, and so on. Here's a great way to log what you eat if you're on a diet, or to keep a list of movies people recommend that you rent.

If you share an iCloud account with another family member, you might create a different Reminder list for each person. (Of course, now you run the risk that your spouse might sneakily add items to *your* to-do list!)

If you have an Exchange account, one of your lists can be synced to your corporate Tasks list. It doesn't offer all the features of the other lists in Reminders, but at least it's kept tidy and separate.

> **Tip** This feature is especially cool on the iPhone 4S, because you can add things to individual lists by name. You can say, for example, "Add low-fat cottage cheese to the Groceries list."

To create a new list, tap the button at the top-left corner of the Reminders screen. You arrive at the list of Lists. At the outset, it lists only two lists: Completed and Reminders. But if you tap Edit and then Create New List, you can create and name that Groceries list, Movies list, whatever you like. (You can also tap the ⊖ button to delete a list.)

Once you've created some lists, you have two ways to switch among them:

- **Swipe your finger across the screen.** The lists slide into view as though they're successive photos in a slideshow.

- **Tap the ☰ button to see the Lists list,** and then tap the one you want to open.

Later, you can assign a task to a different list by tapping List on its Details screen.

Stocks

This one's for you, big-time day trader. The Stocks app tracks the rise and fall of the stocks in your portfolio. It connects to the Internet to download the very latest stock prices.

(All right, maybe not the *very* latest. The price info may be delayed as much as 20 minutes, which is typical of free stock-info services.)

When you first fire it up, Stocks shows you a handful of sample high-tech stocks—or, rather, their abbreviations. (They stand for the Dow Jones Industrial Index, the NASDAQ Index, the S&P 500 Index, Apple, Google, and Yahoo. AT&T, one of the starter listings on the original iPhone, has been dumped.)

Next to each, you see its current share price, and next to *that,* you see how much that price has gone up or down today. As a handy visual gauge to how elated or depressed you should be, this final number appears on a *green* background if it's gone up, or a *red* one if it's gone down.

Tap a stock name to view its stock-price graph at the bottom of the screen. You can even adjust the time scale of this graph by tapping the little interval buttons along the top edge: 1d means "one day" (today); 1w means "one week"; 1m, 3m, and 6m refer to numbers of months; and 1y and 2y refer to years.

Finally, to get more detailed information about a stock, tap its name and then tap the 🅨! button in the lower-left corner. The iPhone fires up its Web browser and takes you to the Yahoo Finance page for that particular stock, showing the company's Web site, more detailed stock information, and even recent news articles that may have affected the stock's price.

Landscape View

If you turn the iPhone sideways, you get a much bigger, more detailed, wide-screen graph of the stock in question. (Flick horizontally to view the previous or next stock.)

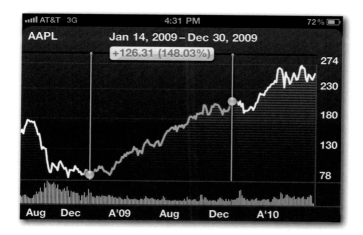

Better yet, you can pinch with two fingers or two thumbs to isolate a certain time period; pop-up bubbles show you how much of a bath you took (or how much of a windfall you received) during the interval you highlighted. Cool!

Customizing Your Portfolio

It's fairly unlikely that *your* stock portfolio contains just Apple, Google, and Yahoo. Fortunately, you can customize the list of stocks to reflect the companies you *do* own (or you want to track).

To edit the list, tap the ❸ button in the lower-right corner. You arrive at the editing screen, where the following choices await:

- **Delete a stock** by tapping the ⊖ button and then the Delete confirmation button.

- **Rearrange the list** by dragging the grip strips on the right side.

- **Add a stock** by tapping the **+** button in the top-left corner; the Add Stock screen and the keyboard appear.

    The idea here is that you're not expected to know every company's stock-symbol abbreviation. So type in the company's *name,* and then tap Search. The iPhone shows you, just above the keyboard, a scrolling list

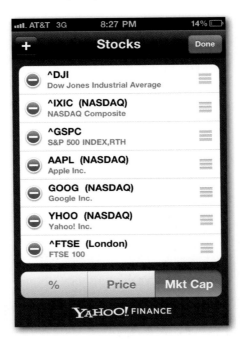

of companies with matching names. Tap the one you want to track. You return to the stocks-list editing screen.

- **Choose %, Price, or Numbers.** You can specify how you want to see the changes in stock prices in the far-right column: as *percentages* ("+ 0.65%"), *numbers* ("+2.23") or as *market capitalization* ("120.3B," meaning $120.3 billion total corporate value). Tap the corresponding button at the bottom of this screen.

When you're finished setting up your stock list, tap Done.

Voice Memos

This audio app is ideal for recording lectures, musical performances, notes to self, and cute child utterances. The best part: When you sync your iPhone, all of your voice recordings get copied back to the Mac or PC automatically. You'll find them in iTunes, in a folder called Voice Memos.

 Tip On a new iPhone, the Voice Memos app comes in a folder called Utilities on the first Home screen.

Start by doing a "testing, testing" check, and make sure the VU meter's needle is moving. (If it's not, maybe the iPhone thinks you're recording from the wrong source—a Bluetooth headset, for example.)

Tap the red Record button to start recording. You can pause at any time by pressing the same button—which now bears a pause symbol (**II**). Stop recording by tapping the Stop button (■) on the right.

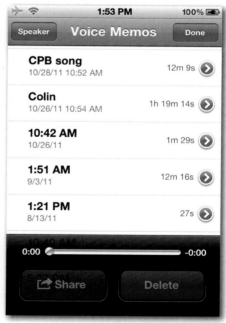

You can also switch out of the app to do other work. A red banner across the top of the screen reminds you that you're still recording. (You can make *very*

long recordings with this thing. Let it run all day, if you like. Even your most long-winded friends can be immortalized.)

To review your recordings, tap what used to be the Stop button, which now looks like a list (☰). This opens the Recordings list. Tap one to hear it; tap Delete to get rid of it; tap Share to send it by email or MMS. (If the recording is too long for email or MMS, you're offered the chance to edit it, as described next.)

Editing Your Recording

You might not guess that such a tiny, self-effacing app might actually offer some basic editing functions, but it does. Tap the ⊙ button to the right of any recording to open its Info screen.

Here, you can give yourself some clue what it is by choosing a label (Podcast, Interview, and so on, shown below at left). Or tap Custom and type in any name you prefer.

If you tap Trim Memo, you get the display shown below at right. Drag the endpoints of the scroll bar inward to cut the dead air off the beginning and end, playing the sound as necessary to guide you (▶). Tap Trim Voice Memo.

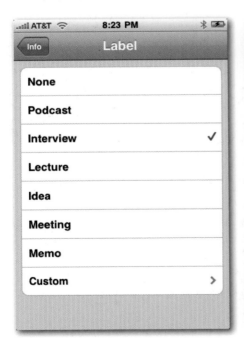

Weather

This little widget shows a handy current-conditions display for your city (or any other city) and, at your option, even offers a six-day forecast.

In iOS 5, you don't even have to tell the app what weather you want; it uses your location and assumes you want the *local* weather forecast (below, left).

Tip This is a wicked-cool new feature in iOS 5: If you tap the weekly forecast (or drag downward on it), you reveal an hour-by-hour forecast hiding underneath (below, right). You can then swipe to scroll the hourly forecast.

Return to the weekly forecast by tapping once (or swiping up repeatedly until the little "Hourly" light dims).

But you can also get the weather for other cities—great if you're going to be traveling, or you're wondering how life is for distant relations.

Tap the ❶ button at the lower-right corner; the widget flips around.

On the back panel, you can delete the sample city (Cupertino, California, which is Apple's headquarters) by tapping ⊖ and then Delete. And you can add your own city, or cities of interest, by tapping ✚. The Add Location screen and keyboard appear so you can type your city and state or Zip code. You can rearrange the sequence of cities by dragging the grip strips up or down.

> **Tip** This Weather widget is world-friendly. You can type the name of any reasonably sized city on earth to find out its weather. Remember to check before you travel.

When you tap Search, you're shown a list of matching cities; tap the one whose weather you want to track. When you return to the configuration screen, you can also specify whether you prefer degrees Celsius or degrees Fahrenheit. Tap Done.

Now the front of the widget displays the name of your town, today's predicted high and low, the current temperature, a six-day forecast, and a graphic representation of the sky conditions (sunny, cloudy, rainy, and so on).

There's nothing else to tap here except the ⓨ! icon at lower left. It fires up the Safari browser, which loads itself with Yahoo's information page about that city. Depending on the city, you might see a City Guide, city news, city photos, and more.

If you've added more than one city to the list, by the way, just flick your finger right or left to shuffle through the weather screens for the different cities on your list. The tiny bullets beneath the display correspond to the number of cities you've set up—and the white bold one indicates where you are in the sequence.

YouTube

YouTube, of course, is the stratospherically popular video-sharing Web site where people post short videos of every description: funny clips from TV, homemade blooper reels, goofy short films, musical performances, bite-sized serial dramas, and so on. YouTube's fans watch 200 million little videos a day.

Of course, there's a Web browser on the iPhone. So why does it need a special YouTube *program?* (Especially now that YouTube offers a specialized Web site, *m.youtube.com*, that many iPhoners actually prefer to the app?)

Long story: When the iPhone debuted, YouTube movies were in a format called Flash, which the iPhone didn't (and still doesn't) recognize. (Apple says Flash video is a buggy battery-drainer.)

So Apple persuaded YouTube to re-encode all its millions of videos into H.264, a *much* higher-quality format. Amazingly enough, YouTube agreed—and you are the lucky benefactor.

Finding a Video to Play

The YouTube program is basically a collection of lists. Tap one of the icons at the bottom of the screen, for example, to find videos in any of these ways:

- **Featured.** A scrolling, flickable list of videos handpicked by YouTube's editors. You get to see the name, length, star rating, and popularity (viewership) of each one.

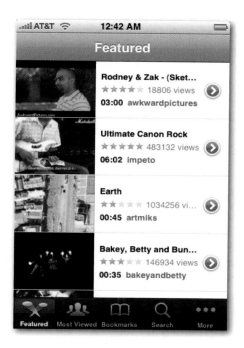

- **Most Viewed.** A popularity contest. Tap the buttons at the top to look over the most-viewed videos Today, This Week, or All (meaning "of all time"). Scroll to the bottom of the list and tap Load 25 More to see the next chunk of the list.

- **Search.** Makes the iPhone keyboard appear so you can type a search phrase. YouTube produces a list of videos whose titles, descriptions, keywords, or creator names match what you typed.

- **Favorites.** A list of videos you've flagged as your own personal faves, as described in a moment.

If you tap More, you get some additional options:

- **Most Recent.** These are the very latest videos posted on YouTube.

- **Top Rated.** Whenever people watch a video on YouTube, they have the option of giving it a star rating. (You can rate videos right from the iPhone, too.) This list rounds up the highest-rated videos. Beware—you may be disappointed in the taste of the masses.

- **History.** This is a list of videos you've viewed recently on the iPhone— and a Clear button that nukes the list, so people won't know what you've been watching.

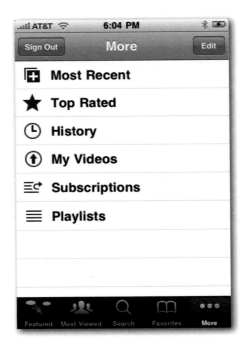

- **My Videos, Subscriptions, Playlists.** These options appear only if you have a YouTube account (which is free at *www.youtube.com*) and have logged into it on your iPhone. My Videos are, of course, the videos you've posted on YouTube. Subscriptions are videos you've signed up to receive in installments (many YouTubers produce a new video every week, for example). And Playlists are handpicked sets of videos you've grouped together yourself. Details follow.

Tip Once you've tapped More to see the additional options, you also get an Edit button. It opens a Configure screen that works exactly like the one described on page 165. That is, you can now rearrange the four icons at the bottom of the YouTube app's screen, or you can replace those icons with the ones that are usually hidden (like Most Recent or Top Rated) just by dragging them into place.

Each list offers a ⊙ button at the right side. Tap it to open the Details screen for that video, featuring a description, date, category, tags (keywords), uploader name, play length, number of views, links to related videos, and so on.

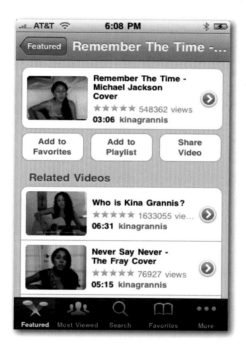

Also on this screen: Add to Favorites, which adds this video to your own personal list of favorites (tap Favorites at the bottom of the screen to see it); Add to Playlist, which opens a Playlist screen where you can add, edit, and delete these self-playing sequences of videos; and Share Video, which creates an outgoing message containing a link to that video.

Address it and send it along to anyone you think would be interested, thus fulfilling your duty as a cog in the great viral YouTube machine.

Playing YouTube Videos

To play a video, tap its row in any of the lists. Turn the iPhone 90 degrees counterclockwise—at least if you want to see the video full-screen. The video begins playing automatically; you don't have to tap the ▶ button. (You *can* turn the iPhone upright once the video starts, but that makes it play all shrunken in the screen, with huge, black, empty areas above and below.)

Here you'll discover a basic truth about the YouTube app on the iPhone: Videos look *great* if you're connected to the Internet through a WiFi hotspot or the 3G network. They look *not* so great if you're connected over your cell company's older, non-3G network. In that case, you get a completely different version of the video—smaller, coarser, and grainier. In fact, you may not be able to get videos to play at all.

When you first start playing a video, you get the usual iPhone playback controls (▶▶I, I◀◀, II) the volume slider, and the progress scrubber at the top. Here again, you can double-tap the screen (or tap the 🔳 button) to magnify the video just enough to eliminate the black bars on the sides of the screen.

The controls fade away after a moment so they don't block your view. You can make them appear and disappear with a single tap on the video.

There are two icons on these controls, however, that *don't* also appear when you're playing iPod videos. First is the 📖 button, which adds the video you're watching to your Favorites list so you won't have to hunt for it later.

Second is the ✉ button, which pauses the video and sends you to the Mail app, where a link to the video is pasted into an outgoing message for you.

The Done button at the top-left corner takes you out of the video you're watching and back to the list of YouTube videos.

 **10** # Getting Online

T he iPhone's concept as an all-screen machine is a curse and a bless-
ing. You may curse it when you're trying to type text, wishing you
had real keys. But when you're online—oh, baby. That's when the
Web comes to life, looming larger and clearer than on any other cellphone.
That's when you see real email, full-blown YouTube videos, hyper-clear
Google maps, and all kinds of Internet goodness, larger than life.

Well, at least larger than on most other cellphones.

A Tale of Three Networks

The iPhone can get onto the Internet using any of three methods—three kinds of wireless networks. Which kind you're on makes a huge difference to your iPhone experience; there's nothing worse than having to wait until the next ice age for some Web page to arrive when you need the information *now*. Here they are, listed from slowest to fastest.

- **Old, slow cellular network.** Your iPhone can connect to data over the same airwaves that carry your voice, thanks to AT&T's EDGE cellular data network or Verizon's and Sprint's 1xRTT version of the same thing. The good part is that it's almost everywhere, so your iPhone can get online almost anywhere you can make a phone call.

  The bad news is that it's slow. *Dog* slow—sometimes dial-up slow.

  You can't be on a phone call while you're online using EDGE or 1xRTT, either.

- **3G cellular network.** For several years, cellphone companies have quietly built high-speed cellular data networks—so-called *3G* networks. (3G stands for "third generation." The ancient analog cellphones were the first generation; EDGE-type networks were the second.) Geeks refer to the 3G network standard by its official name: HSDPA, for High-Speed Downlink Packet Access.

  Baby, when you're on 3G, the iPhone is awesome. Web pages that take 2 minutes to appear using EDGE or 1xRTT show up in about 20 seconds. Email downloads much faster, especially when there are attachments involved. Voice calls sound better, too, even when the signal strength is very low, since the iPhone's 3G radio can communicate with multiple towers at once.

  Oh, and on AT&T, you can talk on the phone and use the Internet simultaneously, which can be very handy indeed.

  3G is not all sunshine and bunnies, however; it has two huge downsides.

  First: coverage. In an attempt to serve the most people with the least effort, cell companies always bring 3G service to the big cities first. 3G coverage is available in hundreds of U.S. cities, which is a good start. But that still leaves most of the country, including several entire states, without any 3G coverage at all. For example, here's AT&T's coverage map; whenever you're outside the blue chicken pox, your iPhone falls back to the old EDGE speeds.

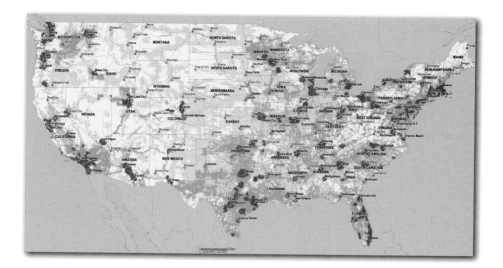

The second big problem with 3G is that, to receive its signal, a phone's circuitry uses a lot of power. That's why AT&T's iPhone 4 gets *twice* the talk time (14 hours instead of 7) when you turn off 3G. (That option isn't available on the 4S or on Verizon's iPhones.)

- **WiFi hotspots.** WiFi, known to geeks as 802.11, is the fastest of all. It's wireless networking, the same technology that laptops get online at high speed in any WiFi *hotspot.*

Hotspots are everywhere these days: in homes, offices, coffee shops (notably Starbucks), hotels, airports, and thousands of other places. Unfortunately, a hotspot is a bubble about 300 feet across; once you wander out of it, you're off the Internet. So WiFi is for people who are sitting still.

 At *www.jiwire.com*, you can type an address or a city and find out exactly where to find the closest WiFi hotspots. Or, quicker yet: Open Maps on your iPhone and type in, for example, *wifi austin tx* or *wifi 06902.* Pushpins on the map show you the closest WiFi hotspots.

When you're in a WiFi hotspot, your iPhone has a *very* fast connection to the Internet, as though it's connected to a cable modem or DSL. And when you're online this way, you can make phone calls and surf the Internet simultaneously. And why not? Your iPhone's WiFi and cellular antennas are independent.

So those are the three networks, from slowest to fastest; the iPhone looks for them from fastest to slowest. (You'll always know which kind of network you're on, thanks to the icons on the status bar: 📶 for WiFi, **3G** for 3G, and **E** or ° for superslow cellular.)

> **Tip** No cellular icon (**E**, °, or **3G**) appears on the status bar if you have a WiFi signal.

And how much faster is one than the next? Well, network speeds are measured in kilobits per second (which isn't the same as the more familiar *kilobytes* per second; divide by 8 to get those).

The EDGE/1xRTT network is supposed to deliver data from 70 to 200 kbps, depending on your distance from the cell towers. 3G gets 300 to 700 kbps. And a WiFi hotspot can spit out 650 to 2,100 kbps. You'll never get speeds near the high ends—but even so, you can see that there's quite a difference.

The bottom line: 3G and WiFi are *awesome.* EDGE/1xRTT—not so much.

> **Tip** Your iPhone is technically capable of getting onto even faster cellular networks—something called *7.2 Mbps HSDPA,* if you're scoring at home—once AT&T installs them. Check back here in 2013.

Sequence of Connections

The iPhone isn't online all the time. To save battery power, it opens the connection only on demand: when you check email, request a Web page, and so on. At that point, the iPhone tries to get online following this sequence:

- **First, it sniffs around for a WiFi network** that you've used before. If it finds one, it connects quietly and automatically. You're not asked for permission, a password, or anything else.

- **If the iPhone can't find a previous hotspot,** but it detects a *new* hotspot, a message appears. It displays any new hotspots' names, as shown at left on the facing page; tap the one you want. (If you see a 🔒 icon, then that hotspot has been protected by a password, which you'll have to enter.)

- **If the iPhone can't find any WiFi hotspots to join,** or if you don't join any, it connects to the cellular network, like 3G or EDGE/1xRTT.

Silencing the "Want to Join?" Messages

Sometimes, you might be bombarded by those "Do you want to join?" messages at a time when you have no need to be online. You might want the iPhone to stop bugging you—to *stop* offering WiFi hotspots. In that situation, from the Home screen, tap Settings→Wi-Fi, and then turn off Ask to Join Networks. When this option is off, the iPhone never interrupts your work by bounding in, wagging, and dropping the name of a new network at your feet. In this case, to get onto a new network, you have to visit the aforementioned Settings screen and select it, as described next.

The List of Hotspots

At some street corners in big cities, WiFi signals bleeding out of apartment buildings sometimes give you a choice of 20 or 30 hotspots to join. But whenever the iPhone invites you to join a hotspot, it suggests only a couple of them: the ones with the strongest signal and, if possible, no password requirement.

But you might sometimes want to see the complete list of available hotspots—maybe because the iPhone-suggested hotspot is flaky. To see the full list, from the Home screen, tap Settings→Wi-Fi. Tap the one you want to join, as shown above at right.

Commercial Hotspots

Tapping the name of the hotspot you want to join is generally all you have to do—if it's a home WiFi network. Unfortunately, joining a *commercial* WiFi hotspot—one that requires a credit-card number (in a hotel room or airport, for example)—requires more than just connecting to it. You also have to *sign into* it, exactly as you'd do if you were using a laptop.

To do that, return to the Home screen and open Safari. You'll see the "Enter your payment information" screen, either immediately or as soon as you try to open a Web page of your choice.

Supply your credit-card information or (if you have a membership to this WiFi chain, like Boingo or T-Mobile) your name and password. Tap Submit or Proceed, try *not* to contemplate the cost, and enjoy your surfing.

 Tip Mercifully, the iPhone memorizes your password. The next time you use this hotspot, you won't have to enter it again.

How to Turn Off 3G (AT&T iPhones)

3G is a power hog; it *cuts your iPhone's battery life in half.* Therefore, be grateful that AT&T iPhone 3GS and 4 models, upgraded to iOS 5, even *have* an on/off switch for their 3G radio; that's a luxury most 3G phone owners don't have.

You might consider turning off 3G when, for example, you're not in a 3G area anyway, or you're not using the Internet. Or maybe you're getting the "20% battery left" warning, and you're many hours away from a chance to recharge.

Turning off 3G forces the iPhone to use the older, less-congested AT&T network, which sometimes means you can complete a call in a crowded place where a 3G attempt would fail.

In those situations, from the Home screen, tap Settings→General→Network; where it says Enable 3G, tap to turn it Off. Now, if you want to get online, your phone will use only WiFi and the slow EDGE network.

Airplane Mode and WiFi Off Mode

To save even more battery power, you can turn off all three of the iPhone's network connections in one fell swoop. You can also turn off WiFi alone.

- **To turn all radios off.** In Airplane Mode (tap Settings, turn on Airplane Mode), you turn off *both* the WiFi *and* the cellular circuitry. Now you can't make calls or get onto the Internet. You're saving power, however, and also complying with regulations that ban cellphones in flight.

- **To turn WiFi on or off.** From the Home screen, tap Settings→Wi-Fi. Tap the On/Off switch to shut this radio down (or turn it back on).

> **Tip** Once you've turned on Airplane Mode, you can actually tap Wi-Fi and turn that feature back *on* again. Why on earth? Because some airlines offer WiFi on selected flights. You'll need a way to turn WiFi *on,* but your cellular circuitry *off.*
>
> Conversely, you sometimes might want to do the opposite: turn *off* WiFi, but leave cellular *on.* Why? Because sometimes, the iPhone bizarrely won't get online at all. It's struggling to use a WiFi network that, for one reason or another, isn't connecting to the Internet. By turning WiFi off, you force the iPhone to use its cell connection—which may be slower, but at least it works!

In Airplane Mode, anything that requires voice or Internet access—text messages, Web, email, and so on—triggers a message. "Turn off Airplane Mode or use WiFi to access data." Tap either OK (to back out of your decision) or Settings (to turn off Airplane Mode and get online).

You can, however, enjoy all the other iPhone features: iPod, Camera, Clock, Calculator, and so on. You can also work with stuff you've *already* downloaded to the phone, like email and voicemail messages.

Personal Hotspot (Tethering)

Tethering means using your iPhone as a glorified Internet antenna, so that your laptops, iPod Touches, iPads, game consoles, and other Internet-connectables can get online. (The other gadgets can connect to the phone over a WiFi connection, a Bluetooth connection, or a USB cable.) In fact, several laptops and other gadgets can all share the iPhone's connection simultaneously. Your phone becomes a personal cellular router, like a MiFi.

That's incredibly convenient. Many other app phones have it, but Apple's execution is especially nice. For example, the hotspot shuts itself off 90 seconds after the last laptop disconnects. That's hugely important, because these personal hotspot features are merciless battery drains.

The hotspot feature costs $20 a month extra, which buys only 2 gigabytes of data for all those laptops (that's in addition to your existing iPhone data plan). Think email, not YouTube. Additional gigabytes are $20 each.

To get this feature, you have to sign up for it by calling your cellular company or visiting its Web site (if you didn't already do that when you signed up for service).

Turning On the Hotspot

On the phone, open Settings→General→Network→Personal Hotspot.

 Tip Once you've turned on Personal Hotspot for the first time, you won't have to drill down as far to get to it. A new Personal Hotspot item appears right there on the main Settings screen from now on.

The Personal Hotspot screen contains details on connecting other computers. It also has the master on/off switch. Turn Personal Hotspot On.

(If you see a button that says, "Set Up Personal Hotspot," it means you haven't yet added the monthly tethering fee to your cellular plan. Contact your wireless carrier to get that change made to your account.)

You have to use a password for your personal hotspot; it's to ensure that people sitting nearby can't surf using your connection and run up your cell bill. Apple suggests a hard-to-crack password, but you can edit it and make up one of your own. (It has to be at least eight characters long and contain letters, numbers, and punctuation. Don't worry—in general, your laptop or other WiFi gadget can memorize it for you.)

Your laptops and other gadgets can connect to the Internet using any of three connections to the iPhone: WiFi, Bluetooth, or a USB cable. The USB connection ("tethering") is always available, but you can't share your connection over WiFi or Bluetooth unless those iPhone antennas are turned on (duh).

If one or both (WiFi or Bluetooth) are turned off, a message appears to let you know—and offers to turn them on for you. To save battery power, turn on only what you need.

Connecting via WiFi

After about 10 seconds, the iPhone shows up on your laptop or other gadget as though it's a WiFi network. Just choose the iPhone's name from your computer's WiFi hotspot menu (on the Mac, it's the 🛜 menu). Enter the password, and bam—your laptop is now online, using the iPhone as an antenna.

You can leave the iPhone in your pocket or purse. You'll surf away on your laptop, baffling every Internet-less soul around you. Your laptop can now use email, the Web, chat programs—anything it could do in a real WiFi hotspot (just a little slower).

Connecting via Bluetooth

There's no compelling reason to use Bluetooth instead of WiFi, especially since Bluetooth slows down your Internet connection. But anyway.

To connect wirelessly over Bluetooth, you first have to *pair* your laptop with the phone—a one-time procedure. It varies by laptop. For example:

- **Mac OS X.** On the Mac, open System Preferences→Bluetooth. Click the + button in the lower-left corner; when your iPhone's name shows up in the list, click it and then click Continue. After a moment, a huge six-digit number appears on both the Mac screen and the iPhone screen; on the phone, tap Pair, and on the Mac, click Continue and then Quit.

 Tip You can make life a lot easier later if, before you click Quit, you turn on "Show Bluetooth status in the menu bar." You'll see why in a moment.

- **Windows 7.** Open the Start menu; type *Bluetooth*. Click Add a Bluetooth Device. When your iPhone's name shows up in the list, click it and then click Next. After a moment, a huge six-digit number appears on both the PC screen and the iPhone screen; on the phone, tap Pair, and on the PC, tap Close.

Now, the pairing business is a one-time operation, but you still have to connect to the phone manually each time you want to go online.

- **On the Mac,** click the ❈ icon in the menu bar (which appears there because you wisely followed the preceding tip). Choose iPhone→Connect to Network. (The menu lists whatever your actual iPhone's name is, which might not be "iPhone.")

- **In Windows,** click the ❈ icon on the system tray and connect to the iPhone.

Connecting via USB Cable

If you can connect your laptop to your iPhone using the white charging cable, you should. Tethering eats up a lot of the phone's battery power, so keeping it plugged into the laptop means you won't wind up with a dead phone when you're finished surfing.

Once You're Connected

On the iPhone, a blue bar appears at the top of the screen to make you aware that the laptop is connected; in fact, it shows how many laptops or other gadgets are connected at the moment, via any of the three connection methods. (You can tap that bar to open the Personal Hotspot screen in Settings.)

If you have AT&T, you can still use all functions of the iPhone, including making calls and even surfing the Web, while it's channeling your laptop's Internet connection.

If you have Verizon or Sprint, your CDMA network can't handle Internet connections and voice calls simultaneously. So if a phone call comes in, the iPhone suspends the hot-spot feature until you're finished talking; when you hang up (or if you decline the call), all connected gadgets regain their Internet connections automatically.

Turning Off Personal Hotspot

If you're connected wirelessly to the iPhone, the Personal Hotspot feature is a battery hog. It'll cut your iPhone's battery longevity in half. That's why, if no laptops are connected for 90 seconds, the iPhone turns the Hotstpot off automatically.

You can also turn off the Hotspot manually, in either of two ways:

- In Settings→WiFi, a new button appears that says Disconnect WiFi Clients. Tap it to bump the laptops off your phone, perhaps so that you can get your phone onto a public WiFi hotspot you've found.

- In Settings→Personal Hotspot, tap Off.

Turning Personal Hotspot Back On

About 90 seconds after the last gadget stops using the hotspot, your iPhone shuts off the feature to save its own battery. To fire it back up again later, open Settings and tap Personal Hotspot. That's it—just visit the Personal Hotspot screen and then back right out again to make the iPhone resume broadcasting its WiFi or Bluetooth network to your laptops and other gadgets.

Twitter

Twitter, of course , is a free service (sign up at *twitter.com*) that lets you send out short messages, like text messages, to anyone who wants to get them from you. Meanwhile, you sign up to receive other people's tweets (as they're called). Twitter is a fantastic way for people to spread news, links, thoughts, and observations directly to the people who care—incredibly quickly.

Twitter apps, which let you read and send tweets, have been popular on the iPhone for years. You might try Twitter (Twitter's own, official app), Twitterrific, or Twittelator. But in iOS 5, Twitter is woven into the built-in iPhone apps.

Start by visiting Settings→Twitter. Here you can enter your Twitter name and password (Twitter names always begin with the @ symbol, like @smith), or sign up for a Twitter account. Here, too, you're offered the chance to download the actual Twitter app mentioned above. You can also tap Update Contacts, which attempts to add the Twitter addresses of everybody in your Contacts app to their information cards.

Once you've set up Twitter in this way, you'll find some nifty tweeting buttons built into your other apps. For example:

- **Camera, Photos.** When you tap the  button below a photo, you're offered a Tweet button. It sends out that photo (and adds a comment that you type, if you like) to your followers.

- **YouTube, Maps, Safari.** Tap the , and then tap Tweet, to send a link to the YouTube video, map location, or Web page that's currently open.

When you tweet something, you get the new "Tweet sheet." Here you can add a comment to the link or photo, or attach your current location. You'll notice that the keyboard here offers dedicated @ and # keys. (The # is for creating hashtags—searchable keywords on a tweet like #iphone4sbugs—that Twitter fans can use when searching for tweets about certain topics.)

11 The Web

The iPhone's Web browser is Safari, a lite version of the same one that comes with every Macintosh and is also available for Windows. It's fast, simple to use, and very pretty indeed. You see the real deal—the actual fonts, graphics, and layouts—not the stripped-down, bare-bones mini-Web on cellphones of years gone by.

Safari Tour

You get on the Web by tapping Safari on the Home screen. As noted in the previous chapter, the Web on the iPhone can be either fast (when you're in a WiFi hotspot), medium (in a 3G coverage area) or excruciating (on the EDGE cellular network). Even so, some Web is usually better than no Web at all.

 Tip You don't have to wait for a Web page to load entirely. You can zoom in, scroll, and begin reading the text even when only part of the page has appeared.

Safari has most of the features of a desktop Web browser: bookmarks, auto-complete (for Web addresses), scrolling shortcuts, cookies, a pop-up ad blocker, password memorization, and so on. (It's missing niceties like streaming music, Java, Flash, and other plug-ins.)

Here's a quick tour of the main screen elements, starting from the upper right:

- **(Google).** Tap this word (which you can change to say "Bing" or "Yahoo") to open the search bar and the keyboard; see page 351.

- **Address bar.** This empty white box is where you enter the *URL* (Web address) for a page you want to visit. (URL is short for the even-less-self-explanatory *Uniform Resource Locator*.)

- **✕, ↻ (Stop, Reload).** Tap **✕** to interrupt the downloading of a Web page you've just requested (if you've made a mistake, for instance, or if it's taking too long).

  Once a page has finished loading, the **✕** button turns into a **↻** button. Click it if a page doesn't look or work quite right. Safari re-downloads the Web page and reinterprets its text and graphics.

- **◀, ▶ (Back, Forward).** Tap the **◀** button to revisit the page you were just on. Once you've tapped **◀**, you can then tap the **▶** button to return to the page you were on *before* you tapped the **◀** button.

- **⤴ (Share/Bookmark).** When you're on an especially useful page, tap this button. It offers six choices: Add Bookmark (page 344), Add to Reading List (page 346), Add to Home Screen (page 347), Mail Link to this Page, Tweet (page 336), and Print (page 220).

- **⊞ (Bookmarks).** This button brings up your list of saved bookmarks.

- **⊡, ⊟ (Page Juggler).** Safari can keep multiple Web pages open, just like any other browser. Page 352 has the details.

Zooming and Scrolling

These two gestures—zooming in on Web pages and then scrolling around them—have probably sold more people on the iPhone than any other demonstration. It all happens with a fluid animation, and a responsiveness to your finger taps, that's positively addicting.

When you first open a Web page, you get to see the *entire thing.* Unlike most cellphones, the iPhone crams the entire Web site onto its 3½-inch screen, so you can get the lay of the land.

At this point, of course, you're looking at .004-point type, which is too small to read unless you're a microbe. So the next step is to magnify the *part* of the page you want to read.

The iPhone offers three ways to do that:

- **Rotate the iPhone.** Turn the device 90 degrees in either direction. The iPhone rotates and magnifies the image to fill the wider view.

- **Do the two-finger spread.** Put two fingers on the glass and drag them apart. The Web page stretches before your very eyes, growing larger. Then you can pinch to shrink the page back down again. (Most people do several spreads or several pinches in a row to achieve the degree of zoom they want.)

- **Double-tap.** Safari is intelligent enough to recognize different *chunks* of a Web page. One article might represent a chunk. A photograph might qualify as a chunk. When you double-tap a chunk, Safari magnifies *just that chunk* to fill the whole screen. It's smart and useful.

  Double-tap again to zoom back out.

Double-tap

Once you've zoomed out to the proper degree, you can then scroll around the page by dragging or flicking with a finger. You don't have to worry about "clicking a link" by accident; if your finger's in motion, Safari ignores the tapping action, even if you happen to land on a link.

Tip Once you've double-tapped to zoom in on a page, you can use these little-known tricks: Double-tap anywhere on the *upper* half of the screen to scroll up, or the *lower* half to scroll down. The closer you are to the top or bottom of the screen, the more you scroll.

By the way, you'll occasionally encounter a *frame* (a column of text) on a page—an area that scrolls independently of the main page. The iPhone has a secret, undocumented method for scrolling one of these frames without scrolling the whole page: the *two-finger drag.* Try it out.

The Address Bar

As on a computer, this Web browser offers several tools for navigating the Web: the address bar, bookmarks, the History list, and good old link-tapping. These pages cover each of these methods in turn, along with the Reading List and Web Clips.

The address bar is the strip at the top of the screen where you type in a Web page's address. And it so happens that *four* of the iPhone's greatest tips and shortcuts all have to do with this important navigational tool:

- **Insta-scroll to the top.** You can jump directly to the address bar, no matter how far down a page you've scrolled, just by tapping the very top edge of the screen (on the status bar). That "tap the top" trick is timely, too, when a Web site is designed to *hide* the address bar.

- **Don't delete.** There *is* a ⊗ button at the right end of the address bar whose purpose is to erase the entire current address so you can type another one. (Tap inside the address bar to make it, and the keyboard, appear.) But the ⊗ button is for suckers.

  Instead, whenever the address bar is open for typing, *just type.* Forget that there's already a URL there. The iPhone is smart enough to figure out that you want to *replace* that Web address with a new one.

- **Don't type** *http://www or .com.* Safari is also smart enough to know that most Web addresses use that format—so you can leave all that stuff out, and it will supply them automatically. Instead of *http://www.cnn.com*, for example, you can just type *cnn* and hit Go.

- **Don't type *.net, .org,* or *.edu,* either.** Safari's canned URL choices can save you four keyboard taps apiece. To see their secret menu, hold your finger down on the .com button. Then tap the common suffix you want.

Otherwise, this address bar works just like the one in any other Web browser. Tap inside it to make the keyboard appear. (If the address bar is hidden, then tap the top edge of the iPhone screen.)

The Safari Keyboard

In Safari, the keyboard works just as described in Chapter 2, with a couple of exceptions.

First, there are no spaces allowed in Internet addresses; therefore, in the spot usually reserved for the space bar, this keyboard has three keys for things that *do* appear often in Web addresses: period, slash, and ".com." These nifty special keys make typing Web addresses a lot faster.

Second, tap the blue Go key when you're finished typing the address. That's your Enter key. (Or tap Cancel to hide the keyboard *without* "pressing Enter.")

As you type, a handy list of suggestions appears beneath the address bar (facing page, left). These are all Web addresses that Safari already knows about, because they're either in your Bookmarks list or in your History list (meaning you've visited them recently).

If you see the address you're trying to type, then by all means tap it instead of typing out the rest of the URL. The time you save could be your own.

By the way, remember that you can *rotate* the keyboard into landscape orientation, as shown here. This is a big deal; when it's stretched out the wide way, you get much bigger, broader keys, and typing is much easier and faster.

Bookmarks

Safari comes prestocked with bookmarks—that is, tags that identify Web sites you might want to visit again without having to remember and type their URLs. Amazingly, all these canned bookmarks are interesting and useful to *you* in particular! How did it know?

Easy—it copied your existing desktop computer's browser bookmarks from Internet Explorer (Windows) or Safari (Macintosh) when you synced the iPhone (Chapter 13). Sneaky, eh?

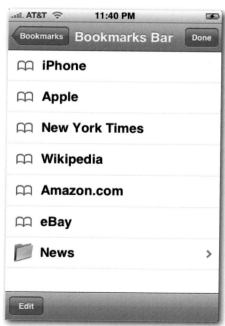

To see them, tap 📖 at the bottom of the screen. You see the master list of bookmarks. Some may be "loose," and many more are probably organized into folders, or even folders *within* folders.

Tapping a folder shows you what's inside, and tapping a bookmark begins opening the corresponding Web site.

Creating New Bookmarks

You can add new bookmarks right on the phone. Any work you do here is copied *back* to your computer the next time you sync the two machines—or instantaneously, if you've turned on iCloud bookmark syncing.

When you find a Web page you might like to visit again, tap the 📤 button (bottom of the screen) and then tap Add Bookmark. The Add Bookmark screen appears. You have two tasks here:

- **Type a better name.** In the top box, you can type a shorter or clearer name for the page than the one it comes with. Instead of "Bass, Trout & Tackle—the Web's Premier Resource for the Avid Outdoorsman," you can just call it "Fish site."

  The box below this one identifies the underlying URL, which is totally independent from what you've *named* your bookmark. You can't edit this one.

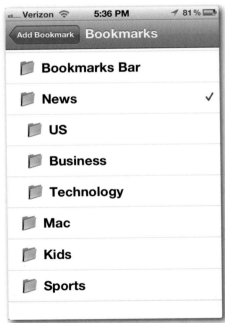

- **Specify where to file this bookmark.** If you tap Bookmarks >, you open Safari's hierarchical list of bookmark folders, which organize your bookmarked sites. Tap the folder where you want to file the new bookmark so you'll know where to find it later.

 Tip Here's a site worth bookmarking: *http://google.com/gwt/n*. It gives you a bare-bones, superfast version of the Web, provided by Google for the benefit of people on slow connections (like EDGE). You can opt to hide graphics for even more speed. Yeah, the iPhone's browser is glorious and all—but sometimes you'd rather have fast than pretty.

Editing Bookmarks and Folders

It's easy enough to massage your Bookmarks list within Safari—to delete favorites that aren't so favorite anymore, to make new folders, to rearrange the list, to rename a folder or a bookmark, and so on.

The techniques are the same for editing bookmark *folders* as editing the bookmarks themselves—after the first step. To edit the folder list, start by opening the Bookmarks (tap the 𝄞 button), and then tap Edit.

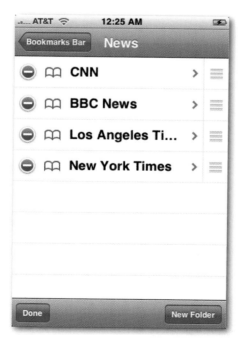

To edit the bookmarks themselves, tap 𝄞, tap a folder, and *then* tap Edit. Now you can get organized:

- **Delete something.** Tap the ⊖ button next to a folder or bookmark, and then tap Delete to confirm.

- **Rearrange the list.** Drag the grip strip (☰) up or down in the list to move the folders or bookmarks around. (You can't move or delete the top three folders—History, Bookmarks Bar, and Bookmarks Menu.)

- **Edit a name and location.** Tap a folder or bookmark name. If you tap a folder, you arrive at the Edit Folder screen; you can edit the folder's name and which folder it's inside of. If you tap a bookmark, Edit Bookmark lets you edit the name and the URL it points to.

Tap the Back button (upper-left corner) when you're finished.

- **Create a folder.** Tap New Folder in the lower-right corner of the Edit Folders screen. You're offered the chance to type a name for it and to specify where you want to file it (that is, in which *other* folder).

Tap Done when you're finished.

The Reading List

The Reading List is a handy list of Web pages you want to read later.

It doesn't actually store the pages on the phone; it just stores *links* to the pages. You can't read them later unless you're actually online.

If it sounds like the Reading List is a lot like bookmarks, well, you're right—but there are some differences. For example, it's faster to flag a Web page you like—you don't have to make up a name or a location for it, as with a bookmark. The Reading List also keeps track of what you've read; you can use the All/Unread buttons at the top of the list to view everything, or just what you haven't yet read. You might treat the Reading List as a list of pages you'll want to read *once* later, and use bookmarks for pages you like to revisit *frequently*.

> **Tip** To make matters even sweeter, iCloud synchronizes your Reading List among your Mac, iPhone, iPad, and so on—as long as you've turned on bookmark syncing. It's as through the Web always keeps your place.

To add a page to the Reading List, tap the button (bottom of the screen) and then tap Add to Reading List. Or just hold your finger down on a link until a set of buttons appears, including Add to Reading List.

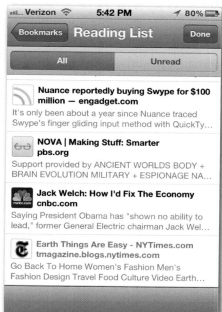

Once you've added a page to the Reading List, you can get to it by tapping the 🔖 button, and then tapping Reading List. Tap an item on your list to open and read it.

Web Clips

If there's a certain Web site you visit all the time, like every day, then even the four taps necessary to open it in the usual way (Home, Safari, Bookmarks, your site's name) can seem like an overwhelming amount of red tape. That's why Apple made it simple to add the icon of a certain Web page right on your Home screen.

Start by opening the page in question. Tap the ✚ button at the bottom of the screen. In the button list, tap Add to Home Screen. Now you're offered the chance to edit the icon's name; finally, tap Add.

When you return to your Home screen, you'll see the new icon. You can move it around, drag it to a different Home screen, and so on, exactly as you would any other app.

Or, to delete it, touch its icon until all the Home icons begin to wiggle. Tap the Web Clip's ⊗ badge to remove its icon.

Tip You can turn *part* of a Web page into one of these Web Clips, too. You might want quick access to *The New York Times'* "most emailed" list, or the bestselling children's books on Amazon, or the most-viewed video on YouTube, or the box scores for a certain sports league.

All you have to do is zoom and scroll the page in Safari *before* you tap the **+** button, isolating the section you want. Later, when you open the Web Clip, you'll see exactly the part of the Web page you wanted.

The History List

Behind the scenes, Safari keeps track of the Web sites you've visited in the past week or so, neatly organized into subfolders like Earlier Today and Yesterday. It's a great feature when you can't recall the address for a Web site you visited recently—or when you remember it had a long, complicated address and you get the psychiatric condition known as iPhone Keyboard Dread.

To see the list of recent sites, tap the 🕮 button, and then tap the History folder, whose icon bears a little clock to make sure you know it's special. Once the History list appears, just tap a bookmark (or a folder name and *then* a bookmark) to revisit that Web page.

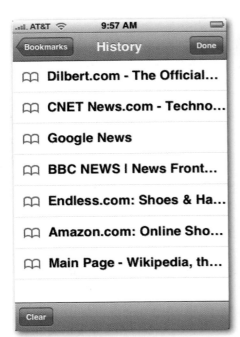
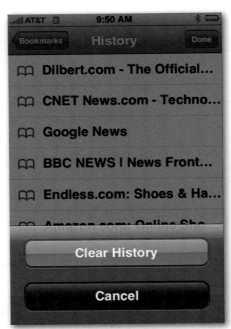

Erasing the History List

Some people find it creepy that Safari maintains a complete list of every Web site they've seen recently, right there in plain view of any family member or coworker who wanders by. They'd just as soon their wife/husband/boss/parent/kid not know what Web sites they've been visiting.

You can't delete just one particularly incriminating History listing. You can, however, delete the *entire* History menu, thus erasing all your tracks. To do that, tap Clear; confirm by tapping Clear History.

You've just rewritten History.

Tapping Links

Here's the fourth and final method of navigating the Web: tapping links on the screen, much the way you'd click them if you had a mouse. As you know from desktop-computer browsing, not all links are blue and underlined. Sometimes, in fact, they're graphics.

The only difference is that on the iPhone, not all links take you to other Web pages. If you tap an email address, it opens up the iPhone's Mail program (Chapter 12) and creates a preaddressed outgoing message. If you tap a phone number you find online, the iPhone calls it for you. There's even such a thing as a *map* link, which opens the Maps app.

Each of these links, in other words, takes you out of Safari. If you want to return to your Web browsing, then you have to return to the Home screen, or the task switcher, and tap Safari. The page you had open is still there, waiting.

 Tip If you hold your finger on a link for a moment—touching rather than tapping—a handy sliding panel appears. At the top, you see the full Web address that will open. There are some useful buttons: Open, Open in New Page, Add to Reading List, and Copy (meaning "copy the link address"). Oh, there's also Cancel.

Saving Graphics

In the original iPhone software, if you found a picture online that you wished you could keep forever, you had only one option: Stare at it until you'd memorized it.

Now, however, life is much easier. Just keep your finger pressed on the image, very still, for about a second. A sheet appears, offering a Save Image button. (If the graphic is also a tappable link, an Open Link button is on this sheet as well.)

If you tap Save Image, the iPhone thoughtfully deposits a copy of the image in your Camera Roll (page 194) so it will be copied back to your Mac or PC at the next sync opportunity. If you tap Copy, you nab that graphic and can now paste it into another program.

AutoFill

On the real Safari—on the Mac or PC—a feature called AutoFill saves you an awful lot of typing. It fills out your name and address automatically when you're ordering something online. It stores your passwords so you don't have to re-enter them every time you visit passworded sites.

On the iPhone, where you're typing on glass, the convenience of AutoFill goes to a whole new level.

To turn on AutoFill, visit Settings→Safari→AutoFill. Two features await (shown on the facing page at left):

- **Use Contact Info.** Turn this On. Then tap My Info. From the address book, find your own listing. You've just told Safari *which* name, address, city, state, Zip code, and phone number belong to you.

  From now on, whenever you're asked to input your address, phone number, and so on, you'll see an AutoFill button at the top of the keyboard. Tap it to make Safari auto-enter all those details, saving you no end of typing. (It works on *most* sites.) If there are extra blanks that AutoFill doesn't fill, then you can tap the Previous and Next buttons to move your cursor from one to the next instead of tapping and scrolling manually.

- **Names & Passwords.** If you turn this on, then Safari will offer to memorize each name and password you enter on a Web site. You can tap Yes (a good idea for your PTA or library account), Never for this Website (a good idea for your bank), or Not Now (you'll be asked again next time).

Searching the Web

You might have noticed that whenever the address bar appears, so does a search bar just to the right of it. (It bears the name of your chosen search service—Google, for example.)

That's an awfully handy shortcut. It means you can perform a search without having to leave whatever page you're already on. Just tap into that box, type your search phrase (or speak it, if you have an iPhone 4S), and then tap the big blue Search button in the corner.

You can tell the iPhone to use a Yahoo or Bing search instead of Google, if you like. From the Home screen, tap Settings→Safari→Search Engine, as shown on the next page.

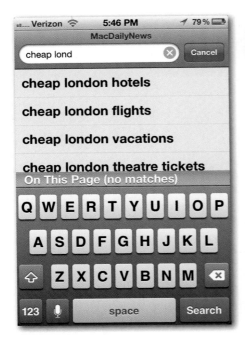

Tip There are all kinds of cool things you can type here—special terms that tell Google, "I want *information,* not Web-page matches."

You can type a movie name and Zip code or city/state (*Titanic Returns 10024*) to get a list of today's showtimes in theaters near you. Get the forecast by typing *weather chicago* or *weather 60609*. Stock quotes: Type the symbol (*AMZN*). Dictionary definitions: *define schadenfreude*. Unit conversions: *liters in 5 gallons*. Currency conversions: *25 usd in euros*. Then tap Search to get instant results.

Manipulating Multiple Pages

Like any self-respecting browser, Safari can keep multiple pages open at once, making it easy for you to switch among them. You can think of it as a miniature version of tabbed browsing, a feature of browsers like Safari Senior, Firefox, Chrome, and the latest Internet Explorer. Tabbed browsing keeps a bunch of Web pages open simultaneously—in a single, neat window.

The beauty of this arrangement is that you can start reading one Web page while the others load into their own tabs in the background.

On the iPhone, it works like this:

- **To open a new window,** tap the button in the lower right. The Web page shrinks into a mini version. Tap New Page to open a new, untitled Web-browser tab; now you can enter an address, use a bookmark, or whatever.

> **Note** Alternatively, hold your finger down on a link instead of tapping it. You get a choice of three commands, one of which is Open in New Page. (The others are Open and Copy, meaning copy the Web address.)
>
> Sometimes, Safari sprouts a new window *automatically* when you click a link. That's because the link you tapped is programmed to open in a new window. To return to the original window, read on.

- **To switch back to the first window,** tap again. Now there are two dots (• •) beneath the miniature page, indicating that *two* windows are open. (The boldest, whitest dot indicates where you are in the horizontal row of windows.) Bring the first window's miniature onto the screen by flicking horizontally with your finger. Tap it to open it full-screen.

You can open a third window, and a fourth, and so on, and jump among them, using these two techniques. The ⬚ icon sprouts a number to let you know how many windows are open; for example, it might say ⬚.

- **To close a window,** tap ⬚. Flick over to the miniature window you want to close, and then tap the ⊗ button at its top-left corner.

 Note Safari requires at least one window to be open. If you close the very last window, Safari gives you a blank, empty window to take its place.

Reader

How can people read Web articles when there's Times-Square blinking going on all around them? Fortunately, you'll never have to put up with that again.

The Reader button in the address bar is amazing. With one tap, it eliminates *everything* from the Web page you're reading except the text and photos. No ads, toolbars, blinking, links, banners, promos, or anything else.

The text is also changed to a clean, clear font and size, and the background is made plain white. Basically, it makes any Web page look like a printed book page, and it's glorious. Here's the before and after. Which looks easier to read?

 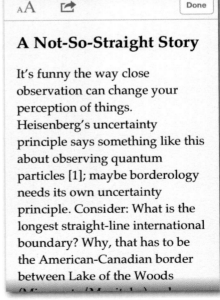

To exit Reader, tap the Reader button again. Best. Feature. Ever.

The fine print: The Reader doesn't appear until the page has fully loaded. It doesn't appear on "front page" pages, like the *nytimes.com* home page—only when you've opened an article within. It may not appear on sites that are already specially designed for access by cellphones.

Audio and Video on the Web

In general, streaming audio and video on the iPhone is a bust. The iPhone doesn't recognize the Real, Windows Media, or Flash file formats. This means the iPhone can't play the huge majority of online video and audio recordings. That's a crushing disappointment to news and sports junkies.

But the iPhone isn't *utterly* clueless about streaming online goodies. It can play some QuickTime movies, like movie trailers, as long as they've been encoded (prepared) in certain formats (like H.264).

It can also play MP3 audio files right off the Web. That can be extremely handy for people who like to know what's going on in the world, because many European news agencies offer streaming MP3 versions of their news broadcasts. Here are a few worth bookmarking:

- **BBC News.** You can find 5-minute news bulletins at *www.bbc.co.uk/ worldservice/programmes/newssummary.shtml*. (Here's a shortcut: *http:// bit.ly/2xhEKF.*)

- **Deutsche Welle.** English-language news, sports, arts, and talk from Germany. *www.dw-world.de/dw/0,2142,4703,00.html*. (Shortcut: *http://bit. ly/HHwog.*)

- **Radio France.** English-language broadcasts from France. *www.rfi.fr/ langues/statiques/rfi_anglais.asp*. (Shortcut: *http://bit.ly/10ol5A.*)

- **Voice of America.** The official external radio broadcast of the U.S. government. *www.voanews.com/english/*.

Actually, any old MP3 files play fine right in Safari. If you've already played through your 4 or 8 gigabytes of music from your computer, then you can always do a Web search for *free mp3 music.*

RSS: The Missing Manual

In the beginning, the Internet was an informational Garden of Eden. There were no banner ads, pop-ups, flashy animations, or spam messages. Back then, people thought the Internet was the greatest idea ever.

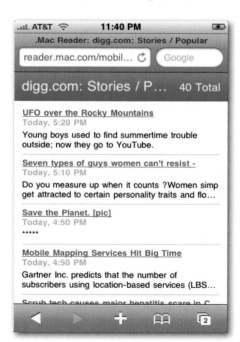

Those days, alas, are long gone. Web browsing now entails a constant battle against intrusive advertising and annoying animations. And with the proliferation of Web sites of every kind—from news sites to personal weblogs (*blogs*)—just reading your favorite sites can become a full-time job.

Enter RSS, a technology that lets you subscribe to *feeds*—summary blurbs provided by thousands of sources around the world, from Reuters to Apple to your nerdy next-door neighbor. The result: You spare yourself the tediousness of checking for updates manually, plus you get to read short summaries of new articles without ads or blinking animations. And if you want to read a full article, you just tap its headline.

 Note RSS stands for either Rich Site Summary or Really Simple Syndication. Each abbreviation explains one aspect of RSS—either its summarizing talent or its simplicity.

Safari, as it turns out, doubles as a handy RSS reader. Whenever you tap an "RSS Feed" link on a Web page, or whenever you type the address of an RSS feed into the address bar (it often begins with *feed://*), Safari automatically displays a handy table-of-contents view that lists all the news blurbs on that page.

Scan through the summaries. When you see an article that looks intriguing, tap its headline. You go to the Web page to read the full-blown article.

 Tip It's worth bookmarking your favorite RSS feeds. One great one for tech fans is *feed://www.digg.com/rss/index.xml*, a constantly updated list of the coolest and most interesting tech and pop-culture stories of the day. Most news publications offer news feeds, too. (Your humble author's own daily *New York Times* blog has a feed that's *http://pogue.blogs.nytimes.com/?feed=rss2*.)

Web Security

Safari on the iPhone isn't meant to be a full-blown Web browser like the one on your desktop computer, but it comes surprisingly close—especially when it comes to privacy and security. Cookies, pop-up blockers, parental controls…they're all here, for your paranoid pleasure.

Pop-Up Blocker

The world's smarmiest advertisers have begun inundating us with pop-up and pop-under ads—nasty little windows that appear in front of the browser window, or, worse, behind it, waiting to jump out the moment you close your window. Fortunately, Safari comes set to block those pop-ups so you don't see them. It's a war out there—but at least you now have some ammunition.

The thing is, though, pop-ups are sometimes legitimate (and not ads)—notices of new banking features, seating charts on ticket-sales sites, warnings that the instructions for using a site have changed, and so on. Safari can't tell these from ads—and it stifles them, too. So if a site you trust says, "Please turn off pop-up blockers and reload this page," then you know you're probably missing out on a *useful* pop-up message.

In those situations, you can turn off the pop-up blocker. From the Home screen, tap Settings→Safari. Where it says Block Pop-ups, tap the On/Off switch.

Cookies

Cookies are something like Web page preference files. Certain Web sites—particularly commercial ones like Amazon.com—deposit them on your hard drive like little bookmarks so they'll remember you the next time you visit. Ever notice how Amazon.com greets you with, "Welcome, Chris" (or whatever your name is)? It's reading its own cookie, left behind on your hard drive (or in this case, on your iPhone).

Most cookies are perfectly innocuous—and, in fact, are extremely useful, because they help Web sites remember your tastes. Cookies also spare you the effort of having to type in your name, address, and so on, every time you visit these Web sites.

But fear is widespread, and the media fan the flames with tales of sinister cookies that track your movement on the Web. If you're worried about invasions of privacy, Safari is ready to protect you.

From the Home screen, tap Settings→Safari→Accept Cookies. The options here are like a paranoia gauge. If you click Never, you create an acrylic shield around your iPhone. No cookies can come in, and no cookie information can go out. You'll probably find the Web a very inconvenient place; you'll have to re-enter your information upon every visit, and some Web sites may not work properly at all. The Always option means, "Oh, what the heck—just gimme all of them."

A good compromise is From Visited, which accepts cookies from sites you *want* to visit, but blocks cookies deposited on your phone by sites you're not actually visiting—cookies an especially evil banner ad gives you, for example.

This screen also offers a Clear Cookies button (deletes all the cookies you've accumulated so far), as well as Clear History (page 477) and Clear Cache.

The *cache* is a patch of the iPhone's storage area where pieces of Web pages you visit—graphics, for example—are retained. The idea is that the next time you visit the same page, the iPhone won't have to download those bits again. It already has them on board, so the page appears much faster.

If you worry that your cache eats up space, poses a security risk, or is confusing some page (and preventing the most recent version of the page from appearing), then tap this button to erase it and start over.

Parental Controls

If your child (or employee) is old enough to have an iPhone but not old enough for the seedier side of the Web, then don't miss the Restrictions feature in Settings. The iPhone makes no attempt to separate the good Web sites from the bad—but it *can* remove the Safari icon from the iPhone altogether so that no Web browsing is possible at all. See page 463 for instructions.

Web Applications

For the first year of the iPhone, there was no App Store. No add-on programs, no way to make the iPhone do new, cool stuff (at least not without hacking it). Apple gave iPhone programmers only one bit of freedom: They could write iPhone-shaped *Web pages* tailored for the iPhone.

Some of these iPhone Web applications look like desktop widgets that do one thing really well—like showing you a Doppler radar map for local weather. Some are minipages that tap directly into sites like Flickr and Twitter. Some even let you tap into Web-based word processing sites if you need to create a document *right this very instant.*

Today, regular iPhone programs do everything those Web apps once did. Web apps were essentially a workaround, a placeholder solution until Apple could get its App Store going. So Web apps have pretty much faded away now that the App Store is in business.

If you're still interested, you can read about these antique iPhone artifacts in the free downloadable appendix to this chapter. It's available from this book's "Missing CD" page at *www.missingmanuals.com.*

12 Email

You ain't never seen email on a phone like this. It offers full formatting, fonts, graphics, and choice of type size; file attachments like Word, Excel, PowerPoint, PDF, Pages, Numbers, and photos; and compatibility with Yahoo Mail, Gmail, AOL Mail, iCloud mail, corporate Microsoft Exchange mail, and just about any standard email account. Dude, if you want a more satisfying portable email machine than this one, buy a laptop.

This chapter covers the basic email experience. If you've gotten yourself hooked up with iCloud or Exchange ActiveSync, though, you'll soon find out how wireless email syncing makes everything better. Or at least different. (See Chapters 14 and 15 for details.)

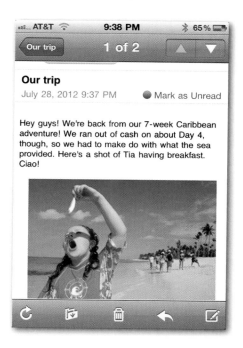

Setting Up Your Account

If you play your cards right, you won't *have* to set up your email account on the phone. The first time you set up the iPhone to sync with your computer (Chapter 13), you're offered the chance to *sync* your Mac's or PC's mail with the phone. That doesn't mean it copies actual messages—only the email settings, so the iPhone is ready to start downloading mail.

You're offered this option if your Mac's mail program is Mail or Outlook/Entourage, or if your PC's mail program is Outlook, Outlook Express, or Windows Mail.

But what if you don't use one of those email programs? No sweat. You can also plug the necessary settings right into the iPhone.

Free Email Accounts

If you have a free email account from Google, AOL, or Yahoo; an iCloud account (Chapter 14); or a Microsoft Exchange account run by your employer (Chapter 15), then setup on the iPhone is easy.

From the Home screen, tap Settings→Mail, Contacts, Calendars→Add Account. Tap the colorful logo that corresponds to the kind of account you have (Google, Yahoo, or whatever).

Now you land on the account-information screen. Tap into each of the four blanks and, when the keyboard appears, type your name, email address, account password, and a description (that one's optional). Tap Save.

Your email account is ready to go!

 Tip If you don't have one of these free accounts, they're worth having, if only as a backup to your regular account. They can help with spam filtering, too, since the iPhone doesn't offer any; see page 384. To sign up, go to Google.com, Yahoo.com, AOL.com, or iCloud.com.

POP3 and IMAP Accounts

Those freebie, Web-based accounts are super-easy to set up. But they're not the whole ball of wax. Millions of people have a more generic email account, perhaps supplied by their employers or Internet providers. They're generally one of two types:

- **POP accounts** are the oldest, most compatible, and most common type on the Internet. (POP stands for Post Office Protocol, but this won't be on the test.) But a POP account can make life complicated if you check your mail on more than one machine (say, a PC and an iPhone), as you'll discover shortly.

  A POP server transfers incoming mail to your computer (or iPhone) before you read it, which works fine as long as you're using *only that machine* to access your email.

- **IMAP accounts** (Internet Message Access Protocol) are newer and have more features than POP servers, and they're quickly catching up in popularity. IMAP servers keep all your mail online, rather than making you store it on your computer; as a result, you can access the same mail from any computer (or phone) . IMAP servers remember which messages you've read and sent, and they even keep track of how you've filed messages into mail folders. (Those free Yahoo email accounts are IMAP accounts, and so are Apple's iCloud accounts and corporate Exchange accounts. Gmail accounts *can* be IMAP, too.)

  There's really only one downside to this approach: If you don't conscientiously delete mail after you've read it, your online mailbox eventually overflows. On IMAP accounts that don't come with a lot of storage, the system sooner or later starts bouncing new messages, annoying your friends.

The iPhone can communicate with both kinds of accounts, with varying degrees of completeness.

If you haven't opted to have your account-setup information transferred automatically to the iPhone from your Mac or PC, then you can set it up manually on the phone.

From the Home screen, tap Settings→Mail, Contacts, Calendars→Add Account. Tap Other, tap Add Mail Account, and then enter your name, email address, password, and an optional description. Tap Next.

Apple's software attempts to figure out which kind of account you have (POP or IMAP) by the email address. If it can't make that determination, then you arrive at a second screen, where you're asked for such juicy details as the Host Name for Incoming and Outgoing Mail servers. (This is also where you tap either IMAP or POP, to tell the iPhone what sort of account it's dealing with.)

If you don't know this stuff offhand, you'll have to ask your Internet provider, corporate tech-support person, or next-door teenager to help you.

When you're finished, tap Save.

To delete an account, open Settings→Mail, Contacts, Calendars→[account name]. At the bottom of the screen, you'll find the Delete Account button.

 Tip In iOS 5, for the first time, you can edit your IMAP or Exchange mailboxes (mail folders) right on the phone.

View the mailbox list for the account and then tap Edit. Tap the New Mailbox button to create a new folder. To edit an existing mailbox, tap its name; you can then rename it, tap the Mailbox Location folder to move it, or tap Delete Mailbox. Tap Save to finish up.

The "Two-Mailbox Problem"

It's awesome that the iPhone can check the mail from a POP mail account, which is the sort offered by most Internet providers. This means, however, that now you've got *two* machines checking the same account—your main computer and your iPhone.

Now you've got the "two-mailbox problem." What if your computer downloads some of the mail and your iPhone downloads the rest? Will your mail stash be split awkwardly between two machines? How will you remember where to find a particular message?

Fortunately, the problem is halfway solved by a factory setting deep within the iPhone that says, in effect: "The iPhone may download mail, but it will leave a copy behind for your desktop computer to download later."

 Tip If you must know, this setting is at Settings→Mail, Contacts, Calendars→[your account name]→Advanced→Delete from server→Never.

Unfortunately, that doesn't stop the opposite problem. It doesn't prevent the *computer* from downloading messages before your *iPhone* can get to them. When you're out and about, therefore, you may miss important messages.

Most people would rather not turn off their computers every time they leave their desks. Fortunately, there's a more automatic solution: Turn on the Leave messages on server option in your Mac or PC email program. Its location depends on which email program you use. For example:

- **Outlook for Mac/Entourage.** Choose Tools→Accounts. Double-click the account name; click Advanced or Options. Turn on Leave a copy of each message on the server.

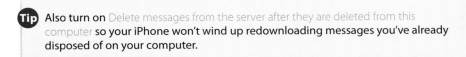

Tip Also turn on Delete messages from the server after they are deleted from this computer so your iPhone won't wind up redownloading messages you've already disposed of on your computer.

- **Mail.** Choose Mail→Preferences→Accounts→[account name]→ Advanced. Turn off Remove copy from server after retrieving a message.

- **Outlook.** Choose Tools→E-mail Accounts→E-mail. Click View or Change E-Mail Accounts→Next→[your account name]→Change→More Settings→Advanced. Turn on Leave a copy of messages on the server.

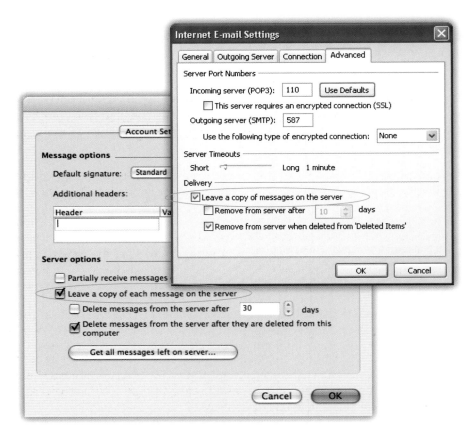

- **Outlook Express.** Choose Tools→Accounts→[your account name]→ Properties→Advanced. Turn on Leave a copy of messages on the server.

With this arrangement, both machines download the same mail; messages aren't deleted until you delete them from the bigger computer.

 Tip Here's another idea that may help: Turn on Always Bcc Myself (in Settings→Mail, Contacts, Calendars). It ensures that when you send a message from your iPhone, it fires off a copy to your own email address—so that when you return to your desk, you'll have copies of all the messages you wrote from the road. (Yeah, they'll be in your inbox and not your Sent Mail, but at least it's something.)

And consider getting (or forwarding your mail to) an IMAP account like iCloud, Gmail, or Yahoo Mail to avoid this whole mess. Then any changes you make on one machine are magically reflected on the other.

Downloading Mail

If you have "push" email (Yahoo, iCloud, or Exchange), then your iPhone doesn't *check* for messages; new messages show up on your iPhone *as they arrive,* around the clock.

If you have any other kind of account, then the iPhone checks for new messages automatically on a schedule—every 15, 30, or 60 minutes. It also checks for new messages each time you open the Mail program, or whenever you tap the Check button (Ç) within the Mail program.

You can adjust the frequency of these automatic checks or turn off the "push" feature (because it uses up your battery faster) in Settings; see page 468.

When new mail arrives, you'll know it at a glance; all the new Notification Center options described on page 36 work well in Mail. For example, if your phone is off, you can tap the Sleep or Home button to view the sender, subject, and the first line of the message right on the Lock screen. (Swipe across one, right there on the Lock screen, to jump to it in Mail.)

If your phone is on, a new message can alert you by appearing briefly at the top of the screen, without disturbing your work (page 35).

At the Home screen, Mail's icon sprouts a circled number that tells you how many new messages are waiting. (If you routinely leave a lot of unread messages in your inbox, and so you don't really care about this "badge," you can turn it off in Settings→Notifications→Mail→Badge App Icon.)

You'll also hear the iPhone's little "You've got mail" sound, unless you've turned that off in Settings. To read your new mail, tap Mail.

 Note If you have more than one email account, then this number shows you the *total* number of new messages, from all accounts. The Accounts screen, shown below, shows the breakdown by account.

The Unified Inbox

If you have more than one email address, then you're in luck. The iPhone offers a *unified inbox*—an option that displays all the incoming messages from all your accounts in a single place. (If you don't see it—if Mail opened up to some other screen—keep tapping the upper-left button until you do.)

This Mailboxes page has two sections:

- **Inboxes.** To see all the incoming messages in one unified box, tap All Inboxes. You can, of course, also view the inbox for any *individual* account in the top section shown here at left.

- **Accounts.** Farther down the Mailboxes screen, you see your accounts listed again. Tap one to view the traditional mail folders: Inbox, Drafts

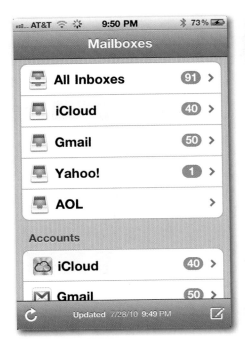
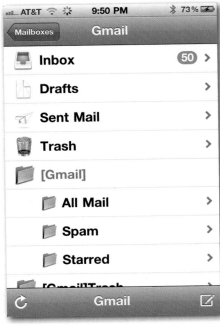

(emails written but not sent), Sent, Trash, and any folders you've created yourself (Family, Little League, Old Stuff, whatever), as shown on the facing page at right. If you have a Yahoo, iCloud, Exchange, or another IMAP account, then these folders are automatically created on the iPhone to match what you've set up online.

 Note Not all kinds of email accounts permit the creation of your own filing folders, so you may not see anything but Inbox, Sent, and Trash.

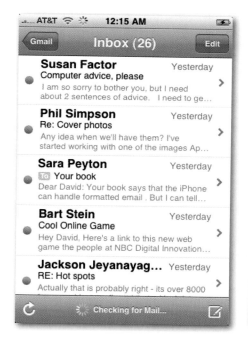

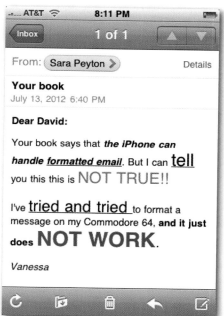

The Message List—and Threading

If you tap an inbox's name, you wind up face to face with the list of incoming messages. At first, you see only the subject lines of your messages, plus, in light-gray type, the first few lines of their contents; that way, you can scan through new messages and see if there's anything important. You can flick your finger to scroll this list, if it's long. Blue dots indicate messages you haven't yet opened. Tap a message to read it in all its formatted glory.

Here and there, you may spot a little number at the right side of the message list, like this: **3** >. That means you're looking at some *threaded* messages. That's where several related messages—back-and-forths on the same sub-

ject—appear only once, in a single, consolidated Inbox entry. (The number indicates the number of volleys in this exchange.) The idea is to reduce inbox clutter and to help you remember what people were talking about.

To read a normal message in the message list, you just tap it. But when you tap a threaded message, you first open an intermediate screen that lists the messages in the thread. Tap one of those to read, at last, the message itself.

Of course, this also means that to return to the inbox, you have more back-tracking to do (tap the upper-left button twice).

In general, threading is a nice feature, even if it accidentally clumps in a message that has nothing to do with the others from time to time.

But if it bugs you, you can turn it off. Open Settings→Mail, Contacts, Calendars, scroll down, and turn off Organize By Thread.

What to Do with a Message

Once you've opened a message, you can respond to it, delete it, file it, and so on. Here's the drill.

Read It

The type size in email messages can be pretty small. Fortunately, you have some great iPhoney enlargement tricks at your disposal. For example:

- **Spread two fingers** to enlarge the entire email message.

- **Double-tap a narrow block of text** to make it fill the screen, if it doesn't already.

Drag or flick your finger to scroll through or around the message.

It's nice to note that links are "live" in email messages. Tap a phone number to call it, a Web address to open it, a YouTube link to watch the video, an email address to write to it, a time and date to add it to your calendar, and so on.

Tip If you're using a Gmail account—a great idea—then any message you send, reply to, delete, or file into a folder is reflected on the Web at Gmail.com. Whether deleting a message really deletes it (after 30 days) or adds it to Gmail's "archived" stash depends on the tweaky settings described at *http://tinyurl.com/yokd27*.

Reply to It

To answer a message, tap the Reply/Forward icon (◄) at the bottom of the screen. You're asked if you want to Reply or Forward; tap Reply. If the message

was originally addressed to multiple recipients, then you can send your reply to everyone simultaneously by hitting Reply All instead.

A new message window opens, already addressed. As a courtesy to your correspondents, Mail places the original message at the bottom of the window.

 Tip If you select some text (page 54) before you tap, then the iPhone pastes only that selected bit into the new, outgoing message. In other words, you're quoting back only a portion—just the way it works on a full-sized computer.

At this point, you can add or delete recipients, edit the subject line or the original message, and so on. When you're finished, tap Send.

 Tip Use the Return key to create blank lines in the original message. (Use the loupe—page 44—to position the insertion point at the proper spot.)

Using this method, you can splice your own comments into the paragraphs of the original message, replying point by point. The brackets by each line of the original message help your correspondent keep straight what's yours and what's hers.

Forward It

Instead of replying to the person who sent you a message, you may sometimes want to pass the note on to a third person. To do so, tap the ← button at the bottom of the screen. This time, tap Forward.

 Tip If there's a file attached to the inbound message, the iPhone says, "Include attachments from original message?" and offers Include and Don't Include buttons. Rather thoughtful, actually—the phone can forward files it can't even open.

A new message opens, looking a lot like the one that appears when you reply. You may wish to precede the original message with a comment of your own, like, "Frank: I thought you'd be interested in this joke about your mom."

Finally, address and send it as you would any outgoing piece of mail.

Flag It

Sometimes you'll receive email that prompts you to some sort of action, but you may not have the time (or the fortitude) to face the task at the moment.

("Hi there… it's me, your accountant. Would you mind rounding up your expenses for 1999 through 2011 and sending me a list by email?")

That's why, in iOS 5, Mail lets you flag a message, summoning a little flag icon in a new column next to the message's name. (You can see the flag in the first message below at right.) It can mean anything you like—it simply calls attention to certain messages.

To flag an open message, tap Details at the top. Then tap the word Mark that appears in the subject line; in the resulting box, tap Flag. The flag symbol appears in the body of the message, next to the message's name in your message list, and even on the corresponding message in your Mac or PC email program, thanks to the miracle of wireless syncing.

You can also rapidly flag messages in a message list (the inbox, for example). Tap Edit, tap the little circles next to the messages you want to flag, tap Mark, and then tap Flag.

Filing or Deleting One Message

As noted earlier, some mail accounts let you create filing folders to help manage your messages. Once you've opened a message that's worth keeping, you file it by tapping the 📁 button at the bottom of the screen. Up pops the list of your folders (next page, left); tap the one you want.

It's a snap to delete a message you no longer want, too. If it's open in front of you, simply tap the 🗑 button at the bottom of the screen. Frankly, it's worth deleting tons of messages just for the pleasure of watching the animation as they funnel down into that tiny icon, whose lid pops open and shut accordingly (below, right).

Tip If that one-touch Delete method makes you a little nervous, you can ask the iPhone to display a confirmation box before trashing the message forever. Visit Settings→Mail, Contacts, Calendars→Ask Before Deleting.

You can also delete a message from the message *list*—the inbox, for example. Just swipe your finger across the message listing, in either direction. (It doesn't have to be an especially broad swipe.) The red Delete button appears; tap it to confirm, or tap anywhere else if you change your mind.

Tip In a Gmail account, swiping like this produces a button that says Archive, not Delete. That's the Gmail way: It wants you to save everything. But you can change the button back so it says Delete. Tap Settings→Mail, Contacts, Calendars→[your Gmail account name]. Here you can turn off Archive Messages. The button will now say Delete, and the messages you delete will really be deleted.

There's a long way to delete messages from the list, too, as described next. But for single messages, the finger-swipe method is *much* more fun.

Filing or Deleting Batches of Messages

You can also file or delete a bunch of messages at once. In the message list, tap Edit. A dot appears beside each message title. You can tap as many of these circles as you like, scrolling as necessary, adding a ✓ with each touch.

Finally, when you've selected all the messages in question, tap either Delete or Move. (The number in parentheses shows how many you've selected).

If you tap Move, you're shown the folder list so you can say where you want them moved. If you tap Delete, the messages disappear.

 When you delete a message, it goes into the Deleted folder. In other words, it works like the Macintosh Trash or the Windows Recycle Bin. You have a safety net.

Email doesn't have to stay in the Deleted folder forever, though. You can ask the iPhone to empty that folder every day, week, or month. From the Home screen, tap Settings→Mail, Contacts, Calendars. Tap your account name and then Advanced→Remove. Now you can change the setting from "Never" to "After one day" (or week, or month).

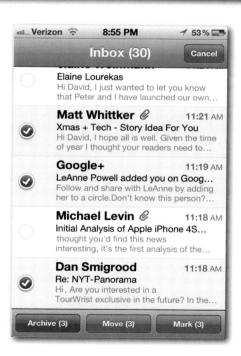

Add the Sender to Contacts

When you get a message from someone new who's worth adding to your iPhone's Contacts address book, tap the blue, oval-shaped email address (where it says "From:"). You're offered two buttons: Create New Contact and Add to Existing Contact. Use the second button to add an·email address to an existing person's "card."

Open an Attachment

The Mail program downloads and displays the icons for *any* kind of attachment—but it can *open* only documents from Microsoft Office (Word, Excel, PowerPoint), those from Apple iWork (Pages, Keynote, Numbers), PDFs, text, RTFs, VCFs, graphics, and un-copy-protected audio and video files.

Just scroll down, tap the attachment's icon, wait a moment for downloading, and then marvel as the document opens up, full screen. You can zoom in and out, flick, rotate the phone 90 degrees, and scroll just as though it were a Web page or a photo.

 Tip If you hold your finger down on the attachment's name, you get a list of ways to open it. Quick Look means the same non-editable preview as you'd get with a quick tap. But you might also see Open in iBooks, for example, or the name of another app that can open it. Tap the one you want.

 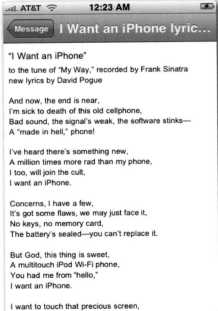

When you're finished admiring the attachment, tap Message (top-left corner) to return to the original email message.

Snagging a Graphic—Two Ways

One of the great joys of iPhone mail is its ability to display graphics that the sender embedded right in the message. If you get sent a particularly good picture, just hold your finger still on it. You're offered two choices:

- **Save Image.** Tap this button to copy the photo into your Photos program, along with the pictures you've taken yourself. To see it later, tap Photos on the Home screen, and then tap Camera Roll.

- **Copy.** Here's another place where Copy and Paste pay off. After tapping Copy, you can paste the photo into another email message, into an outgoing picture message (MMS), or anywhere fine graphics are pasted.

View the Details

When your computer's screen measures only 3½ inches diagonally, there's not a lot of extra space. So Apple designed Mail to conceal the details that you might need only occasionally. They reappear, naturally enough, when you tap Details in the upper-right corner of a message.

Now you get to see a few more details about the message. For instance:

- **Who it's to.** Well, duh—it's to *you,* right? Yes, but it might have been sent to other people, too. When you open Details, you see who else got this note—along with anyone who was Cc'd (sent a copy).

 Tip When you tap the person's name in the blue oval, you open the corresponding info card in Contacts. It contains one-touch buttons for calling someone back (tap the phone number) or sending a text message (tap Text Message)—which can be very handy if the email message you just received is urgent.

- **Mark as Unread.** In the inbox, any message you haven't yet read is marked by a blue dot (●). Once you've opened the message, the blue dot goes away.

  By tapping Mark and then Mark as Unread, however, you make that blue dot *reappear.* It's a great way to flag a message for later, to call it to your own attention. The blue dot can mean not so much "unread" as "un–dealt with."

- **Flag.** As noted above, you can also add a little "don't forget me" flag to a message. Tap Mark and then Flag.

Tap Hide to collapse these details.

Move On

Once you've had a good look at a message and processed it to your satisfaction, you can move on to the next (or previous) message in the list by tapping the ▲ or ▼ button in the upper-right corner.

Or you can tap the button in the upper-left corner to return to the inbox (or whatever mailbox you're in).

Searching

Praise be—there's a search box in Mail. It's hiding *above* the top of every mail list, like your inbox. To see it, scroll up, or just tap the status strip at the top of the screen.

Tap inside the search box to make the keyboard appear. As you type, Mail hides all but the matching messages; tap any one of the results to open it.

The iPhone can reliably search the From, To, or Subject fields, or all three at once. In iOS 5, it's also supposed be able to search the *body* of your messages (when you tap All). At least in version 5.0.1, though, this feature rarely works—

it generally comes up empty-handed, even when you know for a fact that the searched-for word is right there in the body of an inbox message.

At the very bottom, you may see a link called Continue Search on Server. It doesn't appear for all email accounts, but it's there when you're in iCloud, Gmail, and most other IMAP accounts. It's intended to let you continue your search on email that's not on your iPhone—but that's still out there on the Internet, usually because it's so old that it's scrolled off your phone. If the message you seek hasn't appeared, Continue Search on Server is worth a try.

 If, after typing a few letters, you tap Search, the keyboard goes away and an Edit button appears. Tapping it lets you select a whole bunch of the search results— and then delete or file them simultaneously.

Writing Messages

To compose a new piece of outgoing mail, open the Mail program, and then tap the ☑ icon in the lower-right corner. A blank new outgoing message appears, and the iPhone keyboard pops up.

Tip Remember: You can turn the phone 90 degrees to get a much bigger widescreen keyboard for email. It's *much* easier to type this way. Remember, too: Dictating (on an iPhone 4S) is much, *much* faster than typing.

Here's how you go about writing a message:

❶ **In the "To:" field, type the recipient's email address—or grab it from Contacts.** Often, you won't have to type much more than the first couple of letters of the name *or* email address. As you type, Mail automatically displays all matching names and addresses so you can tap one instead of typing. (It thoughtfully derives these suggestions by analyzing both your Contacts *and* which people you've recently exchanged email with.)

Tip If you hold your finger down on the period (.) key, you get a pop-up palette of common email-address suffixes, like .com, .edu, .org, and so on.

Alternatively, tap the ⊕ button to open your Contacts list. Tap the name of the person you want. (Note, though, that the Contacts list shows you *all* names, even those of people who don't have email addresses.)

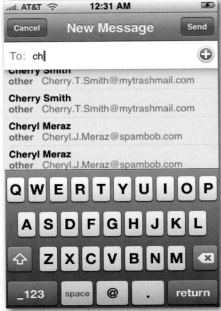

You can add as many addressees as you like; just repeat the procedure.

Incidentally, if you've set up your iPhone to connect to a corporate Exchange server (Chapter 15), then you can look up anybody in the entire company directory at this point. Page 440 has the instructions.

❷ **To send a copy to other recipients, enter the address(es) in the Cc or Bcc fields.** If you tap Cc/Bcc, From, the screen expands to reveal two new lines beneath the To line: Cc and Bcc.

Cc stands for *carbon copy.* Getting an email message where your name is in the Cc line implies: "I sent you a copy because I thought you'd want to know about this correspondence, but I'm not expecting you to reply."

Bcc stands for *blind carbon copy.* It's a copy that goes to a third party secretly—the primary addressee never knows you sent it. For example, if you send your coworker a message that says, "Chris, it bothers me that you've been cheating the customers," you could Bcc your supervisor to clue her in without getting into trouble with Chris.

Each of these lines behaves exactly like the To line. You fill each one up with email addresses in the same way.

❸ **Change the email account you're using, if you like.** If you have more than one email account set up on your iPhone, you can tap Cc/Bcc, From to expand the form and then tap From to open up a spinning list of your accounts. Tap the one you want to use for sending this message.

❹ **Type the topic of the message in the Subject field.** It's courteous to put some thought into the subject line. (Use "Change in plans for next week," for instance, instead of "Yo.") Leaving it blank only annoys your recipient. On the other hand, don't put the *entire* message into the subject line, either.

❺ Type your message in the message box. All the usual iPhone keyboard tricks apply (Chapter 2). Don't forget that you can use Copy and Paste, within Mail or from other programs. Both text and graphics can appear in your message.

 You can't attach anything to an outgoing message—at least not directly. You can email a photo or a video from within the Photos program (page 223), though; you can *forward* a file attached to an incoming piece of mail; and you can *paste* a copied photo or video (or several) into an open email message. Close enough.

❻ Format the text, if you like. In iOS 5, for the first time, you can apply bold, italic, or underlining to mail text you've typed. The controls aren't easy to find, though.

The trick is to select the text first (page 54). When the button bar appears, tap the ▶ to bring the **B / U** button into view. Tap that to make the Bold, Italics, and Underline buttons appear on the button bar; tap away. Not terribly efficient, but it works.

 You can use the same trick to summon the new Quote Level controls. Select text; tap the ▶ to bring the Quote Level button into view; tap it to reveal the Increase and Decrease buttons. These buttons indent or un-indent those cluttery blocks of quoted and re-quoted text that often appear when you're replying to a message. (One tap affects the entire paragraph, not just the selected bit of it.)

If you really can't stand those quote indentations, you can now stop the iPhone from adding them in the first place when you forward or reply to a message. The on/off switch for that feature is in Settings→Mail, Contacts, Calendars→Increase Quote Level.

❼ Tap Send (to send the message) or Cancel (to back out of it). If you tap Cancel, the iPhone asks if you want to save the message. If you tap Save Draft, then the message lands in your Drafts folder.

Later, you can open the Drafts folder, tap the aborted message, finish it up, and send it.

 If you *hold down* the ✑ button for a moment, the iPhone automatically opens your most recently saved draft. Wicked cool!

Signatures

A *signature* is a bit of text that gets stamped at the bottom of your outgoing email messages. It can be your name, a postal address, or a pithy quote.

Unless you intervene, the iPhone stamps "Sent from my iPhone" at the bottom of every message. You may be just fine with that, or you may consider it the equivalent of gloating (or free advertising for Apple). In any case, you can change the signature if you want to.

From the Home screen, tap Settings→Mail, Contacts, Calendars→Signature. The Signature text window appears, complete with a keyboard, so you can compose the signature you want.

 Tip In iOS 5, you can use bold, italic, or underline formatting in your signature. Just follow the steps on the facing page for formatting a message: select the text, tap the ▶ to bring the **B I U** button into view, and so on.

Surviving Email Overload

If you don't get much mail, you probably aren't lying awake at night trying to think of ways to manage so much information overload on your tiny phone.

If you do get a lot of mail, here are some tips.

The Spam Problem

Mail is an awfully full-fledged email program for a *phone.* But compared with a desktop email program, it's really only half-fledged. You can't send file attachments, can't create mail rules—and can't screen out spam.

Spam, the junk mail that makes up more than 80 percent of email, is only getting worse. So how are you supposed to keep it off your iPhone?

The following solution will take 15 minutes to set up, but it will make you very happy in the long run.

Suppose your regular email address is *iphonecrazy@comcast.net.*

❶ **Sign up for a free Gmail account.** You do that at *www.gmail.com.*

The idea here is that you're going to have all your *iphonecrazy@comcast.net* messages sent on to this Gmail account, and you'll set up your iPhone to check the *Gmail* account instead of your regular account.

Why? Because Gmail has excellent spam filters. They'll clean up the mail mess before it reaches your iPhone.

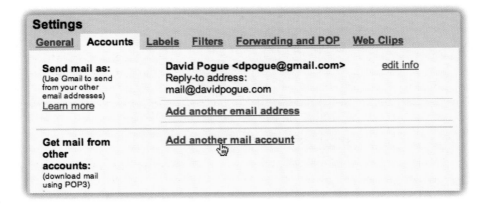

Unfortunately, just *forwarding* your mail to the Gmail account won't do the trick. If you do that, then the return address on every message that reaches your iPhone will be *iphonecrazy@comcast.net.* When you tap

Reply on the iPhone, your response won't be addressed to the original sender; it'll be addressed right back to you!

But the brainiacs at Google have anticipated this problem, too.

❷ **Sign into Gmail. Click Settings→Accounts→"Add another mail account," and fill in the email settings for your main address. Turn on "Leave a copy of retrieved message on the server."** What you've just done is told Gmail to *fetch the mail* from your main address. The return addresses of your incoming messages remain intact!

As you complete the setup process in Gmail, you'll see a message that says: "You can now retrieve mail from this account. Would you also like to be able to send mail as *iphonecrazy@comcast.net*?"

If you click "Yes, I want to be able to send mail as [your real email address]," your iPhone should not only *receive* spam-filtered mail from your main account—but when you reply, the return address will also be your main email address (*iphonecrazy@comcast.net*) and not your Gmail address. In theory, at least.

This feature turns Gmail into a convenient, automatic, behind-the-scenes spam filter for your iPhone that leaves little trace of its involvement. (You can always change the outgoing account on a per-message basis; see page 381.) In the meantime, at least, all mail sent to your main address will come to your iPhone prefiltered.

And as an added, *added* bonus, you can check your *iphonecrazy@comcast.net* email from any computer that has a Web browser—at Gmail.com.

 Tip Next time, keep your email address out of spammers' hands in the first place. Use one address for the public areas of the Internet, like chat rooms, online shopping, Web site and software registration, and newsgroup posting. Spammers use automated software robots that scour these pages, recording email addresses they find. Create a separate email account for person-to-person email—and *never* post that address on a Web page.

How Many Messages

In Settings→Mail, Contacts, Calendars→Show, you can specify how many messages you want to appear in the list before scrolling off the screen: 25, 50, 200, whatever.

It's only a false sense of being on top of things—you can always tap the Load 25 More Messages button to retrieve the next batch—but at least you'll never have a 2,000-message inbox.

Condensing the Message List

As you may have noticed, the messages in your inbox are listed with the subject line in bold type *and* a couple of lines, in light-gray text, that preview the message itself.

You can control how many lines of the light-gray preview text show up here. From the Home screen, tap Settings→Mail, Contacts, Calendars→Preview. Choosing None means you fit a lot more message titles on each screen without scrolling; choosing 5 Lines shows you a lot of each message but means you'll have to do more scrolling.

Spotting Worthwhile Messages

The iPhone can display a little **To** or **Cc** logo on each message in your inbox. At a glance, it helps you identify which messages are actually intended for *you.* Messages without those logos are probably spam, newsletters, mailing lists, or other messages that weren't specifically addressed to you.

To turn on these little badges, visit Settings→Mail, Contacts, Calendars and turn on Show To/CC Label. There's no downside to using this feature.

Managing Accounts

If you have more than one email account, you might want to deactivate one for a while—for example, to accommodate your travel schedule. You can also delete an account.

Visit Settings→Mail, Contacts, Calendars. In the list of accounts, tap the one you want. At the top of the screen, you see the On/Off switch; Off makes an account dormant. And at the bottom, you see the Delete Account button.

 Tip If you have several accounts, which one does the iPhone use when you send mail from other apps—like when you email a photo from Photos or a link from Safari?

It uses the *default* account, of course. You determine which one is the default account in Settings→Mail, Contacts, Calendars→Default Account.

13 Syncing with iTunes

Just in case you're one of the six people out there who've never heard of it, iTunes is Apple's multifunction, multimedia jukebox software. It's been loading music onto iPods since the turn of the 21st century.

Most people use iTunes to manipulate their digital movies, photos, and music, from converting songs off a CD into iPhone-ready music files to buying songs, audiobooks, and movies online.

But as an iPhone owner, you need iTunes even more urgently, because it's the most efficient way to get masses of music, videos, apps, email, addresses, appointments, ringtones, and other stuff *onto* the phone. It also backs up your iPhone automatically.

If you've never had a copy of iTunes on your computer, then fire up your Web browser and go to *www.apple.com/itunes/download*. Once the file lands on your computer, double-click the installer icon and follow the onscreen instructions to add iTunes to your life.

This chapter gives you a crash course in iTunes and tells you how to sync it with your iPhone.

> **Tip** In iOS 5, iTunes is no longer *required*. It's perfectly possible to use all of an iPhone's features without even owning a computer. You can download all that stuff—music, movies, apps—right from the Internet, and you can back up your phone using iCloud (described in the next chapter).
>
> Using iTunes, however, is still more efficient, and it's nice to know that your stuff is backed up on a machine that's within your control. Besides: In iOS 5, you can keep using your iPhone even while it's syncing—a very nice new perk.

The iTunes Window: What's Where

Here's a quick tour of the main iTunes window and what all its parts do.

The Source panel on the left side lists all the audio and video sources you can tap into at the moment. Clicking a name in the Source list makes the main song-list area change accordingly, like so:

- **Library.** As you add movies, App Store downloads, music, podcasts, ringtones, and other stuff to iTunes, subheadings appear under the Library heading (like Music, TV Shows, Podcasts, Ringtones, and so on). Click one to see what audio, video, or software your computer has in that category.

- **Store.** Click the icons to shop for new stuff in the iTunes Store (music, movies, apps, TV shows, free podcasts) or to see the list of things you've already bought.

- **Devices.** If there's a CD in the computer's drive, an iPod or iPhone connected to the computer, or an Apple TV on your network, you'll see its icon here. Click to see its contents.

Source list

- **Shared.** This list lets you browse the music libraries of *other* iTunes addicts on your network and play their music on your own computer. (Yes, it's legal.)

- **Playlists.** *Playlists* are lists of songs that you assemble yourself, mixing and matching music from different CDs and other sources as you see fit (page 394). Here's where you see them listed.

Here's the basic rule of using iTunes: Click one of these headings in the Source list to reveal what's *in* that source. The contents appear in the center part of the iTunes window.

The playback and volume controls, which work just as they do on the iPhone, are at the top-left corner of iTunes. At the upper-right corner is a search box that lets you pluck one track out of a haystack. Next to it, you'll find handy buttons to change views within the window. (Cover Flow, which works just as it does on the iPhone, is the third button in this grouping.)

Five Ways to Get Music and Video

Once you have iTunes, the next step is to start filling it with music and video so you can get all that goodness onto your iPhone. iTunes gives you at least five options right off the bat.

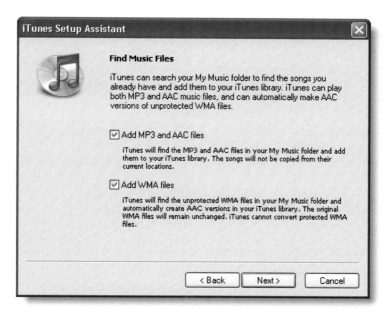

Let iTunes Find Your Existing Songs

If you've had a computer for longer than a few days, you probably already have some songs in the popular MP3 format on your hard drive, perhaps from a file-sharing service or a free music Web site. If so, the first time you open iTunes, it offers to search your PC or Mac for music and add it to its library. Click Yes; iTunes goes hunting around your hard drive.

 Tip If you use Windows, you may have songs in the Windows Media Audio (WMA) format. Unfortunately, iTunes and the iPhone can't play WMA files. But when iTunes finds nonprotected WMA files, it offers to convert them automatically to a format that it *does* understand. That's a convenient assurance that your old music files will play on your new toy. (iTunes/iPhone can *not,* however, convert *copy-protected* WMA files like those sold by some music services.)

Visit the iTunes Store

Another way to feed your iPhone is to shop at the iTunes Store.

Click the iTunes Store icon in the list on the left side of the iTunes window. Once you land on the store's main page and set up your iTunes account, you can buy and download songs, audiobooks, and videos. This material goes straight into your iTunes library, just a sync away from the iPhone.

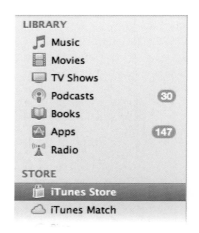

After years of conflict and controversy, the record companies have finally allowed Apple to start selling songs that aren't copy protected. Today, there's almost nothing left in the music department of iTunes that still has copy protection.

Your iPhone, of course, can also get to the iTunes Store, wirelessly; just tap that alluring purple iTunes icon on the Home screen. Any songs you buy on the phone get copied back to iTunes the next time you sync.

Not everything in the iTunes Store costs money, by the way. In addition to free iPhone apps, there are plenty of free audio and video podcasts, suitable for your iPhone, in the Podcasts area of the store. And there are tons of iPhone-compatible movie trailers to download at *www.apple.com/trailers/*. Hit that link on your iPhone's browser and watch the trailers stream down, perfectly formatted to the palm of your hand.

 Tip iTunes doesn't have a monopoly on music sales for your iPhone. Amazon, Google, Rhapsody, and other services sell songs in MP3 format, meaning no copy protection (and iPhone compatibility). eMusic.com has great MP3 prices, but the music comes from lesser-known bands. Amazon's MP3 Downloader software for Mac and PC can whip your purchases right into iTunes; Rhapsody has similar helper software for Windows.

Import Music from a CD

iTunes can also convert tracks from audio CDs into iPhone-ready digital music files. Just start up iTunes, and then stick a CD into your computer's CD drive. The program asks if you want to convert the songs to audio files for iTunes. (If it doesn't ask, click Import CD at the bottom of the window.)

Once you tell it to import the music, iTunes walks you through the process. If you're connected to the Internet, the program automatically downloads song titles and artist information from the CD and begins to add the songs to the iTunes library.

If you want time to think about which songs you want from each CD, then you can tell iTunes to download only the song *titles,* and then give you a few minutes to ponder your selections. To do that, choose iTunes→Preferences→General (Mac) or Edit→Preferences→General (Windows). Use the When you insert a CD: pop-up menu to choose Show CD.

From now on, if you don't want the entire album, you can exclude the dud songs by turning off their checkmarks. Then click Import CD in the bottom-right corner of the screen.

 Tip You can ⌘-click (Mac) or Ctrl-click (Windows) any box to turn *all* the checkboxes on or off. This technique is ideal when you want only one or two songs in the list. First, turn all the checkboxes off, and then turn just those two back on again.

In that same Preferences box, you can also click Import Settings to choose the *format* (file type) and *bit rate* (amount of audio data compressed into that format) for your imported tracks. The factory setting is the AAC format at 128 kilobits per second.

Most people think these settings make for fine-sounding music files, but you can change your settings to, for example, MP3, which is another format that lets you cram big music into a small space. Upping the bit rate from 128 kbps to 256 kbps makes for richer-sounding music files—which also happen to take up more room because the files are bigger (and the iPhone's "hard drive" doesn't hold as much as your computer's). The choice is yours.

As the import process starts, iTunes moves down the list of checked songs, ripping each one to a file in your Home→Music→iTunes→iTunes Music folder (Mac) or Documents→Music→iTunes→iTunes Media→Music folder (Windows). An orange squiggle next to a song name means that the track is currently converting. Feel free to switch into other programs, answer email, surf the Web, and do other work while the ripping is under way.

Once the importing is finished, each imported song bears a green checkmark, and iTunes signals its success with a melodious flourish. Now you have some brand-new files in your iTunes library.

 Tip If you always want *all* the songs on that stack of CDs next to your computer, then change the iTunes CD import preferences to Import CD and Eject to save yourself some clicking. When you insert a CD, iTunes imports it and spits it out, ready for the next one.

Download Podcasts

The iTunes Store houses thousands upon thousands of *podcasts,* those free audio (and video!) recordings put out by everyone from big TV networks to a guy in his barn with a microphone.

To explore podcasts, click the Podcasts tab at the top of the store's window. Now you can browse shows by category, search for podcast names by keyword, or click around until you find something that sounds good.

Many podcasters produce regular installments of their shows, releasing new episodes onto the Internet when they're ready. You can have iTunes keep a look out for fresh editions of your favorite podcasts and automatically download them for you, where you can find them in the Podcasts area in the iTunes Source list. All you have to do is *subscribe* to the podcast, which takes a couple of clicks in the store.

If you want to try out a podcast, click the price button (Free) near its title to download just that one show. If you like it (or know that you're going to like it before you even download the first episode), then there's also a Subscribe button that signs you up to receive all future episodes.

You play a podcast just like any other file in iTunes: Double-click the file name in the iTunes window and use the playback controls in the upper-left corner. On the iPhone, podcasts show up in their own list.

Buy Audiobooks

Some people like the sound of a good book, and iTunes has plenty to offer; click the Audiobooks tab at the top of the Store window. You can find verbal versions of the latest best sellers here, usually priced lower than the hardback version of the book—which would be four times the size of your iPhone anyway.

If iTunes doesn't offer the audiobook you're interested in, you can find a larger collection (over 50,000 of them) at Audible.com. This Web store sells all kinds of audiobooks, plus recorded periodicals like *The New York Times* and radio shows. To purchase Audible's wares, though, you need to go to the Web site and create an Audible account.

If you use Windows, then you can download from Audible.com a little program called Audible Download Manager, which catapults your Audible downloads into iTunes for you. On the Mac, Audible files land in iTunes automatically when you buy them.

And when those files do land in iTunes, you can play them on your computer or send them over to the iPhone with a quick sync.

Playlists

A *playlist* is a list of songs you've decided should go together. It can be any group of songs arranged in any order, all according to your whims. For example, if you're having a party, you can make a playlist from the current Top 40 and dance music in your music library. Some people may question your taste if you, say, alternate tracks from *La Bohème* with Queen's *A Night at the Opera,* but hey—it's your playlist.

To create a playlist, press ⌘-N (Mac) or Ctrl+N (Windows). Or choose File→New Playlist, or click the + button below the Source list.

> **Tip** You can also create playlists right on the phone; see page 162.

A freshly minted playlist starts out with the impersonal name "Untitled Playlist." Fortunately, the renaming rectangle is open and highlighted. Just type a better name: "Cardio Workout," "Shoe-Shopping Tunes," "Hits of the Highland Lute," or whatever you want to call it. As you add them, your playlists alphabetize themselves in the Source window.

Once you've created this new playlist, you're ready to add your songs or videos. The quickest way is to drag their names directly onto the playlist's icon.

> **Tip** Instead of making an empty playlist and then dragging songs into it, you can work the other way. You can scroll through a big list of songs, selecting tracks as you go by ⌘-clicking (on the Mac) or Ctrl-clicking (in Windows)—and then, when you're finished, choose File→New Playlist From Selection. All the songs you selected immediately appear on a brand-new playlist.

When you drag a song title onto a playlist, you're not making a copy of the song. In essence, you're creating an *alias* or *shortcut* of the original, which means you can have the same song on several different playlists.

iTunes even starts you out with some playlists of its own devising, like "Top 25 Most Played" and "Purchased" (a convenient place to find all your iTunes Store goodies listed in one place).

Editing and Deleting Playlists

A playlist is easy to change. Here's what you can do with just a little light mousework:

- **Change the order of songs in the playlist.** Click at the top of the first column in the playlist window (the one with the numbers next to the songs) and drag song titles up or down within the playlist window to reorder them.

- **Add new songs to the playlist.** Tiptoe through your iTunes library and drag more songs into a playlist.

- **Delete songs from the playlist.** If your playlist needs pruning, or that banjo tune just doesn't fit in with the brass-band tracks, you can ditch it quickly: Click the song in the playlist window and then hit Delete or Backspace to get rid of it. When iTunes asks you to confirm your decision, click Yes.

  Deleting a song from a playlist doesn't delete it from your music library—it just removes the title from your *playlist.* (Pressing Delete or Backspace when the Library Music icon is selected gets rid of the song for good.)

- **Delete the whole playlist.** To delete an entire playlist, click it in the Source list and press Delete (Backspace). Again, this zaps only the playlist itself, not all the songs you had in it. (Those are still in your computer's iTunes folder.)

 Tip If you want to see how many playlists a certain song appears on, Ctrl-click (Mac) or right-click (Mac or PC) the track's name; from the shortcut menu, choose Show in Playlist.

Authorizing Computers

Before the iTunes Store moved to not-copy-protected songs, music fans had to suffer through the hostility of computer authorization. Since you may still have some of those older, protected songs, here's the scoop.

When you create an account in iTunes (a requirement of owning an iPhone), you automatically *authorize* that computer to play copy-protected songs from the iTunes Store. Authorization is Apple's way of making sure you don't go playing those music tracks on more than five computers, which would greatly displease the record companies.

You can copy those older songs onto a maximum of four other computers. To authorize each one to play music from your account, choose Store→Authorize Computer. (Don't worry; you have to do this just once per machine.)

When you've maxed out your limit and can't authorize any more computers, you may need to *deauthorize* one. On the computer you wish to demote, choose Store→Deauthorize Computer.

TV, Movies, and Movie Rentals

iTunes hasn't been just about music for years. Nowadays, you can also buy TV episodes ($2 apiece, no ads), movies, and music videos. You can also *rent* movies from iTunes for $3 to $5 apiece. Once you download a movie, you have 30 days to start watching—and once you start, you have 24 hours to finish before it turns into a pumpkin (actually, it deletes itself from your computer and phone).

You can do your renting and buying in two ways. First, you can use the iTunes software on your Mac or PC and then sync it to the iPhone by following the steps later in this chapter.

Second, you can download videos straight to the phone when you're in a WiFi hotspot. (The difference: If you download a rental movie to your phone, you can't move it to any other gadget. If you download it to iTunes, you can move it from computer to phone to iPad, or whatever, although it can exist on only one machine at a time.)

Automatic Syncing—with a Cable

Transferring data between the iPhone and the computer is called *synchroniza-*
tion. Syncing is sometimes a one-way street, and sometimes it's bidirectional,
as you'll find out in a moment.

This section covers the ins and outs—or, rather, the backs and forths—of
iPhone syncing over a USB cable. In iOS 5, you can also sync wirelessly, over
WiFi; that's described later in this chapter.

To sync over a cable, you connect the iPhone to the computer. That's it. As
long as the cable is plugged into your computer's USB port, iTunes opens
automatically, and the synchronization begins. iTunes controls all iPhone synchronization, acting as a software bridge between phone and computer.

 Note Your photo-editing program (like iPhoto or Photoshop Elements) probably springs
open every time you connect the iPhone, too. See page 416 if that bugs you.

When the iPhone and the computer are communicating, the iTunes window
and the iPhone screen both say, Sync in progress.

If you need to use the iPhone for a moment, just drag your finger across the
slide to cancel slider on the screen. The sync pauses. When you reconnect the
phone to the cable, the sync intelligently resumes.

In fact, if someone dares to call you while you're in mid-sync, the iPhone can-
cels the session *itself* so you can pick up the call. Just reconnect it to the computer when you're done chatting so it can finish syncing.

Now, ordinarily, the iPhone-iTunes relationship is automatic and complete. An
automatic sync takes care of all of these details:

- **Contacts, calendars, and Web bookmarks.** These get copied in both directions. That is, after a sync, your computer and phone contain exactly the same information.

  So if you entered an appointment on the iPhone, it gets copied to your computer—and vice versa. If you edited the same contact or appointment on both machines at once while they were apart, your computer displays the two conflicting records and asks you which one "wins."

- **Music, apps, TV, movies, ringtones, and ebooks you bought using iTunes on your computer; photos from your computer; and email account information.** All of this gets copied in one direction: computer→phone.

- **Photos and videos taken with the iPhone's camera; music, videos, apps, ringtones, and ebooks you bought right from the phone.** All of this gets copied the other way: phone→computer.

- **A complete backup.** iTunes also takes it upon itself to back up *everything else* on your iPhone: settings, text messages, call history, and so on. (Details on this backup business are on page 421.)

 Tip If you're in a hurry, you can skip the time-consuming backup portion of the sync. Just click the ⊗ at the top of the iTunes window whenever it says "Backing up." iTunes gets the message and skips right ahead to the next phase of the sync— transferring contacts, calendars, music, and so on.

Manual Syncing

OK, but what if you don't *want* iTunes to fire up and start syncing every time you connect your iPhone? What if, for example, you want to change the assortment of music and video that's about to get copied to it? Or what if you just want to connect the USB cable to charge the phone, not to sync it?

In that case, you can stop the autosyncing in any of three ways:

- **Interrupt a sync in progress.** Click the ⊗ button in the iTunes status window until the syncing stops.

- **Stop iTunes from syncing with the iPhone just this time.** As you plug in the iPhone's cable, hold down the Shift+Ctrl keys (Windows) or the ⌘-Option keys (Mac) until the iPhone pops up in the iTunes window. Now you can see what's on the iPhone and change what will be synced to it—but no syncing takes place until you command it.

- **Stop iTunes from autosyncing any iPhone, ever.** In iTunes, choose Edit→Preferences (Windows) or iTunes→Preferences (Mac). Click the Devices tab and turn on Prevent iPods, iPhones, and iPads from syncing automatically. You can still trigger a sync on command when the iPhone is wired up—by clicking the Sync button.

Once you've made iTunes stop syncing automatically, you've disabled what many people consider the greatest feature of the iPhone: its magical self-updating with the stuff on your computer.

Still, you must have turned off autosyncing for a reason. And that reason might be that you want to control what gets copied onto it. Maybe you're in a hurry to leave for the airport, and you don't have time to sit there for an hour while six downloaded movies get copied to the phone. Maybe you have 50 gigabytes of music but only 16 gigs of iPhone storage.

In any case, here are the two ways you can sync manually:

- **Use the tabs in iTunes.** With the iPhone connected, you can specify exactly what you want copied to it—which songs, which TV shows, which apps, and so on—using the various tabs in iTunes, as described on the following pages. Once you've made your selections, click the Summary tab, and then click Apply. (The Apply button says Sync instead if you haven't actually changed any settings.)

- **Drag files onto the iPhone icon.** Yes, this sneaky little trick is what insiders might recognize as the iPod Paradigm. Once your iPhone is cabled into your computer, you can click its icon and then turn on Manually manage music and videos (on the Summary screen). Click Apply.

  Now you can drag songs and videos directly onto the iPhone's icon to copy them there. Wilder yet, you can bypass iTunes *entirely* by dragging music and video files *from your computer's desktop* onto the iPhone's icon. That's handy when you've just inherited or downloaded a bunch of song files, converted a DVD to the iPhone's video format, or whatever.

  Just two notes of warning here. First, unlike a true iPod, the iPhone accommodates dragged material from a *single* computer only. Second, if you ever turn off this option, all those manually dragged songs and videos will disappear from your iPhone at the next sync opportunity.

Tip Also on the Summary tab, you'll find the baffling little option called Sync only checked songs and videos. This is a global override—a last-ditch "keep the embarrassing songs off my iPhone" option.

When this option is turned on, iTunes consults the tiny checkboxes next to every single song and video in your iTunes library. If you turn off a song's checkbox, it will not get synced to your iPhone, no matter what—even if you use the Music tab to sync All songs or playlists, or explicitly turn on a playlist that contains this song. If the song's or video's checkbox isn't checked in your Library list, then it will be left behind on your computer.

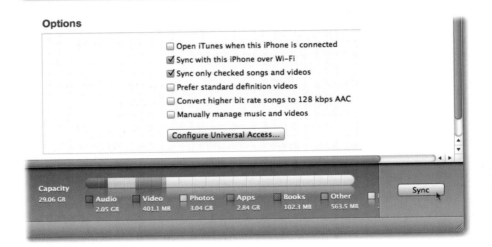

12 Tabs to Glory

Once your iPhone is cabled up to the computer's USB port, click its icon in the iTunes Source list. The middle part of the iTunes window now reveals a horizontal row of file-folder tabs, representing the categories of stuff you can sync to your iPhone.

Here's what each one tells you:

- **Summary.** This screen gives basic stats on your iPhone, like its serial number, capacity, and phone number. Buttons in the middle let you check for iPhone software updates or restore it to its out-of-the-box state. Checkboxes at the bottom of the screen let you set up manual syncing, as described previously.

- **Info.** The settings here control the syncing of your contacts, calendars, email account settings, and bookmarks.

- **Apps.** Those useful and not-useful-but-totally-fun-anyway little programs from the iPhone App Store get synced up here (Chapter 8).

- **Tones.** Any ringtones that you've bought from the iTunes Store or made yourself (Chapter 5) appear here; you can specify which ones you want synced to the iPhone. (This tab is no longer called just "Ringtones," because the iPhone can handle tones for all kinds of different events, like incoming text messages or mail, tweets, reminders, and so on.)

- **Music.** You can opt to sync all your songs, music videos, and playlists here—or, if your collection is more than the iPhone can store, just some of them.

- **Movies, TV Shows.** You can choose both movies and TV shows from the App Store for syncing here, along with other compatible video files in your library.

- **Podcasts.** This screen lets you sync all—or just selected—podcasts. You can even opt to get only the episodes you haven't heard yet.

- **iTunes U.** Free educational podcasts and lectures from universities.

- **Books.** Ebooks and PDF documents you want to read in the iBooks app.

- **Photos.** Here you can get iPhone-friendly versions of your pictures copied over from a folder on your hard drive—or from a photo-management program like Photoshop Elements, Photoshop Album, or iPhoto.

- **Nike + iPod.** This tab appears only if you've bought one of the wireless Nike pedometers that communicates with an iPhone app as you jog.

At the bottom of the screen, a colorful map shows you the amount and types of files: Audio, Video, Photos, Apps, Books, and Other (for your personal data). More importantly, it also shows you how much room you have left, so you won't get overzealous in trying to load the thing up.

The following pages cover each of these tabs, in sequence, and detail how to sync each kind of iPhone-friendly material.

This discussion assumes that you've (a) connected your iPhone to the computer with its USB cable, and (b) clicked the iPhone's icon in the Source list at the left side of the iTunes window.

Info Tab (Contacts, Calendars, Settings)

On this tab, you're offered the chance to copy some distinctly non-entertainment data over to your iPhone: your computer's calendar, address book, email settings, notes, and Web bookmarks. The PalmPilot-type stuff (Rolodex, datebook) is extremely useful to have with you, and the settings and bookmarks save you a lot of tedious setup on the iPhone.

 Note If you're a subscriber to Apple's data-in-the-clouds iCloud service, then you won't see the controls described on the following pages. That's because iCloud, not iTunes, handles synchronization with the iPhone. Instead, all you see is a message to the effect that, for example, "Your calendars are being pushed to your iPhone over the air from iCloud."

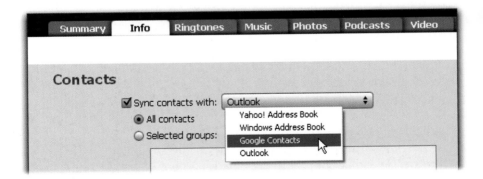

Syncing Notes

Any notes you create on the iPhone can synchronize with the notes in Mail, Outlook (in Windows), or in the Notes folders of Gmail, Yahoo Mail, or AOL. If you're lucky, turning on the Sync notes checkbox is all there is to it. If you're not, try the suggestions at *http://bit.ly/hKPkl*.

Syncing Contacts

If you've been adding to your address book for years in a program like Microsoft Outlook or Mac OS X's Address Book, then you're just a sync away from porting all that accumulated data right over to your iPhone. Once there, phone numbers and email addresses show up as links, so you can reach out and tap someone.

Here's how to sync up your contacts with the iPhone. The steps depend on which program you keep them in.

- **Outlook 2003 and 2007.** Turn on Sync contacts with and, from the pop-up menu, choose Outlook. Finally, click Apply.

  Note that some of the more obscure fields Outlook lets you use, like Radio and Telex, won't show up on the iPhone. All the major data points do, however, including name, email address, and (most importantly) phone number.

 Tip Having weird syncing issues with Outlook's contacts and calendars? In iTunes, go to Edit→Preferences→Syncing and click Reset Sync History. This function doesn't wipe out the data you've synced, just the Windows memory of it. The next time you sync the iPhone, it'll be like the very first time.

- **Outlook Express.** Microsoft's free email app for Windows XP stores your contacts in a file called the Windows Address Book. To sync it with your iPhone, turn on Sync contacts from, choose Windows Address Book from the pop-up menu, and then click Apply.

- **Windows Live Mail.** Windows Live Mail, a free download for Windows 7 (and called Windows Mail in Vista), is essentially a renamed version of Outlook Express. You set it up to sync with the iPhone's Contacts program just as described—except in iTunes, choose Windows Contacts, rather than Windows Address Book, before clicking Apply.

- **Yahoo Address Book.** The Yahoo Address Book is the address book component of a free Yahoo Mail account. It's therefore an *online* address book, which has certain advantages—like the ability to be accessed from any computer on the Internet.

To sync with it, turn on Sync contacts from and then choose Yahoo Address Book from the pop-up menu. (On the Mac, just turn on Yahoo Address Book; no menu is needed.)

Since Yahoo is an *online* address book, you need an Internet connection and your Yahoo ID and password to sync it with the iPhone. Click Configure, and then type your Yahoo ID and password. When finished, click OK. Now click Apply to get syncing.

Because it's online, syncing your Yahoo address book has a couple of other quirks.

First, Yahoo Address Book, ever the thoughtful program, lets you remember both birthdays and anniversaries in a data field. The iPhone, however, grabs only the birthday part, leaving you to remember the anniversary dates yourself. Just don't forget your own!

Furthermore, any custom labels you slap on phone entries on the iPhone side get synced into the Other field when they get to Yahoo. It seems Yahoo is just not as creative as you are when it comes to labeling things.

Finally, Yahoo Address Book doesn't delete contacts during a sync. So if you whack somebody on the iPhone, you still have to log into Yahoo and take 'em out there, too.

- **Google Contacts.** The addresses from your Gmail, Google Mail, and Google Apps accounts can sync up to the iPhone as well. Turn on Sync contacts from and then choose Google Contacts from the pop-up menu. (On the Mac, just turn on Google Contacts; no menu is needed.) Agree to the legal disclaimer about iTunes snatching data.

  Since Google Contacts are kept on the Web, you need an Internet connection and your Gmail/Google ID and password to sync your contacts with the iPhone. In the password box that pops up (click Configure on the Info screen if it doesn't), type your Gmail name and password. When finished, click OK. Now click Apply to get syncing.

  Only one contact per email address gets synced, so if you have multiple contacts with the same address, someone will get left out of the syncing party. Google has a page of troubleshooting tips and info for other Contacts-related questions at *www.google.com/support/contactsync*.

- **Mac OS X Address Book.** Apple products generally love one another, and the built-in contact keeper that comes with Mac OS X is a breeze to sync up with your iPhone. Turn on Sync contacts from and then pick Address Book from the pop-up menu.

If you've gathered sets of people together as *groups* in your address book, you can also transfer *them* to the iPhone by turning on Selected groups and then checking the ones you want. When finished, click Apply to sync things up.

- **Entourage, Outlook for Mac.** Entourage and its Mac successor, Outlook, the email program in Microsoft Office for the Mac, also plays nicely with the iPhone, as long as you introduce it properly first.

  In Entourage, choose Entourage→Preferences. Under General Preferences, choose Sync Services. Turn on Synchronize contacts with Address Book and .Mac.

  In Outlook, choose Outlook→Preferences. Click Sync Services. Turn on Contacts.

  Click OK, and then plug the iPhone into the Mac. Click the iPhone's icon in the iTunes Source list, and then click the Info tab. Turn on Sync contacts from and, from the pop-up menu, choose Address Book. Finally, click Apply to sync.

- **Other programs.** Even if you keep your contacts in a Jurassic-era program like Palm Desktop, you may still be able to get them into the iPhone/iTunes sync dance. If you can export your contacts as vCards (a contacts-exchange format with the extension .vcf), then you can import them into the Windows' Address Book or the Mac's Address Book.

  Now you can sync to your heart's delight.

Syncing Bookmarks

Bookmarks—those helpful shortcuts that save you countless hours of mis-typing Web site addresses—are a reflection of your personality, because they tend to be sites that are important to *you.* Fortunately, they can make the trip to your iPhone, too. In fact, any bookmarks you create on the iPhone can also be copied back to your computer; it's a two-way street.

iTunes can transfer your bookmarks from Internet Explorer or Safari (Windows), or from Safari on a Mac. In iTunes, on the Info tab, scroll down past Contacts and Calendars and Mail Accounts until you get to the section called Web Browser. Then:

- **In Windows,** turn on Sync bookmarks from and then choose either Safari or Internet Explorer from the pop-up menu. Click Apply to sync.

- **On the Mac,** turn on Sync Safari bookmarks and then click Apply.

And what if Firefox is your preferred browser? You can still get those favorites moved over to the iPhone, thanks to an ingenious free Firefox plug-in called Sync. It's available at *www.mozilla.com/en-US/firefox/sync/*, or you can just Google it.

The Sync add-on doesn't just copy your bookmarks to the phone—it creates a live, two-way wireless sync between your computer and your phone. Bookmarks, yes, but also your History list and even your open tabs.

Actually, *most* other browsers can export their bookmarks. You can use that option to export your bookmarks file to your desktop and then use Safari's File→Import Bookmarks command to pull it from there.

Syncing Your Calendar

With its snazzy-looking Calendar program tidily synced with your computer, the iPhone can keep you on schedule—and even remind you when you have to call a few people.

Out of the box, the iPhone's calendar works with Outlook 2003 and later for Windows, and with iCal and Entourage/Outlook on the Mac.

Here again, setting up the sync depends on the calendar program you're using on your computer.

 Note If you have Windows Vista or Windows 7, then you have a built-in calendar program—Windows Live Calendar—but no way to sync it with the iPhone. The reason, according to Apple, is that Microsoft has not made public the format of its calendar program.

- **Outlook Calendar (Windows).** In the Calendars area of the Info tab, turn on Sync calendars from Outlook.

   You can also choose how many days' worth of old events you want to have on your iPhone, since you probably rarely need to reference, say, your calendar from 2002. Turn on Do not sync events older than ___ days, and then specify the number of days' worth of old appointments you want to have on hand.

Events you add on the iPhone get carried back to Outlook when you reconnect to the computer and sync up.

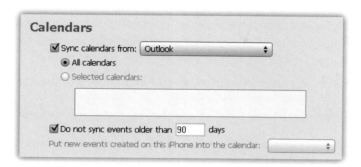

- **iCal (Macintosh).** Mac OS X comes with a nimble little datebook called iCal, which syncs right up with the iPhone. To use it, on the Info tab's Calendars area, turn on Sync iCal calendars.

    If you have several different *calendars* (color-coded categories) in iCal—Work, Home, Book Club, and so on—then you can turn on Selected calendars and choose the ones you want to copy to the iPhone. See page 265 for details on using the categories once they're on the phone.

    Near the bottom of the calendar-sync preferences, there's a place to indicate how far back you want to sync old events.

    Once you get all your calendar preferences set up the way you like, click Apply to get your schedule in sync.

- **Entourage (Mac).** Entourage can sync its calendar events with the iPhone, too. Start by opening Entourage, and then choose Entourage→Preferences. Under General Preferences, choose Sync Services, and then turn on Synchronize events and tasks with iCal and MobileMe. Click OK, and then plug the iPhone into the computer.

    Click the iPhone icon in the iTunes Source list, and then, on the Info tab, turn on Sync iCal calendars. Click the Apply button to sync.

Syncing Email Settings

Teaching a new computer of *any* sort to get and send your email can be stressful; the job entails plugging in all sorts of user-hostile information bits called things like the SMTP Server Address and Uses SSL. Presumably, though, you've got your email working on your Mac or PC—wouldn't it be great if you didn't have to duplicate all that work on your iPhone?

That's exactly what iTunes can do for you. It can transfer the *account setup information* to the iPhone so it's ready to start hunting for messages immediately.

 Note No mail *messages* are transferred to or from the iPhone over the cable. For that sort of magic, you need iCloud or Exchange service. (See Chapters 14 and 15.)

It can do that—*if,* that is, your current email program is Mail or Entourage/ Outlook (on the Mac) or Outlook or Outlook Express (in Windows).

On the iTunes Info tab, scroll down to Mail Accounts. The next step varies by operating system:

- **Windows.** Turn on Sync selected mail accounts from and, from the shortcut menu, choose Outlook or Outlook Express.

- **Macintosh.** Turn on Sync selected Mail accounts.

Finally, if your email program collects messages from multiple accounts, then turn on the checkboxes of the accounts you want to see on your iPhone. Click Apply to start syncing.

The Apps Tab

On this tab, you get a convenient duplicate of your iPhone's Home screens. You can drag app icons around, create and manage folders, shift Home screens into a different order, and otherwise organize your Home life much faster than you'd be able to do on the phone itself (because you have a mouse, a keyboard, and a big screen). Details are on page 240.

At the left side, there's a list of all the iPhone programs you've got on your computer, including programs you just bought in that two-hour shopping frenzy in the App Store. The list also shows all the apps you bought on the iPhone that have since been transferred into iTunes as a backup.

If you don't want to sync *all* those programs at the moment—maybe you want to leave off the Crash Bandicoot game until the weekend because you know you'll never get any work done if you add it on a Tuesday—click Sync Apps. Then turn on the checkboxes for the programs you want to load onto the iPhone right now.

Any programs you leave unchecked will be *removed* from the iPhone when you sync. (Of course, you can always reinstall them by turning their checkboxes back on before the next sync.)

The Tones Tab

Once you click the Tones tab in iTunes, checkboxes await, corresponding to the ringtones (or text tones and other alert tones) you've bought from Apple or made through various do-it-yourself craft projects (Chapter 5). Be sure to sync over any ringtones you've assigned to your frequent callers so the iPhone can alert you with a personalized audio cue, like Pink's rendition of "Tell Me Something Good" when they call you up.

The Music Tab

To copy over the music and audiobooks you want to take along on your phone, click the Music tab. Next, turn on Sync Music. Now you need to decide *what* music to put on your phone.

- If you have a big iPhone and a small music library, you can opt to sync the Entire music library with one click.

- If you have a big music collection and a small iPhone, you'll have to take only *some* of it along for the iPhone ride. In that case, click Selected playlists, artists, and genres. In the lists below, turn on the checkboxes for the playlists, artists, and music genres you want to transfer. (These are cumulative. If there's no Electric Light Orchestra in any of your selected playlists, but you turn on ELO in the Artists list, you'll get all your ELO anyway.)

 Tip Playlists make it fast and easy to sync whole batches of tunes over to your iPhone. But don't forget that you can add individual songs, too, even if they're not in any playlist. Just turn on Manually manage music and videos. Now you can drag individual songs and videos from your iTunes library onto the iPhone icon to install them there.

If you've got music videos, you'll see that they get their own checkbox. As for audiobooks, they already live in their own self-titled playlists. Click the appropriate checkbox to include them in your sync.

Making It All Fit

Sooner or later, everybody has to confront the fact that an iPhone holds only 8, 16, 32, or 64 gigabytes of music and video. (Actually less, because the operating system itself eats up over a gigabyte.) That's enough for around 2,000, 4,000, or 8,000 average-length songs—assuming you don't put any video or photos on there.

Your multimedia stash is probably bigger than that. If you just turn on all Sync All checkboxes, then you'll get an error message telling you that it won't all fit on the iPhone.

One way to solve the problem is to tiptoe through the Music, Podcasts, Photos, Apps, Books, and Videos tabs, turning off checkboxes and trying to sync until the "too much" error message goes away.

If you don't have quite so much time, turn on Automatically fill free space with songs. It makes iTunes use a little artificial Genius intelligence to load up your phone automatically, using your most played and most recent music as a guide. (It does not, in fact, fill the phone completely; it leaves a few hundred megabytes for safety—so you can download more stuff on the road, for example.)

Another helpful approach is to use the *smart playlist,* a music playlist that assembles itself based on criteria that you supply. For example:

❶ **In iTunes, click Music in the Source list; then choose File→New Smart Playlist.** The Smart Playlist dialog box appears.

❷ **Specify the category.** Use the pop-up menus to choose, for example, a musical genre, or songs you've played recently, or *haven't* played recently, or that you've rated highly.

❸ **Turn on the "Limit to" checkbox, and set up the constraints.** For example, you could limit the amount of music in this playlist to 2 gigabytes, chosen at random. That way, every time you sync, you'll get a fresh, random supply of songs on your iPhone, with enough room left for some videos.

4 **Click OK.** The new Smart Playlist appears in your Source list, where you can rename it.

Click it to look it over, if you like. Then, on the Music tab, choose this playlist for syncing to the iPhone.

The Movies and TV Shows Tabs

When it assumes the role of an iPod, one of the things the iPhone does best is play video on its gorgeous, glossy screen. TV shows and movies you've bought or rented from the iTunes Store look especially nice, since they're formatted with iPods in mind. (And if you started watching a rented movie on your computer, the iPhone begins playing it right from where you left off.)

Syncing TV shows and movies works just like syncing music or podcasts. You can have iTunes copy all your stuff to the iPhone, but video fills up your storage awfully fast. That's why you can turn on the checkboxes of just the individual movies or shows you want—or, using the Automatically include pop-up menu, request only the most recent, or the most recent ones you haven't seen yet.

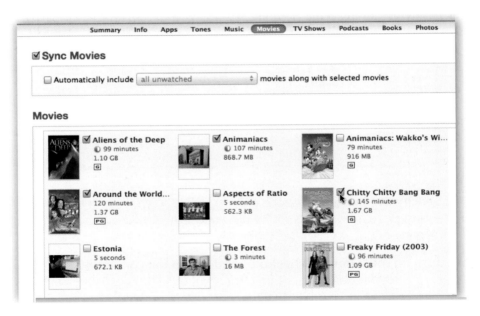

Remember that if you've rented a movie from the iTunes Store and started watching it, you have less than 24 hours left to finish before it turns into a pumpkin.

The Podcasts and iTunes U Tabs

One of the great joys of iTunes is the way it gives you access, in the iTunes Store, to thousands of free amateur and professional *podcasts* (basically, downloadable radio or TV shows), including free college lectures and videos in the iTunes U category.

Here, you can choose to sync all podcast episodes, selected shows, all unplayed episodes—or just a certain number of episodes per sync. Individual checkboxes let you choose *which* podcast series get to come along for the ride, so you can sync to suit your mood at the time.

The Books Tab

Here are the thumbnails of your audiobooks and your ebooks—those you've bought from Apple, those you've downloaded from the Web, and those you've dragged right into iTunes from your desktop (PDF files, for example). You can ask iTunes to send them all to your phone, or only the ones whose checkboxes you turn on.

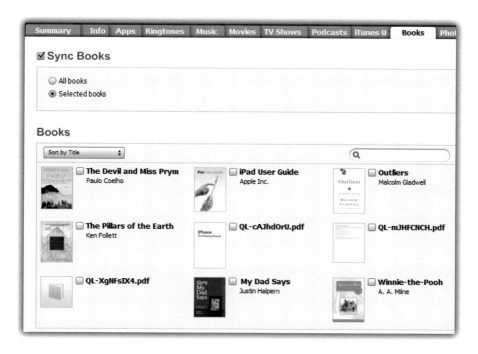

The Photos Tab (Computer→iPhone)

Why corner people with your wallet to show them your kid's baby pictures, when you can whip out your iPhone and dazzle them with a finger-tapping slideshow?

iTunes can sync the photos from your hard drive onto the iPhone. If you use a compatible photo-management program, you can even select individual albums of images that you've already assembled on your computer.

 If you're using iCloud, you might find Photo Stream to be a simpler way to sync the photos between your computer and your phone. (See the next chapter.) You still have to sync with iTunes to transfer your phone's *videos,* though.

Here are your photo-filling options for the iPhone:

- **Photoshop Elements 3.0 or later** for Windows.

- **Photoshop Album 2.0 or later** for Windows.

- **iPhoto 4.0.3 or later** on the Mac.

- **Aperture,** Apple's high-end program for photography pros.

- **Any folder of photos on your hard drive,** like My Pictures (in Windows), Pictures (on the Mac), or any folder you like.

The common JPEG files generated by just about every digital camera work fine for iPhone photos. The GIF and PNG files used by Web pages work, too.

 You can sync photos from only one computer. If you later attempt to snag some snaps from a second machine, iTunes warns you that you must first erase all the images that came from the *original* computer.

When you're ready to sync your photos, click the Photos tab in iTunes. Turn on Sync photos from, and then indicate where you'd like to sync them *from* (Photoshop Elements, iPhoto, or whatever).

If you want only *some* of the albums from your photo-shoebox software, then click Selected albums, events, and faces. Then turn on the checkboxes of the albums, events, and faces you want synced. (The "faces" option is available only if you're syncing from iPhoto or Aperture on the Mac, and only if you've used the Faces feature, which groups your photos according to who's in them.)

Once you make your selections and click Apply, the program computes for a very long time, "optimizing" copies of your photos to make them look great on the iPhone (for example, downsizing them from 10-megapixel overkill to something more appropriate for a 0.6-megapixel screen), and then ports them over.

After the sync is complete, you'll be able to wave your iPhone around, and people will *beg* to see your photos.

Syncing Photos and Videos (iPhone→Computer)

The previous section described copying photos in only one direction: from the computer to the iPhone. But here's one of those rare instances when you can actually *create* data on the iPhone so that you can later transfer it to the computer: photos and videos that you take with the iPhone's own camera. You can rest easy, knowing that they can be copied back to your computer for safekeeping with only one click.

Now, it's important to understand that *iTunes is not involved* in this process. It doesn't know anything about photos or videos coming *from* the iPhone; its job is just to copy pictures *to* the iPhone.

So what's handling the iPhone-to-computer transfer? Your operating system. It sees the iPhone as though it's a digital camera and suggests importing them just as it would from a camera's memory card.

Here's how it goes: Plug the iPhone into the computer with the USB cable. What you'll see is probably something like this:

- **On the Mac.** iPhoto opens. This free photo-organizing/editing software comes on every Mac. Shortly after it notices that the iPhone is on the premises, it goes into Import mode. Click Import All, or select some thumbnails from the iPhone and then click Import Selected.

After the transfer (or before it, in older iPhoto versions), click Delete Photos if you'd like the iPhone's cameraphone memory cleared out after the transfer. (And, yes, both photos and videos get imported together.)

- **In Windows.** When you attach a camera (or an iPhone), a dialog box pops up that asks how you want its contents handled. It lists any photo-management program you might have installed (Picasa, Photoshop Elements, Photoshop Album, and so on), as well as Windows' own camera-management software (Scanner and Camera Wizard in Windows XP; Using Windows in Vista or Windows 7).

Click the program you want to handle importing the iPhone pictures and videos. You'll probably also want to turn on Always do this for this device, so it'll happen automatically the next time.

Shutting Down the Importing Process

Then again, some iPhone owners would rather *not* see some lumbering photo-management program firing itself up every time they connect the phone. You, too, might wish there were a way to *stop* iPhoto or Windows from bugging you every time you connect the iPhone. That, too, is easy enough to change—if you know where to look.

- **Windows XP.** With the iPhone connected, choose Start→My Computer. Right-click the iPhone's icon. From the shortcut menu, choose Properties. Click the Events tab; next, click Take no action. Click OK.

- **Windows Vista, Windows 7.** When the AutoPlay dialog box appears, click Set AutoPlay defaults in Control Panel. (Or, if the AutoPlay dialog box is no longer on the screen, choose Start→Control Panel→AutoPlay.)

  Scroll all the way to the bottom until you see the iPhone icon. From the pop-up menu, choose Take no action. Click Save.

Windows Vista, Windows 7

Windows XP

• **Macintosh.** Open iPhoto. Choose iPhoto→Preferences. Where it says Connecting camera opens, choose No application. Close the window.

From now on, no photo-importing message will appear when you plug in the iPhone. (You can always import its photos manually, of course.)

One iPhone, Multiple Computers

In general, Apple likes to keep things simple. Everything it ever says about the iPhone suggests that you can sync only *one* iPhone with *one* computer.

That's not really true, however. You can actually sync the same iPhone with *multiple* Macs or PCs.

And why would you want to do that? So you can fill it up with material from different places: music and video from a Mac at home; contacts, calendar, ebooks, and iPhone applications from your Windows PC at work; and maybe even the photos from your laptop.

iTunes derives these goodies from different sources to begin with—pictures from your photo program, addresses and appointments from your contacts and calendar programs, music and video from iTunes. So all you have to do is set up the tabs of each computer's copy of iTunes to sync *only* certain kinds of material.

On the Mac, for example, you'd turn on the Sync checkboxes for only the Music, Podcasts, and Video tabs. Sync away.

Next, take the iPhone to the office; on your PC, turn on the Sync checkboxes on only the Info, Books, and Apps tabs. Sync away once more. Then on the laptop, turn off Sync on all tabs except Photos.

And off you go. Each time you connect the iPhone to one of the computers, it syncs that data set according to the preferences set in that copy of iTunes.

One Computer, Multiple iPhones

It's fine to sync multiple iPhones with a single computer, too. iTunes cheer-fully fills each one up, and backs each one up, as they come. In fact, if you open the Preferences box (in the iTunes menu on the Mac, the Edit menu on Windows), the Devices tab lists of all the iPhones (and iPads and iPod Touches) that iTunes is tracking.

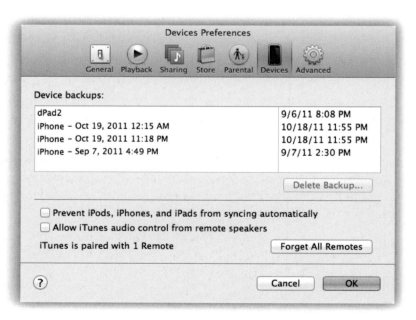

If you use Windows, however, here's a note of warning: You have to use the same sync settings for everyone's phones.

If, for example, you try to switch your Contacts syncing from Google to Outlook Express, an iTunes dialog box informs you that your changes will affect everyone else syncing iPods and iPhones on the PC. (If you really want every family member happy, have each person sign in with his own Windows user account and copy of iTunes.)

 Tip How's this for an undocumented secret? You can use the iPhone to *combine* several different address books—Outlook on a PC and Address Book on a Mac, for example. *All* your contacts wind up on *all* machines—iPhone, Mac, and PC.

Suppose you've synced the iPhone with Computer #1. When you plug it into Computer #2, click the iPhone icon and then the Info tab. Select the additional program you want to sync from—Outlook, Yahoo, whatever. Click Apply.

When iTunes asks if you want to Merge Info or Replace Info, click Merge Info. Now all the iPhone's existing addresses remain in your current address book, but it also copies the contacts from the second computer to the iPhone.

One-Way Emergency Sync

In general, the iPhone's ability to handle bidirectional syncs is a blessing. It means that whenever you modify the information on one of your beloved machines, you won't have to duplicate that effort on the other one.

It can also get hairy. Depending on what merging, fussing, and button-clicking you do, it's possible to make a mess of your iPhone's address book or calendar. You could fill it with duplicate entries, or the wrong entries, or entries from a computer that you didn't intend to merge in there.

Fortunately, as a last resort, iTunes offers a *forced one-way sync* option, which makes your computer's version of things the official one. Everything on the iPhone gets replaced by the computer's version, just this once. At least you'll know exactly where all that information came from.

To do an emergency one-way sync, plug the iPhone into the computer with the USB cable. Click its icon in iTunes. On the Info tab, scroll all the way to the bottom, until you see the Advanced area. There it is: Replace the information on this iPhone, complete with checkboxes for the five things that iTunes can completely replace on the phone: Contacts, Calendars, Bookmarks, Notes, and Mail Accounts. Click Apply to start minty fresh.

WiFi Sync

The iPhone faithful waited for this feature a long, long time: In iOS 5, you can now sync your phone to your computer wirelessly. The phone can be charging in its bedside alarm clock dock, happily and automatically syncing with your laptop somewhere else in the house. It transfers all the same stuff to and from your computer—apps, music, books, contacts, calendars, movies, photos, ringtones—but through the air instead of via your USB cable.

Your phone needs iOS 5, of course; your computer needs iTunes 10.5 or later. The computer has to be turned on and running iTunes. The phone and the computer have to be on the same WiFi network.

Setting Up Wireless Sync

To *set up* wireless sync, you have to connect the phone to your computer using the white USB cable, one last time. Ironic, but true.

Now open iTunes and click the iPhone's icon in the Source list. On the Summary tab, scroll down; turn on Sync with this iPhone over Wi-Fi. Click Apply. You can now detach the phone.

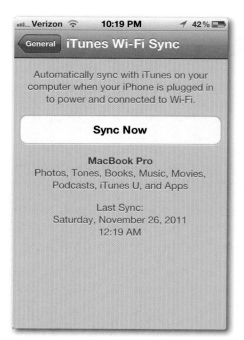

Syncing Over WiFi

From now on, whenever the phone is plugged into power (like a speaker dock, alarm-clock dock, or a wall outlet), and it's on the WiFi network, syncing is automatic. You don't even have to think about it. (Well, OK—you have to think about leaving the computer turned on with iTunes open, which is something of a buzzkill.)

You can also trigger a sync manually—and this time, the iPhone *doesn't* have to be plugged into power. To do that, open Settings→General iTunes→Wi-Fi Sync and tap Sync Now. (You can also trigger a WiFi sync from within iTunes— just click the Sync button. It says "Sync" only if, in fact, anything has changed since your last sync.)

Backing Up the iPhone

You've spent all this time tweaking preferences, massaging settings, and getting everything just so on your brand-new iPhone. Wouldn't it be great if you could *back up* all that work so that if something bad happens to the phone, you wouldn't have to start from scratch?

With iTunes, you can. You get a backup every time the iPhone syncs with iTunes. The backup also happens before you install a new iPhone firmware version from Apple. iTunes also offers to do a backup before you use the Restore option described below. iTunes backs up everything it doesn't already have a copy of: stuff you've downloaded to the phone (music, ebooks, apps, and so on), plus less-visible things, like your iPhone's mail and network settings, your call history, contact favorites, notes, text messages, and other personal preferences that are hard or impossible to recreate.

> **Tip** You can also back up your phone wirelessly and automatically—not to iTunes, but to iCloud, if you've signed up. That method has the advantage of being available even if your computer gets lost or burned to a crisp in a house fire. See the next chapter for details.

Using That Backup

So the day has come when you really need to *use* that backup of your iPhone. Maybe it's become unstable, and it's crashing all over. Or maybe you just lost the dang thing, and you wish your replacement iPhone could have all your old info and settings on it. Here's how to save the day (and your data):

❶ Connect the iPhone to the computer you normally use to sync with.

❷ When the iPhone pops up in the iTunes Source list, click the Summary tab.

❸ Take a deep breath and click Restore. A message announces that after iTunes wipes your iPhone clean and installs a fresh version of the iPhone firmware, you can restore your personal data.

❹ Take iTunes up on its offer to restore all your settings and stuff from the backup. If you see multiple backup files listed from other iPhones (or an iPod Touch), be sure to pick the backup file for *your* phone. Let the backup restore your phone settings and info. Then resync all your music, videos, and podcasts. Exhale.

> **Tip** For the truly paranoid, there's nothing like a *backup* of your backup. Yes, you can actually back up the iTunes backup file, maybe on a flash drive, for safekeeping. On a Mac, look in Home→Library→Application Support→MobileSync→Backup. For Windows Vista or Windows 7, visit C: drive→User→App Data (hidden folder)→ Roaming→Apple Computer→MobileSync→Backup.
>
> If you get in a situation where you need to restore your iPhone through iTunes on a different computer (say, if your old machine croaked), install iTunes on it and then slip this backup file into the same folder on the new computer. Then follow the steps on these pages to restore your data to the iPhone.

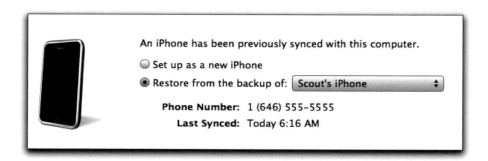

An iPhone has been previously synced with this computer.

○ Set up as a new iPhone

● Restore from the backup of: [Scout's iPhone ◆]

Phone Number: 1 (646) 555-5555
Last Synced: Today 6:16 AM

Deleting a Backup File

Want to delete the existing iPhone backup and start over completely from a little place called Square One? Go to the iTunes preferences (Edit→Preferences in Windows or iTunes→Preferences on the Mac) and click the Devices tab.

Click the dated backup file you don't want and hit Remove Backup. Then connect your iPhone and do one of the things described on page 421 to make yourself a new backup.

14 iCloud

A pple's iCloud service may have opened for business in October 2011, but it's had a long history. It began life as something called iTools, resurfaced as a service called .Mac, popped up again as a $100-a-year entity called MobileMe, and has now become iCloud.

In each case, though, it all stems from Apple's brainstorm that, since it controls both ends of the connection between a Mac and the Apple Web site, it should be able to create some pretty clever Internet-based features.

This chapter concerns what iCloud can do for you, the iPhone owner.

 To get a free iCloud account if you don't already have one, sign up at *www.icloud. com*. Then enter your iCloud email address and password in Settings→iCloud.

What iCloud Giveth

So what is iCloud? Mainly, it's these things:

- **A synchronizing service.** It keeps your calendar, address book, and documents updated and identical on all your gadgets: Mac, PC, iPhone, iPad, iPod Touch (pretty much what MobileMe did).

- **An online locker.** Anything you buy from Apple—music, TV shows, ebooks, and apps—is stored online, for easy access at any time. For example, whenever you buy a song or a TV show from the online iTunes Store, it appears automatically on your iPhone and computers. Your photos are stored online, too.

- **Back to My Mac.** This option to grab files from one of your other Macs across the Internet isn't new, but it survives in iCloud. It lets you access the contents of one Mac from another one across the Internet.

- **Find My iPhone—and Mac.** Find My iPhone pinpoints the current location of your iPhone on a map. In other words, it's great for helping you find your phone if it's been stolen or lost.

  You can also make your lost gadget start making a loud pinging sound for a couple of minutes by remote control—even if it was set to Vibrate mode. That's brilliantly effective when your phone has slipped under the couch cushions.

- **Automatic backup.** iCloud can back up your iPhone—automatically and wirelessly (over WiFi, not over cellular connections). It's a quick backup, since iCloud backs up only the changed data.

  If you ever want to set up a new i-gadget, or if you want to restore everything to an existing one, life is sweet. Once you're in a WiFi hot spot, all you have to do is re-enter your Apple ID and password in the setup assistant that appears when you turn the thing on. Magically, your gadget is refilled with everything that used to be on it.

  Well, *almost* everything. An iCloud backup stores everything you've bought from Apple (music, apps, books); photos and videos in your Camera Roll; settings, including the layout of your Home screen; text messages; and ringtones. Your mail, and anything that came to the gadget from your computer (like music from iTunes and photos from iPhoto), have to be reloaded.

Much of this is based on the central Web site *www.icloud.com*.

Note: iCloud doesn't have all the old MobileMe features. For example, you lose the iDisk, the online photo and video galleries, and iWeb.

If you have a MobileMe account, it will be yours to enjoy, at no charge, until June 30, 2012. At that point, it goes away forever. Your calendar, email, and address book will be auto-converted to the iCloud format. But your iWeb pages, everything on your iDisk, and all your photo galleries go away. Say goodnight, Gracie.

(If you have a MobileMe account, you upgrade it to iCloud by visiting *www.me.com* and following instructions. You'll need Mac OS X Lion if you have a Mac, and Windows Vista or later if you have a PC. When it's all over, tap OK on the iPhone message that says, "Complete your move to iCloud.")

iCloud Sync

For many people, this may be the killer app for iCloud right here: The iCloud Web site, acting as the master control center, can keep multiple Macs, Windows PCs, and iPhones/iPads/iPod Touches synchronized. That offers both a huge convenience factor—all your stuff is always on all your gadgets—and a safety/backup factor, since you have duplicates everywhere.

It works by storing the master copies of your stuff—email, notes, contacts, calendars, Web bookmarks, and documents—on the Web. (Or "in the cloud," as the product managers would say.)

Whenever your Macs, PCs, or i-gadgets are online—over WiFi or 3G cellular— they connect to the mother ship and update themselves. Edit an address on your iPhone, and shortly thereafter, you'll find the same change in Address Book (on your Mac) and Outlook (on your PC). Send an email reply from your PC at the office, and you'll find it in your Sent Mail folder on the Mac at home. Add a Web bookmark anywhere and find it everywhere else. Edit a spreadsheet in Numbers on your iPad, and find the same numbers updated on your Mac.

Actually, there's even another place where you can work with your data: on the Web. Using your computer, you can log in to *www.icloud.com* to find Web-based clones of Calendar, Contacts, and Mail.

To control the syncing, tap Settings→iCloud on your iPhone. Turn on the checkboxes of the stuff you want to be synchronized all the way around:

- **Mail.** "Mail" refers to your actual email messages, plus your account settings and preferences from Mac OS X's Mail program.

- **Contacts, Calendars.** There's nothing as exasperating as realizing that the address book you're consulting on your home Mac is missing somebody you're *sure* you entered—on your phone. This option keeps all your address books and iCal calendars synchronized. Delete a phone number on your computer at home, and you'll find it gone from your phone. Enter an appointment on your iPhone, and you'll find the calendar updated everywhere else.

- **Reminders.** This option refers to the to-do items you create in the phone's Reminders app; very shortly, those reminders will show up on your Mac (in iCal or BusyCal) or PC (in Outlook). How great to make a reminder for yourself in one place and have it reminding you later in another one!

- **Bookmarks.** If a Web site is important enough to merit bookmarking while you're using your phone, why shouldn't it also show up in the Bookmarks menu on your desktop PC at home, your Mac laptop, or your iPad? This option syncs your Safari Reading List, too.

- **Notes.** This option syncs the notes from your phone's Notes app into the email programs on your Mac or PC; to your other i-gadgets; and, of course, to the iCloud Web site.

- **Photo Stream.** Here's the on/off switch for the feature that keeps your last 1,000 photos synchronized among Mac, PC, phone, and other i-gadgets. (There's no Web component of Photo Stream.)

- **Documents & Data.** Some programs are available for more than one machine—including Apple's own iWork suite (Numbers, Pages, Keynote). Those programs are available for Mac, iPhone/iPod Touch, and iPad.

  In that delicious situation, you can create or edit a document on *one* kind of machine, and marvel as iCloud automatically syncs it with all your *other* devices.

  When you fire up one of the iWork programs on the iPhone, the startup screen offers two buttons: Later (don't connect to iCloud now) or Use iCloud (copy your work wirelessly to iCloud, so your other computers and gadgets can get at it).

  From now on, you don't have to do anything special; any document you create or edit appears automatically on your other iCloud-connected machines. If you have iWork for your Mac, your documents are auto-synced to iCloud *if* you've turned on the checkbox in System Preferences.

  On your computer, though, the syncing isn't quite so automatic; you're supposed to use the iWork page of iCloud.com to upload and download Keynote, Numbers, and Pages files to and from your mobile gadgets.

To set up syncing, turn on the switches for the items you want synced. That's it. There is no step 2.

 Note You may notice that there are no switches here for syncing stuff you buy from Apple, like books, movies, apps, and music. They're not so much *synced* as they are *stored* for you online. You can download them at any time to any of your machines.

Photo Stream

This iCloud feature is described in glorious detail in Chapter 7—the photos chapter.

Find My iPhone

Did you leave your iPhone somewhere? Did your laptop get stolen? Has that mischievous 5-year-old hidden your iPad again?

Now you can check into iCloud.com to see exactly where your Mac, iPhone, or iPad is. You can even make it beep loudly for 2 minutes, so you can figure out which couch cushion it's under, or which jacket pocket you left it in. If the missing item is an iPad or iPhone, you can make it beep even if the ringer switch is off, and even if the phone is asleep. You can also make a message pop up on the screen; if you actually left the thing in a taxi or on some restaurant table, you can use this feature to plead for its return. The bottom line: If you ever lose your Apple gear, you have a fighting chance at getting it back.

(That's *if* it's online and still has power, and *if* you turned on Find My iPhone in Settings→iCloud.)

If an ethical person finds your phone, you might get it back. If it's a greedy person who says, "Hey, cool! A free iPhone!" then maybe you can bombard him with so many of these messages that he gives it back in exasperation.

If not, you can either lock the gadget with a password (yes, by remote control) or even avail yourself of one more amazing last-ditch feature: Remote Wipe.

That means **erasing your data by remote control,** from wherever you happen to be. The evil thief can do nothing but stare in amazement as the phone suddenly erases itself, winding up completely empty.

(If you ever get the phone back, you can just sync with iTunes, and presto! Your stuff is back on the phone—at least everything since your last sync.)

Once you've turned this option on in Settings, you can sleep easy. Later, if the worst should come to pass and you can't find your iPhone, go to any computer and call up *www.icloud.com*. Log in with your Apple name and password.

Click the ☁ icon at upper left; in the list of iCloud features, click Find My iPhone. If you're asked for your password again, type it; Apple wants to make sure it's really, *really* you who's messing around with your account settings.

Finally, in the panel on the left side, click the name of your phone.

Immediately, the Web site updates to show you, on a map, the current location of your phone—and Macs, iPod Touches, and iPads. (If they're not online, or if they're turned all the way off, you won't see their current locations.)

If just knowing where the thing *is* isn't enough to satisfy you, click the little ⓘ next to your phone's name, and try one of these three buttons:

- **Play Sound or Send Message.** Click this button, type a message, and then click Send. Instantly, that message appears on the phone's screen, wherever it is, no matter what app was running. Whoever's using it can't miss it, can't do anything without dismissing the message first.

  When it's all over, Apple sends an email confirmation to your @me.com address.

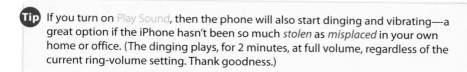

Tip If you turn on Play Sound, then the phone will also start dinging and vibrating—a great option if the iPhone hasn't been so much *stolen* as *misplaced* in your own home or office. (The dinging plays, for 2 minutes, at full volume, regardless of the current ring-volume setting. Thank goodness.)

- **Lock.** What if you worry about the security of your phone's info, but you don't want to erase it completely and just want to throw a low-level veil of casual protection over the thing? Easy: Lock it by remote control. The Lock button lets you make up a four-digit passcode (which overrides the one you already had on the phone, if any). Without it, the sleazy crook can't get into your phone without erasing it.

The passcode works just as though you'd created one yourself on the phone. That is, it remains in place until you, with the phone in hand, manually turn it off in Settings Settings→General→Passcode Lock.

- **Remote Wipe.** This is the last-ditch security option, for when your immediate concern isn't so much the phone as all the private stuff that's on it. Click this button, confirm the dire warning box, and click Erase All Data. By remote control, you've just erased everything from your phone, wherever it may be. (If it's ever returned, you can restore it from your backup.)

Once you've wiped the phone, you can no longer find it or send messages to it using Find My iPhone.

> **Tip** There's an app for that. Download the Find My iPhone app from the App Store. It lets you do everything described above from another iPhone, in a tidy, simple control panel.

Email

Apple offers an email address as part of each iCloud account. Of course, you already *have* an email account. So why bother? The first advantage is the simple address: *YourName@me.com*.

Second, you can read your me.com email from any computer anywhere in the world, via the iCloud Web site, or on your iPhone/iPod Touch/iPad.

To make things even sweeter, your me.com mail is completely synced. Delete a message on one gadget, and you'll find it in the Deleted Mail folder on another. Send a message from your iPhone, and you'll find it in the Sent Mail folder on your Mac. And so on.

Video, Music, Apps: Locker in the Sky

Apple, as if you hadn't noticed, has become a big seller of multimedia files. It has the biggest music store in the world. It has the biggest app store, for both i-gadgets and Macs. It sells an awful lot of TV shows and movies. Its ebook store, iBooks, is no Amazon.com, but it's chugging along.

When you buy a song, movie, app, or book, you've always been allowed to copy it to all your other Apple equipment—no extra charge. But iCloud automates, or at least formalizes, that process. Once you buy something, it's added to a tidy list of items that you can download to all your *other* machines.

Here's how to grab them:

- **iPhone, iPad, iPod Touch.** Open the App Store icon (for apps), the iBooks program (for ebooks), or the iTunes app (for songs or TV shows; tap the category you want). Tap Updates (App Store only). Tap Purchased. Tap Not On This iPhone.

There they are: all the items you've bought on your *other* machines using the same Apple ID. To download anything listed here onto *this* machine, tap the ⊕ button. Or tap an album name to see the list of songs on it so you can download just *some* of those songs.

You can save yourself all that tapping by opening Settings→Store and turning on Automatic Downloads (for Music, Apps, and Books). From now on, whenever you're in WiFi, stuff you've bought on other Apple machines gets downloaded to this one *automatically,* in the background.

 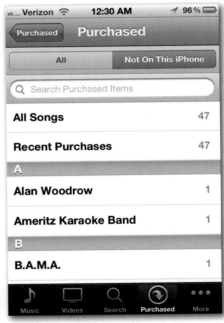

- **Mac or PC.** Open the Mac App Store program (for Mac apps) or the iTunes app (for songs, TV shows, books, and movies). Under the Store heading, there they are: individual subheadings for each gadget you've used to buy stuff: "Purchased on iPhone," "Purchased on Mom's iPad," and so on. Or just click Purchased to view the entire list. There are all your purchases, ready to open or re-download if necessary.

Any bookmark you set in an iBook book is synced to your other gadgets, too. The idea, of course, is that you can read a few pages on your phone in the doctor's waiting room and then continue from the same page on your iPad on the train ride home.

iTunes Match

Anything you've ever bought from the iTunes music store is now available for playing on any Apple gadget you own. You get it.

A lot of people, however, have music in their collections that *didn't* come from the iTunes Store. Maybe they ripped some audio CDs into their computers. Maybe they acquired some music from, ahem, a friend.

What a sad situation! You've got some of your music available with you on your iPhone, and some that's stranded at home on your computer.

Enter iTunes Match. It's an Apple service that lets you store your *entire* collection, including songs that didn't come from Apple, online, for $25 a year.

The iTunes software analyzes the songs in your collection. If it finds a song that's also available in iTunes, then—bing!—that song becomes available for your playback pleasure, without your actually having to transfer your copy to Apple. Apple says, in effect: "Well, our copy of the song is just as good as yours, so you're welcome to listen to our copy on any of your machines."

Truth is, in fact, Apple's copy is probably *better* than your copy. You get to play back the song at iTunes' 256 Kbps quality, no matter how grungy your copy.

If there's a song or two in your collection *not* among Apple's 20 million tracks, then you can upload them to Apple.

The advantages of forking over the $25 a year are (a) you can listen to *all* your music from any computer/phone/tablet, (b) that audio-quality upgrade, and (c) using the song-matching system saves you huge amounts of uploading time. (The rival services from Google and Amazon require uploading your entire music collection, which can take days.)

The disadvantage: You're paying $25 a year.

To get started, make sure you have the latest version of iTunes. Choose Store→Turn On iTunes Match and sign up. Wait awhile as iTunes does its analyzing, matching, and uploading business.

Once that's done, turn on Settings→Music→iTunes Match on your phone. From now on, any songs on the iPhone that are actually sitting online are marked by a icon. And any song you buy on any machine shows up as available to play on any of them.

These songs behave exactly like songs that are stored physically on your phone. (In fact, they often are; if you tap a ☁ song to play it, the iPhone downloads and stores it so it won't have to bother the next time.)

> **Tip** Listening to streaming iTunes Match music over a cellular connection eats up your monthly data limit fast! To protect yourself, turn off Settings→Store→Use Cellular Data; now you can listen only over a WiFi connection.

If you plan to be offline for awhile (like on a flight to Tokyo), you can hide the online songs by turning off Settings→Music→Show All Music.

The Price of Free

A free iCloud account gives you 5 gigabytes of online storage. That may not sound like much, especially when you consider how big some music files, photo files, and video files are.

Fortunately, anything you buy from Apple—like music, apps, books, and TV shows—doesn't count against that 5-gigabyte limit. Neither do the photos in your Photo Stream.

So what's left? Some things that don't take up much space, like settings, documents, and pictures you take with your iPhone, iPad, or iPod Touch—and some things that take up a lot of it, like email, commercial movies, and home videos you transferred to the phone from your computer. (Your iPhone backup might hog space, but you can pare that down in Settings→iCloud→Storage & Backup→Manage Storage. Tap an app's name and then tap Edit.)

You can, of course, expand your storage if you find 5 gigs constricting—for $2 a gigabyte a year. So you'll pay $20, $40, or $100 a year for an extra 10, 20, or 50 gigs. You can upgrade your storage online, on your computer, or right on the iPhone (in Settings→iCloud→Storage & Backup).

The Corporate iPhone

15

No, the chapter name "The Corporate iPhone" is not an oxymoron. Yes, in its younger days, people thought of the iPhone as a *personal* device, meant for consumers and not for corporations. But somebody at Apple must have gotten sick of hearing, "Well, the iPhone is cool, but it's no BlackBerry." These days, among business people, the iPhone is actually more popular than the BlackBerry. The iPhone now has the security and compatibility features your corporate technical overlords require.

Even better, the iPhone can talk to Microsoft Exchange ActiveSync servers, staples of corporate computer departments that, among other things, keep smartphones wirelessly updated with the calendar, contacts, and email back at the office. (Yes, it sounds a lot like MobileMe or iCloud. Which is probably why Apple's MobileMe slogan was, "Exchange for the rest of us.")

The Perks

This chapter is intended for you, the iPhone owner—not for the highly paid, well-trained, exceedingly friendly IT (information technology) managers at your company.

Your first task is to convince them that your iPhone is now secure and compatible enough to welcome into the company's network. Here's some information you can use:

- **Microsoft Exchange ActiveSync.** Exchange ActiveSync is the technology that keeps smartphones wirelessly synced with the data on the mother ship's computers. The iPhone works with Exchange ActiveSync, so it can remain in wireless contact with your company's Exchange servers exactly like BlackBerries and Windows Mobile phones do.

(*Exchange ActiveSync* is not to be confused with regular old *ActiveSync,* which is a much older technology that's designed to update smart-phones and palmtops over a cable.)

Your email, address book, and calendar appointments are now sent wirelessly to your iPhone so it's always kept current—and they're sent in a way that those evil rival firms can't intercept. (It uses 128-bit encrypted SSL, if you must know.)

 Tip That's the same encryption used by Outlook Web Access (OWA), which lets employees check their email, calendar, and contacts from any Web browser. In other words, if your IT administrators are willing to let you access your data using OWA, they should also be willing to let you access it with the iPhone.

- **Mass setup.** Using a free software program for Mac or Windows called the iPhone Configuration Utility, your company's network geeks can set up a bunch of iPhones all at once.

  This program generates iPhone *profiles* (.mobileconfig files): canned iPhone setups that determine all WiFi, network, password, email, and VPN settings.

  The IT manager can email this file to you or post it on a secure Web page; either way, you can just open that file on your iPhone, and presto—you're all configured and set up. And the IT manager never has to handle the phones individually.

  Said manager can now send you new custom apps wirelessly, without your having to sync up to iTunes.

- **Security.** In the event of the unthinkable—you lose your iPhone, or it gets stolen, and vital company secrets are now "in the wild," susceptible to discovery by your company's rivals—network administrators have a handy tool at their disposal. They can erase your entire iPhone by remote control, even though they have no idea where it is or who has it. (iCloud users can do this on a personal iPhone, too.)

  The iPhone can connect to wireless networks using the latest, super-secure connections (WPA Enterprise and WPA2 Enterprise), which are highly resistant to hacker attacks. And when you're using virtual private networking, as described at the end of this chapter, you can use a very secure VPN protocol called IPSec. That's what most companies use for secure, encrypted remote access to the corporate network. Juniper and Cisco VPN apps are available, too.

Speaking of security: Not only does the iPhone let you create much tougher-to-crack passwords than the feeble four-digit passwords of time gone by, but these passwords now encrypt all email, email attachments, and the data of any apps that are written to take advantage of this feature.

 This Data Protection feature requires an iPhone with 32 GB of memory or more. And it requires doing a full Restore from an iTunes backup.

- **Fewer tech-support calls.** Finally, don't forget to point out to the IT staff how rarely you'll need to call them for tech support. It's pretty clear that the iPhone is easier to figure out than, ahem, certain rival smartphones.

And what's in it for you? Complete synchronization of your email, address book, and calendar with what's on your PC at work. Send an email from your iPhone, find it in the Sent folder of Outlook at the office. And so on.

You can also accept invitations to meetings on your iPhone that are sent your way by coworkers; if you accept, they're added to your calendar automatically, just as on your PC. You can also search the company's master address book, right from your iPhone.

The biggest perk for you, though, is just getting permission to *use* an iPhone as your company-issued phone.

Setup

Once you've convinced the IT squad of the iPhone's work-worthiness, they can set up things on their end by consulting Apple's free, downloadable setup guide: the infamous *iPhone OS Enterprise Deployment Guide*. (It incorporates Apple's individual, smaller guides for setting up Microsoft Exchange, Cisco IPSec VPN, IMAP email, and Device Configuration profiles.)

This guide is filled with handy tips, like: "On the Front-End Server, verify that a server certificate is installed and enable SSL for the Exchange ActiveSync virtual directory (require basic SSL authentication)."

In any case, you (or they) can download the deployment guide from this site: *www.apple.com/support/iphone/enterprise*.

At that point, they must grant you and your iPhone permission to access the company's Exchange server using Exchange ActiveSync. Fortunately, if you're already allowed to use Outlook Web Access, then you probably have permission to connect with your iPhone, too.

The steps for *you*, the lowly worker bee, to set up your iPhone for accessing your company's Exchange ActiveSync server are much simpler.

First, set up your iPhone with your corporate email account, if that hasn't been done for you. Tap Settings→Mail, Contacts, Calendars→Add Account→ Microsoft Exchange. Fill in your work email address, user name, and password as they were provided to you by your company's IT person. The Username box is the only potentially tricky spot.

Sometimes, your user name is just the first part of your email address—so if your email address is *smithy@worldwidewidgets.com*, then your user name is simply *smithy.*

In other companies, though, you may also need to know your *Windows domain* and stick that in front of the user name, in the format *domain\user name* (for example, *wwwidgets\smithy*). In some companies, this is exactly how you log into your PC at work or into Outlook Web Access. If you aren't sure, try your user name by itself first; if that doesn't work, then try *domain\ user name.* And if *that* doesn't work, then you'll probably have to ask your IT people for the info.

Incidentally, what's in the Description field doesn't matter. It can be whatever you want to call this particular email account ("Gol-Durned Work Stuff," for example).

When you're finished plugging in these details, tap Next at the top of the screen.

If your company is using Exchange 2007 or later, that should be all there is to it. You're now presented with the list of corporate information that the iPhone can sync itself with: Email, Contacts, and Calendars. This is your opportunity to turn *off* any of these things if you don't particularly care to have them sent to your iPhone. (You can always change your mind in Settings.)

However, if your company uses Exchange 2003 (or 2007/2010 with AutoDiscovery turned off—they'll know what that means), you're now asked to provide the *server* address. It's often the same address you'd use to get to the Web version of your Outlook account, like *owa.widgetsworldwide.com*. But if in doubt, here again, your company techie should be able to assist. Only then do you get to the screen where you choose which kinds of data to sync.

And that's it. Your iPhone will shortly bloom with the familiar sight of your office email stash, calendar appointments, and contacts.

Life on the Corporate Network

Once your iPhone is set up, you should be in wireless corporate heaven:

- **Email.** Your corporate email account shows up among whatever other email accounts you've set up (Chapter 12); you can view it in the new unified inbox, if you like. In fact, you can now have *multiple* Exchange accounts on the same phone. And not only is your email "pushed" to the phone (it arrives as it's sent, without your having to explicitly *check* for messages), but it's also synced with what you see on your computer at work. If you send, receive, delete, flag, or file any messages on your iPhone, you'll find them sent, received, deleted, flagged, or filed on your computer at the office. And vice versa.

All the iPhone email niceties described in Chapter 12 are available to your corporate mail: opening attachments, rotating and zooming into them, and so on. Your iPhone can even play back your office voicemail, presuming your company has one of those unified messaging systems that send out WAV audio file versions of your messages via email.

Oh—and when you're addressing an outgoing message, the iPhone's autocomplete feature consults *both* your built-in iPhone address book *and* the corporate directory (on the Exchange server) simultaneously.

- **Contacts.** In the address book, you gain a new superpower: You can search your company's master name directory right from the iPhone. That's great when you need to track down, say, the art director in your Singapore branch.

  To perform this search, tap Contacts on the Home screen. Tap the Groups button in the upper-left corner. On the Groups screen, a new section appears that mere mortal iPhone owners never see: Directories. Just

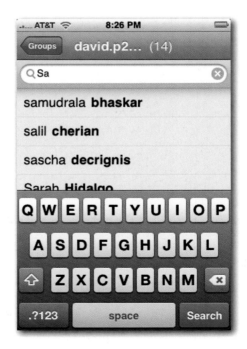

beneath it, tap the name of your Exchange account ("Gol-Durned Work Stuff," for example).

On the following screen, start typing the name of the person you're looking up; the resulting matches appear as you type. (Or type the whole name, and then tap Search.)

In the list of results, tap the name you want. That person's Info screen appears so you can tap to dial a number or compose a preaddressed email message. (You can't send a text message to someone in the corporate phone book, however.)

- **Calendar.** Your iPhone's calendar is wirelessly kept in sync with the master calendar back at the office. If you're on the road and your minions make changes to your schedule in Outlook, you'll know about it; you'll see the change on your iPhone's calendar.

There are some other changes to your calendar, too, as you'll find out in a moment.

 Tip Don't forget that you can save battery power, syncing time, and mental clutter by limiting how much *old* calendar stuff gets synced to your iPhone. (How often do you really look back on your calendar to see what happened more than a month ago?) Page 472 has the details.

Exchange + Your Stuff

The iPhone can display calendar and contact information from multiple sources at once—your Exchange calendar/address book and your own personal data, for example.

Here's how it works: Open your iPhone calendar. Tap the Calendars button at the top left.

Now you're looking at the complete list of calendar *categories*. Here's what you might find there:

- **All Calendars.** This button, at the very top, takes you to your *single, unified* calendar, showing all appointments from your Exchange account, iCloud, maybe your Google or Yahoo calendars, and your Mac's or PC's calendar program. No wonder you've been feeling so busy.

- **iCloud.** Tap this one to see all your iCloud categories on the same calendar (Social, School, Kids, and so on).

- **Google calendar [or another CalDAV subscription].** Tap this one to see all the events listed on some Internet-based calendar to which you've subscribed.

- **[Your Exchange account name].** Tap this button to see only your work calendar. (You may see subcategories, if your company uses them, listed under the Exchange heading, bearing color-coded dots.)

- **Home, Personal, Social....** Tap one of the individual category names to see *only* that category of your iCloud, Exchange, or personal calendar.

You can pull off a similar stunt in Contacts. Whenever you're looking at your list of contacts, you can tap the Groups button (top left of the screen). Here, once again, you can tap All Contacts to see a combined address book—or you can look over only your iCloud contacts, your Exchange contacts, your personal contacts, and so on. Or tap [group name] to view only the people in your tennis circle, book club, or whatever (if you've created groups); or [your Exchange account name] to search only the company listings.

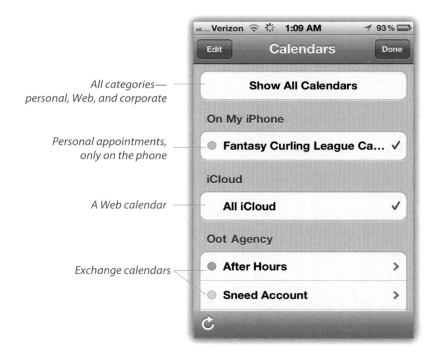

All categories—personal, Web, and corporate

Personal appointments, only on the phone

A Web calendar

Exchange calendars

Invitations

If you've spent much time in the world of Microsoft Outlook (that is, corporate America), then you already know about *invitations.* These are electronic invitations that coworkers send you directly from Outlook. When you get one of these invitations by email, you can click Accept, Decline, or Tentative.

If you click Accept, then the meeting gets dropped onto the proper date in your Outlook calendar, and your name gets added to the list of attendees maintained by the person who invited you. If you click Tentative, then the meeting is flagged *that* way, on both your calendar and the sender's.

Exchange meeting invitations on the iPhone show up in *four places,* just to make sure you don't miss them:

- **In your face.** An incoming invitation pops up as a standard iPhone alert—a blue bubble, a top-of-screen banner, or whatever you've selected in Settings→Notifications→Calendar. Tap View to read what it's about, who else is coming, and where it's taking place.

  Here's also where you can tap Accept, Maybe, or Decline. ("Maybe"= Outlook's "Tentative.")

 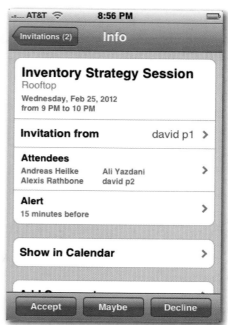

Tapping Decline deletes the invitation from every corner of your iPhone, although it will sit in your Mail program's Trash for a while in case you change your mind.

- **On your Home screen.** The Calendar icon on your Home screen sprouts a red, circled number, indicating how many invites you haven't yet looked at.

- **In email.** Invitations also appear as attachments to messages in your corporate email account, just as they would if you were using Outlook. Tap the name of the attachment to open the invitation Info window.

- **In Calendar.** When your iPhone is connected to your company's Exchange calendars, there's a twist: An Inbox button appears at the lower-right corner of your Calendar program.

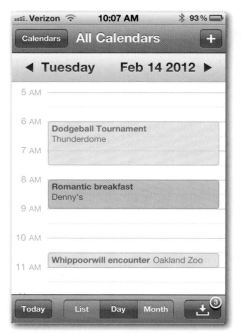

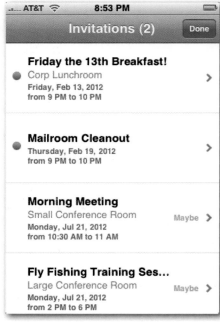

When an invite (or several) is waiting for you, a red, circled number appears on this icon, letting you know you've got waiting invitations to attend to (and telling you how many). Tap the Inbox icon to see the Invitations list, which summarizes all invitations you've accepted, maybe'd, or not responded to yet.

 Tip Invitations you haven't dealt with also show up on the Calendar's list view or day view with a dotted outline. That's the iPhone's clever visual way of showing you just how severely your workday will be ruined if you accept this meeting.

You can also *generate* invitations. When you're filling out the Info form for a new appointment, you get a field called Invitees. Tap there to enter the email addresses of the people you'd like to invite.

Your invitation will show up in whatever calendar programs they use, and they'll never know you didn't send it from some corporate copy of Microsoft Outlook.

A Word on Troubleshooting

If you're having trouble with your Exchange syncing and can't find any steps that work, ask your Exchange administrators to make sure that ActiveSync's settings are correct on their end. You've heard the old saying that in 99 percent of computer troubleshooting, the problem lies between the keyboard and the chair? The other 1 percent of the time, it's between the *administrator's* keyboard and chair.

> **Tip** You can access your company's SharePoint sites, too. That's a Microsoft document-collaboration feature that's also a common part of corporate online life.
>
> The iPhone's browser can access these sites; it can also open Word, Excel, PowerPoint, and PDF documents you find there. Handy indeed!

Virtual Private Networking (VPN)

The typical corporate network is guarded by a team of steely-eyed administrators for whom Job One is preventing access by unauthorized visitors. They perform this job primarily with the aid of a super-secure firewall that seals off the company's network from the Internet.

So how can you tap into the network from the road? Only one solution is both secure and cheap: the *virtual private network,* or VPN. Running a VPN lets you create a super-secure "tunnel" from your iPhone, across the Internet, and straight into your corporate network. All data passing through this tunnel is heavily encrypted. To the Internet eavesdropper, it looks like so much undecipherable gobbledygook.

VPN is, however, a corporate tool, run by corporate nerds. Your company's tech staff can tell you whether or not there's a VPN server set up for you to use.

If there is one, then you'll need to know what type of server it is. The iPhone can connect to VPN servers that speak *PPTP* (Point-to-Point Tunneling Protocol) and *L2TP/IPSec* (Layer 2 Tunneling Protocol over the IP Security Protocol), both relatives of the PPP language spoken by modems. Most corporate VPN servers work with at least one of these protocols.

The iPhone can also connect to Cisco servers, which are among the most popular systems in corporate America, and with a special app, Juniper's Junos Pulse servers, too.

To set up your VPN connection, visit Settings→General→Network→VPN. Tap the On/Off switch to make the VPN configuration screen pop up. Tap L2TP, PPTP, or IPSec (that's the Cisco one), depending on which kind of server your company uses (ask the network administrator).

The most critical bits of information to fill in are these:

- **Server.** The Internet address of your VPN server (for example, *vpn.ferrets-r-us.com*).

- **Account; Password.** Here's your user account name and password, as supplied by the IT guys.

- **Secret.** If your office offers L2TP connections, then you'll need yet another password called a Shared Secret to ensure that the server you're connecting to is really the server you intend to connect to.

Once everything is in place, the iPhone can connect to the corporate network and fetch your corporate mail. You don't have to do anything special on your end; everything works just as described in this chapter.

Some networks require that you type the currently displayed password on an *RSA SecurID card,* which your administrator will provide. This James Bondish, credit-card-like thing displays a password that changes every few seconds, making it rather difficult for hackers to learn "the" password.

VPN on Demand

If you like to access your corporate email or internal Web site a few times a day, having to enter your name-and-password credentials over and over again can get old fast. Fortunately, iOS 5 offers a huge time-saving assist with its introduction of *VPN on Demand.*

That is, you just open up Safari and tap the corporate bookmark; the iPhone creates the VPN channel automatically, behind the scenes, and connects.

There's nothing you have to do, or even anything you *can* do, to make this feature work; your company's network nerds have to turn this feature on at their end.

They'll create a *configuration profile* that you'll install on your iPhone. It includes the VPN server settings, an electronic security certificate, and a list of domains and URLs that will automatically turn on the iPhone's VPN feature.

From now on, whenever you open Safari and try to visit a Web page that's behind the company's firewall, the iPhone makes the VPN connection for you automatically. You're spared the hassle of entering a user name or password.

When your iPhone goes to sleep, it terminates the VPN connection, both for security purposes and to save battery power.

 Clearly, eliminating the VPN sign-in process also weakens the security that the VPN was invented for in the first place. Therefore, you'd be well advised—and probably required by your IT guys—to use the iPhone's password feature, so some evil corporate spy (or teenage thug) can't just steal your iPhone and start snooping through your corporate servers.

16 Settings

Your iPhone is a full-blown computer—well, at least a half-blown one. And like any good computer, it's customizable. The Settings application, right there on your Home screen, is like the Control Panel in Windows, or System Preferences on the Mac. It's a tweaking center that affects every aspect of the iPhone: the screen, ringtones, email, Web connection, and so on. You scroll the Settings list as you would any iPhone list: by dragging your finger up or down the screen.

Most of the items on the Settings page are doorways to other screens, where you make the actual changes. When you're finished inspecting or changing the preference settings, you can return to the main Settings screen by tapping the Settings button in the upper-left corner—or by just pressing the Home button.

In this book, you can read about the iPhone's preference settings in the appropriate spots—wherever they're relevant. But so you'll also have it all in one place, here's an item-by-item walkthrough of the Settings application.

Airplane Mode

As you're probably aware, you're not allowed to make cellphone calls on U.S. airplanes. According to legend (if not science), a cellphone's radio can interfere with a plane's navigation equipment.

But the iPhone does a lot more than make calls. Are you supposed to deprive yourself of all the music, videos, movies, and email that you could be using in flight, just because cellphones are forbidden?

Nope. Just turn on Airplane Mode by tapping the Off button at the top of the Settings list (so the orange On button appears). Now it's safe (and permitted) to use the iPhone in flight—at least after takeoff, when you hear the announcement about "approved electronics"—because the cellular and WiFi features of the iPhone are turned off completely. You can't make calls or get online, but you can do anything else in the iPhone's bag of nonwireless tricks.

WiFi

WiFi—wireless Internet networking—is one of the iPhone's best features. This item in Settings opens the WiFi Networks screen, where you'll find three useful controls:

- **WiFi On/Off.** If you don't plan to use WiFi, turning it off gets you a lot more life out of each battery charge. Tap anywhere on this On/Off slider to change its status.

 Tip Turning on Airplane Mode automatically turns off the WiFi antenna—but you can turn WiFi back on. That's handy when you're on a flight with WiFi on board.

- **Choose a Network.** Here you'll find a list of all nearby WiFi networks that the iPhone can "see," complete with a signal-strength indicator and a padlock icon if a password is required. An Other item lets you access WiFi networks that are invisible and secret unless you know their names. See Chapter 10 for details on using WiFi with the iPhone.

- **Ask to Join Networks.** If this option is On, then whenever you attempt to get online (to check email or the Web, for example), the iPhone sniffs around to find a WiFi network. If it finds one you haven't used before, the iPhone invites you, with a small dialog box, to hop onto it.

  So why would you ever want to turn this feature off? To avoid getting bombarded with invitations to join WiFi networks, which can happen in heavily populated areas, and to save battery power. (The phone will still hop automatically onto hotspots it's joined in the past.)

Carrier

If you see this panel at all, then you're doubly lucky: First, you're enjoying a trip overseas; second, you have a choice of cellphone carriers who have roaming agreements with AT&T, Verizon, or Sprint. Tap your favorite and prepare to pay some serious roaming fees.

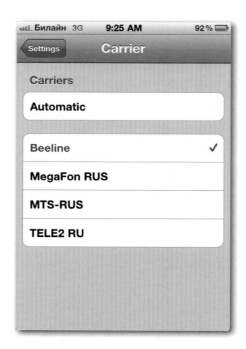

Notifications

This Settings panel, newly beefed up in iOS 5, lists all the apps that think they have the right to nag for your attention. Flight-tracking programs alert you that there's an hour before takeoff. Social-networking programs ping you when someone's trying to reach you. Games let you know when it's your move (in a game against someone else online). Instant-messaging apps ding to let you know that you have a new message. It can add up to a lot of interruption.

On this panel, you can tailor, to an almost ridiculous degree, how you want to be nagged. You can specify which apps notify you in which manner; which apps can leave their notifications on your Lock screen or in the new Notification Center; and more. By turning certain things off, you can reduce that feeling of sensory overload from your phone.

See the end of Chapter 1 for a complete description of these controls.

Location Services

A hullabaloo arose in the spring of 2011, when researchers discovered that the iPhone was keeping a record of your geographical movements.

The information wasn't being transmitted to Apple, the government, or the Warren Commission; it was just sitting there on your hard drive, accessible only with Unix commands. But even so, conspiracy theorists immediately went into hysterics. "Apple is tracking you," went the overblown headlines.

Apple was quick to explain. No, it wasn't tracking you. It was collecting the locations of WiFi hotspots, as described on page 293. Even so, Apple quickly stopped backing up the location database to your computer, changed the duration of the storage to only a week's worth, and stopped collecting hot-spot locations if you turned off Location Services.

Then, in iOS 5, Apple moved the location-tracking controls front and center.

At the top, you'll find the master on/off switch for all Location Services. If you turn it off, the iPhone can no longer determine where you are on a map, geo-tag your photos, find the closest ATM, tell your friends where you're hanging out, and so on.

Furthermore, this screen goes on to list every single app that uses your loca-tion information, and it lets you turn off this feature on a per-app basis. You might want to do that for privacy's sake—or you might want to do that to save battery power, since the location searches sap away a little juice every time. (The little ➹ icon indicates which apps have actually *used* your location data. If it's gray, that app has checked your location in the past 24 hours; if it's purple, it's locating you right now.)

Even more controls await if you tap System Services. Here are the on/off switches for six of the iPhone's own features that use your location. Cell Network Search, for example, lets your phone tap into Apple's database of cellular frequencies by location, which speeds up connections. Diagnostics and Usage sends location information back to Apple along with diagnostic information so that, for example, Apple can see where calls are being dropped

There's even an on/off switch for Status Bar Icon; if it's on, you'll see the ➹ icon right there at the top of the screen, so you'll be aware when some app is using your location.

Sounds

Here's a more traditional cellphone settings screen: the place where you choose a ringtone sound for incoming calls.

- **Silent Vibrate, Ring Vibrate.** Like any self-respecting cellphone, the iPhone has a Vibrate mode—a little shudder in your pocket that might get your attention when you can't hear the ringing. As you can see, there

are two on/off controls for the vibration: one for when the phone is in Silent mode (page 20) and one for when the ringer's on.

- **Ringer and Alerts.** The slider here controls the volume of the phone's ringing.

  Of course, it's usually faster to adjust the ring volume by pressing the up/down buttons on the left edge whenever you're not on a call. But if you find that your volume buttons are getting pressed accidentally in your pocket, you can also turn off Change with Buttons. Now you can adjust the volume *only* with this slider, here in Settings.

- **Ringtone.** Tap this row to view the iPhone's list of 25 built-in ringtones, plus 27 "alert tones," plus any new ones you've added yourself. (There's even a Buy More Tones button at the top. It takes you straight to the iTunes Store, where you can buy a 30-second pop-song snippet for $1.30 each.)

  Tap a ring sound to hear it. After you've tapped one you like, confirm your choice by tapping Sounds to return to the Sounds screen.

 Note Of course, you can choose a different ringtone for each person in your phone book (page 75). You can also set up a "vibrate, then ring" effect (page 149).

- **Text Tone, New Voicemail, New Mail, Sent Mail, Tweet...** For some people, these controls represent the most important advance in all of iOS 5. Yes, after all those years on the market, the iPhone finally lets you choose your own sounds for all those different phone events. You can choose individual sounds for the arrival of a new voicemail, text message, or email; the successful sending of an outgoing email message; and calendar or Reminders alarms.

  This is a big deal—not just because you can express your individuality through your choice of ringtones, text tones, reminder tones, and so on, but because you can finally distinguish your iPhone's blips and bleeps from somebody else's in the same family or workplace.

  You can also turn on or off the Lock Sounds (the sounds you get when you tap the Sleep/Wake switch on the top of the phone) and the Keyboard Clicks that play when you type on the virtual keyboard.

Brightness

Ordinarily, the iPhone controls its own screen brightness. An ambient-light sensor hidden behind the smoked glass at the top of the iPhone's face samples the room brightness each time you wake the phone and adjusts the brightness automatically: brighter in bright rooms, dimmer in darker ones.

When you prefer more manual control, here's what you can do:

- **Brightness slider.** Drag the handle on this slider to control the screen brightness manually, keeping in mind that more brightness means shorter battery life.

  If Auto-Brightness is turned on, then the changes you make here are relative to the iPhone's self-chosen brightness. In other words, if you goose the brightness by 20 percent, then the screen will always be 20 percent brighter than the iPhone would have chosen for itself.

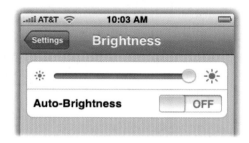

- **Auto-Brightness On/Off.** Tap anywhere on this switch to disable the ambient-light sensor completely. Now the brightness of the screen is under complete manual control.

Wallpaper

Wallpaper can mean either the photo on the Unlock screen (what you see when you wake the iPhone up), or the background picture on your Home screen. On this panel, you can change the image used for either one. Page 220 has step-by-step instructions.

General

The General pages offer a *huge,* motley assortment of settings governing the behavior of the virtual keyboard, the Bluetooth transmitter, the password-protection feature, and about six trillion other things.

- **About.** Tapping this item opens a page for the statistics nut. Here you can find out how many songs, videos, and photos your iPhone holds; how much storage your iPhone has; techie details like the iPhone's software and firmware versions, serial number, model, WiFi and Bluetooth addresses, and so on. (It's kind of cool to see how many applications you've installed.)

 Tip At the very top, you can tap the phone's name to rename it. That's part of iOS 5's "PC-free" initiative; it used to be that you could change the iPhone's name only in iTunes.

- **Software Update.** Here's another part of Apple's "you don't need a computer anymore" master plan. Now, when Apple releases a new software update for your iPhone, you can download it directly to the phone. You don't need to connect to a Mac or PC for that job.

You'll know when an update is waiting for you, because you'll see a little number badge on the Settings icon (previous illustration, left), as well as on the word General in Settings. Tap it, and then tap Software Update, to see and install the update. (If no number badge is waiting, then tapping Software Update just shows you your current iOS 5 version.)

- **Usage.** This screen is clear proof that the iPhone is an obsessive-compulsive. You find out here that it knows everything about you, your apps, and your iPhone activity.

  For example, the Storage section lists every single app on your iPhone, along with how much of your storage it's eating up. (Biggest apps are at the top.) Better yet, you can tap an app to see how much it and its associated documents consume—and there's a Delete App button staring you in the face.

  The idea, of course, is that if you're running out of space on your iPhone, this display makes it incredibly easy to see what the space hogs are—and delete them.

The next section, iCloud, also reports on storage—but in this case, it shows you how much storage you're using on your iCloud account. (Remember, you get 5 gigabytes free; after that, you have to pay.) If you tap

Manage Storage, you get to see how much of that space is used up by which apps—Mail is usually one of the biggest offenders.

The next item, Battery Percentage, appears on this screen for no apparent reason; still, it's nice. Turn it On to see your battery gauge with a numeric percentage readout (for example, "89%").

The Usage readout shows, in hours and minutes, how much time you've spent using all iPhone functions since the last time it was charged up (although it's not broken down by activity, alas). Standby is how much time the iPhone has spent in sleep mode, awaiting calls.

Finally, the statistics under Cellular Usage break down how much time you've spent talking on the iPhone, both in the Current Period (that is, this billing month) and in the iPhone's entire Lifetime. That's right, folks: For what's probably the first time in history, a cellphone actually keeps track of your minutes, to help you avoid exceeding the number you've signed up for (and therefore racking up 45-cent overage minutes).

Similarly, the Sent and Received tallies indicate how much you've used the Internet, expressed as kilobytes or megabytes of data, including email messages and Web-page material. These are extremely important statistics, because your iPhone plan is probably capped at, for example, 250 megabytes or 2 gigabytes a month. If you've signed up for the

Personal Hotspot feature, which gets you another 2 gigabytes a month, those usage stats appear here, too.

If you exceed your monthly maximum, you're instantly charged another $15 or $20 for another chunk of data. So keeping an eye on these statistics is a very good idea.

The Reset Statistics button, of course, sets all these counters back to zero.

- **Siri.** If you have an iPhone 4S, you have this item. It's the master on/off switch for Siri, the amazing voice-commanded virtual-assistant feature described in Chapter 4. (If you turn it off, your iPhone 4S turns back into an iPhone 4—that is, it offers the older, more limited Voice Control feature that controls only dialing and music playback.)

  Also on this panel: a choice of languages; an option to have Siri's responses read aloud only when you're on headset (so you don't disturb those around you); an option to choose your own Contacts card, so Siri knows, for example, where to go when you say "give me directions home"; and Raise to Speak (which is described on page 104).

- **Network.** Tap Network to open a screen containing five items.

  One may be Enable 3G. On certain AT&T iPhone models, this switch lets you turn off the iPhone's 3G radio when you'd rather have battery life than high Internet speed.

  Another is Cellular Data. It's a reaction to the cell carriers' capped-monthly-data plans. For example, if you see that you've already used up 248 of your monthly 250-meg allotment, you might want to turn your Internet features off for a couple of days to make sure you don't go over the limit. Your smartphone becomes a dumbphone, suitable for making calls but not getting online, but at least you won't trigger an overage fee. (You can still get online in a WiFi hotspot.)

  Then there's Data Roaming, which refers to the iPhone's ability to get online when you're outside your cell company's U.S. network. Unless you're particularly wealthy, leave this item turned off. Otherwise, you might run up unexpectedly massive charges (like $5,000 for two weeks) when you're overseas because your iPhone continues to check for new mail every few minutes.

  Up next: Personal Hotspot, the on/off switch for the iPhone's ability to act as an Internet antenna for your laptop; see page 332.

The next is VPN, for virtual private network. A VPN is a secure, encrypted tunnel that carries the data from one computer, across the Internet, and into a company's computers; see page 446.

The final item on the Network page is Wi-Fi, which is an exact duplicate of the WiFi controls described on page 450.

- **Bluetooth.** Here's the on/off switch for the iPhone's Bluetooth transmitter, which is required to communicate with a Bluetooth earpiece, keyboard, laptop (for tethering), or hands-free system in a car. When you turn the switch on, you're offered the chance to pair the iPhone with other Bluetooth equipment; the paired gadgets are listed here for ease of connecting and disconnecting.

- **iTunes Wi-Fi Sync.** Here's where you can sync your phone with iTunes wirelessly. The full scoop appears on page 420.

- **Spotlight Search.** Here you can control which kinds of things Spotlight finds when it searches your phone. Tap to turn off the kinds of data you don't want it to search: Mail, Notes, Calendar, whatever.

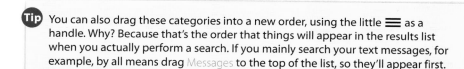

Tip You can also drag these categories into a new order, using the little ☰ as a handle. Why? Because that's the order that things will appear in the results list when you actually perform a search. If you mainly search your text messages, for example, by all means drag Messages to the top of the list, so they'll appear first.

- **Auto-Lock.** As you may have noticed, the iPhone locks itself after a few minutes of inactivity on your part. In locked mode, the iPhone ignores screen taps.

All cellphones (and iPods) offer locked mode. On the iPhone, however, locking is especially important because the screen is so big. Reaching into your pocket for a toothpick or a ticket stub could, at least theoretically, fire up some iPhone program or even dial a call from the confines of your pocket.

On the Auto-Lock screen, you can change the interval of inactivity before the auto-lock occurs (1 minute, 2 minutes, and so on), or you can tap Never. In that case, the iPhone locks only when you send it to sleep.

- **Passcode Lock.** Here you can make up a password that you have to enter whenever you wake up the iPhone. If you don't know the password, you can't use the iPhone (except for limited tasks like taking a photo or using Siri). It's designed to keep your stuff private from other people in the house or the office, or to protect your information in case you lose the iPhone.

You can have either a four-digit number, as in years past—convenient, but not so impossible to guess—or a full-blown, longer, alphanumeric password. You decide, using the Simple Passcode on/off switch.

Now tap Turn Passcode On. You're asked to type in the password you want, either on the number keypad (for Simple Passcodes) or the alphabet keyboard. You're asked to do it again to make sure you didn't make a typo.

 Note Don't kid around with this passcode. It's a much more serious deal than the iPod passcode. If you forget the iPhone code, you'll have to restore your iPhone (page 505), which wipes out everything on it. You've still got most of the data on your computer, of course (music, video, contacts, calendar), but you may lose text messages, mail, and so on.

Once you confirm your password, you return to the Passcode Lock screen. Here you have a few more options.

For example, the Require Passcode option lets you specify how quickly the password is requested before locking somebody out: immediately after the iPhone wakes or 1, 15, 30, 60, or 240 minutes later. (Those options are a convenience to you, so you can quickly check your calendar or missed messages without having to enter the passcode—while still protecting your data from, for example, evildoers who pick up your iPhone while you're out getting coffee.)

The on/off switch for Siri (or, if you don't have Siri, Voice Dial) is here, too. It's a huge convenience that you can voice-dial or speak to Siri even when the phone is locked—but that's also, technically, a security risk. Somebody who finds your phone on your desk could, in theory, blindly voice-dial your colleagues or use Siri to, for example, send a text. If you turn this item off, then you won't be able to use Siri or voice control until after you've entered your password.

Finally, here is Erase Data—an option that's scary and reassuring at the same time. When this option is on, then if someone makes 10 incorrect guesses at your passcode, your iPhone erases itself. It's assuming that some lowlife burglar is trying to crack into it to have a look at all your personal data.

This option, a pertinent one for professional people, presents potent protection from patient password prospectors.

 Even when the phone is locked and the password unguessable, a tiny blue Emergency Call button still appears on the Unlock screen. It's there just in case you've been conked on the head by a vase, you can't remember your own password, and you need to call 911.

- **Restrictions.** This means "parental controls." (Apple called it "Restrictions" instead so as not to turn off potential corporate customers. Can't you just hear it? " 'Parental controls?' This thing is for *consumers!?*")

  Anyway, if you tap Enable Restrictions, then you're asked to make up a four-digit password (not the same as the passcode described above) that permits only you, the all-knowing parent, to make changes to these settings. (Or you, the corporate IT administrator who's doling out iPhones to the white-collar drones.)

Once you've changed the settings described below, the only way to change them again (when your kid turns 18, for example) is to return to the Restrictions page and correctly enter the password. That's also the only way to turn off the entire Restrictions feature (tap Disable Restrictions and correctly enter the password). To turn it back on, you'll have to make up a password all over again.

Once Restrictions is turned on, you can put up data blockades in a number of different categories.

For starters, you can turn off access to iPhone features that locked-down corporations might not want their employees—or parents might not want their children—to use, because they're considered either security holes or time drains: Safari (can't use the Web at all), YouTube, iTunes, the Camera, FaceTime, iTunes, Ping (Apple's music-discussion online network), the ability to go Installing Apps or Deleting Apps, Siri, or Explicit Language (meaning Siri's ability to understand, display, and speak naughty words).

Most of these restrictions work by *removing icons altogether* from the iPhone's Home screen: Safari, YouTube, iTunes, Ping, Camera, and Installing Apps (that is, the App Store). (When the switch says Off, the corresponding icon has been taken off the Home screen and can't be found even by Spotlight searches.)

Next comes Allow Changes: on/off switches that permit or prohibit this phone's operator from making changes to certain aspects of the phone. First comes Location settings; you can block any changes to any Location settings (Don't Allow Changes), or you can block changes only to specific apps, which are listed here. Then come the options to prevent changes to your email/calendar Accounts and your Find My Friends settings.

At the bottom of the screen, you'll find the Allowed Content options—better known as parental controls. Here you can spare your children's sensitive eyes and ears by blocking inappropriate material.

Ratings are a big deal; they determine the effectiveness of the parental controls described below. Since every country has its own rating schemes (for movies, TV shows, games, raunchy song lyrics, and so on), you use the Ratings For control to tell the iPhone which country's rating system you want to use.

Once that's done, you can use the Music & Podcasts, Movies, TV Shows, and Apps controls to specify what your kid is allowed to watch, play, and listen to. For example, you can tap Movies and then tap PG-13; any movies rated "higher," like R or NC-17, won't play on the iPhone now. (And if your sneaky offspring try to buy these naughty songs, movies, or TV shows wirelessly from the iTunes Store, they'll discover that the Buy button is dimmed and unavailable.)

Turn off Explicit to prevent the iPhone from playing songs that have naughty language in the lyrics. (This works only on songs bought from the iTunes Store.)

In-App Purchases permits you to buy new material (game levels, book chapters, and so on) from within an app that you've already bought. In other words, even if you've shut down access to your offspring's ability to install new apps, as described above, this loophole remains. That's why it has its own Off switch, and an option to Require Password (so that you, the wise adult, can step in to permit a certain purchase without having to turn Restrictions off).

Finally, the Game Center controls let you stop your kid from playing multiplayer games (against strangers online, in other words) or adding game-playing friends to the center.

- **Date & Time.** At the top of this screen, you'll see an option to turn on 24-hour time, also known as military time, in which you see "1700" instead of "5:00 PM." (You'll see this change everywhere times appear, including at the top edge of the screen.)

Set Automatically refers to the iPhone's built-in clock. If this item is turned on, then the iPhone finds out what time it is from an atomic clock out on the Internet. If not, then you have to set the clock yourself. (Turning this option off makes two more rows of controls appear automatically: a Time Zone option so you can specify your time zone and Set Date & Time, which opens a "number spinner" so you can set the clock.)

- **Keyboard.** Here you can turn off some of the very best features of the iPhone's virtual keyboard. (All these shortcuts are described in Chapter 2.)

  It's hard to imagine why you wouldn't want any of these tools working for you and saving you time and keystrokes, but here you go: Auto-Capitalization is where the iPhone thoughtfully capitalizes the first letter of every new sentence for you. Auto-Correction is where the iPhone suggests spelling corrections as you type. Check Spelling, of course, refers to the pop-up spelling suggestions. Enable Caps Lock is the on/off switch for the Caps Lock feature, in which a fast double-tap on the Shift key turns on Caps Lock. Finally, "." Shortcut turns on or off the "type two spaces to make a period" shortcut for the ends of sentences.

  Below those options is International Keyboards. Tap it to view the 46 keyboard layouts and languages the iPhone offers for your typing pleasure. See page 51 for details on how you rotate among them.

 There are some crazy keyboard options in here. For example, you can add a new keyboard, like English UK, and then tap its name to change its layout independently for the software keyboard (onscreen); you can also specify the layout of a wireless Bluetooth keyboard that you've attached.

Finally, you get iOS 5's new typing-shortcuts feature, which expands abbreviations that you set up (like "sys") to longer phrases (like "See you soon!"). See page 50.

- **International.** The iPhone: It's not just for Americans anymore. The Language screen lets you choose a language for the iPhone's menus and messages; Voice Control determines what language the iPhone listens for when you utter spoken commands (on non-Siri phones). The Keyboards item here opens the same keyboard-choosing screen described above. Region Format controls how the iPhone displays dates, times, and currencies. (For example, in the U.S., Christmas is on 12/25; in Europe, it's 25/12.)

  And Calendar, new in iOS 5, lets you choose which kind of calendar system you want to use: Gregorian (that is, "normal"), Japanese, or Buddhist.

- **Accessibility.** These options are intended for people with visual, hearing, and motor impairments, but they might come in handy now and then for almost anyone. All these features are described in Chapter 5.

- **Profile.** Here's where you choose a configuration profile that may have been distributed to you by your corporate overlords, as described in Chapter 15.

- **Reset.** On the Reset screen, you'll find six ways to erase your tracks. Reset All Settings takes all the iPhone's settings back to the way they were when it came from Apple. Your data, music, and videos remain in place, but the settings you've changed all go back to their factory settings.

Erase All Content and Settings is the one you want when you sell your iPhone, or when you're captured by the enemy and want to make sure they will learn nothing from you or your iPhone.

 Note This feature takes a while to complete—and that's a good thing. The iPhone doesn't just delete your data; it also overwrites the newly erased memory with gibberish to make sure the bad guys can't see any of your deleted info, even with special hacking tools.

Reset Network Settings makes the iPhone forget all the memorized WiFi networks it currently autorecognizes.

Reset Keyboard Dictionary has to do with the iPhone's autocorrection feature, which kicks in whenever you're trying to input text. Ordinarily, every time you type something the iPhone doesn't recognize—some name or foreign word, for example—and you don't accept the iPhone's suggestion, it adds the word you typed to its dictionary so it doesn't bother you with a suggestion again the next time. If you think you've entered too many words that aren't legitimate terms, you can delete from its little brain all the new words you've "taught" it.

Reset Home Screen Layout undoes any icon-moving you've done on the Home screen. It also consolidates all your Home-screen icons, fitting them, 20 per page, onto as few screens as possible.

Finally, Reset Location Warnings refers to the "OK to use location services?" warning that appears whenever an iPhone program, like Maps or Camera, tries to figure out where you are. This button makes the iPhone forget all your responses to those permission boxes. In other words, you'll be asked permission all over again the first time you use each of those programs.

iCloud

Here's where you enter your iCloud name and password—and where you find the on/off switches for the various kinds of data synchronization that iCloud can perform for you. Chapter 14 tells all.

Mail, Contacts, Calendars

There's a lotta stuff going on in one place here. Breathe deeply; take it slow.

Accounts

Your email accounts are listed here; this is also where you set up new ones. See page 362 for details.

Fetch New Data

More than ever, the iPhone is a real-time window into the data stream of your life. Whatever changes are made to your calendar, address book, or email back on your computer at home (or at the office) can magically show up on your iPhone, seconds later, even though you're across the country.

That's the beauty of "push" email, contacts, and calendars. You get push email if you have a free Yahoo Mail account. You get all three if you've signed up for an iCloud account (Chapter 14), or if your company uses Microsoft Exchange (Chapter 15).

Having an iPhone that's updated with these critical life details in real time is amazingly useful, but there are several reasons why you might want to use the Off button here. Turning off the push feature saves battery power, saves you money when you're traveling abroad (where every "roaming" Internet use can run up your cellular bill), and spares you the constant "new mail" jingle when you're trying to concentrate (or sleep).

 If you tap Advanced, you can specify either push (real-time syncing over the air) or fetch (checking on a schedule) for each type of program—Mail, Contacts, and Calendars—for each account you have.

And what if you don't have a push email service, or if you turn it off? In that case, your iPhone can still do a pretty decent job of keeping you up to date. It can check your email every 15 minutes, every half-hour, every hour, or only on command (Manually). That's the decision you make in the Fetch panel here. (Keep in mind that more frequent checking means shorter battery life.)

 The iPhone always checks email each time you open the Mail program, regardless of your setting here. If you have a push service like iCloud or Exchange, it also checks for changes to your schedule or address book each time you open Calendar or Contacts—again, no matter what your setting here.

Mail

Here you set up your email account information, specify how often you want the iPhone to check for new messages, change the font size for email, and more.

- **Show.** Using this option, you can limit how much mail the Mail program shows you, from the most recent 25 messages to the most recent 1,000. This feature doesn't stop you from getting and seeing all your mail—you can always tap Download More in the Mail program—but it may help to prevent the sinking feeling of Email Overload.

- **Preview.** It's cool that the iPhone shows you the first few lines of text in every message. Here you can specify how many lines of text appear. More means you can skim your inbound mail without having to open many of them; less means more messages fit without scrolling.

- **Minimum t Size.** Anyone with fading vision will appreciate this option. It lets you scale the type size of your email from Small to Giant.

- **Show To/Cc Label.** If you turn this option on, a tiny, light-gray logo appears next to many of the messages in your inbox. The **To** logo indicates that this message was addressed directly to you; the **Cc** logo means you were merely "copied" on a message primarily intended for someone else.

  If there's no logo at all, then the message is in some other category. Maybe it came from a mailing list, or it's an email blast (a Bcc), or the message is from you, or it's a bounced message.

- **Ask Before Deleting.** Ordinarily, you can delete an open message quickly and easily, just by tapping the icon. But if you'd prefer to see an "Are you sure?" confirmation box before the message disappears, then turn this option on.

- **Load Remote Images.** Spammers, the vile undercrust of lowlife society, have a famous trick. When they send you email that includes a picture, they don't actually paste the picture into the message. Instead, they include a "bug"—a piece of code that instructs your email program to *fetch* the missing graphic from the Internet. Why? Because that gives the spammer the ability to track who has actually opened the junk mail, making their email addresses much more valuable for reselling to other spammers.

That's a long explanation for a simple feature: If you turn this option off, then the iPhone does not fetch "bug" image files at all. You're not flagged as a sucker by the spammers. You'll see empty squares in the email where the images ought to be. (Graphics sent by normal people and legitimate companies are generally pasted right into the email, so they'll still show up just fine.)

- **Organize By Thread.** This is the on/off switch for the feature that clumps related back-and-forths into individual items in your Mail inbox, as described on page 367.

- **Always Bcc Myself.** If this option is on, then you'll get a secret copy of any message you send.

- **Signature.** A signature is a bit of text that gets stamped at the bottom of your outgoing email messages. Here's where you can change yours.

- **Default Account.** Your iPhone can manage an unlimited number of email accounts. Here, tap the account you want to be your *default*—the one that's used when you create a new message from another program, like a Safari link, or when you're on the All Inboxes screen of Mail.

Contacts

Contacts is a first-class citizen with an icon of its own on the Home screen, so it gets its own little set of options in Settings.

- **Sort Order, Display Order.** The question is: How do you want the names in your Contacts list sorted—by first name or by last name?

Note that you can have them *sorted* one way, but *displayed* another way. This table shows how a very short Contacts list would appear, using each of the four combinations of settings:

	Display "Last, First"	Display "First, Last"
Sort order "First, Last"	O'Furniture, Patty Minella, Sal Peace, Warren	Patty O'Furniture Sal Minella Warren Peace
Sort order "Last, First"	Minella, Sal O'Furniture, Patty Peace, Warren	Sal Minella Patty O'Furniture Warren Peace

As you can see, not all of these combinations make sense.

- **My Info.** Tap here to tell the phone which card in Contacts represents *you.* Knowing who you are is useful to the phone in a number of places—for example, it's how Siri knows what you mean when you say, "Give me directions home."

- **Import SIM Contacts.** If you came to the iPhone from another, lesser GSM phone, then your phone book may be stored on its little SIM card instead of in the phone itself. In that case, you don't have to retype all those names and numbers to bring them into your iPhone. This button can do the job for you. (The results may not be pretty. For example, some phones store all address-book data in CAPITAL LETTERS.)

Calendars

Your iPhone's calendar can be updated by remote control, wirelessly, through the air, either by your company (via Exchange, Chapter 15) or by somebody at home using your computer (via iCloud, Chapter 14).

- **New Invitation Alerts.** Part of that wireless joy is receiving invitations to meetings, which coworkers can shoot to you from Outlook or even the iPhone—wirelessly, when you're thousands of miles apart. Very cool.

  Unless, that is, you're getting a lot of these invitations, and it's beginning to drive you a little nuts. In that case, turn New Invitation Alerts off.

- **Sync.** If you're like most people, you refer to your calendar more often to see what events are *coming up* than the ones you've already lived through. Ordinarily, therefore, the iPhone saves you some syncing time and storage space by updating only relatively recent events on your iPhone calendar. It doesn't bother with events that are older than 2 weeks, or 6 months, or whatever you choose here. (Or you can turn on All Events if you want your entire life, past and future, synced each time— storage and wait time be damned.)

- **Time Zone Support.** Now, here's a mind-teaser for you world travelers. If an important event is scheduled for 6:30 p.m. New York time, and you're in California, how should that event appear on your calendar? Should it appear as 3:30 p.m. (that is, your local time)? Or should it remain stuck at 6:30 (East Coast time)?

  It's not an idle question, because it also affects reminders and alarms.

  Out of the box, Time Zone Support is turned on.

  That is, everything stays on the calendar just the way you entered it, even as you travel from time zone to time zone.

If you turn Time Zone Support off, then the iPhone automatically translates all your appointments into the local time. If you scheduled a reminder to record a TV movie at 8:00 p.m. New York time, and you fly to California, the reminder will pop up at 5:00 p.m. local time. The iPhone actually learns (from the local cell towers) what time zone it's in, changes its own clock automatically, and literally slides appointments around on your calendar. Handy—but dangerous if you forget what you've done.

 Note If Time Zone Support is turned on, you can still make it shift your appointments to the local time—by setting the time zone manually. You do that by tapping Time Zone on this screen. (Of course, this control's real purpose is for you to establish the "home" time zone, so the iPhone knows those calendar appointments' *real* times.)

- **Default Calendar.** This option lets you answer the question: "When I add a new appointment to my calendar on the iPhone, which *calendar* (category) should it belong to?" You can choose Home, Work, Kids, or whatever category you use most often.

Reminders

Here are the preference settings for the new Reminders app.

- **Sync.** This option answers the question: How far back do you want Reminders to go when it syncs its to-do lists with your computer, iCloud, and various other calendar programs?

- **Default List.** Suppose you've created multiple Reminder lists (Groceries, Movies to Rent, To Do, and so on). When you create a new item—for example, by telling Siri, "Remind me to fix the sink"—which list should it go onto? Here's where you specify.

Twitter

Now that you can send Twitter posts directly from apps like Camera, Photos, Safari, and Maps, the phone needs a central place where you can fill in your Twitter name and password (or sign up for an account if you don't already have one). This is the place. Details are at the end of Chapter 10.

This is also the place where you can stop various iPhone apps from accessing your Twitter account, using the on/off switches here.

Phone

These settings have to do with your address book, call management, and other phone-related preferences.

- **My Number.** Here's where you can see your iPhone's own phone number. You can even edit it, if necessary (just how it appears—you're not actually changing your phone number).

- **TTY.** A TTY (teletype) machine lets people with hearing or speaking difficulties use a telephone—by typing back and forth, or sometimes with the assistance of a human TTY operator who transcribes what the other person is saying. When you turn this iPhone option on, you can use the iPhone with a TTY machine, if you buy the little $20 iPhone TTY adapter from Apple.

- **Change Voicemail Password.** Yep, pretty much just what it says.

- **International Assist.** When this option is turned on, and when you're dialing from another country, the iPhone automatically adds the proper country codes when dialing U.S. numbers. Pretty handy, actually.

- **SIM PIN.** As noted on page 21, your SIM card (AT&T iPhones, or Sprint/ Verizon phones when you travel overseas) stores all your account information. SIM cards are especially desirable abroad, because in most countries, you can pop yours into any old phone and have working service. If you're worried about yours getting stolen or lost, turn this option on. You'll be asked to enter a passcode.

  Then, if some bad guy ever tries to put your SIM card into another phone, he'll be asked for the password. Without the password, the card (and the phone) won't make calls.

 And if the evildoer guesses wrong three times, the words "PIN LOCKED" appear on the screen, and the SIM card is locked forever. You'll have to get another one from AT&T. So don't forget the password.

- **[Your carrier] Services.** This choice opens up a cheat sheet of handy numeric codes that, when dialed, play the voice of a robot providing useful information about your cellphone account. For example, *225# lets you know the latest status of your bill, *646# lets you know how many airtime minutes you've used so far this month, and so on.

 The button at the bottom of the screen opens up your account page on the Web, for further details on your cellphone billing and features.

FaceTime

These options pertain to FaceTime, the video calling feature described in Chapter 3. Here, for example, is the on/off switch for the entire feature; a place to enter your Apple ID, so people can make FaceTime calls to you; and a place to enter email addresses and a phone number, which can also be used to reach you.

Finally, the Caller ID section lets you specify how you want to be identified when you place a call to somebody else: either as a phone number or an email address.

Safari

Here's everything you ever wanted to adjust in the Web browser but didn't know how to ask.

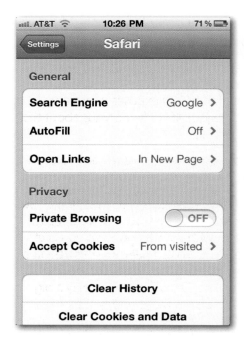

- **Search Engine.** Your choice here determines who does your searching from the search bar: Google, Bing, or Yahoo.

- **AutoFill.** Safari's AutoFill feature saves you tedious typing by filling in your passwords, name, address, and phone numbers on Web forms automatically (just for the sites you want). Here's the on/off switch.

- **Open Links.** When you tap a link with your finger, should the new page open in front of the current page—or behind it? Answer here.

- **Private Browsing.** *Private Browsing* lets you surf the Web without adding any pages to your History list, searches to your Google search box, passwords to Safari's saved password list, or autofill entries to Safari's memory. In other words, it lets you use the Web without leaving any tracks. (You know who you are.)

The trick is to turn this option on before you start browsing. When you're ready to browse "publicly" again, turn this option off. Safari again begins taking note of the pages you visit—but it never remembers the earlier ones. In other words, what happens in Private Browsing stays in Private Browsing.

- **Accept Cookies.** These options let you limit how many cookies (Web preference files) are deposited on your iPhone.

- **Clear History.** Like any Web browser, Safari keeps a list of Web sites you've visited recently to make it easier for you to revisit them: the History list. And like any browser, Safari therefore exposes your tracks to any suspicious spouse or crackpot colleague. If you're nervous about that prospect, tap Clear History to erase your tracks.

- **Clear Cookies and Data.** This feature, similarly, deletes all the cookies that Web sites have deposited on your "hard drive."

- **Fraud Warning.** *Phishing* is a scheme to separate you from your money. You get an email message that purports to be from your bank, or eBay, or PayPal. Apparently there's a problem with your account! So you click the provided link for the account-verification Web page—which, behind the scenes, is a fake. The bad guy's computers collect your name and password as you "log in." This Safari feature is supposed to display a big warning box when you attempt to visit one of these phony sites.

- **JavaScript.** JavaScript is a programming language whose bits of code frequently liven up Web pages. If you suspect some bit of code is choking Safari, however, you can turn off its ability to decode JavaScript here.

- **Block Pop-ups.** In general, you want this turned on. You really don't want pop-up ad windows ruining your surfing session. Now and again, though, pop-up windows are actually useful. When you're buying concert tickets, for example, a pop-up window might show the location of the seats. In that situation, you can turn this option off.

- **Advanced.** Safari now recognizes HTML5, a Web technology that lets Web sites store data on your phone, for accessing even when you're not online (like your Gmail stash). In Website Data, you can see which Web apps have created these databases on your phone, and delete them if necessary.

The Debug Console is an information strip at the top of the Safari screen. It's intended to display errors, warnings, tips, and logs for HTML, Java-Script, and CSS—solely for the benefit of people who are designing and debugging Web pages or Web apps for the iPhone.

Messages

These options govern text messages (SMS) and iMessages, both of which are described in Chapter 5:

- **iMessage.** This is the on/off switch for iMessages. If it's off, then your phone never sends or receives these handy, free messages—only regular text messages.

- **Send Read Receipts.** If this is on, then people who send you iMessages will know when you've seen them. They'll see a tiny gray text notification beneath the iMessage bubble that contains their message. If you're creeped out by them being able to know when you're ignoring them, turn this item off.

- **Send as MMS.** If you try to send an iMessage to somebody when there's no Internet service, what happens? If this item is on, then the message goes to that person as a regular text message, using your cell carrier's network. If it's off, then the message won't go out at all.

- **Receive At.** Here you can enter additional email addresses that people can use to send your phone iMessages.

   This screen also offers a Caller ID item that lets you indicate what you want to appear on the other guy's phone when you send a text: your phone number or email address.

- **MMS Messaging.** This is the on/off switch for picture and video messages (as opposed to text-only ones).

- **Group Messaging, Show Subject Field, Character Count.** These options are described on page 136.

 There used to be additional options here called Show Preview and Repeat Alert. They've been moved to Settings→Notifications→Messages.

Music

On this panel, you can adjust a bunch of iPod playback features. Most of them—Shake to Shuffle, Sound Check, EQ, Volume Limit, Lyrics & Podcast Info, and Group By Album Artist—are described on page 177. What's left?

- **iTunes Match.** Do you want your iPhone to have access to your entire music collection online? You're paying $25 a year for it (page 433)—why on earth not?

- **Home Sharing.** Conveniently enough, you can access your iTunes music collection, upstairs on your computer, right from your iPhone, over your home WiFi network. Or at least you can if both machines are signed into the same Apple ID. Here's where you enter the Apple ID that matches your iTunes setup.

Video

In iOS 5, the Video app is now separate from the Music app (they used to be combined in one app called iPod). Here's what you can adjust:

- **Start Playing.** When you play a video you've seen before, you can have it begin either from Where Left Off or From Beginning.

- **Closed Captioning.** You can opt to see dialogue subtitles, when available (which is almost never).

- **Home Sharing.** You can also access your iTunes video collection, as described a few paragraphs ago. Same deal here.

Photos

Here's a motley collection of photo-related settings:

- **Photo Stream.** This is the master on/off switch for Photo Stream, which is one of iCloud's marquee features (page 201).

- **Play Each Slide For.** How long do you want each photo to remain on the screen? You can choose 2, 3, 5, 10, or 20 seconds. (Hint: 2 is plenty, 3 at most. Anything more than that will bore your audience silly.)

- **Repeat, Shuffle.** These options work just as they do for music. Repeat makes the slideshow loop endlessly; Shuffle plays the slides in random order.

- **Keep Normal Photo.** See the tip on page 193.

Notes

At long last, you can now change the typeface used for your random jottings in the Notes app. You have a choice of three.

As noted in Chapter 9, Notes can sync with various online services: iCloud, Gmail, Yahoo, and so on. Tap Default Account here to specify which one should receive new notes you create if you haven't specifically chosen one.

Store

If you've indulged in a few downloads (or a few hundred) from the App Store (Chapter 8), then you may well find some settings of use here Settings→Store. For example:

- **Automatic Downloads.** If you have an iCloud account (and you probably should), then a very convenient option is available to you: automatic downloads of music, apps, and ebooks you've bought on other iOS 5 gadgets. For example, if you buy a new album on your iPad, turning on Music here means that your iPhone will download the same album automatically, next time it's in a WiFi hotspot.

  (If you turn these items off, then you can always download them manually, one at a time, as described on page 234.)

- **Use Cellular Data.** Those downloads are big. They can eat up your cellphone's monthly data allotment right quick, and send you deep into Surcharge Land. That's why the iPhone does that automatic downloading only when you're in a WiFi hotspot—unless you turn this item on. Hope you know what you're doing.

- **[Magazines & Newspapers].** Next on the Store settings screen, you may find a list of newsstand periodicals to which you've subscribed—newspapers and magazines. These are on/off switches for automatic downloading of new issues when they come out.

If you tap your Apple ID at the bottom of the panel, you get these buttons:

- **View Apple ID.** This takes you to the Web, where you can look over your Apple Account information, including credit-card details.

- **Sign Out.** Tap when, for example, a friend wants to use her own iTunes account to buy something on your iPhone. As a gift, maybe.

- **iForgot.** If you've forgotten your Apple ID password, tap here. You'll be offered a couple of different ways of establishing your identity—and you'll be given the chance to make up a new password.

App Preferences

At the bottom of the Settings app screen, you see a list of apps that have installed setting screens of their own. For example, here's where you can edit your screen name and password for the AIM chat program, change how many days' worth of news you want the NY Times Reader to display, and so on. Each one offers a motley assortment of changeable preference options.

It can get to be a very long list.

Appendixes

A Signup and Setup

You gotta admit it: Opening up a new iPhone brings a certain excitement. There's a prospect of possibility, of new beginnings. Even if you intend to protect your iPhone with a case, there are those first few minutes when it's shiny, spotless, free of fingerprints or nicks—a gorgeous thing.

This chapter is all about getting started, whether that means buying and setting up a new iPhone, or upgrading an iPhone 3GS or iPhone 4 to the new iOS 5 software that's described in this book.

Buying a New iPhone

Just because the iPhone 4S is now the big kid on the block doesn't mean its ancestors are suddenly worthless. At this writing, you can still buy an iPhone 4 (for $100 with a 2-year cell contract) or even an iPhone 3GS ($1 with a contract).

Of course, each newer version of the phone is faster, has a better camera and screen, and comes packed with more features. You could make the argument that the incredible camera and Siri virtual assistant of the iPhone 4S justify its $100 price premium all by themselves.

In any case, once you've chosen the model you want, you also have to choose which cellphone company you want to provide its service: AT&T (any of the three phones), Verizon (iPhone 4 or 4S), or Sprint (iPhone 4 or 4S).

Verizon has the best cellular coverage—the fewest dropped calls—but its Internet speeds are much lower than AT&T's. Sprint offers some of the best deals but doesn't cover as much of the country. Research the coverage where you live and work. (Each company's Web site shows a map of its coverage.)

You can buy your iPhone from a phone store (Verizon, Sprint, AT&T), an Apple store, or from the Apple Web site. You can buy the phone either with or without a 2-year contract. Yes, that surprises many people—but most people still opt for the contract, because the 16-gigabyte phone's initial price is $200 that way. Without the contract, it costs $600 or more.

With a contract, the phone is locked to the cellphone company you're choosing; it works *only* with that company's network. For example, a locked AT&T phone won't work with Verizon, Sprint, T-Mobile, or any other carrier, and you can't insert the SIM card from a non-AT&T phone and expect it to work. (The exception: When you travel overseas with a Sprint or Verizon iPhone 4S, you can insert a different country's SIM card into it for use while you're there.)

Hackers have succeeded in unlocking the iPhone so it can be used on other cell companies' networks; their primary motivation for doing so was to be able to use it in countries where the iPhone hasn't been available. But now that the iPhone is sold legitimately in 90 countries (and counting), there may be less reason to go that questionable route.

All right then: Here you are in the phone store, or sitting down to do some ordering online. Here are some of the decisions you'll have to make:

- **Transferring your old number.** You can bring your old cellphone or home phone number to your new iPhone. Your friends can keep dialing your old number—but your iPhone will ring instead of the old phone.

  It usually takes under an hour for a cellphone-number transfer to take place, but it may take several hours. During that time, you can make calls on the iPhone, but you can't receive them.

 Note Transferring a land-line number can take several *days*.

- **Select your monthly calling plans.** Signing up for cellphone service involves more red tape than a government contract. In essence, you have to choose *three* plans: one for voice calls (required), one for Internet service (required), and one for text messages (optional).

  AT&T's plans are typical. There's a $40 monthly plan, which offers 450 weekday calling minutes. But there's a 900-minute plan for $60, and an unlimited calling plan for $70.

  The AT&T plans offer *rollover minutes*. That is, if you don't use up all your minutes this month, the unused ones are automatically added to your allotment for next month, and so on.

  All three cell companies offer unlimited free calls to other phones from the same company. All but the cheapest plan offer unlimited calls on nights and weekends.

Next, you have to choose an Internet data plan for your iPhone's email, Web, iCloud, and app-downloading pleasure. AT&T and Verizon offer *capped* data plans, in which you pay a monthly fee (for example, $30) for a certain amount of Internet uploading and downloading (for example, 2 gigabytes). If you opt for the Personal Hotspot feature (page 335), you usually pay about $20 more.

Of course, who has any idea what 2 gigabytes of data is? How much of that do you eat up with email alone? How much is one YouTube video?

As you approach your monthly limit, you'll get warnings by text message. You can also check the Web site or dial a code on your phone. Yes, it's a pain to have to worry about data limits, but at least monitoring them is fairly easy. If you use more than your allotted amount, you're automatically billed a surcharge—for example, $10 for each additional gigabyte.

At this writing, Sprint offers unlimited text messages and Internet use—a huge relief to most people. Its voice plans cost more than its rivals', but the total monthly bill is usually lower as a result.

AT&T and Verizon's voice and Internet plans don't include any text messages. For those, you'll have to pay (for example) $5 more for 200 messages, or $20 for unlimited messages. Of course, you can always pay à la carte, too: 20 cents for each message sent or received.

 Note: If the people you'll be texting also have Apple gadgets, don't spend a lot on a texting plan. Remember that all messages you send to other iOS 5 machines automatically turn into iMessages, which are unlimited and free. See page 139.

All iPhone plans require a two-year commitment and an "activation fee" (ha!).

 Tip: The choice you make here isn't etched in stone. You can change your plan at any time. If you have AT&T, for example, visit *www.wireless.att.com*, where you can log in with your iPhone number and make up a password. Click My Account, and then click Change Rate Plan to view your options.

As you budget for your plan, keep in mind that, as with any cellphone, you'll also be paying taxes as high as 22 percent, depending on your state. Ouch.

Most people choose the individual plans described above. There are, however, business plans and multiple-iPhone family plans that might be worth considering. (In a typical family plan, you pay only $10 more per month per person. All your phones share a pool of minutes. Each phone still has to have its own Internet data plan, though.)

A New iPhone: "PC-Free" Setup

Before iOS 5 came along, you couldn't use a new iPhone at all without hooking it up to a computer. That first date with iTunes was mandatory to set up the basic iPhone settings.

Now, though, the setup process takes place entirely on the phone's screen.

That's part of Apple's much larger *PC-free* initiative, which aims to eliminate the need for a computer altogether. You don't need a computer to back up your phone, because iCloud backs it up. You don't need a computer to store your music and video collections, because the Apple Store remembers what you've bought and lets you redownload it at any time. You don't need a computer to download and install iPhone software updates, because they come straight to the phone now. You don't even need a computer to edit photos or create mail folders, because all that's on the phone, too.

And you don't need a computer to set up the iPhone anymore.

The first time you turn on a brand-new iPhone—or an older one that you've erased completely—the setup wizard appears. Swipe your finger where it says slide to set up. Now you're asked some important questions:

- **Language; Country.** You won't get very far setting up your phone if you can't understand the instructions. So the very first step here is to tell it what language you speak. When you tap the blue Next arrow, you tell the phone where in the world you live. (It proposes the country where you bought the phone. Clever, eh?)

- **Location Services.** The iPhone knows where you are. That's how it can pinpoint you on a map, tag the photos you take with their geographical locations, find you a nearby Mexican restaurant, and so on.

  Some people are creeped out by the phone's knowing where they are, worrying that Apple, by extension, also knows where you are (it doesn't). So here's your chance to turn off all the iPhone's location features. Tap either Enable or Disable Location Services, and then tap Next.

- **Wi-Fi Networks.** Here's where you're shown a list of wireless networks nearby and given the chance to join one. Apple wants your high-speed Internet experience to begin right away.

- **Set Up iPhone.** If this is a brand-new phone (or you're using the Restore method of updating an older one), this important screen wants to know if you're upgrading from an older iPhone—one that you backed up in advance. If that's true, tap Restore from iCloud Backup (if your backup was on iCloud) or Restore from iTunes Backup (if your backup was on your computer, in iTunes). Since you can't even access iCloud from an iOS 4 phone, your backup is probably in iTunes.

- **Apple ID.** A million features require an Apple ID—just about any transaction you make with Apple online. Buying anything from Apple, from a song to a laptop. Signing up for an iCloud account (Chapter 14). Playing games against other people online. Making an Apple Store appointment at the Genius Bar.

    If you already have one (and if you've ever bought anything from Apple or iTunes or the App Store, you do), enter it here. If you don't have one, you can create one. You'll be asked to provide your name, birthday, email address (or you can create a new iCloud email address), a password of your choice, a security question (you'll have to answer it correctly if you ever forget your password), and if you'd like the honor of receiving junk email from Apple.

    (You can tap Skip This Step if you don't want an Apple ID, at least for now. You can get one later in Settings.)

- **Set Up iCloud.** You get this screen, and the next two, only if you did sign in with your Apple ID .

    Since you've had a glance at Chapter 14, you already know how useful Apple's free iCloud service can be. Here's where you indicate whether or not you want to use iCloud at all.

- **iCloud Backup.** If you just tapped Use iCloud, then this screen appears, offering the opportunity to back up your iPhone wirelessly and automatically to iCloud (page 421).

- **Find My iPhone.** If you did opt into iCloud, you're also asked if you'd like to tap Use Find My iPhone. If you do, you'll be able to locate your lost iPhone on a map, using any Web browser. You'll also be able to command it to start pinging loudly, so you can find where you left it in the house. It's a pretty great feature (page 428).

- **Terms and Conditions.** You agree with everything Apple's lawyers say, or you can't play.

- **Siri.** If you have an iPhone 4S, here's your chance to turn off Siri, the single greatest new phone feature in 15 years. So why would you ever want to turn it off? Because it works by sending your voice utterances to Apple's computers for processing, and that thought alarms the privacy-obsessed.

- **Diagnostics & Usage.** Behind the scenes, your iPhone sends records back to Apple, including your location and what you're doing on your iPhone. By analyzing this data en masse, Apple can figure out where the dead spots in the cellular network are, how to fix bugs, and so on. The information is anonymous—that is, it's not associated with you in particular. But if the very idea seems invasive to you, here's your chance to prevent this data from being sent.

- **Thank you.** One last closing remark from Apple, and you're ready to go. Your phone is set up. Tap Start Using iPhone.

Upgrading an Older iPhone to iOS 5

If you bought an iPhone 4S, great! The iOS 5 software comes on it preinstalled.

But you can also upgrade an iPhone 3GS or iPhone 4 to this new software—in either of two ways:

- **Upgrade it.** That means installing iOS 5 on top of whatever's already on your iPhone. All the data and settings on the phone are preserved.

  To begin, connect the phone to your computer and open iTunes. iTunes probably alerted you some time ago that a free upgrade to iOS 5 is available. Just click Update. (If you're not getting that notification, click Check for Update instead. It's on the Summary pane for your iPhone in iTunes.)

- **Restore it.** This is a more dramatic step, which you should choose only if you've been having problems with your phone or, for some other reason, would like to start completely fresh. This step backs up the phone, erases it completely, installs iOS 5, and then copies your stuff back onto the phone.

  Connect the phone to your computer, open iTunes, and then click Restore.

The updating or restoring process takes awhile. You'll see the iPhone restart. When it's all over, the PC-free setup process described on the previous pages begins automatically.

Software Updates

As you're probably aware, phone software like the iPhone's is a perpetual work in progress. Apple constantly fixes bugs, adds features, and makes tweaks to extend battery life and improve other services.

In the olden times (2010 and earlier), you downloaded these iOS updates on your computer, in iTunes, and synced them from there to your phone. But in the PC-free era, the updates go directly from Apple to your phone.

One day you'll be minding your own business, and you'll see, for the first time in iPhone history, a red numbered badge appear on the *Settings* app's icon. Open Settings→General→Software Update to read about the new update and install it. You can download this update either in a WiFi hot spot or in a 3G cellular area. Note, though, that unless it's plugged into a power source, your phone won't install an iOS update unless its battery is at least half full.

Install Updates from Your Computer

Maybe you're not that adventurous, and you'd prefer to install your software update the old-fashioned way. No problem: Just connect your device to your computer and check for updates in iTunes. (If you're using Wi-Fi Sync, you can also do this by plugging your device into a power source and connecting it and your computer to the same WiFi network, and then opening iTunes.)

 Tip You can still install iOS updates from iTunes, if you like. It works just as it did in the old days. Connect the iPhone to iTunes, wirelessly or not (Chapter 13). Then click the iPhone's icon in iTunes; on the Summary pane, tap Check for Update.

B Accessorizing the iPhone

Like the iPods that came before it, the iPhone has inspired a torrent of accessories that seems to intensify with every passing month. Stylish cases, speakers, docks, cables—the list goes on.

This appendix gives you a tiny representative sampling. It also points you in the right direction so you can find iPhone accessories that look good, sound good, and most importantly—fit.

Proper Shopping for the iPhone

This is the most important thing to remember when you're looking for iPhone hardware: *Not all iPod and iPhone accessories are created equal.* (Or, as Yoda might say: *Created equal, not all iPod and iPhone accessories are.*)

For example:

- The iPhone 4/4S is shaped differently from the iPhone 3GS. Form-fitting cases, sockets, and accessories designed for the older model don't fit the newer ones.

- The iPhone is also a phone, with components inside that can cause static and interference when used with external speakers (which have their own electronic innards). So accessories for the iPod may not work.

To help you identify products that are compatible with the iPhone, Apple has its own "Works with iPhone" logo program. As the company puts it, products bearing the logo are "electronic accessories designed to connect specifically to iPhone and certified by the developer to meet Apple performance standards."

Getting stuff with the "Works with iPhone" logo should save you the grief that comes with "Buying the Wrong Thing."

Some good places to look:

- **Apple's iPhone Accessories Web page and, even better, the Apple Store app.** Here are all of Apple's own, official white plastic cables, the optional iPhone dock adapters, and power plugs, alongside tons of iPhone-friendly products from other manufacturers. Click the link for iPhone Accessories on the main store page to see the goods—and ratings from other customers. Some products feature a helpful question-and-answer forum as well. *http://store.apple.com*

- **Incase.** Incase has been turning out handsome iPod cases practically since the little white MP3 player took the first spin of its scroll wheel. Somehow, they had iPhone cases and other accessories in stock before the first iPhone hit the street. *www.goincase.com*

- **iPhoneAccessories.com.** The site's name says it all—and the site itself pretty much *sells* it all if you're looking for iPhone stuff. You can find cables, cases, speakers, headphones, and more from all the major iPhone accessory manufacturers, along with frequent clearance sales. *www.iphoneaccessories.com*

- **Griffin Technology.** Cables, cases, and many audio accessories. *www.griffintechnology.com*

- **Belkin.** From acrylic cases to sporty armbands, Belkin markets several iPhone items. *www.belkin.com*

- **EverythingiCafe.** If it works with an iPhone, you can probably find it here by clicking the Store tab: cleaning cloths, screen protectors, Bluetooth headsets, cases, and on and on. It's not just a shopping center; user forums, reviews, and news make the site live up to its all-encompassing name. *http://store.everythingicafe.com*

Tip Inventive and exciting iPhone products are coming out all over the place. If you don't have time to keep up, let the gadget blogs do it for you. A few to hit regularly if you want to see the latest in cool: Gizmodo (*www.gizmodo.com*), Engadget (*www.engadget.com*), and Crave (*news.cnet.com/crave*). And for a thorough examination of just about every major iPhone and iPod accessory hitting the shelves, don't miss the news and reviews over at iLounge (*www.ilounge.com*).

If you're looking for specific categories of products, say a not-too-geeky belt case or a Bluetooth headset for hands-free dialing, the next few pages give you an idea of what's out there.

Protecting Your iPhone

It should be called the iPhone Paradox: People buy the thinnest, sleekest, shiniest, most gorgeous smartphone in existence—and then bury it in an ugly, fat, thick carrying case. There's just something so wrong about that.

On the other hand, this thing is made of a layer of breakable glass on both the front and the back; the instinct to protect it is perfectly understandable. Two types of accessories in particular can bring an extra layer of protection (and peace of mind): cases and screen protectors.

Cases

When you shop for a case, consider how you use your iPhone. Into sports and activity? A brightly colored rubberized covering that lets you dial without taking it out of the case might work best. Using it as you stroll around the office all day? Consider a leather holster-style case with a belt clip. Some examples:

- **Apple Bumper case.** Made from "durable rubber" and "molded plastic," the Bumper case is the first Apple-created iPhone case (and was Apple's answer to the iPhone 4 antenna issue). The bumpers come in six (bright) colors: black, white, blue, orange, green, and pink. ($30; *http://store.apple.com*)

- **Case-Mate ID Credit Card Case.** This case is the perfect accessory for a night out on the town: The case's built-in slot can fit two credit card–size items (like an ID and a credit card). A bonus: It comes with a free screen protection kit. ($35; *www.case-mate.com*)

- **Speck Products Fitted case.** This form-fit two-piece hardshell case offers the best of both worlds: fashion and protection. And the case's original fabric-wrapped patterns afford the iPhone some serious style points. ($35; *www.speckproducts.com*)

- **Sena Case UltraSlim leather case.** The UltraSlim leather case is one of the thinnest cases on the market—perfect for the minimalist crowd. Available in an eccentric 18 different color combinations, the UltraSlim offers high-quality luxury for an affordable price. ($30; *www.senacases. com*)

- **OtterBox cases.** The OtterBox Defender is famous for being bulky but nearly indestructible. If you work in a rough job, or you're just a klutz, it might be worth the mass. The OtterBox Commuter gives your iPhone protection in a slimmer case. (Defender $40; Commuter $35; *www.otterbox.com*)

Lens Attachment Cases

With each new iPhone model, Apple makes the camera better. What's next—interchangeable lenses? For your phone? Exactly!

- **Griffin Clarifi.** Add a built-in close-up lens to your iPhone 3GS, built right in to this protective case. When you want to get in really close to an object, just slide the lens into place and shoot. ($10; *https://store.griffin-technology.com/clarifi*)

These cases are only for iPhone 4 and iPhone 4S:

- **iPhone SLR Mount.** This crazy adapter/case lets you use actual Nikon and Canon SLR lenses with an iPhone. Lenses not included. ($250; *photojojo. com/store/awesomeness/ iphone-slr-mount*)

- **iPhone Lens Dial.** If one lens is good, three must be better, right? The iPhone Lens Dial from Photojojo adds three optical-quality coated glass lenses to your iPhone: wide angle, fisheye, and telephoto. The lenses are included and give the back of your iPhone the look of an old-fashioned three-turret-lens movie camera. Rotate the lenses on the back of the case to the lens. ($250; *photojojo.com/store/awesomeness/iphone-lens-dial*)

- **Holga iPhone Lens Filter Kit.** Maybe adding nine filters to your iPhone is what you have in mind. The Holga iPhone Lens Filter Kit looks like you've grafted an old rotary dial telephone onto the back of your iPhone, but instead of a dial, you spin to differ-ent filters and effects, giving you the retro-crappy images and videos all the

kids are wild about nowadays. ($25; *http://shop.holgadirect.com/products/ holga-iphone-lens-filter-kit-for-iphone-slft-ip4*)

Screen Protectors

People who've used stylus-based Palms, Pocket PCs, or smartphones are big fans of screen protectors—thin sheets of sticky plastic that lie smoothly over the glass to provide a protective barrier.

- **ZAGG invisibleSHIELD.** Designed to protect both the front and back of your iPhone, this screen-protector has a formidable pedigree: Its thin polyurethane film was originally created for the military to protect the leading edge of helicopter blades. ZAGG also sells its invisibleSHIELD for only the back, only the front, and only the sides (where it works as a Death Grip fix!) ($15-$25; *www.zagg.com*)

- **Fusion of Ideas Stealth Armor.** Like ZAGG, Fusion of Ideas offers some pretty great screen protection, especially with its "nano-fusion technology" protective screen films. And if you're not in the mood for boring old clear, the company offers some fun, unconventional faux-texture alternatives like leather, tungsten, carbon fiber, and brushed aluminum. ($15-$35; *www.fusionofideas.com*)

Making the iPhone Heard

Your iPhone comes with a pair of wired, mike-equipped earbuds and a not-very-powerful external speaker. But not everyone likes the earbuds Apple provides with iPhones, and some people's ears simply can't hold them in place. If you want a bump up from this factory equipment, you can find plenty of other options. For example:

- **V-MODA Remix Remote.** Because these earbuds come with four pairs of silicon ear fittings in both clear and black, you'll be able to create a better-fitting earbud that seals in the music and blocks out background noise. The earbuds also come with a built-in three-button remote, which packs an omnidirectional microphone. A control button lets you make and take calls. The V-MODAs should last you a while, too—the cables are reinforced with Kevlar, and they have a two-year warranty. ($80; *www.v-moda.com*)

- **BlueAnt S4 True Handsfree Bluetooth speakerphone.** The iPhone's speakerphone isn't all that loud, even when it's cranked up all the way—and you still have to take a hand off the steering wheel to pick up a call. With the BlueAnt S4, you can pair up your iPhone, clip it to the car's sun visor, and just say "OK" to pick up incoming calls the next time the phone rings. Or let the speakerphone's Bluetooth transmitter play music right from your iPhone, or give turn-by-turn directions using your favorite navigation app, without any extra cables. ($100; *www.myblueant.com*)

- **Jawbone Jambox wireless speaker.** You want loud volume and great sound? Delivering up to 85 decibels of rich sound you can hold in your hand, the Jambox works over Bluetooth, so you don't have to leave your beloved i-device chained to the confines of your hi-fi. Better yet, the Bluetooth doubles as a speakerphone. Combined with its built-in microphone, Jambox also provides crisp, clean-sounding conference calls ($200; *www.jawbone.com*)

- **Jawbone Icon Bluetooth headset.** CNET's highest-rated headset ever, the Jawbone Icon, almost looks like something out of the prop department on a sci-fi movie. But there's good stuff inside, including noise-cancellation circuitry to help eliminate wind and background chatter for improved call clarity. ($100; *www.jawbone.com*)

Tip For advice about a wide variety of iPhone headphones, check out the reviews and recommendations at Headphones.com.

- **Tascam iM2 stereo microphone.** Despite the hundreds of improvements Apple has made to the iPhone over the years, its built-in mike still can't record stereo sound. This microphone solves that problem nicely, both for audio and video recordings. The iM2 plugs into the iPhone's 32-pin dock connector and is powered by the iPhone, but there's a USB port in case you want to charge the phone with the iM2 attached. It features two rotating condenser microphones, CD-quality digital recording, a built-in analog-to-digital converter, an integrated mike preamp, and a side-mounted adjustable input volume knob. ($80; *www. tascamcontractor.com/product/im2/*)

Power to the iPhone

Every year, the newest iPhone isn't out for more than a day before people start complaining about the battery life. If you're on the road for hours and away from your charger, here are a few products designed to boost your battery and keep that iPhone running as long as you are:

- **Exogear exolife battery case.** It's an iPhone case! No, it's a backup battery! Wait, it's both. Exogear's form-fitting lithium polymer battery (housed in a sleek polycarbonate hardshell case) adds 5 hours of talk time and 5 hours of Internet time when you're on the go and connected to the 3G network. A pass-through USB port lets you charge and sync the iPhone without having to extract it from the case, and you can also charge the phone and the case at the same time. Available in both black and white. ($80; *www.exogear.com*)

- **mophie juice pack air and juice pack plus.** More on-the-go power, courtesy of a combination case and battery pack. ($80 for juice pack air; $100 for juice pack plus. *www.mophie.com*)

- **Richard Solo 1800 battery.** Snap-on batteries like this one may add a couple of inches onto the end of your iPhone, but they also add on extra hours of useful battery time. The Solo 1800 can recharge a completely dead iPhone and still have juice left over. The kit comes with a wall charger, a dual USB car charger, and a retractable USB cable so that you can charge it in the wall, in your car, or from your computer. ($30; *www.richardsolo.com*)

- **Splash O2 Lite Slim Extended Rechargeable Battery Case.** With this slim, soft-touch case, you'll experience up to two days or more of uninterrupted iPhone power. ($80; *www.splashproducts. com*)

- **Kensington Mini Battery Pack and Charger.** Sometimes you just want a boost to your iPhone battery from something that doesn't take up a lot of space in your pocket or purse. The price of this Kensington plug-in battery pack is small, too. ($40; *www.kensington.com*)

- **Kingston Wi-Drive.** If you've run out of room for music and videos on your phone, you can buy this flash-memory "hard drive." It's about the same size and shape as an iPhone 3G and has its own 4-hour battery. It acts like extra storage for your iPhone—actually, for up to three iOS devices simultaneously. ($110 for 16 GB; *www.kingston.com*)

- **Kensington PowerBolt Duo Car Charger.** Plug this into your car's accessory power socket (where a cigarette lighter was found in the old days) and quickly charge an iPhone and an iPad, or two mobile devices of any kind. Its LED power indicator lets you know when it is fully plugged in—and is a handy reminder to unplug it when not in use so you're not draining your car's electrical system unnecessarily. ($30; *www.kensington.com*)

Health & Fitness

Your iPhone can be your electronic personal trainer, or at least conveniently provide the tunes while you're exercising:

- **iHealth Digital Scale.** Thanks to Bluetooth, this digital scale measures and records your weight on your iPhone wirelessly, via the free iHealth Scale app. You and your family can share one-time readings or long-term trends. Send the results to your doctor or friends who might inspire you to reach your weight goal. ($70; *www.ihealth99.com*)

- **Withings blood pressure monitor.** Wrap the blood pressure monitor around your arm, plug it into your iPhone, measure, and then share your latest blood pressure results with friends via Twitter and Facebook, or even send the results to your doctor via email. ($130; *www.withings.com*)

- **iHealth Blood Pressure Dock.** This system lets you track your blood pressure and heart rate at home or in a relaxed environment anywhere. The device includes a cuff that fits around your arm for the readings, a dock to charge your iPhone, and a free app to graph and share your results with your doctor and caring friends. ($100; *www.ihealth99.com*)

Armbands hold your iPhone close to you while jogging, walking, or doing other exercises. Here are good places to find a wide variety of sporty workout cases that strap onto your arm: *www.belkin.com*, *www.dlo.com*, *www.griffin.com*, *www.goincase. com*, *www.marware.com*, and *www.PDOstore.com*.

Snap-On Accessories

It seems as if iPhone add-ons, like apps and dongles (snap-on hardware accessories) are advancing just as fast as the iPhone itself. Three wild examples:

- **Square card reader.** The Square is a tiny, white, snap-on credit-card reader for the iPhone. It lets anyone—even ordinary people—process credit cards, even for small amounts. Perfect for garage sales, bake sales, Craigslist sales, piano lessons, babysitting, whatever. Once you're paid, Square automatically deposits the dough into your bank account (after assessing a small fee, of course). The little reader plugs right into the iPhone's headphone jack. Receipts arrive instantly via email or mobile phone and can include a photo  of the item, a photo of the buyer, and the buyer's signature. (Card reader and app free, 2.75 percent per swipe; *www.squareup.com*)

- **RedEye mini.** Imagine being able to control your entire home entertainment system, TV, stereo, cable box, and Blu-ray player with something the size of the index finger you're using to change the channels. This mini dongle does just that. Its infrared blaster can control just about any other device that receives standard infrared signals. No real setup required: Plug the RedEye mini into your iPhone's headphone jack, and run the free RedEye application. The RedEye mini comes backed by ThinkFlood's online infrared code database, so you can control devices even if you don't have the original remote at hand. ($50; *www.thinkflood.com*)

- **mophie marketplace.** Here's another way that little people can accept cards: Put your phone in a case with swiping features built right in. Since the mophie marketplace is a case and not a dongle, you won't lose it (unless you lose your iPhone, too). ($80 for the mophie marketplace, then $13 a month for GoPayment service from Intuit; *www. mophie.com*)

Video Output

If you want to play your iPhone's videos, presentations, and games on a TV or a projector, you just need the right cable. You can read more about this topic on page 184, but here's the basic rundown. Each is available at the Apple store:

- **Apple Digital AV Adapter.** Mirrors anything on your iPhone 4S screen to an HDTV over an HDMI cable (not included). ($40)

- **Apple Component AV Cable.** Sends the iPhone's video output to your TV's component inputs—red (Pr), green (Y), and blue (Pb), and red/white analog audio sockets. ($40)

- **Apple Composite AV Cable.** If your TV is really old, this cable connects to your TV set's yellow video input and red/white audio inputs. ($40)

- **Apple VGA Adapter.** Connects the iPhone's video (not audio) to a VGA-equipped TV, projector, or other compatible display. ($30)

- **Griffin eXport In-Flight Video Cable.** Sends the phone's video to common airlines' in-flight entertainment systems. ($40)

iPod Accessories

Often, iPod accessories work with the iPhone, too—these gadgets have the same 30-pin connectors on the bottom—but not always. One thing to remember: electronic interference. If you forget, the iPhone will remind you. If it senses that you're seating it in a non–"Works with iPhone" speaker system, you'll see a message suggesting that you put it in Airplane Mode. Doing so takes care of the interference, but it also prevents you from making or getting phone calls. You can blow past the warning and keep Airplane Mode off, but you may get some unwanted static blasts with your music.

Troubleshooting & Maintenance

The iPhone is a computer, and you know what that means: Things can go wrong. This particular computer, though, is not quite like a Mac or a PC. It runs a spin-off of the Mac OS X operating system, but that doesn't mean you can apply the same troubleshooting techniques.

Therefore, let this appendix be your guide when things go wrong.

First Rule: Install the Updates

There's an old saying: "Never buy version 1.0 of anything." In the iPhone's case, the saying could be: "Never buy version 5.0 of anything."

The very first version (or major revision) of anything has bugs, glitches, and things the programmers didn't have time to finish the way they would have liked. The iPhone is no exception.

The beauty of this phone, though, is that Apple can send it fixes, patches, and even new features through software updates. One day you'll connect the phone to your computer for charging or syncing, and—bam!—there'll be a note from iTunes that new iPhone software is available.

So the first rule of trouble-free iPhoning is to accept these updates when they're offered. With each new software blob, Apple removes another few dozen tiny glitches.

Remember that within the first two months of the original iPhone's life, software updates 1.0.1 and 1.0.2 came down the pike, offering louder volume, security fixes, bug fixes, and many other subtle improvements. The big-ticket updates, bringing more actual features, came tumbling after (1.1.1 through 1.1.4). The same thing happened with the 2.0, 3.0, and 4.0 cycles—and now that iOS 5 is here, a similar flurry of fixes has followed.

Reset: Six Degrees of Desperation

The iPhone runs actual programs, and as actual programs do, they actually crash. Sometimes, the program you're working in simply vanishes and you find yourself back at the Home screen. Just reopen the program and get on with your life.

If the program you're in just doesn't seem to be working right—it's frozen or acting weird, for example—then one of these seven resetting techniques usually clears things right up.

 Note Proceed down this list in order! Start with the easy ones.

- **Exit the app.** On an iPhone, you're never aware that you're launching and exiting programs. They're always just *there*, like TV channels, when you switch to them. There's no Quit command. But if a program starts acting glitchy, you can make it quit, so that you can reopen it afresh.

  To do that, double-press the Home button to bring up the app switcher. Hold your finger down on the icon of the troubled app until its icon starts to wiggle. Then tap the ⊗ button. The program quits. Try reopening it to see if the problem has gone away.

- **Force quit the app.** If the phone is so frozen that you can't even bring up the app switcher, you'll have to *force* quit the stuck app. Hold down the Sleep switch until the slide to power off message appears. Then hold down the Home button for 10 seconds, or until the frozen program quits. The next time you open the troublesome program from the Home screen, it should be back in business.

 Note These steps have changed since the first couple of iPhone generations.

- **Turn the phone off and on again.** If it seems something more serious has gone wrong, then hold down the Sleep switch for a few seconds. When the screen says, slide to power off, confirm by swiping. The iPhone shuts off completely.

  Turn it back on by pressing the Sleep switch for a second or two.

- **Force restart the phone.** If you haven't been able to force quit the program, and you can't shut the phone off either, you might have to force a restart. To do that, hold both the Home button and the Sleep switch for 10 seconds. Keep holding, even if the screen goes black or you see the "power off" slider. Don't release until you see the Apple logo appear, meaning that the phone is restarting.

- **Reset the phone's settings.** Relax. This procedure doesn't erase any of your data—only the phone's settings. From the Home screen, tap Settings→General→Reset→Reset All Settings.

- **Erase the whole phone.** From the Home screen, tap Settings→ General→Reset→Erase All Content and Settings. Now, *this* option zaps all your stuff—*all* of it. Music, videos, email, settings, apps, all gone, and all overwritten with random 1's and 0's to make sure it's completely unrecoverable. Clearly, you're getting into last resorts here. Of course, you can sync with iTunes to copy all that stuff back onto your iPhone.

- **Restore the phone.** If none of these steps seem to solve the phone's glitchiness, it might be time for the Nuclear Option: erasing it completely, resetting both hardware and software back to a factory-fresh condition.

> **Tip** If you're able to sync the phone with iTunes *first,* do it! That way, you'll have a backup of all those intangible iPhone data bits: text messages, call logs, Recents list, and so on. iTunes will put it all back onto the phone the first time you sync after the restore.

To restore the phone, connect it to your computer. In iTunes, click the iPhone icon and then, on the Summary tab, click Restore.

The first order of business: iTunes offers to make a backup of your iPhone (all of its phone settings, text messages, and so on) before proceeding. Accepting this invitation is an excellent idea. Click Back Up.

> **Tip** If you've opted to back up your phone onto iCloud (page 421), you can also restore it from Apple's online backups. (You can restore this way only if your iPhone is completely wiped empty. If it's not, manually erase it using iTunes first.)
>
> During the setup screens described on page 488, tap Restore from iCloud Backup.... You're shown a list of the three most recent backups; tap the one you want. The phone goes right to work downloading your settings and account information. Then it restarts and begins to download your apps; if you're in a hurry for one particular app, tap its icon to make iCloud prioritize it. At any time, you can check the restore process's status in Settings→iCloud→Storage and Backup.
>
> When that's all over, you can get to work downloading your music (if you're an iTunes Match subscriber).

What Else to Try

If the phone is still glitchy, try to remember what changes you made to it recently. Did you install some new App Store program, add a new video, mess around with your calendar?

It's worth fishing through iTunes, turning off checkboxes, hunting for the recently changed items, and resyncing, in hopes of figuring out what's causing the flakiness.

iPhone Doesn't Turn On

Usually, the problem is that the battery's dead. Just plugging it into the USB cord or USB charger doesn't bring it to life immediately, either; a completely dead iPhone doesn't wake up until it's been charging for about 10 minutes. It pops on automatically when it has enough juice to do so.

If you don't think that's the trouble, then try the resetting tactics on the previous pages.

Doesn't Show Up in iTunes

If the iPhone's icon doesn't appear in the Source list at the left side of the iTunes window, you've got a problem. You won't be able to load it up with music, videos, or photos from your computer.

- **The USB factor.** Trace the connection from the iPhone to its cradle (if you're using one) to the USB cable to the computer, making sure everything is seated. Also, don't plug the USB cable into a USB jack on your keyboard, and don't plug it into an unpowered USB hub. Believe it or not, just trying a different USB jack on your computer often solves the problem.

- **The iPhone factor.** Try turning the phone off and on again. Make sure its battery is at least partway charged; if not, wait 10 minutes, until it's sucked in enough power from the USB cable to revive itself.

 Tip If you're having trouble charging the iPhone, check the battery icon at the top of the screen. If it bears a little lightning-bolt icon, then you're charging; the iPhone will be 80 percent charged in about an hour.

But if the red part of the battery icon on the iPhone screen flashes three times and the screen goes black, then the iPhone is not getting power and won't charge.

Phone and Internet Problems

How can the phone part of the iPhone go wrong? Let us count the ways.

- **Can't make calls.** First off, do you have enough cellular signal to make a call? Check your signal-strength bars. Even if you have one or two, flakiness is par for the course, although one bar in a 3G area is much better than one bar in a non-3G area. Try going outside, standing near a window, or moving to a major city (kidding).

Also, make sure Airplane Mode isn't turned on (page 331). Try calling somebody else, to make sure the problem isn't with the number you're dialing.

In areas where everyone is using phones at once (airports, conferences, New York, San Francisco), consider turning off 3G, if that's an option on your iPhone model (page 331). Often, you'll have a better chance of connecting using the older, slower network.

Finally, be aware of the Death Grip (page 24). Nestling the lower-left corner of the iPhone 4 in the palm of your left hand can lower the signal strength (unless your phone is in a case or has a "bumper"). (The problem doesn't occur on the iPhone 4S.)

If nothing else works, try the resetting techniques described at the beginning of this chapter.

- **Can't get on the Internet.** Remember, the iPhone can get online in three ways: via a WiFi hot spot, via the 3G network, and via the much slower EDGE or 1xRTT network. If you're not in a hot spot *and* you don't have a cell signal—that is, if there's no ▁▅▇█, **E**, or **3G** icon at the top of the screen—then you can't get online at all.

- **Can't send text messages.** Make sure, of course, that you've signed up for a texting plan. Make sure you haven't turned on Show Subject Field (page 136) and forgotten to fill out the body of the message.

Email Problems

Getting your email settings right the first time isn't easy. There are all kinds of tweaky codes and addresses that you have to enter—if they weren't properly synced over from your computer, that is.

If email isn't working, here are some steps to try:

- Sometimes, there's nothing for it but to call your Internet provider (or whoever's supplying the email account) and ask for help. Often, the settings you use at home won't work when you're using a mobile gadget like the iPhone. Open Settings→Mail, Contacts, Calendars and tap your email account's name to view the Settings screen.

- If you're getting a "user not recognized" error, you may have typed your password wrong. (It's easy to do, since the iPhone converts each character you type into a • symbol about a second after you type it.) Delete the password in Settings and re-enter it.

- If you're having trouble connecting to your company's Exchange server, see the end of Chapter 15.

- Oh—and it probably goes without saying, but remember that you can't get email if you can't get online, and you can't get online unless you have a WiFi or cellular signal.

Messages Are Disappearing

Strange but true: Unbeknownst to just about everyone but Apple programmers, there's a hidden setting that controls how many messages are allowed to pile up in your Sent, Drafts, and Trash email folders. And it comes set to 50 messages each.

If any more messages go into those three folders, then the earlier ones are auto-deleted from the iPhone (although not from the server on the Internet). The idea is to keep your email stash on the phone manageable, but if you're not prepared, it can be somewhat alarming to discover that messages have vanished on their own.

To see this setting, tap Settings→Mail, Contacts, Calendars; under Mail, you can adjust the Show item to keep 50, 100, 200, 500, or 1,000 recent messages. This feature is intended to keep the number of messages in your *inbox* to a reasonable number; most people don't realize, however, that it also applies to the Sent, Drafts, and Trash folders in all your POP and IMAP email accounts.

Can't Send Email

It's your settings. It's got to be your settings in Settings→Mail, Contacts, Calendars. Double-check every one of those geeky boxes (SMTP server, authentication method, and so on) with your Internet provider on the line.

Problems that Aren't Really Problems

There's a difference between "things not working as they were designed to" and "things not working the way I'd *like* them to." Here are a few examples:

- **Rotation sensor doesn't work.** As you know, the screen image is supposed to rotate into horizontal mode when you turn the iPhone itself. But this feature works only in certain programs, like Safari, Mail, Notes, the iPod music-playback mode, and when viewing photos or email attachments.

Furthermore, the iPhone has to be more or less upright when you turn it. It can't be flat on a table, for example. The orientation sensor relies on gravity to tell it which way you're holding the phone.

Finally, if the display isn't rotating the way you'd like it to, it may be that you've turned on the rotation lock. If so, you'll see the icon at the top of the screen. See page 14 for the details.

- **The phone volume is low—even the speakerphone.** Actually, the recent iPhone models have surprisingly loud, clear audio volume, so something must be wacky. With all due respect, did you remove the plastic film from your brand-new iPhone? (This plastic, intended to be on the phone only during shipping, covers up the earpiece.)

> **Tip** The speaker volume is a lot better when it's pointed at you, either on a table or with your hand cupped around the bottom of the phone to direct the sound.

iPod Problems

The iPhone is a great iPod, but even here, things can go wrong:

- **Can't hear anything.** Are the earbuds plugged in? They automatically cut the sound coming from the iPhone's built-in speaker.

  Is the volume up? Press the Up volume key on the side of the phone. Also make sure that the music is, in fact, supposed to be playing (and isn't on Pause).

- **Can't sync music or video files to the iPhone.** They may be in a format the iPhone doesn't understand, like WMA, MPEG-1, MPEG-2, or Audible Format 1.

  Convert them first to something the iPhone does understand, like AAC; Apple Lossless; MP3; WAV; Audible Formats 2, 3, or 4; AIFF (these are all audio formats); H.264; or MPEG-4 (video formats).

- **Something's not playing or syncing right.** It's technically possible for some corrupted or incompatible music, photo, or video file to jam up the entire syncing or playback process. In iTunes, experiment with playlists and videos, turning off checkboxes until you figure out which one is causing the problem.

Warranty and Repair

The iPhone comes with a one-year warranty and 90 days of phone tech support. If you buy an AppleCare+ contract ($100), you're covered for a second year.

 Tip AT&T, Sprint, or Verizon tech support is free for both years of your contract. They handle questions about your iPhone's phone features.

If, during the coverage period, anything goes wrong that's not your fault, Apple will fix it free. (In fact, AppleCare+ even covers damage if it *is* your fault, for $50 each time—even if you drop the phone or get it wet. Maximum: Twice.)

You can either take the phone to an Apple Store, which is often the fastest route, or call 800-APL-CARE (800-275-2273) to arrange shipping back to Apple. In general, you'll get the fixed phone back in three business days.

 Note *Sync the phone before it goes in for repair.* The repair process generally erases the phone completely—Apple very often simply hands you a new (or refurbished) iPhone instead of your original. In fact, if you're worried that someone at Apple might snoop around, you might want to erase the phone *first.* (Use the Restore option—page 505.)

Also, don't forget to remove your SIM card (page 21) before you send in your broken AT&T iPhone—and to put it back in when you get the phone. Don't leave it in the loaner phone. AT&T can get a new card if you lose your original, but it's a hassle.

While your phone is in the shop, you can sign up for a loaner iPhone to use in the meantime for $30. Apple will ship it to you, or you can pick one up at the Apple Store. Just sync this loaner phone with iTunes, and presto—all your stuff is right back on it.

You can keep this service phone until seven days after you get your fixed phone back.

Out-of-Warranty Repairs

Once the year or two has gone by, or if you damage your iPhone in a way that's not covered by the warranty (backing your car over it comes to mind), Apple charges $200 to repair an iPhone (they usually just replace it).

The Battery Replacement Program

Why did Apple seal the battery inside the iPhone, anyway? Everyone knows lithium-ion batteries don't last forever. After 300 or 400 charges, the iPhone battery begins to hold less charge (perhaps 80 percent of the original). After a certain point, the phone will need a new battery. How come you can't change it yourself, as on any normal cellphone?

Apple's reply: A user-replaceable battery takes up a lot more space inside the phone. It requires a plastic compartment that shields the guts of the phone from you and your fingers; it requires a removable door; and it needs springs or clips to hold the battery in place.

In any case, you can't change the battery yourself. If the phone is out of warranty, you must send it to Apple (or take it to an Apple Store) for an $85 battery-replacement job. (As an eco-bonus, Apple properly disposes of the old batteries, which consumers might not do on their own.)

Where to Go from Here

At this point, the iPhone is such a phenomenon that there's no shortage of resources for getting more help, news, and tips. Here are a few examples:

- **Apple's official iPhone User Guide.** Yes, there is an actual download-able PDF user's manual. *http://manuals.info.apple.com/en/iPhone_User_Guide.pdf*

- **Apple's official iPhone help Web site.** Online tips, tricks, and tutorials; troubleshooting topics; downloadable PDF help documents; and, above all, an enormous, seething treasure trove of discussion boards. *www.apple.com/support/iphone/*

- **Apple's service site.** All the dates, prices, and expectations for getting your iPhone repaired. Includes details on getting a temporary replacement unit. *www.apple.com/support/iphone/service/faq/*

- **iPhone blog.** News, tips, tricks, all in a blog format. *www.TiPb.com/*

- **iLounge.** Another great blog-format site. Available in an iPhone format so you can read it right on the device. *www.iLounge.com/*

- **MacRumors/iPhone.** Blog-format news; accessory blurbs; help discussions; iPhone wallpaper. *www.macrumors.com/iphone/*

- **iPhone Atlas.** Discussion, news, apps, how-tos. *www.iphoneatlas.com*

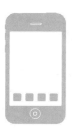

Index